The Essential
CATHOLIC
CATECHISM

A Readable, Comprehensive Catechism
of the Catholic Faith

DR. ALAN SCHRECK

NIHIL OBSTAT: Reverend James Dunfee
Censor Liborum

IMPRIMATUR: Most Reverend Gilbert I. Sheldon
Bishop of Steubenville
August 10, 1999

The NIHIL OBSTAT and IMPRIMATUR are a declaration that a book or pamphlet is considered to be free from doctrinal or moral error. It is not implied that those who have granted the NIHIL OBSTAT and IMPRIMATUR agree with the contents, opinions, or statements expressed.

This reprint edition published by TAN Books in 2019.

ISBN: 978-1-5051-1322-8

Published in the United States by
TAN Books
PO Box 269
Gastonia, NC 28053
www.TANBooks.com

Printed in India

CONTENTS

FOREWORD

It is a joy to be able to welcome a new edition of Alan Schreck's *The Essential Catholic Catechism*. It is no easy task to write a catechism that engages the interest and refreshes the understanding and does so without compromising the depth of treatment of the content; a catechism that focuses on the essentials while also feeding the soul with a rich and satisfying fare. Alan Schreck has the rare gift of combining a compelling sense of the Holy Spirit's formative role in each of our lives, as members of Christ's Body, with a constant educative attention to the sources of the faith in Scripture and Tradition and also a pleasing and accessible style.

Every catechism written after 1992 must take as its reference point, in a special way, the *Catechism of the Catholic Church*. In promulgating that Catechism, St. John Paul II wrote that its publication was intended to encourage the development of new local catechisms: "It is meant to encourage and assist in the writing of new local catechisms, which must take into account various situations and cultures, while carefully preserving the unity of faith and fidelity to Catholic doctrine" (Apostolic Constitution, *Fidei Depositum*). Dr. Schreck's *Essential Catholic Catechism* stands in relation to the *Catechism of the Catholic Church* in part as a commentary on that universal Catechism, constantly referencing its treatment of topics back to that work, unpacking and explaining key terms and taking the opportunity to explain something of the development of doctrine in relation to its teaching, amplifying some of the historical notes found in the Catechism itself. Two representative examples would be the sections on the origin of the New Testament and on the development of the sacraments.

In addition to providing some additional historical background to particular doctrines, briefly tracing their development through Tradition, the *Essential Catholic Catechism* has a particularly strong focus on the scriptural underpinning of Catholic teaching in all areas. The *Catechism of the Catholic Church* has itself been described as the most scriptural of all catechisms and this attentiveness to the biblical sources of doctrine characterizes Dr. Schreck's work as well. This point, together with a constant willingness to engage with questions about the Church's teaching that would be of particular interest to members of Protestant ecclesial communities, makes the *Essential Catholic Catechism* an excellent companion volume to Alan Schreck's well-known work *Catholic and Christian*. With regard to the sources of the faith employed in this catechism, alongside the Scriptures, there is also a constant advertence to the sixteen documents of the Second Vatican Council and post-conciliar magisterial teaching. This balancing of sources towards the more contemporary expressions of the faith is in part what makes for the particular readability of this catechism.

There are also number of features of this work that make it especially helpful not only for those wishing to understand better the living truths of the faith for themselves but also for those seeking to educate and catechize others, to transmit the faith in parish, family, or school settings. One such feature is the rich treatment of the Person and work of the Holy Spirit—the only One who can "initiate and sustain" catechesis in the Church, as St. John Paul II reminded us (*Catechesi tradendae* 72). Alan Schreck's catechism once again follows the *Catechism of the Catholic Church* in this respect and consistently highlights the inseparability of the Holy Spirit from the work of the Lord Jesus in the history of salvation, in the liturgy, and in the lives of Jesus' disciples. The reminder of the Holy Spirit's indwelling and constant presence in his Church communicates a powerful and dynamic impetus towards mission throughout the text.

It is also helpful that the structure of *The Essential Catholic Catechism* follows God's saving pedagogy so closely, in creation and in the history of his Chosen People and of the Church. This catechism, Dr. Schreck notes, "seeks to tell the *story* of God and his loving relationship with the human race." The *narratio* of the faith, as the Fathers of the Church described it, the overarching story of God's covenants with humanity and his unceasing work to draw us up from the misery of our sins and from death into his everlasting happiness, provides the framework within which all of the individual doctrines are presented. This "golden thread" of narration, as Sophia Cavalletti calls it, enables one to see clearly the coherence and the beauty of the works of the Lord, all of them having but one purpose, to draw us upwards towards the "love that never ends" (CCC 25).

Petroc Willey
Professor of Catechetics, Franciscan University of Steubenville

FOREWORD TO THE FIRST EDITION

It is a real joy for me to read and recommend this catechism, *The Essential Catholic Catechism*, which its author, Alan Schreck, Ph.D., Professor in Theology at the Franciscan University of Steubenville, has now revised according to the *Catechism of the Catholic Church*.

The Essential Catholic Catechism presents the Catholic faith for people of today. It is written in everyday language that makes it easy and agreeable to read, without sacrificing the meaning of its content to its facility. Its concordance with the teaching of the *Catechism of the Catholic Church* makes it a good example of those "new local catechisms, which take into account various situations and cultures, while carefully preserving the unity of faith and fidelity to Catholic doctrine" (John Paul II, Apost. Const. *Fidei depositum*) and which were meant to proceed from the edition of the above mentioned *Catechism*, itself a fruit of the Second Council of the Vatican. I wish *The Essential Catholic Catechism* a large extension and a joyful reception in the English-speaking world.

Cardinal Christoph Schönborn
General Editor of the
Catechism of the Catholic Church

ACKNOWLEDGMENTS

I offer special thanks and gratitude for the typing and production of this book to Patricia Maher, without whose assistance this work could not have been produced. I also thank Maria Fedoryka, Mary Kray, and Larissa Sension for their time and help in typing and corrections.

I extend deep and heartfelt gratitude to my wife, Nancy, and to my children—Paul, Jeanne, Mark, Margaret, and Peter—who faithfully supported and prayed for me. They know best the extra time and energy that writing requires of a husband and father. Thank you!

I would like to thank and acknowledge my former student Conor Gallagher of TAN Books/St. Benedict Press and his team including, Nick Vari and John Moorehouse, for their initiative and work in the publication of this new edition of *The Essential Catholic Catechism*.

I also deeply appreciate the long-standing support and encouragement of my friend and colleague Dr. Petroc Willey, Director of the Catechetical Institute and Professor of Catechetics at Franciscan University of Steubenville, and thank him for contributing the foreword to this new edition.

Alan Schreck, Ph.D.
February, 2019

ABBREVIATIONS

AA	*Apostolicam actuositatem*	LH	*Liturgy of the Hours*
AAS	*Acta Apostolicae Sedis*	LXX	Septuagint
AF	J.B. Lightfoot, ed., *The Apostolic Fathers* (New York: Macmillan, 1889-1890)	MC	*Marialis cultus*
		MD	*Mulieris dignitatem*
		MF	*Mysterium fidei*
AG	*Ad gentes*	MM	*Mater et magistra*
Bende Benedictionibus (Book of Blessings)		NA	*Nostra aetate*
CA	*Centesimus annus*	NCCB	National Conference of Catholic Bishops (U.S.A.)
Catech. R.	*Catechismus Romanus*		
CCEO	Corpus Canonum Ecclesiarum Orientalium	ND	Neuner-Dupuis, *The Christian Faith in the Doctrinal Documents of the Catholic Church*
CCL	Corpus Christianorum, Series Latina (Turnhout, 1953-)		
		OBA	*Ordo baptismi adultorum*
CD	*Christus Dominus*	OC	*Ordo confirmationis*
CDF	Congregation for the Doctrine of the Faith	OCF	*Order of Christian Funerals*
		OCM	*Ordo celebrandi Matrimonium*
CELAM	Consejo Episcopal Latinoamericano	OCV	*Ordo consecrationis virginum*
CIC	Codex Iuris Canonici	OE	*Orientalium ecclesiarum*
CL	*Christifideles laici*	OP	*Ordo paenitentiae*
COD	*Conciliorum oecumenicorum decreta*	OR	Office of Readings
CPG	*Solemn Profession of Faith:* Credo of the People of God	OT	*Optatam totius*
		PG	*Perfectae caritatis*
CSEL	Corpus Scriptorum Ecclesiasticorum Latinorum (Vienna, 1866-)	PG	J.P. Migne, ed., Patrologia Graeca (Paris, 1857-1866)
CT	*Catechesi tradendae*	PL	J.P. Migne, ed., Patrologia Latina (Paris: 1841-1855)
DeV	*Dominum et Vivificantem*		
DH	*Dignitatis humanae*	PLS	J.P. Migne, ed., Patrologia Latina Supplement
DM	*Dives in misericordia*		
DS	Denzinger-Schönmetzer, *Enchiridion Symbolorum, definitionum et declarationum de rebus fidei et morum (1965)*	PO	*Presbyterorum ordinis*
		PP	*Populorum progressio*
		PT	*Pacem in terris*
		RBC	*Rite of Baptism of Children*
DV	*Dei Verbum*	RCIA	*Rite of Christian initiation of adults*
EN	*Evangelii nuntiandi*	RH	*Redemptor hominis*
EP	Eucharistic Prayer	RomM	*Roman Missal*
FC	*Familiaris consortio*	RM	*Redempturis Mater*
GCD	*General Catechetical Directory*	Rmiss	*Rredemptoris Missio*
GE	*Gravissimum educationis*	RP	*Reconciliatio et paenitentia*
GILH	General Introduction to LH	SC	*Sacrosanctum concilium*
GIRM	General Instruction to RomM	SCG	Summa Contra Gentiles
GS	*Gaudium et spes*	SCh	Sources Chrétiennes (Paris: 1942-)
HV	*Humanae vitae*	SRS	*Sollicitudo rei socialis*
ICEL	International Commission on English in the Liturgy	STh	Summa Theologiae
		UR	*Unitatis redintegratio*
IM	*Inter mirifica*		
LE	*Laborem exercens*		
LG	*Lumen gentium*		

CHAPTER 1

God's Revelation and Our Response

This catechism aspires to be a "reader's edition" of the truths conveyed in the *Catechism of the Catholic Church*. Before we can begin to tell the "story" of our faith, it is necessary to introduce:

- the author and source of these truths (God),
- how he has chosen to communicate the truth to us (revelation), and
- the fitting response to the truths God has revealed (faith).

Everything else in this catechism hinges on our understanding and believing these truths.

To some, these three "essentials" are less interesting and more technical than other truths revealed in the *Catechism*. However, like the foundation of a building, the Catholic faith cannot "stand" and be understood without the support of these three underlying truths.

God: The Source and the Center of All

The goal of this catechism is to relate the truths of the Christian faith in a "living," readable fashion.[1] Like much of the Bible, it seeks to tell the *story* of God and his loving relationship with the human race, and of his plan to unite us with himself forever in the joy of heaven. Before beginning to tell this story, however, we will follow the order of the *Catechism of the Catholic Church* and examine the *source* and *authority* of Catholic teaching.

Catholics hold that the ultimate source of Catholic teaching, the "author" of the Catholic faith, is God himself, who is the origin and source of all truth and goodness. If this is true, then the teaching of the Catholic Church is based on the highest authority possible and is unquestionably reliable.

This is a bold claim. How can anyone claim to know with certainty things about God and his will for the human race? Though many people have a natural longing or desire for God, others question whether God exists, or doubt that we can know anything about God with absolute certitude. Even committed Christians and other religious people may have doubts and questions at times about the nature and even the existence of God.

The Bible and Christian tradition affirm that God may be known through reflection on the things he has created, such as the beauty and order of the universe (see Rom 1:19-20; Ps 19:2). We can also discover God as the source of the highest qualities of the human person: "his openness to truth and beauty, his sense of moral goodness, his freedom and the voice of his conscience, with his longings for the infinite and for happiness" (*Catechism of the Catholic Church*, paragraph 33, henceforth CCC 33).

The existence of these qualities points to a spiritual principle or "soul" in man, which must originate in a superior spiritual being, God. For example, Christian author C.S. Lewis observes that all people have a sense of fairness or "fair play" which points to someone (God) who is the source of this universal moral "law" or principle.[2]

In the Judeo-Christian tradition, such indications of God's existence have become formal arguments, so-called proofs for the existence of God. They are not scientific demonstrations, but are "converging and convincing arguments" (CCC 31) that, taken together, may lead a reasonable person to conclude that a reality exists that is the first cause and final end of all things "that everyone calls 'God.'"[3] These arguments do not necessarily lead people to a life-giving relationship with a personal, loving God, but they can help people to understand why faith in such a God is reasonable and even necessary (see CCC 35).

How Can We Know God When Our Concepts Fall Short?

Christian tradition recognizes human limitations in thinking and speaking about God. The God we speak of transcends anything the human intellect can grasp. Human language "always fall[s] short of the mystery of God" (CCC 42).

For my thoughts are not your thoughts,
    nor are your ways my ways, says the LORD.
As high as the heavens are above the earth,
    so high are my ways above your ways
    and my thoughts above your thoughts.

ISAIAH 55:8-9, NAB

Even when that which we think or say about God is true, our words cannot adequately express his perfection or simplicity. The best human concepts and images are more *unlike* God than like him.

Nonetheless, this should not deter us. We can rejoice in the glimpses of God and his presence that we find in his creation, in what we term "natural revelation." Even when God chooses to reveal himself more directly, in what we call "divine revelation," he still presents himself within the limits of human perception and understanding. God condescends to reveal himself through events in history or by words or visions given to prophets or other chosen messengers.

God's most amazing revelation to us was the Incarnation, for by that event God himself assumed our humanity! As "one of us," Jesus, the God-man, continued to employ images and metaphors to reveal to us truths about God and divine things. For example, he used the image of a wedding banquet to describe heaven, and human fatherhood to reflect the perfect love and fatherhood of God, "from whom every family in heaven and on earth is named" (Eph 3:15, NAB).

Human understanding of God will remain imperfect until we come face to face with God in heaven (the "beatific vision"):

At present we see indistinctly, as in a mirror, but then face to face. At present I know partially; then I shall know fully, as I am fully known.

1 CORINTHIANS 13:12, NAB

The Purpose of God's Revelation

Happily, the purpose of revelation—both natural and divine—is not that we might understand God completely. What, then, is the purpose of revelation? The "Dogmatic Constitution on Divine Revelation" (*Dei Verbum*) of Vatican II teaches:

In His goodness and wisdom, God chose to reveal Himself, and to make known to us the hidden purpose of His will.... Through this revelation,... the invisible God out of the abundance of His love speaks to men as friends and lives among them, so that He may invite and take them into fellowship with Himself.[4]

This statement emphasizes that God reveals himself and his will "out of the abundance of His love" for this purpose: to invite us into a living, personal relationship of friendship and fellowship with our Father and creator. Here we find the true meaning and joy of life. As St. Augustine observed, "You have made us for yourself, and our heart is restless until it rests in you."[5]

God did not merely announce his loving plan for the human race. He demonstrated his love and his longing for intimate union with us by coming to live among us as a man—Jesus Christ. Thus, God's revelation is personal because it comes to us through the person of Jesus. Jesus invites each of us to come to know God as our Father and to live in fellowship with him. Revelation leads to life: true, abundant life in this world (see Jn 10:10) and eternal life with God in the age to come.

Eternal life is not something that human beings can merit or presume to receive. Jesus indicated that many people would not attain eternal life, but be eternally separated from God (see Mt 7:13,14). Jesus came not "to condemn the world but to save the world" (Jn 12:47, NAB) by speaking the Word the Father had given him to speak. "Whoever rejects me and does not accept my words has something to judge him: the word that I spoke, it will condemn him on the last day" (Jn 12:48, NAB). The fullness of this all-important Word—this revelation—that has come to us from God the Father is found in Jesus Christ.

God Speaks to Us Through History

Dei Verbum explains that God reveals himself through both *words* and *deeds* (see CCC 33).[6] The faith of Christians and Jews is based on the belief that God acts in unique and specific ways in human history, and that he also speaks to humanity in various ways.

The first "phase" of divine revelation, the Old Testament, recounts many saving acts of God, such as his deliverance of the Hebrew people from captivity in Egypt. These writings also report that God revealed himself to Abraham, Moses, the prophets, and other men and women of the Old Covenant through dreams, visions, voices, angelic messengers, and other means.

The Christian Scriptures (New Testament) tell of Jesus' mighty works of healing, expelling demons, and finally redeeming the human race through his death on the cross. The New Testament proclaims that in Jesus Christ God spoke to the human race in a unique and unsurpassable way. "Christ, the Son of God made man, is the Father's one, perfect, and unsurpassable Word. In him he has said everything; there will be no other word than this one" (CCC 65). Jesus' words and teaching present to us God's pure, perfect revelation, for "in him all the fullness was pleased to dwell ..." (Col 1:19, NAB).

The Holy Spirit Reveals God's Truth

God entered our history as a man, Jesus of Nazareth. Yet, it is impossible to recognize who Jesus is without the enlightenment of the Spirit of Truth, the Holy Spirit. St. Paul wrote that "no one can say, 'Jesus is Lord,' except by the holy Spirit" (1 Cor 12:3, NAB). Likewise, it is only the Holy Spirit that enables anyone to recognize and address God as "Abba—dear Father (see Rom 8:15, 16, Gal 4:6).

In St. John's Last Supper discourse, Jesus told his apostles that it was to their advantage that he was leaving them, for when he departed he would be able to send them the Holy Spirit.

> I have much more to tell you, but you cannot bear it now. But when he comes, the Spirit of truth, he will guide you to all truth.
>
> JOHN 16:12-13, NAB

For this reason, we can speak of the Holy Spirit as the revealer, the faithful source of God's revelation in the church. The Gospel of John affirms that the Holy Spirit will call to mind the words and teachings of Jesus (see Jn 14:26). He will "instruct you in everything" (Jn 14:26) and "declare to you the things that are coming" (Jn 16:13, NAB).

The Catholic Church has always emphasized that the ultimate *source* of revelation is not a book (the Bible), or a thing (tradition), or even a human group or person (the Magisterium or the pope), but is God himself, particularly in the person of the Holy Spirit. The Holy Spirit reveals God's truth through the channels just mentioned. It is also the Spirit of God who guides the church through these channels into the fullness of truth.

Public Revelation: The Foundation of Christian Truth

How does the Holy Spirit reveal the truth to God's people? A primary work of the Spirit is to testify to Jesus Christ, who is the apex and summation of God's revelation of himself to mankind. Jesus is "the way, and the truth, and the life" (Jn 14:6). The fullness of human life in this age, and eternal life in the age to come, is received only through Jesus.

The Catholic Church recognizes that the lifetime of Jesus and of his apostles was a privileged time of God's foundational (or "public") revelation. God revealed himself in an unsurpassed way in Jesus and through the teaching of his apostles. Hence, the Second Vatican Council proclaims that "we now await no further new public revelation before the glorious manifestation of our Lord, Jesus Christ."[7]

This means that God will send no new savior to mankind, nor will there be any further revelation of God bearing the same authority or significance as his revelation in and through Jesus Christ.[8] As St. Paul warned, "But even if we or an angel from heaven should preach [to you] a gospel other than the one that we preached to you, let that one be accursed!" (Gal 1:8, NAB). No other revelation is valid if it contradicts the Good News received through the apostles and in the traditions that they have passed on to us. As St. Paul exhorted the Thessalonians, "Stand firm and hold fast to the traditions that you were taught, either by an oral statement or by a letter of ours" (2 Thess 2:15, NAB).

God's Word in Sacred Tradition

If a person accepts that Jesus is God's ultimate revelation, his "last (and definitive) Word" to mankind, then it is reasonable to ask: "Why has the church defined 'new' doctrines?" and "Why does the church need the Holy Spirit to teach her and to lead us into the fullness of truth about God?" The *Catechism of the Catholic Church* explains:

> Yet even if Revelation is already complete [in Jesus], it has not been made completely explicit; it remains for Christian faith gradually to grasp its full significance over the course of the centuries. (CCC 66)

The truth that is found in Jesus Christ is something like a gold mine. We have discovered the mine (or rather, God has *revealed* the mine to us), yet we still have the task of digging out all the gold. This means that the Holy Spirit is enabling the church over the course of centuries to "uncover" the truth revealed in Christ, and at times along the way to define the truth that she has come to understand.

Jesus is that "gold mine"—the full revelation of God is found in him. Yet, Jesus is no longer physically present in the world to teach us directly. Where is the fullness of God's truth to be discovered today? The Catholic Church understands that the ultimate revelation of God, coming to us through Jesus Christ and in his Holy Spirit, is communicated to the church in two ways: through sacred Scripture and sacred tradition.

Dei Verbum states that "Sacred tradition and sacred Scripture form one sacred deposit of the word of God, which is committed to the church."[9] The phrase "the word of God" is used by many Christians to refer only to the Bible, but Catholics understand that both the Bible and sacred tradition are God's revealed Word:

> For both of them, flowing from the same divine wellspring, in a certain way merge into a unity and tend toward the same end. For sacred Scripture is the word of God inasmuch as it is consigned to writing under the inspiration of the divine Spirit. To the successors of the apostles, sacred tradition hands on in its full purity God's word which was entrusted to the apostles by Christ the Lord and the Holy Spirit.[10]

It is simpler to think of the entirety of God's Word as a neatly bound book— the Bible. However, many aspects of Christian life, worship, and belief coming from the time of the apostles were not written in the Bible. They were handed on (which is the literal meaning of "tradition") by the apostles and their successors as essential parts of the life of God's New Covenant people, the church. As the Second Vatican Council states:

> The apostles, handing on what they themselves had received, warn the faithful to hold fast to the traditions which they have learned either by word or mouth or by letter (see 2 Thess 2:15), and to fight in defense of the faith handed on once and for all (see Jude 3). Now what was handed on by the apostles includes everything which contributes to the holiness of life, and the increase in faith of the People of God; and so the Church, in her teaching, life, and worship, perpetuates and hands on to all generations all that she herself is, and all that she believes.[11]

For the sake of clarity, the Second Vatican Council distinguishes sacred tradition from the Bible or sacred Scripture, even though the New Testament itself is a compilation of primitive Christian tradition about Jesus, and of his teaching. Sacred tradition, sometimes called apostolic tradition or simply the Tradition, includes every aspect of God's revelation outside of the Bible that God intends to be believed and followed by the whole church in every age: "all that she herself is, and all that she believes."

Some aspects of sacred tradition pass on the fullest way to worship God in the church, or the proper way to honor the angels and the saints, including Mary, the Mother of God. Other aspects of sacred tradition present God's will about how we are to live (the moral life), which is not always explicitly or fully spelled out in the Bible. Part of the role of sacred tradition is to safeguard the true meaning of the sacred Scripture by presenting the church's authoritative interpretation of certain passages of the Bible.

Some Christians mistakenly think that Catholics are diminishing the importance of the Bible by also following sacred tradition. To the contrary, Catholics express their great respect for the Bible by acknowledging that we often must rely on sacred tradition to preserve the true meaning of the Bible. No element of sacred tradition can contradict the teaching of the Bible, since both are expressions of the one truth of God. However, sacred tradition sometimes enables us to interpret certain passages of the Bible correctly (especially those that appear difficult to understand).

The Holy Spirit also uses sacred tradition to present the church with a fuller and deeper understanding of sacred Scripture. Certain themes that are only briefly mentioned or implied in the Bible often are presented in greater fullness and depth through sacred tradition. An example of this is the Catholic beliefs about Mary's Immaculate Conception and Assumption into heaven, which are not explicitly stated in the Bible but which flow out of and deepen our understanding of the biblical teaching about Mary.

Nowhere does the Bible teach that the Scripture *alone* is inspired by God. Concerning sacred tradition and its place in the church, *Dei Verbum* teaches:

> This tradition which comes from the apostles develops in the Church with the help of the Holy Spirit. For there is a growth in the understanding of the realities and the words which have been handed down. This happens through the contemplation and study made by believers, who treasure these things in their hearts (see Lk 2:19, 51), through the intimate understanding of spiritual things they experience, and through the preaching of those who have received through episcopal succession the sure gift of truth. For, as the centuries succeed one another, the Church constantly moves forward toward the fullness of divine truth until the words of God reach their complete fulfillment in her.[12]

Even though the church received its foundational "public revelation" during the lifetimes of Jesus and his apostles, the Holy Spirit is active in the church, as Jesus promised, to provide us with an even fuller and more complete understanding of God's truth. It is through sacred tradition that God accomplishes this.

Not every tradition that develops within the church is part of the divine revelation that Catholics refer to as sacred tradition or Tradition. There are many human traditions that are part of the church's life that are subject to change. Such traditions may be merely human customs, or they may be part of God's will and intention for the church for a particular situation or period of time in the life of God's people, but not for all time and every situation. The bishops of the church, who comprise the Magisterium or the teaching office of the church, have the responsibility and gift (charism) of discerning the difference between authentic sacred tradition and other traditions. The Magisterium faithfully preserves, interprets, and proclaims God's revelation as it comes to us from the Holy Spirit through both sacred Scripture and sacred tradition.

A final question often asked is where the sacred tradition of the church may be found. There is no single volume that contains all of what the Catholic Church considers sacred tradition, since this tradition includes much of the life of God's people, such as ways of worship, devotion, moral teaching and wisdom, and the interpretation of the Bible. Sacred tradition may be described as all the essential, unchangeable elements of the church's "way of life," and the doctrinal definitions of the Magisterium that give us an authentic understanding of all that the church believes and practices.

There are books that summarize the official teachings of ecumenical councils and popes of the Catholic Church. These represent a large portion of sacred tradition, where formal definitions of Catholic belief and practice have been made by the Magisterium over the course of history. However, sacred tradition also includes things that have been consistently taught by the Fathers, doctors, and saints of the church that the Magisterium has not found necessary or appropriate to formally define. Some Catholic beliefs in the area of Christian living and morality fall into this category, such as the rejection of abortion, euthanasia, and infanticide.[13] From the beginning of the church Christians have rejected these and other immoral practices.

Catholics should be eager to grow in their understanding of God's revelation through sacred tradition. Along with the sacred Scripture, it is the primary way that God's truth comes to us to guide and encourage us in our Christian lives. Let us now examine more fully how God addresses us through his written word, the Bible.

God's Revelation in Sacred Scripture

In order to reveal himself, God in his wisdom and goodness has spoken to us in human language. "For in the sacred books the Father who is in heaven comes lovingly to meet his children, and speaks with them."[14] The one great Word of God, Jesus Christ, is revealed in these words that have been consigned to writing by various authors.

The sacred Scripture provides constant nourishment and strength for the church because she accepts it, not as the word of men, "but, as it truly is, the word of God" (1 Thess 2:13, NAB).[15] Because of this, the Catholic Church "has always venerated the divine Scriptures as she venerated the Body of the Lord" (Vatican II, "Dogmatic Constitution on Divine Revelation," *Dei Verbum,* no. 21). When we pray in the "Our Father" for the Lord to give us "our daily bread," we are praying to receive Jesus, the bread of life, as well as the food our bodies need (see Jn 16:27). In the Mass, we receive Jesus from the one table of God's Word in sacred Scripture, *and* of the body of Christ in the Eucharist, a foretaste of the great "banquet" of heaven in which God will fill us completely.

The Value of the Old Testament

Christians accept the Old Testament as inspired by God and thus important for instruction and guidance (CCC 121). However, there is a potential misunderstanding (held, for example, by Marcion in the second century A.D.) which sees the Old Testament as unimportant or dispensable because it has been surpassed by the New Testament, God's revelation of himself in Jesus Christ. The Catholic Church vigorously opposes this idea, because these inspired writings of the Old Testament "are a storehouse of sublime teaching on God and of sound wisdom on human life, as well as a wonderful treasury of prayers; in them, too, the mystery of our salvation is present in a hidden way."[16]

St. Augustine affirmed that the New Testament is hidden in the Old, and the Old Testament is made manifest in the New.[17] It is important, then, for Catholics to study the Old Testament books in order to fully and properly understand the New Testament, and to receive the Old Testament's own unique and valuable divine teaching.

As we study the unfolding story of God's saving plan in history, we must begin this story with the writings of the Old Testament. An unfortunate result of the rift between Catholics and Protestants is the disagreement over the canon (official list of inspired writings) of the Old Testament. Catholics recognize as divinely inspired the writings included in the ancient Greek version of the Old Testament that was used in the early church, known as the Septuagint. Protestants accept only the writings found in an early Hebrew version of the Bible, which did not include the books of Tobit, Judith, Wisdom, Sirach,

Baruch, and 1 and 2 Maccabees. These books are sometimes referred to by Protestants as "the Apocrypha." Many Protestants read and respect these writings, although they do not consider them divinely inspired. Catholics often refer to these books as deutero-canonical (a second canon) because they have been disputed. Even so, Catholics accept them as divinely inspired works that are fully part of the canon of the Old Testament.

The Origins of the New Testament

The forty-six writings that Catholics recognize as the Old Testament were written, edited, and handed down over a period of many centuries. The twenty-seven writings that both Catholics and Protestants accept as the canon[18] of the New Testament took relatively less time to advance from their initial form to their general recognition by the church as a set of inspired writings—only about three hundred years!

How did the New Testament, our primary witness to Jesus, come into being? For about three hundred years, Christians had no universally recognized "New Testament." During this period, letters from the apostles and other close followers of Jesus were circulated among the local Christian churches. Also, various traditions (literally "things passed on") recounting aspects of the life and teaching of Jesus were spread among these churches either as stories or in preaching ("oral tradition"), and eventually in short written accounts about Jesus ("written tradition"). Beginning twenty or thirty years after Jesus' death and resurrection, some of his followers compiled these traditions into unified accounts of Jesus' life and ministry, known as gospels (the "Good News"). One of these evangelists, St. Luke, describes his task in the introduction to his Gospel:

> Inasmuch as many have undertaken to compile a narrative of the things which have been accomplished among us, just as they were delivered to us by those who from the beginning were eyewitnesses and ministers of the word, it seemed good to me also, having followed all things closely for some time past, to write an orderly account for you, most excellent Theophilus, that you may know the truth concerning the things of which you have been informed.
>
> LUKE 1:1-4

Unfortunately, not all of these gospels were reliable or in agreement on certain important points, even though they bore names such as "The Gospel of Thomas" or "The Gospel of Truth." How did Christians determine which gospels and which letters, all claiming to be from apostles or disciples of Christ, were totally true and inspired by God?

The early Christians knew that Jesus had promised the Holy Spirit to guide the church into all truth, enabling her to recognize the teaching and writing he had inspired. How did the Holy Spirit guide the church in this crucial matter? The church believed that the Holy Spirit would guide the chief teachers and elders of God's people, the bishops, to make this judgment and to preach and teach the true meaning of God's written word.

In caring for the flock of Christ, one of the bishop's chief tasks was to ensure that correct doctrine was taught. So it was the bishops who needed to discern which writings and teachings being widely distributed were truly God's word for the whole church—and which were not.[19]

Their determination was officially announced in a decree of the Council of Rome in A.D. 382, under Pope Damasus, and confirmed by the Third Council of Carthage in A.D. 397. The present list of New Testament writings was first founded in the *Codex Vaticanus* from Rome around A.D. 340, and in St. Athanasius' Thirty-Ninth Festal Letter of A.D. 367.

By the fifth century, then, the bishops of the church had reached a general agreement about which letters and gospels were truly inspired by God, even though the status of some writings was still disputed after this time. Thus was the New Testament "born" substantially the same as we know it today. Catholics regard the Bible as the "book of the church," because it came into being as a product of the tradition of the church and through the judgment and discernment of the church's bishops.

Catholics believe that the bishops continue their role of authentically proclaiming and interpreting the Bible through the guidance of the Holy Spirit.[20] As different letters and gospels that claimed to have apostolic origins were read within the early Christian churches, the bishops of these churches prayerfully discerned their authenticity, and oftentimes discussed this subject with other bishops in the region. Over time, the bishops came to agree upon which letters and gospels were truly in harmony with the traditions they had received from the apostles. When the traditionally accepted canon was challenged in the sixteenth century, the Catholic bishops formally defined the present canon of both the Old and New Testaments, at the Council of Trent in 1546.

The Meaning of Inspiration

What does it mean that the Bible, or a particular book of the Bible, is inspired by God? To say that a writing is inspired means that God is, in some way, its author. Vatican II's *Dei Verbum* affirms this when it states:

> The books of the Old and New Testament, whole and entire, with all their parts... (were) written under the inspiration of the Holy Spirit ... they have God as their author and have been handed on as such to the Church herself.[21]

Inspiration also has another dimension, however. The human persons who wrote the sacred Scriptures were not just passive recipients of God's Word who merely served as secretaries for what God was dictating. Rather, God "made use of their powers and abilities" and calls them "true authors," even though they "consigned to writing everything and only those things which He wanted."[22] Thus, the author of the Bible is both God and the human writer.

Interpreting the Bible

In recent times, the Catholic Church has identified two common erroneous approaches to interpreting the Bible. These may be termed *rationalism* and *literalism*.

Rationalism limits the meaning of the Bible to what is commonly thought to be reasonable or possible. It excludes interpretations of the Bible, for example, affirming that God does extraordinary things (mighty works or "miracles") that can't be explained scientifically and that are not part of everyday, common human experience. The rationalist attempts to give a rational, "nonmiraculous" interpretation of biblical texts based on the presupposition that God does not intervene in history in extraordinary or miraculous ways.

This presupposition, of course, excludes the traditional Christian understanding of the incarnation of the Word of God, the resurrection of Jesus from the dead and his ascension into heaven, and all the Gospel accounts of Jesus' "miracles" or mighty works.

Literalism, on the other hand, seeks to interpret Scripture without taking into consideration the original intent of the author or the culture in which the text was written. Literalists believe that the Bible "means what it says"—and although many do this out of respect for God's authorship, their "interpretations" may vary widely, and in many cases lose the author's original intent altogether.

For example, each of the four Gospels gives a slightly different account of the discovery of the empty tomb. In Matthew, one angel comes to roll back the stone (Mt 28:2); in Mark there is a young man at the tomb dressed in white (Mk 16:5); in Luke, two men are there in dazzling apparel (Lk 24:4); and in John there are two angels in white (Jn 20:12). The accounts differ in other details, as well.

The literalist will insist that each of the accounts is historically accurate, and so the apparent discrepancies can be reconciled—proven to be in agreement factually and historically. The rationalist will argue that those differences are irrelevant because the accounts are not historical; they were written to proclaim the church's faith that Jesus is no longer in the tomb, that he is risen. The Catholic Church will consider both her tradition and the contribution of modern scholarly approaches to understanding the sacred Scripture as explained below. Catholics will recognize the basic factual agreement of the accounts (differing only in details), and also the centrality of the *message* of the white-clad witnesses: that the tomb is empty and Jesus is risen!

The Catholic Church teaches that in order to determine what God intends to say to us in the Bible, we must first seek out what the inspired author intended to communicate through the particular language, culture, historical situation, and type of writing (historical writing, poetic texts, etc.) in which the teaching was presented and from which it emerged (see CCC 109-10).[23] To do this requires diligent study and wisdom, in addition to prayer and enlightenment from the Holy Spirit.

Beginning with the encyclical letter of Pope Pius XII in 1943, *Divino Afflante Spiritu,* the Catholic Church has given positive encouragement to biblical scholars to employ modern methods of biblical criticism in order to understand more fully the human dimension of the Bible and its composition. *Dei Verbum* confirmed this encouragement, but also implicitly warned that the findings of biblical scholars, using the so-called historical-critical method or any other modern scientific approach to Scripture, are not enough in themselves to determine the authentic meaning of God's Word. The Constitution insists that the "holy Scripture must be read and interpreted according to the same Spirit by whom it was written."[24]

Three Principles for Sound Interpretation of Scripture

The *Catechism* highlights three criteria, taken from Vatican II, for interpreting Scripture in accordance with the Holy Spirit, who inspired it.

1. Be especially attentive "to the content and unity of the whole Scripture" (CCC 112). The meaning of the sacred text, and consequently the meaning of an individual section of Scripture, can be understood rightly only when viewed in the light of the whole of Scripture and its unity. Individual passages cannot be isolated from the overall message of Scripture if they are to be interpreted correctly.

2. Read the Scripture within "the living Tradition of the whole Church" (CCC 113). To insure that the Tradition of the Catholic Church would be taken into account in interpreting the Bible, Pope Pius XII strongly urged Scripture scholars to study assiduously the Fathers and doctors of the church, as well as renowned interpreters of the past ages.[25]

The 1985 Extraordinary Synod of Catholic Bishops affirmed that "the exegesis of the original meaning of Sacred Scripture, most highly recommended by the Council ... cannot be separated from the living tradition of the Church"[26] All this is simply to recognize that modern approaches to biblical study, as valuable as their findings may be, are not adequate by themselves to elucidate the full meaning of the Bible.

3. Be attentive to the analogy of faith (see Rom 12:6). By "analogy of faith" we mean the coherence of the truths of faith among themselves and within the whole plan of Revelation (CCC 114).

The Inerrancy of the Bible

Biblical inspiration means that God has spoken his Word to humanity through the medium of human authors. Even though fallible human authors were involved in the composition of the Bible, however, the Catholic Church has continually insisted that there is a sense in which the sacred Scripture is without error.[27]

The Second Vatican Council states that, "the books of Scripture firmly, faithfully, and without error, teach that truth which God, for the sake of our salvation, wished to see confided to the Sacred Scriptures."[28]

If this is so, how can we reconcile biblical inerrancy with apparent discrepancies or contradictions in the Bible? For example, the four Gospels present different (and sometimes even conflicting) reports of when and where things happened in Jesus' public ministry and after his resurrection. However, in studying the context of these biblical texts carefully, using sound scholarship, we have come to a deeper understanding of the meaning of such texts. Catholic scholars have observed that the Gospel writers had definite theological and pedagogical reasons for how and in what order they recounted events in Jesus' life.[29]

The same questions have been raised concerning the inerrancy of the Old Testament. Sometimes these questions are related to historical accuracy. Occasionally differing accounts of the same event are recorded, such as the order of creation in Genesis 1:1–2:3 and in Genesis 2:4-25, or the way God parted the Red Sea in Exodus 14:21 and 14:22-29.

The fact that the final editor of the text placed two historically different accounts side by side without explanation or apology should tell us something. That is, the question of historical accuracy is apparently not what (they believed) God was seeking to reveal through the accounts. The inerrancy of the Bible is not called into question by such discrepancies. A more pressing question in recent times is whether the Bible is "inerrant" when it appears to teach things that differ from the findings of modern experimental science.

Recall the teaching of *Dei Verbum* "that the books of Scripture must be acknowledged as teaching firmly, faithfully, and without error that truth which God wanted put into the sacred writings *for the sake of our salvation.*"[30] The phrase, "for the sake of our salvation," is essential to understanding this correctly. The official footnote to this passage in the Vatican II document refers to a statement of St. Thomas Aquinas:

> Any knowledge which is profitable to salvation may be the object of prophetic inspiration. But things which cannot affect our salvation do not belong to inspiration.[31]

As an example of this principle, St. Augustine says that "although the sacred writers may have known astronomy, nevertheless the Holy Spirit did not intend to utter through them any truth apart from that which is profitable to salvation." He adds that this may concern either teachings to be believed or morals to be practiced.[32]

Pope John Paul II has called it an "error" of the theologians in the past

> ... to think that our understanding of the physical world's structure was, in some way, imposed by the literal sense of Sacred Scripture.... In fact, the Bible does not concern itself with the details of the physical world, the understanding of which is the competence of human experience and reasoning. There exist two realms of knowledge, one which has its source in revelation and one which reason can discover by its own power. To the latter belong especially the experimental sciences and philosophy. The distinction between the two realms of knowledge ought not to be understood as an opposition. The two realms are not altogether foreign to each other; they have points of contact. The methodologies proper to each make it possible to bring out different aspects of reality.[33]

The Catholic Church has learned this principle from long reflection and experience. At the time of the emergence of modern astronomy, for example, the Catholic Church mistakenly condemned the scientific teaching of Galileo Galilei that the sun, not the earth, was the center of the solar system. Galileo's theory appeared to contradict the Bible's teaching on this point. Since then, modern science has blossomed with the encouragement and support of the Catholic Church, and a clearer understanding of the interrelationship of science, history, and Christian faith has developed.[34]

Recognizing the legitimate autonomy of the human sciences, the Catholic

Church today holds that the inerrancy of the Bible (and the teaching authority of the church) must apply to science or history with a proper understanding of the text and of God's purpose in revelation. God has inspired the sacred Scriptures primarily to reveal himself, and his plan for all his creation in relationship to himself. The Bible infallibly reveals how we are to relate to God and to each other in this world in order to fulfill God's plan and attain eternal salvation. The Bible is absolutely without error when it speaks of these things. There may be other truths contained in the Bible, but the Catholic Church believes that only these are without error as a result of God's inspiration of the sacred Scripture.

Even in matters regarding salvation, faith, and morality, the Catholic Church rarely defines the exact meaning of particular passages of the Bible (as if to say, the passage means *this* and no more). This leaves room for the contributions of saints, biblical scholars, and others who prayerfully reflect on the meaning of the Scriptures.

In his encyclical letter *Divino Afflante Spiritu* in 1943, Pope Pius XII taught that "in questions of doctrine regarding faith and morals ... there remain, therefore, many things, and of the greatest importance, in the discussion and exposition of which the skill and genius of Catholic commentators may and ought to be freely exercised, so that each may contribute his part to the advantage of all, to the continued progress of the sacred doctrine and to the defense and honor of the Church."[35]

While the Catholic Church has encouraged those who seek out the true meaning of God's Word in the sacred Scripture, it has also issued some necessary warnings and cautions. Pope Pius XII's encyclical letter *Humani Generis* (1950) warned against relying on human reason alone in interpreting the Bible and stressed that we need to consider "the analogy of faith and the Tradition of the Church."[36] As we have mentioned, the church must also be wary of rationalistic prejudices that deny the possibility of God's intervention in history in miraculous ways.

Those who wish to learn more about the meaning of the Bible should seek out books and authors that utilize the best in modern biblical scholarship, along with the Fathers and doctors of the church, in the framework of loyalty to the Catholic Church's teaching office in case of any disputed interpretation.[37]

The *Catechism of the Catholic Church* also encourages Catholics to be aware of the two "senses" of Scripture—two types or levels of meaning present in the biblical text. These are the *literal* sense ("the meaning conveyed by the words of Scripture and discovered by exegesis") and the *spiritual* sense. The spiritual sense may be further divided into three senses:

1. The *allegorical* sense, which are events or images in Scripture that are signs or "types" of spiritual realities, especially of Christ;
2. The *moral* sense, which is instruction given by God leading us to act justly; and
3. The *analogical* sense, in which biblical events or images are seen as signs of their fulfillment in heaven, in terms of their eternal significance. (See CCC 115-17.)

All of these meanings may be explored by the faithful or proposed by exegetes (biblical scholars), but the final judgment about the manner of interpreting Scripture is reserved to the official teaching office of the church.

The Magisterium Defines and Proclaims Christian Doctrine

The Magisterium, or teaching office of the church, is composed of the Catholic bishops in union with the pope. It is a great gift of God in helping us to understand the true and full meaning of God's Word. "This teaching office is not above the word of God, but serves it, teaching only what has been handed on, listening to it devoutly, guarding it scrupulously, and explaining it faithfully by divine commission and with the help of the Holy Spirit; it draws from this deposit of faith everything which it presents for belief as divinely revealed."[38]

Although the teaching office of the church seldom gives exact definitions of the meaning of God's Word, at times disputes over Scripture have led the bishops or the popes to condemn false or erroneous interpretations, or to define truths of the faith based upon God's Word (either in sacred Scripture or in sacred Tradition). For example, erroneous Scripture interpretations of Arius in the fourth century were condemned by the First Ecumenical Council of Nicea (A.D. 325); and the errors of the twentieth-century Modernists were condemned by Pope St. Pius X (1907). The Council of Chalcedon (A.D. 451) positively defined the church's understanding of Jesus being "one person in two natures," while Pope Pius XII in 1950 solemnly defined the dogma of Mary's bodily Assumption into heaven, based on sacred tradition—the church's consistent belief.

Catholics believe that the Holy Spirit enables the bishops and the pope to recognize God's revelation and even to solemnly declare certain teachings to be true (i.e., to define dogma), based on the "sacred deposit" of the faith (*depositum fidei*) which is contained in sacred Scripture and sacred tradition. This is a special gift of God to the church, who gives her, in the Magisterium, a living source of discernment, teaching, and guidance in each age.

The *Catechism* notes the "organic connection" between dogmas defined by the church and our spiritual lives. "Dogmas are lights along the path of faith; they illuminate it and make it secure" (CCC 89). Dogmas may be thought of as channel markers in a river, warning of the danger of error in going too far in one direction or another in the interpretation of Scripture and Tradition, but also showing the path in the middle where the church's faith, in all its richness, may be understood in different ways.

The *Catechism* also reminds us that not all revealed truths are of equal importance. "In Catholic doctrine there exists an order or 'hierarchy' of truths, since they vary in their relation to the foundation of Christian faith."[39] The church's Magisterium helps us to understand every truth that God has revealed (the full gospel), but by her preaching and teaching she focuses our attention on those truths that are most central to the gospel of Jesus Christ, and therefore most important for our salvation.

Tripod of Truth: The Magisterium, the Bible, and Tradition

It may be said that God's revelation is presented in its fullness through a "tripod of truth": sacred Scripture, sacred tradition, and the teaching office or Magisterium of the church. The relationship between these channels of God's truth emerged in the early years of the church. Scripture and Tradition were both aspects of the Word of God, the "sacred deposit" of faith that Jesus entrusted to the church he founded. As the Second Vatican Council explains:

Sacred Scripture is the word of God as it is put down in writing under the inspiration of the Holy Spirit. And sacred tradition transmits in its entirety the word of God which has been entrusted to the apostles by Christ the Lord and the Holy Spirit. It transmits it to the successors of the apostles so that they may faithfully preserve this word of God, explain it, and make it more widely known....[40]

The living teaching office of the church, "whose authority is exercised in the name of Jesus Christ," has "the task of authentically interpreting the word of God, whether in its written form or in the form of tradition."[41] The Magisterium has carried out this task faithfully since the very beginning of Christianity. The apostles of Jesus were the first authorized proclaimers and interpreters of the faith that Jesus left them, followed by the bishops they appointed to lead and teach the churches.

The Second Vatican Council summarizes the relationship of these channels of God's revelation:

It is clear, therefore, that sacred tradition, sacred scripture, and the teaching authority of the church, in accord with God's most wise design, are so linked and joined together that one cannot stand without others, and that all together and each in its own way under the action of the Holy Spirit contribute effectively to the salvation of souls.[42]

Sacred Scripture, Tradition, and the teaching authority of the church are like three legs of a tripod; they are mutually dependent and support each other. Without sacred Scripture, we would have no reliable record of God's dealing with man and the fullness of his revelation of himself in Jesus Christ. Without Tradition, the way Scripture has been understood and interpreted over the centuries by the church would disappear, leaving us to interpret Scripture according to societal or personal biases. Without the teaching authority of the church, there is no united way that either sacred Scripture or Christian tradition could be authoritatively interpreted and applied to practical situations in the present. Confusion and disunity would be the result.

But God, in his goodness, has provided not only the revelation of himself and his plan in the Bible but also the means by which revelation is to be faithfully preserved, passed on, fully understood, and authentically interpreted from the time of Christ down to the present day.

Private Revelation and Its Forms

Earlier in the chapter we noted that there has been "no new public revelation" since the time of Jesus and his apostles. However, this does not mean that God has ceased speaking or revealing himself to the human race. The Holy Spirit provides ongoing revelation and guidance to God's people through various means, building upon the foundational revelation that God has given in Jesus.

One form of the Holy Spirit's ongoing activity in the church is termed "private revelation." There are certain truths that God reveals through the Holy Spirit that either are not intended for the entire church or are not intended to be truths relevant for all times in the church's life. These are truths either directed toward a particular individual or group within the church or intended for a particular time or period in human history.

Private revelation includes such things as words spoken through the gift of prophecy; messages from God spoken to an individual or a group through angels, saints, or Mary, the Mother of God; visions, dreams, or voices that present a word from God to a person or persons; or even a word or appearance of God himself. The Catholic Church insists that such private revelations must be discerned or tested carefully to ensure that they are truly from God, lest some people be deceived.

One important test is that no private revelation can contradict or disagree with "public revelation," that is, what God has revealed through the Bible or sacred tradition. Genuine private revelation always complements and supports God's public revelation to his people.

Even when the church, after discernment, finds no objection to a private revelation, the Catholic Church does not require any of its members to believe in it or its message, since it is not part of the foundational public revelation of God. However, God often has an important purpose in presenting a special private revelation, such as to awaken the church to a part of public revelation that he desires his people to pray and act upon or to call attention to his work and plan during a particular time in human history.

A good example of the Catholic Church's painstaking discernment of private revelation is its approach to the many reported appearances of Mary, the Mother of God. Some reported apparitions of Mary investigated by the Catholic Church have been judged to be false. Others, such as appearances of Mary at Guadalupe (Mexico), Lourdes (France), and Fatima (Portugal), have received widespread approval in the Catholic world, and some popes even have made pilgrimages to these sites.

Nonetheless, Catholics are not required to believe that Mary has appeared and spoken a word from God because these apparitions still remain in the realm of private revelation. However, if it is possible that God is speaking prophetically or sending messengers, such as Christ's Mother, to speak special words from him for our time, it is wise to be attentive to them and to consider them prayerfully. Authentic private revelation, like public revelation, is a gift of God and should be received with thanksgiving.

God not only continues to speak to his people but also continues to reveal himself and his presence by performing mighty acts among his people. Miracles, healings, exorcisms, and other mighty works are done in the name of Jesus and by his power. This should not surprise us, for Jesus told his followers that they would perform even greater works than his (see Jn 14:12). Christians should rejoice and be grateful that God has not chosen to remain hidden, but instead has made himself known to us in both his words and his deeds, in the past and today.

Faith: Our Response to God's Revelation

God so desires our friendship and our salvation that he has revealed himself to the human race. If creation, which "declare[s] the glory of God" (Ps 19:1), and his manifestations in history to his chosen people Israel are not enough to convince us of his existence and his love, then his personal entry into time and matter as a man, Jesus Christ, should be an unmistakable sign of the reality of God and of his love for us.

Jesus reveals fully the one true God and enables us to know God as a Trinity of three divine persons: the Father, the Son, and the Holy Spirit. The only adequate human response to God as he reveals himself to us in so many ways is what is known as *faith*. Faith in God is the foundation of all authentic religion, including Christianity.

But what is faith? It is expressed in the personal form, "I believe" (the Apostle's Creed), or in the expression of the community, the church, "We believe" (the Nicene Creed). The creeds express faith or belief first in God himself, and then, by extension, to all that God has revealed. "Faith is first of all a personal adherence of man to God. At the same time, and inseparably, it is *a free assent to the whole truth that God has revealed*" (CCC 150).

Faith as a personal adherence to God means submitting one's whole life—intellect and will, "heart, mind, and soul"—completely to God, recognizing him as the source of our life, the one who constantly sustains us in existence, and as the final end and goal of our life. To have faith in God is to *trust* God, and to *entrust* our lives to him by what Scripture calls the "obedience of faith" (see Rom 1:5; 16:26; see also CCC 143).

God longs for each person to make this decision. Jesus wept over Jerusalem because his people would not believe in him, and cried out, "Jerusalem, Jerusalem, you who kill the prophets and stone those sent to you, how many times I yearned to gather your children together as a hen gathers her brood under her wings, but you were unwilling!" (Lk 13:34, NAB).

Models of Faith

Faith and the "obedience of faith" may be best understood by considering the lives of those who possessed this virtue. In the Old Covenant, Abraham is presented by Scripture as a model of faith. He led his entire family on a "pilgrimage of faith" from his native land, and responded in faith at every step of that journey, even to the point of being ready to sacrifice his only son at God's command. (This prefigured the sacrifice of the heavenly Father of his only Son for our sake.) Hence, Abraham is still known as our father in faith, as the "father of all who believe" (Rom 4:11), whose faith was "reckoned to him as righteousness" (Gen 15:6; Rom 4:22).

In the New Testament, "the Virgin Mary most perfectly embodies the obedience of faith" (CCC 148). From the moment Mary was first introduced in Scripture at the Annunciation, until the end of her life, Mary's faith in God never wavered, even when she witnessed her Son's abandonment and crucifixion. Her cousin Elizabeth's greeting to Mary was prophetic: "Blessed are you who believed that what was spoken to you by the Lord would be fulfilled" (Lk 1:45, NAB; see also CCC 148). Mary's faith was most perfect, an ideal model for all Jesus' followers.

All of the saints are also examples of faith that encourage the church. As St. Paul wrote: "Yet I live, not longer I, but Christ lives in me; insofar as I now live in the flesh, I live by faith in the Son of God who has loved me and given himself up for me" (Gal 2:20, NAB).

Dimensions of Faith

What is faith? Where does it come from? What is its relation to reason? These questions require an explanation of the many dimensions of faith.

First, faith itself is both a gift of God (grace), and a human act. To believe, "man must have the grace of God to move and assist him; he must have the interior helps of the Holy Spirit, who moves the heart and converts it to God...."[43] No one can believe in God without his grace and the interior action of the Holy Spirit.

And yet, while God offers to every person the grace to believe in him in some way, he does not force anyone to believe. As with a decision to marry a particular person or enter a religious community by a free act, each person must decide whether to put his or her trust in God and turn over his or her life completely to him in the "obedience of faith." In this sense, faith is not just an intellectual assent, but commitment of the whole person to God. It is done in response to his revelation and thanks to the grace of God which makes this faith possible.

For some, it is important or even necessary to pray for the gift of faith, beseeching God for the help and the grace to believe in him, even if this prayer seems to be a cry in the darkness. Jesus promised, "Ask and you will receive; seek and you will find; knock and the door will be opened to you" (Lk 11:9, NAB).

Faith and Reason

To believe in God is not unreasonable. To the contrary, it is a most reasonable human act to acknowledge and to submit to the loving, all-powerful God who created us and everything that is. God enables each person to believe in him by the interior help of the Holy Spirit joined to external evidences or signs such as "the miracles of Christ and the saints, prophecies, the Church's growth and holiness, and her fruitfulness and stability"(CCC 156). Jesus himself is reported as saying: "Believe me that I am in the Father and the Father is in me, or else, believe because of the works themselves" (Jn 14:11, NAB).

Faith, then, is not a "leap in the dark," but a most reasonable act. In fact, the *Catechism* insists that "faith is *certain* ... because it is founded on the very word of God who cannot lie" (CCC 157).

Faith in the Truth God Has Revealed

Not only do Christians believe in God himself, but also in all the *truth* that he has revealed. This is another dimension of Christian faith. St. Thomas Aquinas refers to this when he defines faith: "Believing is an act of the intellect assenting to the divine truth by command of the will and moved by God through grace."[44]

The intellect seeks to *understand* what one believes, which is the classic definition of theology, *"fides quarens intellectum"* (faith seeking understanding). The *Catechism* observes, "a more penetrating knowledge will in turn call forth a greater faith, increasingly set afire by love" (CCC 158). It is the Holy Spirit, God's love personified, who "constantly perfects faith by his gifts, so that Revelation may be more and more profoundly understood."[45] Thus, "the grace of faith opens 'the eyes of your hearts' (Eph 1:18) to a lively understanding of the contents of Revelation: that is, of the totality of God's plan and the mysteries of faith, of their connection with each other and with Christ, the center of the revealed mystery" (CCC 158).

Faith enables us to understand God's revealed truth, and to understand it ever more deeply. Through this work of the Holy Spirit, the Catholic Church has been able to come to understand more clearly the relationship between revealed truths known by faith and human knowledge attained by reason, such as science. Since God is the ultimate source of all reality and truth, there can be no contradiction between revealed truths and truths discovered through study, reason, or scientific research. (Of course, the distinction must be made between "fact" and hypotheses.) As we will see later, the Catholic Church has always been a patron of learning, and encourages research and study, as long as it is not prejudiced against truth that is perceived by faith. Our faith in God makes known a spiritual realm that really exists, but which is not accessible to scientific investigation since it is not material (see CCC 159).[46]

The Necessity of Faith

Faith is necessary in order to attain to the knowledge of the invisible God, and also to attain eternal life with God.

The Gospels record many instances of Jesus teaching his followers the importance of believing in God the Father and in him (Jesus), who is the only way to the Father, in order to enter into eternal life with God—to be "saved" (see Mk 16:16; Jn 3:36; 6:40; 14:6; Acts 4:12). To be sure, Jesus also speaks of the judgment and the salvation of some of those who, through no fault of their own, do not know God and yet have acted in charity (see Mt 25:31-46). However, Jesus reveals that the normal way of salvation is through faith. In fact, through faith, we already know and "see" God, even if only as "in a mirror dimly" (1 Cor 13:12). So the faith we possess now is a foretaste of heaven, and "the beginning of eternal life" (CCC 163).

Growing in Faith—Immersing Ourselves in God's Revelation

Faith is a free gift of God. Faith is also a gift that must be nourished in order to grow. For faith to be strong and flourish, it must be "watered" by constant prayer, and "fed" by the sacraments and by immersing ourselves in God's Word. How can Catholics better come to know God and his revealed truth, and hence grow in faith?

1. Prayerfully reading and studying the Word of God in the Bible. "And such is the force and power of the Word of God that it can serve the Church as her support and vigor, and the children of the Church as strength for their faith, food for their soul, and a pure and lasting fount of spiritual life."[47] The Second Vatican Council also has taught,

> Easy access to Sacred Scripture should be provided for all the Christian faithful…. This sacred Synod earnestly and specifically urges all the Christian faithful … to learn by frequent reading of the divine Scriptures of the "excelling knowledge of Jesus Christ" [Phil 3:8]. "For ignorance of the Scriptures is ignorance of Christ" [St. Jerome]. Therefore, they should gladly put themselves in touch with the sacred text itself, whether it be through the liturgy … through devotional reading, or through instructions suitable for the purpose and other aids…. And let them remember that prayer should accompany the reading of Sacred Scripture, so that God and man may talk together; for "we speak to Him when we pray; we hear Him when we read the divine sayings" [St. Ambrose].[48]

The primary way that Catholics should come to know God's revealed truth is through reading the Bible daily. Even though the Bible is not the *only* source of God's revelation; it is a *primary* source that is normally accessible to every believer (see 2 Tim 3:16-17).

Some Catholics (and other Christians) may ask whether the Catholic Church has ever prohibited its members from reading the Bible. Because the meaning of the Bible was being disputed and misinterpreted by some at the time of the Protestant Reformation, in 1564 Pope Pius IV declared that lay Catholics had to obtain permission from their bishop to read the Bible in their native language—the vernacular. Reading the official Catholic Bible of the time, the Latin Vulgate, was never prohibited.

Later, Catholics had to obtain permission from the Sacred Congregation of the Index in Rome, or from the pope himself, in order to read the Bible in the vernacular. This was done to protect Catholics from inaccurate translations and from misinterpreting the Bible. Catholics still heard the Scriptures proclaimed and explained at Mass and in other contexts by the clergy, as they always had.

In the nineteenth century, the Catholic hierarchy lifted all restrictions on reading the Bible in the vernacular, as long as a Catholic edition was used. In 1896, Pope Leo XIII encouraged Bible reading among Catholics by granting a plenary indulgence to all Catholics who read Scripture for fifteen minutes a day.[49]

2. Studying teachings of past councils and popes. God's revelation of himself also includes his truth passed on in the authentic tradition of the Catholic Church. This tradition may be found in the decisions and declarations of the ecumenical councils of the church, and in the teachings of past popes.

All Catholics today should become familiar with the teachings of the Second Vatican Council by reading the sixteen documents of the council or by studying the council's teaching as it is contained in the *Catechism of the Catholic Church* (CCC). This council presents the tradition of the Catholic Church and the guidance of the church's Magisterium, directed specifically to us who live at this era of history. Through reading and studying the documents of councils of the church and past popes, we become familiar with the rich tradition and life of the Catholic Church.

3. Hearing the teaching of our present pope and bishops. Finally, we encounter God's revelation of himself and his will through keeping in touch with the teachings and statements of the Magisterium—our present pope and bishops. We can do this by reading reliable publications of diocesan or national Catholic publication offices, and magazines and newspapers containing current teachings of the popes and bishops.

It should be noted that there are different levels of authority among the teaching of the pope and the bishops. Some teaching contains specific directives in the area of faith and morals that are binding on the conscience of Catholics. Other teachings, such as general political or economic reflections, do not have the same authority but are to be respectfully received and considered by Catholics. The reading of these teachings, of whatever level of authority, will enable Catholics to be informed about God's current direction and the guidance of the Catholic Church through those who have been set apart to carry on the apostles' task of faithfully preaching and teaching the Word of God.

All of these means, especially the prayerful reading and study of sacred Scripture, will enable the Christian to grow in faith, to persevere in faith, and with God's help finally obtain the goal of faith—full knowledge of God in heaven. There we will see him "face to face" (1 Cor 13:12)—the glory of the "beatific vision," the direct vision of God that brings perfect happiness.

Now that we have spoken in this introductory chapter about the existence of God, God's revelation of himself to humanity, and our response to his revelation, faith, let us recount from the beginning what God has revealed about himself and his loving and merciful plan of salvation for the human race.

CHAPTER 2

God, His Creation, and Man's Rebellion

In the beginning God created the heavens and the earth....

GENESIS 1:1

Now that we have studied how Catholics interpret God's revelation, let us apply these principles to the biblical teaching about the origins of the universe and the human race.

Although the Book of Genesis was not the first book of the Bible to be written, it is placed first in the Old Testament because it tells of the genesis, of the beginning, of God's work of creation and salvation (CCC 289). This revelation from God about our beginnings is the foundation of the Christian faith. If the basic truth presented in the Book of Genesis is distorted or misunderstood, so too will be the rest of the teachings of the Bible.

Genesis teaches us the basic truths about the origin and nature of man, the introduction of evil into the world, and about God and the beginning of his saving plan.

Interpreting Genesis

Many people today, even some Christians, consider Genesis a fascinating story springing from the mythology of a primitive people. Every primitive people developed some story about the origin of the universe and the human race. It stands to reason, they say, that the Book of Genesis resembles other ancient stories, such as the Babylonian myths, the "Epic of Gilgamesh," or *Enuma Elish*.

The Catholic Church, along with many other Christian churches, acknowledges that the Book of Genesis is presented in the form of a story or myth that is similar to other such stories in the ancient world. However, Catholics insist that the content of Genesis, properly understood, contains the absolute and unfailing truth about God's action and plan in creating the universe and the human race. Why? Because Genesis is part of the collection of books, known as the Bible or the sacred Scriptures, that has been inspired and preserved in truth by the author of the universe, God himself. The Catholic Church affirms that:

> The books of Scripture must be acknowledged as teaching firmly, faithfully, and without error that truth which God wanted put into the sacred writings for the sake of our salvation.[1]

and

> The books of the Old Testament, in accordance with the state of mankind before the time of salvation established by Christ, reveal to all men the knowledge of God and of man and the ways in which God, just and merciful, deals with men....[2]

It is important to understand that the Book of Genesis is more than an interesting ancient story. It teaches essential truths about God, his creation, and the beginnings of humanity. As we discussed in the preceeding chapter, Catholics look at Genesis and the other writings of the Bible as theological (God-centered) works that God inspired in order to reveal the truth about himself, his will and plan, and his relationship and dealings with his creatures (including humanity). The Catholic understanding of the Bible differs from that of some other Christians in this regard.

The Existence of God

Before discussing the origin of the universe, we will address the question of God's existence. How do we know there is a God? If there is a God, what is he like?

The Catholic tradition basically recognizes two ways that we can come to know that God exists, and what he is like. The first way is through observing and thinking about the universe, in order to discover the God behind it. This is sometimes called natural revelation—God revealing himself through nature or the universe. "The heavens declare the glory of God..." the psalmist proclaims (Ps 19:2). St. Paul taught that, "Since the creation of the world, [God's] invisible attributes of eternal power and divinity have been able to be understood and perceived in what he has made" (Rom 1:20, NAB).

In the Middle Ages, St. Thomas Aquinas developed five celebrated "proofs" for the existence of God, based on reasoning about the universe. Aquinas argued that since everything has a cause, there must be a "first cause" that brought the material universe into being, and an "unmoved mover" that set it in motion. The magnificent order and beauty of the universe implies the existence of a great intelligent artist who designed it. For Aquinas, the existence of matter and of the universe points to the existence of a superior power and intelligence, God, who created it and set it in motion (CCC 31-34).

This philosophical approach does not conflict with most scientific theories about the origin of the universe. A current theory proposes that the universe began with a "big bang"—a primordial explosion producing matter and energy. Yet, science has not yet determined where the matter came from that exploded in the "big bang." Christians answer that God is ultimately the source of the universe coming into being, however or whenever this occurred. Catholics may accept any scientific theory of the origin of the cosmos, as long as it does not deny that God is finally and ultimately the source and creator of whatever exists. However, science is incapable of answering the basic philosophic questions about the universe, such as, "Why is it there?" and "Why is there something rather than nothing?" Christian doctrine answers these questions by claiming that the universe itself points to the existence of a God who created it.[3]

God Has Revealed Himself

If all we had to rely upon was natural revelation—the existence of the universe pointing to God—we would know God existed, but not much about him or what he is like. So, God has provided a second and more complete way of coming to know him. After speaking about the ability to know God by reflecting on created things, the First Vatican Council (1870) added:

Yet it pleased His [God's] wisdom and goodness to reveal Himself and the eternal decrees of His will to mankind in another, supernatural manner. As the Apostles say: "In many and various ways God spoke of old to our fathers by the prophets; but in these last days he has spoken to us by His Son" (Heb 1:1-2).

Because of this divine revelation, all men are able ... to know with readiness, with firm certitude, and without admixture of error, whatever in divine matters is not of itself beyond the grasp of human reason.[4]

This constitution explains that divine revelation is contained, "in written books [of the Old and of the New Testament] and in the unwritten traditions, which have been received by the apostles themselves, at the dictation of the Holy Spirit, [and] have come down even to us, transmitted as it were, from hand to hand...."[5]

Thus, God has revealed himself and his mind to us. He has done this most fully by becoming a man, Jesus Christ, and by inspiring the testimony of the apostles, the authors of the sacred Scripture and those "faithful witnesses" (the bishops) who have been chosen and authorized by God to hand on their teaching down through the centuries.

How do we know that God spoke or revealed himself to the human race in this way? Such a claim cannot be proven by reason or science. Ultimately, we know with assurance only that God has spoken and revealed himself to us through *faith*. We believe the writings and witnesses who testify that God has spoken and made himself known.

However, this assurance is not a result of "blind faith." The truth has a way of proving itself to the human heart without rational or scientific demonstration. One Christian author, J.B. Phillips, wrote that the Bible is convincing, even to nonbelievers, because it has the "ring of truth"[6]—it rings true with our human experience. As the Letter to the Hebrews describes it:

Indeed, the word of God is living and effective, sharper than any two-edged sword, penetrating even between soul and spirit, joints and marrow, and able to discern reflections and thoughts of the heart.

HEBREWS 4:12, NAB

Faith in God's revelation is a light that illumines God and his presence among us. Just as scientific observation and experimentation are the light that enables us to see and know about electrons and distant stars, faith in the truth that God reveals is the light or medium that enables us to see and know God and spiritual reality.

The One, True God

It is possible, through natural and divine revelation, to come to know that there is a God, and what he is like. What do we know about God through these sources? The foundational affirmation about God, which for centuries distinguished the Jews from their polytheistic neighbors, is that there is one and only one God.

No other people in the ancient world spoke of only one God. The traditional daily prayer of the Jewish people, the *Shema*, begins, "Hear, O Israel: The Lord our God is one Lord..." (Deut 6:4). Christians, too, reject the belief in many gods (polytheism), based on Jesus' clear teaching (see Mk 12:29).[7]

Today we might be tempted to laugh at a primitive people who believed in many gods. Yet, the truth is that even today in modern Western societies, those who do not really know the one, true God pay homage to other gods, whether consciously or not. Most don't worship the earth, the stars, or graven images made of stone or metal. The "gods" of modern Western society include economic, psychological, social, or historical laws; self, money, pleasure, popularity, power; Wall Street, the banking and marketing system, military might, the mass media, multinational corporations and governments. Some even hold up secular ideologies as the ultimate and inviolable source of truth and meaning—whether it be capitalism, socialism, Marxism, or feminism.

Though some of these things may not be evil in themselves, for many Western men and women these are the forces that dominate or rule their lives and decisions, instead of faith and life in the one, true God. Salvation, as we shall see, is not only a matter of the next life, but of being freed in this life from the domination of every "god"—freed to serve the one, true God.

Some people turn to other gods having consciously rejected the existence of God. Atheism, the denial of God's existence, has been designated by the Second

Vatican Council as "among the most serious problems of this age."[8] The council discussed the various forms and causes of atheism, and noted that atheism can emerge from the failure of believers in God to live according to their beliefs:

> To the extent that they [believers] neglect their own training in the faith, or teach erroneous doctrine, or are deficient in their religious, moral, or social life, they must be said to conceal rather than reveal the authentic face of God and religion.[9]

However, those who deny the existence of God finally bear the responsibility for their choice, for as Psalm 53 tells us, only the fool says, "there is no God" (Ps 53:2).

Another category of nonbelievers are agnostics, those who claim that it is impossible to know for certain whether or not God exists. Sometimes it is effective to ask such people (if they are serious about finding out whether God exists) to attempt an experiment. Ask them to go off by themselves sometime and earnestly ask God, if he is there, to reveal himself to them in some way that they will *know* if he exists.

This may sound like putting God to the test, but if the person is truly seeking God, Christians have good reason to believe that God will answer. St. James wrote, "Draw close to God and he will draw close to you" (Jas 4:8). The Book of Revelation says, "Behold, I stand at the door and knock. If anyone hears my voice and opens the door, [then] I will enter his house and dine with him, and he with me" (Rev 3:20, NAB). Jesus, during his life on earth, insisted, "And I tell you, ask and you will receive; seek and you will find; knock and the door will be opened to you. For everyone who asks, receives; and the one who seeks, finds; and to the one who knocks, the door will be opened" (Lk 11:9-10, NAB).

God does not try to hide himself from the human race or from any individual. Just the opposite is true. God desires each person to come to know him and to receive his abundant life in this world and in eternity (see John 10:10; 1 Tim 2:3). As Francis Thompson described so beautifully in his famous poem, God is "the hound of heaven," who does not rest from his pursuit of us until he catches us—when we turn to him.[10]

Specifically, as Christians, we know that God desires to reveal himself to humanity and to show his love for each person. He actually became a man, Jesus Christ, and loved us—even though it meant accepting an unjust and horrible death in order to free us from our sin and rebellion against him. What more could God have done to reveal to us his existence and his love, without over-powering us or otherwise violating our freedom?

All people strive to find the ultimate meaning or purpose of their lives and of human existence. St. Augustine tried it for years, but as he finally told God in his *Confessions*, "You have made us for Yourself, and our hearts are restless until they rest in You."[11] We have been created with a God-shaped vacuum in our hearts, and will find our fulfillment and peace only in knowing, loving, and serv-ing him.

God Is Spirit

Who is this God who Jews and Christians so confidently claim is the fulfillment of all human needs and desires? Even believers sometimes yield to the skepti-cism of those who doubt God's existence because he cannot be observed with-out the eyes of faith.

Soviet cosmonauts triumphantly announced on their first space flight that God was nowhere to be seen, instead of praising the beauty of God's creation. They failed to understand that God belongs to a different order of being. Jesus told the Samaritan woman near Jacob's well, "God is spirit" (Jn 4:24). "Spirit" is a form of being that is nonmaterial but that possesses intellect and free will— the ability to think and reason, to choose and decide. Pope John Paul II, in a general audience on September 11, 1986, summarized the basic Catholic teach-ing on God's nature as defined by the First Vatican Council:

"God is a unique spiritual *substance*, utterly simple and immutable"; and again, "God is infinite in *intellect, will, and in every perfection....*"

The Divine Being is by its own essence absolutely spiritual. Spirituality sig-nifies intellect and free will. God is *Intelligence, Will, and Liberty* in an infi-nite degree, just as He is also *all perfection* in an infinite degree.[12]

It is a difficult thing for most modern people to conceive of a realm of existence that is not material; they tend to think that intelligence and will are dependent upon the existence of a biological organ, the human brain. Yet, God does not have a brain, or any other material part. He is pure, infinite, unbounded spirit.

St. Anselm simply said God is "something ... than which a greater cannot be conceived."[13] In other words, God is greater than the greatest thing we can imagine, whether it be love, truth, justice, beauty, or goodness (which are other examples of realities that cannot be perceived with the senses).

The simplest way to describe God is by his positive attributes: he is omnipotent (all-powerful); omniscient (all-knowing) and all-wise; eternal (having no beginning and no end); omnipresent (present everywhere simultaneously); immutable (unchanging in his being); all-loving; holy (transcending his creation); and perfect in goodness, beauty, truth, justice, and mercy.

Some people object that this view of God is merely a projection of humanity's highest ideals. However, from where did human beings get these ideals? Did they produce them? No! Our highest ideals—even our very being and nature—are a reflection of God, the creator, who is the source of all existence and ideals. The only reason humanity can have some idea of God at all is because human beings are not merely material or physical; we possess a spiritual nature, for we were made in the image of God (see Gen 1:26; CCC 362-63).

A Personal God

Envisioning God as spirit could leave us thinking of God as a vast, impersonal force pervading the universe, like electricity or cosmic energy. Fortunately, God has revealed not only *what* he is—spirit—but also *who* he is. God is neither a human invention nor a cosmic force; God is a personal being.

We all have some idea of what a person is because each of us is one. God is the ultimate source and model of personhood; he defines what a person is. We are called persons only because we reflect the personhood of God. The Bible says we are made in God's "image" and "likeness" (Gen 1:26).

There is one word in the Bible, in both the Old and the New Testaments, that is most often used to describe God as a person. That word is *father*.[14] God is the Father of the universe, of the human race, of his chosen people, and of each individual human person. The word *father* refers to God as both the origin or source of all that is, and also to his fatherly care as the protector and provider for all being.

While it is possible to determine that God exists through reason, no one could know with certainty the divine Fatherhood of God unless God had chosen to reveal this to us. One of the main purposes of his sending the Son of God into our world was to reveal himself as our Father: "No one has ever seen God. The only Son, God, who is at the Father's side, has revealed him." (Jn 1:18, NAB, see also Mt 11:27; Jn 6:46; 14:11; CCC 2798).

The Trinity

The Bible also reveals something about God's personhood that is surprising. The first and fundamental belief of Jews and Christians about God is that God is one; there is only one God. As we have just seen, the Hebrew people often referred to this one God as father. However, the New Testament completes the Old Testament revelation of God by stating clearly, through Jesus Christ, that the one God is actually three Persons: the Father, the Son (or the Word), and the Holy Spirit. Christians have traditionally called this mystery of three Persons in one God the Trinity. "The mystery of the Most Holy Trinity is the central mystery of Christian faith and life" (CCC 234).

It is easy to misunderstand this doctrine. People ask, "Is God one, or is he three?" or "Don't Christians pray to three Gods: Father, Son, and Holy Spirit?" The key to resolving this is to consider in what sense God is one, and in what sense, three. Christian theology has clarified this by the use of the terms *nature* and *person*. God is one because he possesses a single, divine nature, the nature of God. Nature, in this sense, is what makes something what it is. As Pope John Paul II has explained:

> Nature (essence) is all that whereby that which concretely exists is what it is. Thus, for example, when we speak of "human nature," we indicate what makes a man a man, with his essential components and his properties.
>
> Applying this distinction to God, we recognize the unity of nature, the unity of the Divinity, which belongs in an absolute and exclusive way to Him

Who exists as God.[15]

The one God exists as three Persons who are distinct but undivided, since each Person fully possesses the same divine nature, the nature of God. A human person "is he or she who exists as a concrete human being, as an individual possessing humanity, that is, human nature."[16] In God, the Persons are distinct, and yet are united in a far deeper way than any human persons because of the perfection and integrity (unity) of the divine nature, the being of God. The unity of the three Persons of God is so great and profound that it is incorrect to say they are divided in any way. "The Christian faith confesses that God is one in nature, substance, and essence."[17]

How, then, are the three Persons of God related to each other? The church teaches that the "relations" among the three Persons of the Trinity are the only thing that distinguishes them. In other words, the Father generates or begets the Son, the Son is begotten of the Father, and the Holy Spirit proceeds from the Father and the Son.[18] "He is eternally Father by his relationship to his only Son ..." (CCC 246).

Except for these relations by which the Persons of the blessed Trinity are distinguished, everything in God is common and one.[19] We know this only because God chose to reveal to us the secrets of his inner life through Jesus Christ. This revelation is found especially in the great Trinitarian passages in the Gospel of John (see Jn 10:30; 14:10-11; 15:26).

The particular works of God outside of himself are called "missions" of the Trinity. These missions, by which God's plan or "economy" for his creation is carried out, are an "overflow" of God's superabundant love and an expression of the relations of the Persons within the blessed Trinity. Each Person of the Trinity carries out his mission according to his unique personal properties. The Father is the origin and source of the divine life and activity; the Son alone is incarnate; and the Holy Spirit comes forth from the Father and the Son as the greatest gift given to man, resulting from and carrying forward the works of the Son in his incarnation.

The goal or end of God's plan is that all of God's creatures finally enter into the perfect unity of the blessed Trinity. This begins for us even in this life: "'If a man loves me,' says the Lord, 'he will keep my word, and my Father will love him, and we will come to him, and make our home with him'" (Jn 14:23; CCC 260). The Holy Spirit, too, makes his home in us, as in a temple (see 1 Cor 3:16; 6:19; 2 Cor 6:16). Much more could be said about the development of the Christian understanding of the Trinity, but as Pope John Paul II has said:

Even after Revelation it remains the most profound mystery of faith, which the intellect by itself can neither comprehend nor penetrate.... The intellect, however, enlightened by faith, can in a certain way grasp and explain the meaning of the dogma. Thus it can bring close to man the mystery of the inmost life of the Triune God.[20]

Through the study of the Bible and the creeds of the early church, Catholics can come to a fuller appreciation and understanding of the mystery of the Trinity. Through faith, we can hold onto this truth about God as he has revealed it to us. For example, one of the ancient Christian creeds, known as the *Quicumque* Creed, refers to God as "uncreated, immense, eternal, omnipotent ... not three omnipotents, but only one omnipotent: thus God the Father, God the Son, God the Holy Spirit.... There do not exist three Gods, but only one God."

God Is Love

God has a personal nature, and therefore personal qualities. The greatest personal attribute of God is found in the First Letter of John: "God is love" (1 Jn 4:8).

The Bible repeatedly testifies that the inner life of God—the Father, Son, and Holy Spirit—is especially characterized by their mutual love. Jesus, the Son, is constantly honoring the Father who sent him (see Jn 12:27-28, 49-50). God the Father cries out, "This is my beloved Son" (Mt 3:17). The Holy Spirit also glorifies Jesus: "He [the Holy Spirit] will glorify me, because he will take from what is mine and declare it to you" (Jn 16:14, NAB). The Father and the Son send the Holy Spirit to us, giving us a share in their perfect, mutual love: "The love of God has been poured out into our hearts through the holy Spirit that has been given to us" (Rom 5:5, NAB). These texts should lead us to understand that the persons of the Trinity, because of their perfect, mutual love and unity, constantly exalt and glorify each other.

What does it mean to say that God "loves"? God's love is not a passing emotion or feeling, nor does it overlook or excuse unrepented injustice, sin, or rebellion. God's merciful love does not deny or contradict his justice. To understand what love truly is, we should study how God acts in relation to his creatures. The Bible speaks constantly of God's love:

Praise the Lord, all nations! Extol him, all peoples! For great is his steadfast love toward us; and the faithfulness of the Lord endures for ever. Praise the Lord!

PSALM 117:1-2

The steadfast love of the Lord never ceases, his mercies never come to an end; they are new every morning; great is thy faithfulness.

LAMENTATIONS 3:22-23

God so loved the world that he gave his only Son....

JOHN 3:16, NAB

In this is love: not that we have loved God, but that he loved us and sent his Son as expiation for our sins.

1 JOHN 4:10, NAB

Believing in God and loving him have profound practical implications for our lives. This compels us to serve God first and above all others. It leads us to give constant thanks to God, the source of all good and all blessings. It causes us to recognize the unity of all people as sons and daughters of our common father, and to respect their dignity as persons made in God's image and likeness. It requires that we be good stewards, caring for the created things that God has entrusted to us for our use and enjoyment. Finally, knowing and loving God leads us to trust God in all things. As St. Teresa of Avila prayed:

Let nothing trouble you. Let nothing frighten you. Everything passes. God never changes. Patience obtains all. Whoever has God wants for nothing. God alone is enough (see CCC 222-27).[21]

Creation—An Expression of God's Love

Christians believe that God's love is demonstrated by the very existence of the cosmos. Sometimes we forget that there was a time before anything except God existed. Even then, God was not deficient in any way; he was perfectly complete and happy (to use inadequate human concepts).

Why, then, did God create the universe? Because God is love. It is the nature of love to express itself, to give of itself. Love is naturally generous and creative. Christians believe that the universe—so incredibly vast, diverse, majestic, and beautiful—came into being from God's desire to express himself, to give of himself, out of sheer love.[22] "God has no other reason for creating than his love and goodness" (CCC 293).

Some people feel threatened by the immensity of the universe, overwhelmed by a sense of their own insignificance and frailty. A healthy humility should arise from the fact of the limitations and frailty of our human lives. Psalm 144 observes, "[Man is] but a breath; [his] days are like a passing shadow" (v. 4, NAB). Catholics are marked with ashes each year on Ash Wednesday to remind us of the shortness of our lives: "Remember, man, that you are dust, and unto dust you shall return."[23]

Without God this reflection can lead to despair or existential angst. Knowing God should enable us to realize our utter and absolute dependence on him. "You are my God. In your hands is my destiny" (see Ps 31:15-16). Only in realizing our insignificance and weakness can we appreciate God's love. God not only created the universe in the beginning out of love, but sustains it and each one of us in existence at every moment (CCC 301). If God were to forget us, we would cease to exist. Yet God does not forget us. He loves and cares for each of his creatures, individually and personally.

How foolish it is when human beings try to deny or avoid God! Psalm 139 beautifully recounts how God formed each one of us in the womb, knows everything about us, and is present everywhere we could go (CCC 300). Take a moment to read this psalm and reflect on it.

Why should we want to hide from the God who created us, sustains our existence, and loves us so totally? St. Paul told the Athenians, "In him we live and move and have our being" (Acts 17:28). God's deepest desire is for all people to come to know his personal love for them, to accept that love, and to love and obey him in return. In doing this, human nature is perfected; we reach the destiny that God has prepared for us: everlasting life and happiness in his presence.

Paul also wrote, "Indeed, the whole created world eagerly awaits the revelation of the sons of God" (see Rom 8:19). He teaches that even the creation itself "would be set free from slavery to corruption and share in the glorious freedom of the children of God" (Rom 8:21, NAB). God created the world out of love, and he will reveal his love once again by renewing the creation and bringing it to fulfillment in him (see Col 1:15-20).

The Creation and the Fall of the Angels

What do we mean by "creation," or the "created universe"? To create means to produce something out of nothing, to bring forth that which previously did not exist (whether material or spiritual).

Pope John Paul II has written: "The truth of creation expresses the thought that everything existing outside of God has been called into existence by Him.... 'Creation' therefore means: to make from nothing; to call into existence, that is, to form a being from nothing" (see CCC 296, 297).[24]

"In the beginning God created the heavens and the earth" (Gen 1:1). Before the creation of the material universe, only God and other purely spiritual beings existed. God created all things—matter and energy, and even the medium (time) used to measure their duration and change.

The material universe was not the first of God's creations. God also created beings who are pure spirits, like himself, possessing understanding and free will: the angels. The Greek word *angelos* means "messenger." The Bible records that God often sent these spirits as messengers to humanity, bearing important truths or commands. Before time began, before the universe was created, angels gave glory to God, their creator (see Heb 1:6), and served God's will and purposes (see Heb 1:14). These angels "always look upon the face of my heavenly Father" (Mt 18:10, NAB). They are the "mighty ones who do his word, hearkening to the voice of his word" (Ps 103:20; see CCC 329).

However, God has revealed to us a tragedy of cosmic proportions that came to affect the history of the human race. Although God created all of the angels perfectly good and loving, some of the angels used their free will to rebel against

God (CCC 392). The leader of this rebellion has been called by various names in the Bible and Christian tradition: Lucifer, Satan, the devil (CCC 391). The basic sin attributed to Satan is pride, desiring to be God or God's equal. The prophet Isaiah laments:

> How have you fallen from the heavens,
>   O morning star, son of the dawn!...
> You said in your heart:
>   "I will scale the heavens;
> Above the stars of God
>   I will set up my throne;...
>   I will be like the Most High!"
> Yet down to the nether world you go
>   to the recesses of the pit!
>
> ISAIAH 14:12-15, NAB

The Letter of Jude says that, "the angels that did not keep their own position but left their proper dwelling have been kept by him [God] in eternal chains in the nether gloom..." (Jude 6). The Book of Revelation describes the fall of Lucifer, or Satan, more graphically, picturing the angels obedient to God, led by Michael, defeating and casting down Satan and the rebellious angels who followed him:

> Then war broke out in heaven; Michael and his angels battled against the dragon. The dragon and its angels fought back, but they did not prevail and there was no longer any place for them in heaven. The huge dragon, the ancient serpent, who is called the Devil and Satan, who deceived the whole world, was thrown down to earth, and its angels were thrown down with it.
>
> REVELATION 12:7-9, NAB

Thus the angels obedient to God are forever united with him in the joy of heaven, the "dwelling place" of God, while the rebellious angels (or demons) are destined to eternal separation from God as a consequence of their own free choice.

The Origin of Evil

The ultimate origin of evil is the rebellion of powerful spiritual beings against God. Evil may be defined as any rebellion against God, and any consequence of that rebellion. God does not actively will evil (see Jas 1:13-15). Even the idea involves a contradiction—why would God rebel against himself or his own purposes? God is totally good and desires only the perfect harmony and happiness of his creation.

Neither did God create evil. The Book of Genesis observes, "God looked at everything he had made, and he found it very good" (Gen 1:31, NAB). In its origin, evil is a rejection or corruption of the good that comes from God.

God created his highest beings with genuinely free will. In doing so, he took a great risk. He so highly valued the existence of creatures with freedom of choice that he introduced the possibility of these creatures using their free will to rebel against him. Satan and the angels who followed him chose this path. God did not destroy these spirits, which are eternal by nature, but allowed them to receive the inevitable result of their own free choice. They were eternally separated from God and his favor. Their situation is, literally, hell—a condition of eternal torment—for apart from God there is no real happiness or peace.

Is God unjust in allowing Satan and his angelic followers to suffer forever? He is just, for he is giving them what they freely chose. The more difficult question is how God is loving and merciful in allowing this. There is a mystery involved here, but we must realize that Satan and the fallen angels, with their great intelligence, fully realized the possible consequences of their action. They freely chose to rebel against God. The *Catechism* explains:

> It is the *irrevocable* character of their choice, and not a defect in the infinite divine mercy, that makes the angels' sin unforgivable. "There is no repentance for the angels after their fall, just as there is no repentance for men after death."[25]

God is fully loving and merciful. At the same time, he does not impose his love and mercy on any free creature. Since God created beings who are genuinely free, it is certainly possible that some will choose not to accept and obey God. Thus, they separate themselves from his love and mercy.

Good and evil are not equally powerful. There are religions which teach that good and evil are two equally potent cosmic forces (or gods) at war with one another, with the outcome of the struggle still in question. This is called dualism. St. Augustine believed this during his ten years as a Manichee, before his conversion to Christianity. Christianity teaches that the one God, who is totally good, is ultimately victorious, for Satan is but a creature of God whose power is limited.

This being so, why does God allow Satan to continue to influence other creatures, tempting them to rebel against God? Ultimately, this is a great mystery (CCC 395). Perhaps it is a test of the will and the faith of the free creatures that God has created in his image, whom he desires to have freely choose to love and serve him, overcoming temptation and afflictions.

Whatever the reason, followers of Christ have the assurance that God makes all things work together for the good of those who love him (see Rom 8:28, NAB).

The Creation of the Human Race

The Book of Genesis begins with two interwoven accounts of God's creation of the material universe, including the human race. Despite some differences in detail in the accounts, they both affirm that God created all things, and that the climax of the creation of the world was the creation of the human race.[26]

> Then God said "Let us make man in our image, after our likeness. Let them have dominion over [the earth's creatures]...."
> God created man in his image;
>> in the divine image he created him;
>> male and female he created them.
> God blessed them, saying: "Be fertile and multiply; fill the earth and subdue it...."
>
> GENESIS 1:26-28, NAB

There are a number of important truths about the creation and nature of "man" (mankind: from the Hebrew word *adam*) that the church finds in the Book of Genesis and in other biblical writings.

1. Man is created to be in a special relationship with God. Vatican II noted that, "man is the only creature on earth that God has wanted for his own sake,"[27] and of all the beings God made from matter, only the human person is "able to know and love his creator"[28] and share in God's own life. As Pope John Paul II has observed:

> Indeed man, thanks to his spiritual nature and to his capacity for intellectual knowledge and freedom of choice, is, *from the very beginning, in a special relationship with God.* The description of creation (cf. Gn 1-3) permits us to observe that the "image of God" is manifested above all in the relation of the human "I" to the divine "You."[29]

2. Being made in God's "image and likeness," the human person has great dignity. This truth is foundational to Catholic moral teaching, and was especially made clear by the Second Vatican Council in its Pastoral Constitution, *Gaudium et Spes* ("On the Church in the Modern World").

Our dignity comes from God, who made man and woman in his "image and likeness," with an eternal destiny, capable of knowing and possessing oneself, as well as freely giving oneself to others. Further, God calls each person into a living relationship with him, a "covenant of love," in which the person discovers his dignity and finds true freedom, peace, and fulfillment (see CCC 357-358).

3. There is a real unity of the human race, based on its origin in God. Amidst the rich diversity of people in the world with varying languages and cultures, there is an underlying unity through which many people recognize "that all men are truly brethren" (CCC 361). This unity begins with the common origin of the human race, for "from one stock [God] made every nation of mankind to dwell on the face of the earth" (see Acts 17:26; Tob 8:6).

4. Man is created by God with both a corporeal and a spiritual nature, a body and a soul. The term "body" refers to the material or corporeal aspect of man, while "soul signifies the *spiritual principle* in man" (CCC 363). "Human nature" is a unique union of matter and spirit into a single nature, with the human soul, which is directly infused or created by God, as the pattern or "form" of the body.[30]

Even though St. Paul also speaks of man possessing a "spirit," this is actually a way of describing the soul's spiritual nature and supernatural goal, which is communion with God (see CCC 367).

5. *God created the human race as "male and female," and gave them dominion over the earth.* The Book of Genesis affirms God's will that the "image of God" is reflected fully in the creation of "male" and "female" persons, who are equal in dignity and complementary as masculine and feminine.

The first man and the first woman were the prototype of that most beautiful and harmonious community of persons: marriage. Through marriage, man and woman become "one flesh," and bring forth new life ("be fruitful and multiply"). Man and woman also exercise responsible dominion over the earth, as stewards of God's creation.

6. *The key to understanding fully the dignity and vocation of the human person is Jesus Christ.* Jesus is the "second Adam," the beginning of a "new creation" freed from sin, in which man's dignity is restored and his destiny is fully revealed. "In reality it is only in the mystery of the Word made flesh that the mystery of man truly becomes clear."[31]

The Temptation and Fall of Man

One remarkable aspect of man's dignity is his freedom. He is free even in his relationship with his Creator. As Pope John Paul II said, "Man can say 'yes' to God, but he can also say 'no.' He has the capacity to *accept* God and His holy will, but also the capacity to *oppose* it."[32]

According to the Book of Genesis, the only prohibition that God placed on the first man and woman was that they must not eat of the tree of knowledge of good and evil, lest they die (see Gen 2:16-17). Death and even sickness were apparently unknown to them, and all their needs were provided for (see Gen 2:9). Even work was not a burden, but a collaboration with God to bring the visible world to perfection. They enjoyed a rich, full human existence in complete harmony with God, nature, and each other.

This state of humanity before the rebellion against God is called, in Catholic theology, the state of "original justice" or "original innocence." Only through God's revelation do we know this, and recognize sin as an offense against God and an abuse of human freedom, a freedom given that we might freely love and obey God, and love and serve each other.

What more does God reveal about the origin of human sin? The Book of Revelation refers to "the ancient serpent, who is called the Devil and Satan, who deceived the whole world" (Rev 12:9, NAB). The one whom Jesus called "a liar and the father of lies" (Jn 8:44) appears in Genesis 3 in the form of a serpent. He convinces the first woman, Eve, to disobey God's command not to eat of the fruit of that particular tree: "God knows well that the moment you eat of it your eyes will be opened and you will be like gods who know what is good and bad" (Gen 3:5, NAB). Thus, Satan lured the human race into his own sin of pride. He deceived them into wanting to be like God, on their own terms: "In that sin man *preferred* himself to God and by that very act scorned him" (CCC 398).

The image the Book of Genesis uses for the original sin of mankind—eating the fruit of the tree of knowledge of good and evil—may be interpreted in a symbolic way. The original sin was not eating an apple or having sexual relations (which is a gift of God to married couples), but prideful rebellion against God. Although the language used may be figurative, it describes an actual, primeval event—a deed that took place at the beginning of human history.[33]

Satan tempted Eve by telling her that what God commanded was not true, and that she would actually become like God by disobeying him. Rebellion against God and pride are at the heart of humanity's primordial sin. When Eve and Adam sinned, they received part of what Satan promised. They knew good and evil because for the first time they had done evil. This is what Catholics traditionally and rightly call "original sin"—the first sin of the human race. Adam and Eve had disobeyed the God who had loved them so perfectly, so they joined in Satan's rebellion against God and his goodness.

Through this account, the Book of Genesis conveys the basic truth that humanity, like Satan, has turned away from God and his plan by free choice. This sin of our first parents was a rebellion with more than just personal consequences, however. It affected the whole human race that would spring from them biologically. Original sin refers not only to the first human sin, but also to the condition of separation from God into which every human person is born.

Original sin is not transmitted merely by example, but through an actual corruption or distortion of our common human nature. God created our humanity "very good," in his own image and likeness, so it is incorrect to speak of "the total depravity of man," as do some Christian churches. Human nature is essentially good and God-like, but since the first or original rebellion of the human race, it is a fallen nature, distorted and corrupted by sin.[34]

Original sin should be one of the most self-evident of Christian doctrines. Newspapers and other media reports testify daily to the wretched human condition. St. Paul described the root of the problem in his letter to the Romans: "just as through one person sin entered the world, and through sin, death, and thus death came to all, inasmuch as all sinned" (Rom 5:12, NAB; see also Jas 4:1-4). In St. Paul's terminology, original sin is the "law of sin and death" (Rom 8:2) that every person (with the exception of Jesus and his mother, Mary) is subject to from the moment of conception as a result of the Fall of our first parents. We are forced to cry out with the psalmist, "Indeed, in guilt was I born, and in sin my mother conceived me" (see Ps 51:7).

Original sin results in an inherited rebelliousness against God and his ways—"an inclination to evil that is called 'concupiscence.' Baptism, by imparting the life of Christ's grace, erases original sin and turns a man back toward God, but the consequences for nature, weakened and inclined to evil, persist in man and summon him to spiritual battle" (CCC 405).

Each of us experiences this resistance to God fully ruling our lives and the tug of our passions urging us to satisfy their desires. As the Letter of James says:

> Let no one say when he is tempted, "I am tempted by God"; for God cannot be tempted with evil and he himself tempts no one; but each person is tempted when he is lured and enticed by his own desire. Then desire when it has conceived gives birth to sin; and sin when it is full-grown brings forth death.
>
> JAMES 1:13-15

This is the experience and effect of original sin. Yet, some people deny the reality of original sin. The *Catechism* notes:

> Original sin entails "captivity under the power of him who thenceforth had the power of death, that is, the devil" (Council of Trent (1546): DS 1511;

cf. Heb 2:14). Ignorance of the fact that man has a wounded nature inclined to evil gives rise to serious errors in the areas of education, politics, social action (cf. John Paul II, ca 25), and morals. (CCC 407)

How many people do not acknowledge that the *root* cause of social problems is original sin—that man's nature is wounded and in rebellion against God, and that consequently the human race and its institutions are to a great extent in captivity to the power of the devil? This is absolutely true, according to Scripture (see 1 Pet 5:8; 1 Jn 5:19) and Catholic tradition. Yet, to express this truth today and to seek to deal with the root cause of the problems of the world by urging conversion to Christ, deeper faith, and fervent prayer (with action flowing from these), is to invite scorn or skepticism. The sad truth is that much of the Western world has accepted and proclaims a modern form of the Pelagian heresy, denying the absolute need for God and his grace in attempting to solve social problems and create a just and good society (CCC 406).

God's Mercy and Original Sin

When we reflect on the terrible consequences of original sin, there is a temptation to ask, "How could a loving God permit this?" In his love, God gave angels and men the great gift of free will. In his justice, God allowed angels and men to receive the consequences of their free choice. The great Puritan poet, John Milton, characterizes Satan's attitude: "Better to reign in hell, than serve in Heaven."[35] God, in his justice, gave Satan what he wished.

In justice, God also allowed Adam and Eve, and the whole human race, to experience the consequences of sin and rebellion against him. For humanity, this justice is not God's last word. Realizing its weakness and limited understanding, God wills to give the human race another chance, a hope of reconciliation with him. God has offered this second chance to us out of pure mercy and love. In *Summa Theologiae III*, St. Thomas Aquinas wrote:

There is nothing to prevent human nature's being raised up to something greater, even after sin; God permits evil in order to draw forth some greater good. Thus St. Paul says, "Where sin increased, grace abounded all the more"; and the Exultet sings, "O happy fault,...which gained for us so great a Redeemer!"[36]

God gave Adam and Eve a foreshadowing of their deliverance when he told the serpent (Satan) who had just deceived them:

> I will put enmity between you and the woman,
>   and between your offspring and hers;
> He will strike at your head,
>   while you strike at his heel.
>
> GENESIS 3:15, NAB

This passage is known as the *proto-evangelium*—the first glimpse of the good news that an offspring of a woman of our race would strike at the head of the serpent, Satan, and ultimately defeat him (see CCC 410-11). When and how this would happen was not clear to the author of Genesis, nor to Adam and Eve, nor to any other human being until the coming of the one who would fulfill this prophecy, the Savior, Jesus Christ. As Pope John Paul II has summarized salvation history:

> Thus the Bible begins absolutely with a first, and then with a second account of creation, where the origin of all from God, of things, of life, of man (Gen 1:2), is interwoven with the other sad chapter about the origin, this time of man, not without temptation of the devil, of sin and of evil (Gen 3). But God does not abandon His creatures. And so a tiny flame of hope is lit towards a future of a new creation freed from evil (the so-called *proto-evangelium*, Gen 3:15; cf. 9:13). These three threads, God's creative and positive action, man's rebellion, and, already from the beginning, God's promise of a new world, form the texture of the history of salvation, by determining the global content of the Christian faith in creation.[37]

The Problem of Evil and God's Providence

The temptation and fall of the human race leads us inevitably to the deeper question of why God allows such evil and imperfection to exist. The general answer is that God did not bring forth his creation in its complete, perfect, and final form, but in an unfinished form, "a state of journeying." Christian faith, however, affirms that God is inexorably guiding his creation toward an ultimate perfection. This guidance is called "divine providence" (CCC 302).

"Divine providence" is not a vague, beneficent attitude of God toward his creation, but is a love that "is *concrete* and *immediate;* God cares for all, from the least things to the great events of the world and its history" (CCC 303). God expresses this care and directs all things not only directly (as a "first cause"), but also through the decisions and actions of his creatures (as "secondary causes"). *We* are part of God's providence! "For God is at work in you, both to will and to work for his good pleasure" (Phil 2:13). As we proceed to look at God's loving plan to save humanity from its sin and rebellion against him, it will be evident how God works through creatures, especially people that he chooses, to express his providence and to lead all creation to perfection, which is union with him.

How is the existence of evil consistent with this view of God's providence? The "answer" to the problem of evil involves the *whole* of Christian faith—an understanding of all of the truth about God and his creation. Christians affirm that "physical evil" can occur as long as creation has not yet reached its final fulfillment and perfection in God. God permits "moral evil," produced by the choices of his creatures possessing free will, but never actually wills or causes this evil. Christian revelation insists that the key to comprehending and accepting why an all-good God allows evil is that *God brings good out of evil.* As St. Augustine wrote:

> For almighty God ..., because he is supremely good, would never allow any evil whatsoever to exist in his works if he were not so all-powerful and good as to cause good to emerge from evil itself.[38]

St. Paul declares, "We know that all things work for good for those who love God" (Rom 8:28, NAB). The ultimate example of this is how God has brought the greatest good out of the greatest evil. "From the greatest moral evil ever committed—the rejection and murder of God's only Son, caused by the sins of all men—God, by his grace that 'abounded all the more' (cf.Rom 5:20), brought the greatest of goods: the glorification of Christ and our redemption. But for all that, evil never becomes a good" (CCC 312).

Thus it is that Jesus can call all his followers to have a profound yet childlike *trust* in their Father in heaven, in divine providence guiding all things finally to the good and to the perfection of his plan.

Jesus asks for childlike abandonment to the providence of our heavenly Father, who takes care of his children's smallest needs: "Therefore do not be anxious, saying, 'What shall we eat?' or 'What shall we drink?' .... Your heavenly Father knows that you need them all. But seek first his kingdom and his righteousness, and all these things shall be yours as well" (Mt 6:31-33; see also Mt 10:29-31). (CCC 305)

In the coming chapters, we will explore how God's providence, his love, care, and plan, actually *has* unfolded and *is being* unfolded in our human history.

Conclusion

Since the Book of Genesis and the other biblical evidence regarding God and his creation are the foundation of Catholic and Christian faith, let us review some of the basic biblical truths presented in this chapter, "for the sake of our salvation."

1. There is only one God—eternal, almighty, all-loving, and all-wise—who created every spiritual being (such as angels) and the entire material universe out of nothing.

The Catholic Church does allow different views of precisely how and when God created the universe, but insists that only God is the author of creation.

2. There is an angel known as the devil or Satan whose rebellion against God is the ultimate origin of all evil.

Pope Paul VI addressed this issue in a general audience given on November 15, 1973. He said that the greatest need of the church today is, "defense from that evil which is called the Devil.... We know that this dark and disturbing spirit really exists, and that he still acts with treacherous cunning; he is the secret enemy that sows errors and misfortune in human history...."[39]

3. God created man, male and female, in his own image and likeness. Man is a creature composed of both spirit and matter, called by God to an eternal destiny of life with him.

The Catholic Church does not officially teach either that the human race evolved from lower species or that it was created directly by God. To Catholics, the evolution versus creation debate concerning the origin of mankind involves an issue open to scientific investigation rather than a matter of faith necessary to salvation.

The Catholic Church does insist, however, that the soul or spiritual nature of man was directly infused by God into man and woman; it did not evolve. By this act of God, the infusion of the human soul, a distinctive race of human beings with moral responsibility and an eternal destiny was established by God.[40]

4. The first human beings, deceived by Satan, rebelled against God through pride and disobedience and were thereby separated from his friendship. This original sin also introduced suffering, death, and loss of certain gifts and abilities into the human condition.

It is difficult for us to imagine human existence without struggle, pain, and death. Life without them sounds like a utopian fairy tale. But Christians believe that it is a fact that if humanity had not rebelled against God, we would enjoy all the gifts and blessings that the Book of Genesis says Adam and Eve possessed in the Garden of Eden before their sin. We base this belief on God's Word and on the supposition that all evil, including pain and death, is a result of sin. If there had been no original sin, there would be no human struggle, suffering, or death.

5. Each human person ever born (with the exception of Jesus and his mother) is sub-ject to original sin and its effects. Human nature has been corrupted, though not destroyed or irreparably damaged, by original sin.

The effect of original sin on the human condition is pervasive. Human beings cannot avoid doing evil without God's intervention and help. Man alone is powerless to overcome original sin and its effects. Few people have described so well the plight of man after the Fall as St. Paul in his Letter to the Romans:

What I do, I do not understand. For I do not do what I want, but I do what I hate.... So now it is no longer I who do it, but sin that dwells in me. For I know that good does not dwell in me, that is, in my flesh. The willing is ready at hand, but doing the good is not. For I do not do the good I want, but I do the evil I do not want.... Miserable one that I am! Who will deliver me from this mortal body?

ROMANS 7:15, 17-19, 24, NAB

6. *In spite of man's rebellion against him, God gave humanity after the Fall of Adam and Eve a hope of reconciliation with himself.*

Primitive man, though alienated from God and without knowledge of him, sought after God and for ways to please (or appease) him. For centuries, the true God remained hidden from the human race, awaiting the proper time to begin his great plan of reconciliation and restoration. In the next chapter, we will observe how God's plan of salvation began to unfold among the Hebrews, God's chosen people of the first covenant.

CHAPTER 3

God's People of the Old Testament

The last chapter described the rebellion of our first parents against God, who created them and loved them. Their original sin, along with all the subsequent personal (or actual) sins of their offspring, resulted in the estrangement of the human race from its creator.

The plight of humanity at this point seemed hopeless. Man had used God's gift of free will to turn from God, and had rejected God's plan for human life. Once he had rebelled, however, man found that it was beyond his power to reestablish a loving relationship with his creator. He was trapped by the effects of his own sin, just like a man who digs himself into a pit before realizing that he cannot get out by himself.

After Adam and Eve had sinned, only God could save the human race and draw it back into right relationship with himself. God's love and mercy is demonstrated by his desire to reconcile humanity with himself—to rescue us from our sin and its effects. This salvation is totally gratuitous—a free, undeserved gift. If God acted strictly according to justice, the human race clearly would deserve to experience all of the terrible consequences of the sin, including the ultimate consequence of eternal perdition. Instead, God has offered the human race a second chance—an opportunity to be freed from sin and all its effects.

This chapter will describe some major aspects of the first stage of God's plan to save humanity from sin and death. God did not do this in a single act; he prepared the human race over the course of many centuries for the full work of his salvation. This long preparation was necessary due both to the magnitude of the work God had in mind and to humanity's stubborn resistance to God's work.

This process of God calling us back to himself is often called salvation history. Let us recall some of the events of this history of God's saving plan that paved the way for his full deliverance of the human race in Jesus Christ.

God's Plan of Salvation

Conceivably, God could have forgiven man's sin and reconciled humanity to himself simply by decreeing it: "I forgive." However, would this have conveyed to us the seriousness of our offense against God? Would it have expressed God's justice had he overlooked the choice mankind had freely made? Doesn't God desire, even require, a willing and free acceptance of his forgiveness by the human race, which is manifested by heartfelt repentance and a yearning for God's mercy and forgiveness?

God takes our freedom seriously; though he offers us all the grace we need to overcome sin and act righteously, he refuses to obstruct our wrong choices. God desires to forgive and save the human race, but he will not impose forgiveness or reconciliation on anyone. Each person must desire, must choose, to be reconciled to God, and then cry out to God for his forgiveness and love.

In his consummate wisdom, God had a perfect plan for drawing the human race back into right relationship with himself. This plan depended both on God's merciful offer of forgiveness and on man's free response to this offer based on faith and trust in God.

The initial stage of God's plan was to form a specific people who would learn to know God and to live according to his will. Through this people, the whole human race would eventually come to know God, and would learn to love and obey him. In addition, one would emerge from this specific people who would bring God's salvation fully to the human race, a savior for the whole world.

The Covenant Relationship

This grandiose scheme actually had very unlikely and humble beginnings. In fact, at first it looked as if it would never have a chance to begin. Adam and Eve initially violated the covenant relationship of love and trust that God had established between him and them. The sin of Adam and Eve resulted in the corruption of human nature, which manifested itself in all manner of sin, such as Cain's murder of his brother Abel (see CCC 401).

After the Fall, the wickedness of Adam and Eve's descendants was so great that God decided to destroy the human race through a great flood (see Gen

6:5-8). However, there was one righteous man, Noah, to whom God offered the possibility of salvation. If Noah would hear and obey God's instruction to build a huge ark, then he and his family (along with pairs of every living creature) would be saved from the flood. Unlike Adam and Eve, Noah believed what God had spoken to him and obeyed his instruction. As a result, God spared Noah and his family and made his first great covenant with them after the original sin of Adam and Eve.

God's covenant with Noah expresses his relationship with the nations of the world (the "gentes," or Gentiles) up until the time of Christ (see CCC 56, 58). The term *covenant* is essential in understanding God's plan for relating to and saving the human race. The word *covenant* was used in the ancient Near East to describe any solemn agreement between two (or more) parties. The Judeo-Christian tradition believes that God himself initiated a series of covenants with mankind, which became the basis of the relationship between God and a particular people.

In his covenant with Noah, God solemnly agreed never again to attempt to destroy the human race by a flood (see Gen 9:9-11). God set the rainbow in the sky as a "sign of the covenant between me and the earth" (Gen 9:13). The covenant with Noah also signifies that God is at work among the Gentiles, as we see in the great figures of holiness among them that the church venerates even today: the priest-king Melchizedek—a figure of Christ—Noah, Daniel, and Job (see CCC 58).

The story of Noah illustrates certain important points about all of God's covenants with man.

1. *God alone initiates the covenant, but man must accept the covenant and cooperate with it.* As Pope John Paul II has stated, the covenant "is a completely sovereign initiative of God the Creator," and, "Man is the suitable subject for the Covenant, because he was created 'in the image' of God, capable of knowledge and freedom."[1]

2. *God's covenants have a saving purpose,* in this case to preserve the human race from future destruction.

3. *There is often an outward sign (or signs) of a covenant,* in this case the rainbow, which symbolizes and calls to mind the covenant between God and humanity.

The Covenant With Abraham

God's first covenant through Noah foreshadows the great covenant by which God set apart a people to be his own, through which the human race might be restored to God's friendship. The Book of Genesis reports that God revealed himself to a man named Abram, saying:

"Go forth from the land of your kinsfolk and from your father's house to a land that I will show you.

I will make of you a great nation,
and I will bless you;
I will make your name great,
so that you will be a blessing....
All the communities of the earth
shall find blessing in you."
Abram went as the LORD directed him....

GENESIS 12:1-4, NAB

Many years later, God spoke to Abram of a covenant:

My covenant with you is this: you are to become the father of a host of nations. No longer shall you be called Abram; your name shall be Abraham, for I am making you the father of a host of nations.... I will maintain my covenant with you and your descendants after you throughout the ages as an everlasting pact, to be your God and the God of your descendants after you.

GENESIS 17:4-5, 7, NAB

The sign of this covenant was that "every male among you shall be circumcised" (Gen 17:10).

The call of God to Abram set in motion God's saving plan. God was to form a people built upon these "patriarchs"—these fathers of the faith. The descendants of Abraham were to be a nation under God's particular care. Through this people, known at first as the Hebrews, God would eventually bring the blessing of salvation to all humankind. They were "called to prepare for that day when God would gather all his children into the unity of the Church (cf. Rom 11:28; Jn 11:52; 10:16). They would be the root onto which the Gentiles would be grafted, once they came to believe" (cf. Rom 11:17-18, 24; CCC 60).

The Cost of the Covenant

Although this covenant was initiated by God, it required Abraham's full response. Abraham heard and obeyed the call of God to leave his homeland and kinfolk, and settle in a new land, Canaan (see Gen 12:4-6). Later, he had to move to Egypt for a time because of famine. Abraham believed God when God told him that his elderly, barren wife, Sarah, would bear a son, thus fulfilling God's promise that Abraham would be the father of many nations. Then Abraham had to face the severest test of his faith. God asked Abraham to kill his only son, Isaac, as a sacrifice to God, even though Isaac was the key to the fulfillment of God's promise of descendants for Abraham. God sent his angel to stop Abraham's knife-poised hand at the last minute.

Through all these many trials and tests, Abraham remained steadfastly faithful to God: "Abram put his faith in the LORD, who credited it to him as an act of righteousness" (Gen 15:6, NAB). Abraham, like Noah, believed in God and his promises, and obeyed God regardless of the cost. It was through this sort of faith and obedience that God was able to act in history, to reverse the lack of faith and disobedience of Adam and Eve. To this day, Christians, as well as Jews, recognize Abraham as their father in faith (see Rom 4; Gal 3; Heb 11:8-10, 17-19).

This covenant of God with the descendants of Abraham, the Hebrew people, endured for centuries. The content of the covenant was clear and simple: believe in and obey the one God who has revealed himself to Abraham. Circumcise all males as a sign of the covenant, and follow whatever other commands or directives God gives.

Moses and the Covenant at Sinai

Abraham's son, Isaac, fathered two sons, Esau and Jacob, also called Israel. Israel had twelve sons, patriarchs of the twelve tribes of Israel. Jacob's second-youngest son, Joseph, was sold into slavery by his brothers and dwelt in Egypt, where he rose from slavery to the highest position in government next to Pharaoh. When a famine struck the land of Canaan, the other sons of Jacob moved with their families to Egypt, where they prospered for many years due to Joseph's influence.

The story of Joseph is a powerful example of God's providence, bringing good out of evil. "It was not you," said Joseph to his brothers, "who sent me here, but God.... You meant evil against me; but God meant it for good, to bring it about that many people should be kept alive" (Gen 45:8; 50:20) (CCC 312). Joseph's imprisonment and suffering for the sake of God's people is one of the many "types," or foreshadowings, of Christ to be discovered in the Old Testament.

When a new king "who knew nothing of Joseph" (Ex 1:8, NAB) came to power, he began to oppress the Israelites with forced labor, and even ordered the midwives to the Hebrews to kill their male children. One of these children, Moses, was rescued and adopted by Pharaoh's daughter. When Moses grew up, though, he killed an Egyptian and was forced to flee from Egypt to the wilderness of Midian, where he married the daughter of Jethro and became a shepherd of his flocks.

This brief summary of ancient Jewish history is designed to set the stage for one of the most seminal periods in the history of God's plan of salvation. The first key event was God's revelation of himself and his name to Moses. God spoke to Moses from a burning bush, saying:

> I am the God of your father, ... the God of Abraham, the God of Isaac, the God of Jacob.... I have witnessed the affliction of my people in Egypt and ... I have come down to rescue them from the hands of the Egyptians and lead them out of that land into a good and spacious land, a land flowing with milk and honey.... Come, now! I will send you to Pharaoh to lead my people, the Israelites, out of Egypt.
>
> EXODUS 3:6-10, NAB

Moses was unwilling at first, objecting that he would need to know God's name to prove to Pharaoh that he had truly been sent by God. "A name expresses a person's essence and identity and the meaning of this person's life" (CCC 203). Hence the surpassing importance of the event when "God replied, 'I am who am.' Then he added, 'This is what you shall tell the Israelites: I AM sent me to you.'" (Ex 3:14, NAB). This utterance of God is the source of the word YHWH (Yahweh), the personal name of the God of Israel. "This divine name is mysterious just as God is mystery" (CCC 206). The name is considered so sacred by the Jewish people that it is not even pronounced. Substitutes like Adonai ("my Lord") are spoken instead. Books have been written about the precise meaning of this sacred tetragrammaton, YHWH, but the primary point is that God reveals himself as the one who is: he is God.

In the ancient Near East, to know a person's name was thought to provide some influence over the person. It is significant that God would reveal his proper name to Moses. It signifies a major step forward in their relationship and the relationship between God and his Old Covenant people, the Jews.

God demonstrated his love and providential care for his people through concrete historical events. Nothing has shown God's love and care for the Hebrew people more clearly than the series of events that resulted from God's summons to Moses. God sent Moses to Pharaoh, king of Egypt, to demand that he allow the Jews to stop work and worship God in the wilderness. Pharaoh refused, and God sent the plagues upon the Egyptians in an attempt to convince them to heed Moses' request. Finally, Pharaoh relented when an angel of death killed all the firstborn males of the Egyptians, both man and beast, while he "passed over" the homes of the Jews and spared their children. Yahweh demonstrated in deed what he had declared to Moses, that He is "a God merciful and gracious, slow to anger and abounding in steadfast love and faithfulness" (Ex 34:6).

The meal that the Jews ate in haste as they prepared to flee from Egypt is called the Passover meal. It is celebrated annually by the Jewish people to commemorate God's mighty act of leading them out of captivity in Egypt through the miraculous parting of the Red Sea (or Sea of Reeds) when the Egyptians were in hot pursuit.[2]

This Passover of the Jewish people from captivity to freedom has been remembered by them as the most important event illustrating God's salvation and protection of his people. The "Song of Moses" in Exodus 15 and a number of the psalms (66, 78, 105, 106, 136) recall this event and praise God for his mighty acts.

For Christians, God's liberation of the Jewish people from political captivity in Egypt is a great symbol and foreshadowing of God's liberation of humanity from the spiritual captivity of sin and death, accomplished through the dying and rising of Jesus Christ.

By going so far as to give up his own Son for us, God reveals that he is "rich in mercy" (Eph 2:4). By giving his life to free us from sin, Jesus reveals that he himself bears the divine name: "When you have lifted up the Son of man, then you will realize that 'I Am.'"[Jn 8:28 (Gk.)] (CCC 211)

The Commandments

Before Moses, God's covenant with the Hebrew people required their faith in God and obedience to him, but there was no explicitly defined law that governed the life of this people. After the crossing of the Red Sea, the Hebrews wandered in the desert until they reached Mount Sinai, or Horeb, a large peak in the midst of the mountains in the southern Sinai Peninsula. At this mountain, God revealed himself once again to Moses, instructing him to tell the Israelites:

> If you hearken to my voice and keep my covenant, you shall be my special possession, dearer to me than all other people, though all the earth is mine. You shall be to me a kingdom of priests, a holy nation.
>
> EXODUS 19:5-6, NAB

Later, the Lord gave Moses ten commandments or words that were to be the norm of their conduct. These commandments, in summary, are:

1. "I am the Lord your God.... You shall have no other gods before me" (Deut 5:6, 7).
2. "You shall not take the name of the Lord your God in vain" (Deut 5:11).
3. "Observe the sabbath day, to keep it holy, as the Lord, your God commanded you. Six days you shall labor, and do all your work; but the seventh day is a sabbath to the Lord your God" (Deut 5:12-14).
4. "Honor your father and your mother, as the Lord your God commanded you, that your days may be prolonged" (Deut 5:16).
5. "Thou shall not kill" (Deut 5:17).
6. "Neither shall you commit adultery" (Deut 5: 18).
7. "Neither shall you steal" (Deut 5:19).

8. "Neither shall you bear false witness against your neighbor" (Deut 5:20).
9. "Neither shall you covet your neighbor's wife" (Deut 5:21).
10. "You shall not desire your neighbor's house, his field, ... or anything that is your neighbor's" (Deut 5:21).

God's announcement of the Ten Commandments, or Decalogue, is another landmark event in salvation history. God's formation of Israel is similar to parents raising a child. At first it was enough to expect the Hebrews to believe in one God and obey God as he sovereignly directed them in specific circumstances. Now Israel had matured to the point that God could reveal his will more fully, through his Law.

It is important to understand that God's commandments, the Mosaic Law, are not a set of arbitrary, externally imposed regulations. Rather, they codify some of the ways that God had originally created human beings to relate to him and to each other. This is why Jesus says of these commandments:

Not an iota, not a dot, will pass from the law until all is accomplished. Whoever then relaxes one of the least of these commandments and teaches men so, shall be called least in the kingdom of heaven; but he who does them and teaches them shall be called great in the kingdom of heaven.

MATTHEW 5:18-19

It is a disturbing fact that many Catholics today do not even know the Ten Commandments. These commandments are not outdated. Certainly Jesus taught the Jewish people in his day how to interpret these commandments correctly and how to live them more radically, but first he insisted that they be obeyed. When a man questioned Jesus about what he had to do to gain eternal life, Jesus' immediate response was, "If you wish to enter into life, keep the commandments" (Mt 19:17, NAB). When the man asked, "Which ones?" Jesus proceeded to list a number of the Ten Commandments (see Mt 19:18-19).

The first letter of John states the importance of this very directly: "The love of God is this, that we keep his commandments. And his commandments are not burdensome" (1 Jn 5:3, NAB). Those who know God and who want to love him keep his commandments:

The way we may be sure that we know him is to keep his commandments. Whoever says, "I know him," but does not keep his commandments is a liar,... But whoever keeps his word, the love of God is truly perfected in him.

1 JOHN 2:3-5, NAB

In chapter nine we will review in greater depth the meaning of the Ten Commandments as they have been fulfilled in Jesus Christ and the New Covenant.

Israel's Disobedience and God's Steadfast Love

God has given his people guidance for their lives in his Law or commandments, and yet the Hebrews failed to obey it faithfully. No sooner had Moses delivered the Law than the Israelites violated the first commandment by making and worshiping a golden calf (see Deut 9:16). The subsequent history of Israel is a continuous repetition or cycle of a basic pattern of events:

1. The people sin, violating God's commandments;
2. God allows them to suffer the just punishment of their rebellion;
3. The people cry out to God for mercy and forgiveness;
4. The Lord has compassion, removing the punishment and offering forgiveness;
5. The people repent, turning away from their wrongdoing and returning to obedience to God.

A good example of this cycle is presented by the Book of Judges 2:6-23.

The truth that stands out in the history of Israel is the tremendous faithfulness of God to his chosen people in spite of their infidelity. The Hebrew Scriptures repeatedly extol God's steadfast love, *emet:*

I will sing of thy steadfast love, O Lord, for ever;... For thy steadfast love was established for ever, thy faithfulness is firm as the heavens.

PSALM 89:1-2

Psalm 89 goes on to proclaim that God's love and faithfulness are based on his covenant relationship with Israel. Because of this covenant, God always stands ready to forgive and renew his mercy, regardless of the seriousness of Israel's sin and rebellion against him. God is truly portrayed in the Old Testament as both a just and a merciful God, a loving father, a God of steadfast love and faithfulness.

Kings and Prophets

One sign of God's love for Israel was the fulfillment of many of their desires. After Joshua had led the people out of the Sinai Desert and back into the land God had promised to give them, they were ruled by a series of judges. Still, Israel desired to have a king, as the other nations had, so God sent the prophet Samuel to anoint Saul as the first king of Israel. Saul was succeeded by the greatest king of the Old Covenant, David, followed by his son, Solomon, who built the first temple in Jerusalem.

Despite God's blessings, the Hebrew people often violated their covenant with God through sin. God responded by raising up the prophets, whose mission was to call the people to repent, to change their evil ways, and to turn back to faithfulness to the covenant. The task of the prophet is not so much to foretell the future, although prophets may do this through God's inspiration. The prophet is primarily called by God and sent out to challenge God's people to change their lives and return to faithfulness to God and their covenant with him.

The message of the prophets is sometimes a harsh word of conviction for sin (for violation of the covenant), but at other times it is a message of hope and consolation in times of hardship or affliction resulting from the peoples' sin and infidelity. At these times the prophets announce God's covenant of faithfulness and love.

The true prophet speaks not his own word but God's Word, through the inspiration of the Holy Spirit.

The Old Testament canon contains the longer writings of the "major prophets" Isaiah, Ezekiel, and Jeremiah, and the shorter accounts of the "minor prophets" Hosea, Joel, Amos, Obadiah, Micah, Nahum, Habakkuk,

Zephaniah, Haggai, Zechariah, Malachi, Daniel, Baruch, and the Book of Lamentations. The Book of Jonah is also sometimes considered a prophetic book. Through these prophets, God acted to stir up in his people the hope of salvation and the expectation of a new covenant, which would be "written on their hearts" (see Isa 2:2-4; Jer 31:31-34; Heb 10:16). God's salvation would even extend to all nations. However, this would necessitate a radical conversion and purification from sin (see CCC 64; Isa 49:5-6; 53:11; Ezek 36).

The Messianic Prophecies

Another important role of the prophets was to foretell and prepare the people for one who would deliver God's people from all of its bondage—the offspring of Eve whom the Book of Genesis said would crush the head of the serpent. Thus, we find that a number of the writings of the prophets contain messianic prophecies, prophecies foretelling the Messiah or "anointed one" who would deliver Israel from all its captivity.[3]

One of the foundational messianic prophecies was delivered by the prophet Nathan to King David:

> The LORD also reveals to you that he will establish a house for you. And when your time comes and you rest with your ancestors, I will raise up your heir after you, sprung from your loins, and I will make his kingdom firm. It is he who shall build a house for my name. And I will make his royal throne firm forever. I will be a father to him, and he shall be a son to me.
>
> 2 SAMUEL 7:11-14, NAB

As with many prophecies, this one has a dual fulfillment. The immediate fulfillment was in David's son, Solomon, who built a house for the Lord, the first great temple in Jerusalem. The deeper fulfillment of the prophecy was the coming of the Messiah, whose rule would last forever, and who is Son of the Father (God) in the fullest sense, sharing the Father's very own nature.

Christians believe that God spoke through many of the prophets of the Old Testament to point to and prepare the way for the coming of the true Messiah, Jesus Christ. Jesus is the only one who ultimately fulfills all of the prophecies of the Messiah in the Hebrew Scriptures. There are many prophecies speaking of such things as the Messiah's birth of a virgin (see Isa 7:10-14), the place of his birth (see Mic 5:1-3), and of the Messiah himself as "one like a son of man," coming on "the clouds of heaven" (Dan 7:13-14).

There are also Old Testament prophecies that speak of a suffering servant of God who would endure pain, hardship, and even death for the sake of the people (see Isa 52:13-15; 53; Ps 22). "Jesus himself explained the meaning of his life and death in the light of God's suffering Servant" (CCC 601; cf. Mt 20:28). However, few of the Jewish people at the time of Jesus understood these prophecies of the "suffering servant" as messianic because they appeared to contradict their image of the Messiah as a great, triumphant warrior or a magnificent king. Only in the person of Jesus of Nazareth, who both suffered as a man and was glorified as king by his Father, are these two types of prophecies reconciled and perfectly fulfilled.

Prophecies of the New Covenant

Besides foretelling the coming of a Messiah for Israel, the prophets also spoke of God establishing a New Covenant with Israel, a covenant that would fulfill and even exceed the promises of God in the former covenant. The prophet Jeremiah announced:

> The days are coming, says the LORD, when I will make a new covenant with the house of Israel and the house of Judah. It will not be like the covenant I made with their fathers the day I took them by the hand to lead them forth from the land of Egypt.... But this is the covenant which I will make with the house of Israel after those days, says the LORD. I will place my law within them, and write it upon their hearts; I will be their God, and they shall be my people. No longer will they have need to teach their friends and kinsmen how to know the LORD. All, from least to greatest, shall know me, says the LORD, for I will forgive their evildoing, and remember their sin no more.
>
> JEREMIAH 31:31-34, NAB

A sign of this New Covenant would be the sending of God's Spirit in a new and more powerful way upon the people. The prophet Ezekiel compared Israel with an enormous pile of dry bones in the middle of a plain. When God breathed his spirit into them, though, "they came alive and stood upright, a vast army" (Ezek 37:10). As Psalm 104 says, "if you take away their breath, they perish, and return to their dust. When you send forth your spirit, they are created, and you renew the face of the earth" (Ps 104:29-30).

The sending of the Holy Spirit in a new and more powerful way is part of the promise of the New Covenant. In the Old Covenant, only particular people, like prophets and kings, received the spirit of God. But in the New Covenant, as God says through the prophet Joel:

> I will pour out
> my spirit upon all mankind.
> Your sons and daughters shall prophesy,
> your old men shall dream dreams,
> your young men shall see visions;
> Even upon the servants and the handmaids,
> in those days, I will pour out my spirit. JOEL 3:1-2, NAB

The abundant outpouring of the Holy Spirit of God is a sign of the New Covenant predicted by the prophets.

The Relationship of the Old and New Covenants

Pope John Paul II noted that the Old Covenant remained "unchanged throughout the history of salvation, until the definitive and eternal Covenant which God will make (and now has made) with mankind in Jesus Christ."[4]

It is the Messiah, the Savior of Israel, who would come to establish this New Covenant. God's intention in establishing a New Covenant did not necessarily mean totally abandoning his chosen people of the Old Covenant. In fact, the Hebrew people, Israel, were intended to be the principal recipients and beneficiaries of the New Covenant. However, since God does not impose his designs on anyone, even his chosen people were free to reject the New Covenant.

Christians are saddened by the fact that relatively few of God's people of the first covenant accepted the New Covenant that God was offering them. Only a portion or a remnant of the Jewish people accepted Jesus as the Messiah and entered into the New Covenant he established and offered them. This notion of a faithful remnant of the Jewish people who recognize God's work and remain faithful to it is a familiar theme in the Hebrew Scriptures. Each time the Jewish people were taken into captivity, or each time that God sent a prophet, a remnant of the people remained faithful to God and moved ahead with God's plan.

Since many of the Jewish people, even today, have not responded to God's invitation to the New Covenant relationship, Christians have the responsibility to continue to announce to them the message of salvation. The section devoted to the Jewish people in the "Declaration on Non-Christian Religions" *(Nostra Aetate)* of the Second Vatican Council ends by exhorting Catholics to fulfill their duty to preach and proclaim the cross of Christ:

> It is, therefore, the duty of the church's preaching to proclaim the cross of Christ as the sign of God's all embracing love and as the fountain from which every grace flows.[5]

Nonetheless, the council also teaches that Christians must proclaim the gospel of Christ with love and deep respect for these people (the Jews), who remain, "beloved [by God] for the sake of their forefathers. For the gifts and the call of God are irrevocable" (Rom 11:28-29).[6] The Catholic Church vigorously condemns anti-Semitism—any bitterness, discrimination, or persecution directed against the Jewish people. Nevertheless, Christians continue to proclaim to God's people of the first covenant that God has a fuller plan in mind for them that they are always welcome to accept. The Messiah has now come, fulfilling the message of the Law and the prophets, and bringing a New Covenant of life, power, and salvation to all mankind.

The Value of the Old Testament for Christians

The Catholic Church has always valued the Old Testament. We are a people with a history, and our history can be traced back centuries, even millennia, to when God first created us and then formed a people with whom he established a covenant relationship.

The history of the Hebrew people and God's revelation to them is part of our history as Christians. God was at work among them, revealing himself, guiding them, and preparing for the coming of the Messiah. Without this preparation, no one could have recognized or accepted the Savior of the world when he came.

Much that God has revealed about himself and his will is recorded in the Old Testament. We find recorded in those texts the initial covenants of God with mankind, the history of God's mighty acts of salvation and deliverance, the prophetic word that continues to call us back to faithfulness to God, and much practical wisdom of God for our lives, as is recorded in the "wisdom" literature. Thus, the Old Testament is an essential part of God's revealed truth, part of the truth that sets us free (see Jn 8:32).

For Christians the Old Testament must be read in light of the New Testament. Jesus of Nazareth, the Messiah, came to fulfill the first covenant and to interpret it authoritatively. Also, there are some elements of the Old Testament revelation that were intended by God to be relevant and meaningful only for a particular time, but are now no longer binding in light of God's revelation in the New Testament. The dietary laws of the Old Testament are an example of this. Even some moral practices and outlooks found in the Old Testament, such as polygamy or indiscriminate killing through holy wars, are not considered by Christians to be condoned by God's law but a concession to the weakness of the people.

God formed a people much like parents raise a child. There are some things that God permitted or overlooked in the infancy and childhood of his people that he later prohibited or changed because of their increasing maturity. For example, when the Pharisees referred to Moses' practice of allowing divorce, Jesus replied: "Because of your stubbornness Moses let you divorce your wives, ... but at the beginning it was not that way. I now say to you, whoever divorces his wife (lewd conduct is a separate case) and marries another commits adultery" (see Mt 19:8-9).

All of these changes brought about by Jesus through the New Covenant are intended to lead God's people to become increasingly more conformed to God and his will, more holy and righteous. The goal of the Christian life is not simply to keep God's law, but to "be perfect, just as your heavenly Father is perfect" (Mt 5:48, NAB).

The value of the Old Testament for Catholics is, perhaps, best summarized by the bishops of the Second Vatican Council:

> The principal purpose to which the plan of the Old Covenant was directed was to prepare for the coming both of Christ, the universal Redeemer, and of the messianic kingdom, to announce this coming by prophecy (see Lk 24:44; Jn 5:39; 1 Pet 1:10), and to "indicate its meaning through various types" (see 1 Cor 10:11). Now the books of the Old Testament, in accordance with the state of mankind before the time of salvation established by Christ, reveal to all men the knowledge of God and of man and the ways in which God, just and merciful, deals with men. These books, though they also contain some things which are incomplete and temporary, nevertheless show us true divine pedagogy. These same books, then, give expression to a lively sense of God, contain a store of sublime teachings about God, sound wisdom about human life, and a wonderful treasury of prayers, and in them the mystery of our salvation is present in a hidden way. Christians should receive them with reverence.[7]

> God, the inspirer and author of both testaments, wisely arranged that the New Testament be hidden in the Old and the Old be made manifest in the New. For, though Christ established the New Covenant in His blood (see Lk 22:20; 1 Cor 11:25), still the books of the Old Testament, with all their parts, caught up into the proclamation of the gospel, acquire and show forth their full meaning in the New Testament (see Mt 5:17; Lk 24:27; Rom 16:25-26; 2 Cor 3:14-16) and in turn shed light on it and explain it.[8]

The prophecies of the Messiah and of the sending of God's spirit in a new way are examples of how the New Testament is "hidden" in the Old. We will continue in our next chapters to discover how the Old Covenant is made manifest in the New.

CHAPTER 4

Jesus Christ and the New Covenant

"Who do men say that I am?" (Mk 8:27). This question, posed by Jesus almost two thousand years ago, has become one of the most controversial issues in human history. Why? Because Christianity is based primarily on the person and identity of Jesus. Christianity is not, at its root, a philosophy of God, or an ethical system, or a set of religious practices or devotions. Christianity is based on belief in Jesus of Nazareth and on a living relationship with him. For Christians, the question Jesus asked his disciples, But who do you say that I am? (Mk 8:29), is the one question of ultimate importance that confronts each person.

Who Is Jesus?

How have people responded to this question about Jesus' identity? Many of Jesus' contemporaries identified him as one of the great prophets of Israel, either of the past, such as Elijah, or of the present, such as his cousin John the Baptist (see Mk 8:28).

Today we see similar attempts to identify Jesus. Practically everyone agrees that Jesus was a great man. The reason for his greatness, though, is debated. Some say he was an unmatched teacher or moralist, others think of him as a profound mystic, still others as a pioneering social critic or reformer. For some, Jesus is the great teacher of love, or the man born to serve others.

The difficulty with all of these answers is not that they are entirely wrong, but that they are incomplete. Jesus' identity and mission was far more radical and unique than any of these explanations indicate. Christian authors such as C.S. Lewis and Peter Kreeft have noted that only three acceptable alternatives for identifying Jesus are: liar, lunatic, or Lord. If Jesus claimed to be the unique Son of God, possessing the same nature as God his Father, he must have either been consciously deceiving his hearers (a liar), convinced that this was true, but mentally imbalanced to think so (a lunatic), or he was who he claimed to be—Lord of heaven and earth, equal to the Father.

The Christian's answer to Jesus' question, "Who do you say that I am?" can be no less than St. Peter's response to Jesus: "You are the Christ, the Son of the living God" (Mt 16:15-16). It is upon this faith that Christ's church is built (CCC 424). And yet, we must continue to explore the depth of meaning of this profession of faith. In order to discover Jesus' true identity, we must examine the only set of documents that thoroughly records his life—the New Testament and especially the four Gospels.

Approaching the New Testament

Before we look at the accounts of Jesus' life in the New Testament, we must ascertain what type of documents they are. The New Testament is basically the proclamation (*kerygma* in Greek) of the apostles and the early Christian church of their faith or belief in Jesus. Specifically, the New Testament proclaims their belief that Jesus of Nazareth is the long-awaited Messiah or Savior of Israel, and that he is the only divine Son of God the Father. Therefore, the accounts of Jesus in the New Testament are not neutral or purely objective, but present Jesus through the perspective of their faith in him.[1]

The authors of the New Testament were interested in more than just the "bare facts" about Jesus, but we must beware of those who claim that these authors distorted or falsified history. For example, some biblical scholars attempt to produce purely naturalistic explanations of Jesus' miracles, such as how he healed the sick, multiplied food for the hungry, or expelled demons from people. Some even question whether the resurrection of Jesus was a historical event. Much of this theorizing—such as the rejection of the possibility of miracles or the denial of the existence of the devil, of demons, or of any spiritual realm—is based on modern presuppositions and prejudices that began with the Enlightenment.

The Catholic Church does not deny the value of much modern biblical research regarding the identity of Christ, and even praises sound scholarship.

The Second Vatican Council's "Dogmatic Constitution on Divine Revelation" (*DV* 12) acknowledges that the authors of Scripture did shape their presentation of the events of Jesus' life according to their own interests, understanding, and audience. Nevertheless, the Catholic Church officially teaches that the New Testament is a proclamation of faith in Jesus based on reliable historical facts about what Jesus of Nazareth actually did and said. *Dei Verbum* unequivocally states:

> Holy Mother Church has firmly and with absolute constancy held, and continues to hold, that the four Gospels..., whose historical character the church unhesitatingly asserts, faithfully handed on what Jesus Christ, while living among men, really did and taught for their eternal salvation until the day He was taken up into heaven (see Acts 1:1-2)....
>
> The sacred authors wrote the four Gospels, selecting some things from the many which had been handed on by word of mouth or in writing, reducing some of them to a synthesis, explicating some things in view of the situation of their churches, and preserving the form of proclamation, but always in such a fashion that they told us the honest truth about Jesus.[2]

Recognizing the New Testament as a historically reliable set of documents, let us proceed to examine what it teaches, and what the Catholic Church professes, about the person and work of Jesus.

In the Beginning Was the Word

Before Jesus walked the earth as a man, the eternal Son or Word of God existed and was God. As the Second Person of the Blessed Trinity and the Son of the eternal Father, Jesus was able to announce, "before Abraham was, I am" (Jn 8:58), echoing God's revelation of his identity to Moses (Ex 3:13-14). The prologue of the Gospel of John states: "In the beginning was the Word, and the Word was with God, and the Word was God" (Jn 1:1). The Letter to the Hebrews explains: "He reflects the glory of God and bears the very stamp of his nature" (Heb 1:3).

At the Council of Constantinople in A.D. 381, the bishops of the early church formulated a creed or profession of faith to clarify exactly what Christians believe about Jesus as the preexistent Son or Word of God. Catholics profess this Nicene Creed every week at Mass, saying: "We believe in one Lord, Jesus Christ, the only Son of God, eternally begotten of the Father, God from God, Light from Light, true God from true God, begotten, not made, one in being with the Father...."

This part of the Nicene Creed was written to refute the heresy of Arius, who claimed that the Son was not God but only the highest creature of God. The Creed answers this claim by asserting that the Son of God was begotten, or born, of God, not "made," or created. The Son is, therefore, "God from God, Light from Light, true God from True God."

Another way that this Creed affirms that the Son is fully God is the statement that the Son is "one in being" (Greek: *homoousios*) with the Father. Whatever type of being the Father is, so is the Son. Since the Father is God, so is the Son.

When we hear that the Son of God is born or begotten of the Father, it is natural to ask when he was born. Arius reasoned that since the Son is born of God, there must be a time when the Son was not—a time before the Son existed. The Creed says that the Son is "eternally begotten" of the Father, which means that there was never a time when the Son, or Word, of God did not exist. The fact that there is no beginning of the Son's existence challenges us to remember that the Son, because he is God, is eternal.

The Bible and the Creed affirm that with the Father, the Son of God created all that has been made. The Nicene Creed states: "Through him [the Son] all things were made." The Bible also teaches this: all things were made through him, and without him was not anything made that was made (Jn 1:3; see also Col 1:16-17; Heb 1:2). The Son of God brought the universe and each of us into existence, and holds us in existence, for, "in him all things hold together" (Col 1:17).

The Titles of Jesus

We should also pause to reflect on the titles of Jesus that we find in the Creed:

- *Jesus*, in Hebrew, means "God saves," and indicates why the Son of God became man: to bring God's saving plan in history to its climax and fulfillment (see CCC 430).

- *Christ* means anointed, and is the Greek translation of the Hebrew "Messiah." Jesus is the long-awaited Savior who is anointed to redeem Israel and rule over God's people (see CCC 436-40)
- *Son of God*, like "Messiah," was not necessarily a title given only to a divine being, but to those (like God's chosen people, Israel) who had a special relationship with God. However, when Peter called Jesus "Son of the living God," he understood Jesus' sonship as unique and divine. This is indicated by Jesus' response to Peter: "Flesh and blood has not revealed this to you, but my Father who is in heaven" (Mt 16:16-17; see CCC 441, 442).
- *Lord* was used in the Gentile world as a title of respect (like "sir"). However, it also was the Greek translation of the unspeakable Hebrew name of God, YHWH. Thus, the confession that Jesus is Lord (so common in the early church), implied Jesus' divinity, his equality with God (see CCC 446-51).

The Word Became Flesh

The greatest event in human history was inaugurated with the birth of the eternal Word of God into our human condition. God himself became man. This event is called the incarnation of the Word: "the Word became flesh and dwelt among us" (Jn 1:14), or as St. Paul taught, "when the time had fully come, God sent forth his Son, born of woman, born under the law..." (Gal 4:4).

Why did the Son of God become a man, taking on the limitations and pains of our human condition? It was the key to God's plan to redeem the human race from sin and rebellion against him, and to restore us to his friendship:

> For God so loved the world that he gave his only Son, that whoever believes in him should not perish but have eternal life. For God sent the Son into the world, not to condemn the world, but that the world might be saved through him.
>
> JOHN 3:16-17

This is the heart of the Good News! God has loved the human race so much that he has not merely sent angels, prophets, and other messengers to lead us back to himself, but he personally entered into human history to save us from our sin and rebellion against him. What a free, unmerited gift! Who could have imagined that God would have gone to this extreme to show his love and to overcome the sin of the whole human race? Christ has not come to save humanity in general, but to show his love for each one of us individually, to free each person from the bondage of his or her sin. God has come in person, in the flesh, which is the meaning of "incarnation." In this mystery, the depth of God's love and humility is revealed. The primitive Christian hymn about the Son that Paul includes in his letter to the Philippians expresses this most beautifully:

> Though he was in the form of God, [he] did not count equality with God a thing to be grasped, but emptied himself, taking the form of a servant, being born in the likeness of men.
>
> PHILIPPIANS 2:6-7

When the "Word became flesh" and took on our humanity, Jesus also became a *model of holiness* for mankind. By virtue of his becoming man, the Son of God shows us by example how to live and how to love, as the Father has loved us (see CCC 458- 59).

Finally, in becoming man the Son of God gives to humanity a share in his divinity, enabling us to be "partakers of the divine nature" (2 Pet 1:4). He did this by "lifting" the human race to God in his own person, "so that man, by entering into communion with the Word and thus receiving divine sonship, might become a Son of God."[3] St. Athanasius boldly proclaimed: "For the Son of God became man so that we might become God," that is, sharers in God's life by grace through our union with the Son of God.[4]

It is, of course, at Christmas that the church particularly celebrates this mystery of the incarnation of the Word of God. Christmas is a mystery of salvation because Christ shares his divine life with us in taking on our humanity:

> O marvelous exchange! Man's Creator has become man, born of the Virgin. We have been made sharers in the divinity of Christ who humbled himself to share our humanity.[5]

Born of a Virgin

In fulfillment of Isaiah's prophecy, the Son of God became man by his birth "to a virgin betrothed to a man whose name was Joseph, of the house of David; and the virgin's name was Mary" (Lk 1:27).

Jesus had no human father. Joseph is honored by Christians as the guardian, protector, and foster father of Jesus, and head of the holy family. Mary conceived the Son of God in her womb solely by the power of the Holy Spirit (see Lk 1:31, 35). Mary is the true, natural mother of Jesus, and so she has been honored for centuries by Christians as the "Mother of God." This title was defended and confirmed at the Council of Ephesus in A.D. 431 because it attests to the facts that Jesus was truly God and that Mary really bore God himself in her womb. The miraculous circumstances of Jesus' birth teach other things about Mary's privileged role in God's plan which will be explained in the chapter focusing on her.

The sacred Scripture also records many events, following closely upon Jesus' birth, that Christians celebrate and reflect upon: his circumcision on the eighth day, which prefigures Christian baptism (see Lk 2:21); his Epiphany to the Magi, which was his first manifestation as Lord to the nations (see Mt 2:1-12); Jesus' presentation in the temple in which devout Jews Simeon and Anna prophetically recognize Jesus as Messiah (see Lk 2:22-38); and the flight into Egypt and the slaughter of the Holy Innocents, the "proto-martyrs" (see Mt 2:13-21). Truly Jesus' birth was light breaking into a dark world. Although "he came to his own home, and his own people received him not" (Jn 1:11), nonetheless the Scripture has been fulfilled that, "The light shines in the darkness, and the darkness has not overcome it" (Jn 1:5).

Truly God, Truly Man

The Catholic Church has always vigorously affirmed the truth of both Jesus' full divinity and full humanity. Jesus is truly God and truly man. This truth was authoritatively stated by the Council of Chalcedon in A.D. 451. The council declared that Jesus "is perfect both in his divinity and in his humanity, truly God and truly man composed of body and rational soul; that he is the same substance (*homoousios*) with the Father in his divinity, of the same substance (*homoousios*) with us in his humanity, like us in every respect except for sin (see Heb 4:15)."[6]

Jesus possesses two distinct but inseparable natures, the divine and the human, united in one person. Chalcedon's definition leaves one question unanswered: *how* are these two natures perfectly joined into one person? This remains a mystery; Chalcedon could declare only that they *are* joined, not how. Creeds and theological definitions about God or Jesus can distinguish what is true and what is false, but they can never exhaust the mystery of the reality of God and his plan.

When we speak of Jesus' two natures, it would be easy to think of Jesus behaving like a split personality—at one moment doing something human, the next moment doing something that only God could do. Those who followed Jesus did not perceive him in this way because these two natures in Jesus worked together in perfect harmony. John Calvin proposed that Jesus' two natures functioned together like our two eyes: though each eye is distinct, they work together in such perfect unison that our vision is one. Yet even this analogy implies a *separation* of Jesus' divine and human natures that did not exist. Jesus' human nature and human will were so conformed to his divine nature and divine will that the two were joined into an inseparable harmony so that we can truly say that Jesus was one person, not two, but composed of a divine and a human nature.

We can appreciate this truth more fully by reflecting on our own nature. Although we are single, unified persons, we are at the same time both spiritual and physical beings. When we act or decide, it is not just our souls or minds that act, but *we*, as whole persons. My human nature does not decide or do something; *I* do. In the same way, Jesus acted as a single, unified person, even though he is both God and man. It is a person who acts, not a nature. Thus, the *person* of Jesus was the principle of all his actions, not one or the other of his natures.[7]

The divine nature of Jesus Christ is perceived by us only as it is reflected through the fullness and perfection of his human nature. As a man, Jesus came only to do the will of his Father, God. As the Son of God, he alone was capable of doing this perfectly, being the only-begotten divine person, the Son of God incarnate.[8]

Jesus' Human Knowledge and Will

Popes and church councils staunchly defended the humanity of Jesus against those who denied that he had a human soul (such as Apollinarius of Laodicaea in the fourth century), or a distinct human will. Pope Damasus I confessed that the eternal Son also assumed a rational, human soul (CCC 471; cf. Damasus I: DS 149) .

The sixth ecumenical council (Third Council of Constantinople, A.D. 681) affirmed that Jesus possesses two wills, divine and human, which cooperate so perfectly that Jesus, in perfect obedience to the Father and his plan of salvation, always wills humanly whatever his divine will dictates.[9]

That Jesus had a "rational human soul" also means that he had a human mind and knowledge as the Son of God. How these two "minds" work together has long puzzled ordinary Christians and theologians. What did Jesus, as one person, really know when he was on earth? How could his human knowledge, naturally limited, be reconciled with his omniscience as the Son of God?

In becoming a man, the eternal Word of God truly did empty himself—taking "the form of a slave" (Phil 2:7, NAB). In this "kenosis" (self-emptying), just as the Son of God accepted the limitations of a human body (i.e., he was not a "superman"), Christian tradition and Scripture teach that he also accepted the limitations of a human mind. "This is why the Son of God could, when he became man, 'increase in wisdom and in stature, and in favor with God and man' (Lk 2:52), and would even have to inquire for himself about what one in the human condition can learn only from experience" (cf. Mk 6:38; 8:27; Jn 11:34)(CCC 472). In his human nature, Jesus had to grow in knowledge and learn many things from experience, since he was like us in all things, except sin (see Heb 4:15).

Yet, sacred Scripture testifies that Jesus also spoke of things that only God would know, such as his intimate knowledge of his Father in heaven (see Mt 11:27; Mk 14:36; Jn 1:18; 8:55) and "the divine penetration he had into the secret thoughts of human hearts" (cf. Mk 2:8; Jn 2:25; 6:61)(CCC 473).

How do we reconcile these? Simply. Because the Word became flesh in order to reveal the Father and the secrets of God's kingdom, he had to know those things that he was sent by the Father to reveal. In a sense, in these things the human mind of Jesus had "access" to the divine mind. The *Catechism* states this precisely:

By its union to the divine wisdom in the person of the Word incarnate, Christ enjoyed in his human knowledge the fullness of understanding of the eternal plans he had come to reveal (cf. Mk 8:31; 9:31; 10:33-34; 14:18-20, 26-30). What he admitted to not knowing in this area, he elsewhere declared himself not sent to reveal (cf. Mk 13:32; Acts 1:7)(CCC 474).

A clear example of the latter case is found in Mark 13:32. In this text, Jesus was asked directly when the fulfillment of God's kingdom would come about. He answered that not even the Son knew this, but only the Father.

Perhaps the most striking aspect of Jesus' humanity, however, is the *love* that he had for all people. The love of God—divine love—filled his human heart. Devotion to the Sacred Heart of Jesus, pierced for our sins, is a way of honoring God for this great love.[10]

Jesus' Ministry Begins

The Incarnation, the eternal Word of God entering into human history, is one of the greatest mysteries of the Christian faith. By "mystery" is meant something greater than what human reason can grasp. Because of the Incarnation, we could say that Jesus' whole life—everything he did, said, or thought—is a mystery, because it is the Son of God made flesh who is the subject of all that he did, said, and thought. The *Catechism* explains that Jesus' "whole life is a mystery of *revelation, redemption,* and *recapitulation.* That is, everything in Jesus' life *reveals* the Father and his love for us, *redeems* us from our sins, and *restores* fallen man to his original vocation ("recapitulation") (see CCC 516-18). Let us proceed to reflect on these mysteries of Jesus' life so that we may model our life after his, and come to live in him as he lives in us (see CCC 520-21).

Jesus was the Son of God from the moment of his conception in Mary's womb. He was not adopted by God at some point. It is amazing to think that for the first thirty years of his life, Jesus, the Son of God, lived in relative obscurity as a carpenter's son, residing in the small Galilean town of Nazareth. Pope Paul VI, in a speech given there, spoke powerfully of the lessons Nazareth has to teach us: about the dignity of *work,* about the beauty of *family life,* and about the necessity of *silence* for prayer and growth of the kingdom.[11] The silence of the Gospels about the events of Jesus' "hidden life" in Nazareth is broken only by the story of the finding of Jesus in the temple at age twelve (see Lk 2:41-52). We know the Gospels are not modern biographies of Jesus because they tell us relatively little about his early life, before his public ministry.

When Jesus was near thirty years old, his kinsman, John, began to call the Jewish people to repent, to turn from their sins. He began to baptize them in the waters of the Jordan River as a sign of their repentance. John the Baptist was recognized by many of the Jews as a great prophet, and some even claimed he was the Messiah. But John declared, "I baptize you with water; but one mightier than I is coming ... He will baptize you with the holy Spirit and fire" (Lk 3:16, NAB).

One day, Jesus came to receive John's baptism. The Gospels record that at the moment of his baptism, the Spirit of God descended like a dove and hovered over Jesus and a voice from the heavens said, "This is my beloved Son, with whom I am well pleased" (Mt 3:17). John then recognized Jesus as the long-awaited Messiah, the "Lamb of God, who takes away the sin of the world" (Jn 1:29). God began to reveal Jesus' identity even as his public ministry was about to unfold.

Led by the Holy Spirit, Jesus immediately went out into the desert to pray and fast, and was there tempted by Satan. Jesus defeated the devil by ignoring his lies and false promises, and by quoting the Hebrew Scripture, particularly the Book of Deuteronomy, to refute him. "Jesus is the New Adam who remained faithful just where the first Adam had given into temptation ... Jesus' victory over the tempter in the desert anticipates victory at the Passion, the supreme act of obedience of his filial love for the Father" (CCC 539).

After this, Jesus "came into Galilee, preaching the gospel of God, and saying, 'The time is fulfilled, and the kingdom of God is at hand; repent, and believe in the gospel [Good News]'" (Mk 1:14-15). The public ministry of Jesus had begun.

The Message of the Kingdom

The heart of Jesus' teaching, his Good News, is about the reign of God. For centuries, the Jewish people had awaited the Messiah who would fulfill God's promise to establish a kingdom that would overcome all its foes and would endure forever. Jesus electrified his hearers by announcing, "The time is fulfilled, and the kingdom of God is at hand" (Mk 1:15). This implied that he was the one sent by God to establish the kingdom of God!

However, most of the Jews of Jesus' time did not comprehend what Jesus meant by the kingdom of God. Most of them understood the kingdom of God in purely political terms. Jesus never defined what the kingdom was; instead he told numerous parables relating what it was like (see CCC 546). The essence of Jesus' understanding of the kingdom of God is that it is the reign or rule of God over people's hearts and lives. God sent his Son, Jesus, to set people free from anything that would prevent God from ruling over their lives.

Jesus exhorted his hearers to do two things to prepare for the coming of God's kingdom: *repent* (reform your lives by turning away from all sin and wrongdoing) and *believe* the good news that Jesus had come to establish God's reign (see Mk 1:14).

Another radically new dimension of Jesus' proclamation of the kingdom was that the kingdom was for *everyone,* for Jew and Gentile alike, and especially for the materially poor and the poor "in spirit," those who have accepted it with humble hearts (CCC 544). Also, Jesus came to call *sinners* to the kingdom (not those who are righteous in their own eyes; see Mk 2:17), by urging them to turn away from their sin and toward the love of the all-merciful Father. Jesus tells of the great joy in heaven over one sinner who repents (Lk 15:7; see CCC 545; Lk 7:11-32).

The Reign of God: Present in Jesus

When Jesus said that the reign of God was "at hand," did he mean that it was beginning now, or that it was to come in the future? The New Testament indicates that the reign of God began with Jesus' own teaching and ministry.

How do we know this? Jesus' ministry was marked by the full power and authority of God. First Corinthians 4:20 says that the reign of God "does not consist in talk, but in power." Jesus manifested the power of God's reign in a number of ways.

1. Jesus taught with authority. There was spiritual power in his very words. It was the power of absolute, undiluted truth—God's truth. It manifested itself as a profound wisdom that left people in awe, "cut to the heart" (Acts 2:37). The people recognized that Jesus was unlike the other rabbis or teachers of his day because "he taught them as one who had authority, and not as their scribes" (Mt 7:29). Jesus attracted crowds of hundreds and thousands who came to him just to hear his Word.

2. Jesus demonstrated his power over Satan and evil spirits. The Jews recognized that Jesus had the power to cast out demons (exorcism). Some claimed that he did so by the power of the evil one, Beelzebub. Jesus retorted that this made no sense unless Satan were divided against himself. Jesus' power to exorcise must be from God: "if it is by the finger of God that I cast out demons, then the kingdom of God has come upon you" (Lk 11:20).

3. Jesus performed miracles. His mighty works of healing, raising the dead, still-ing storms, multiplying food, and other works, were signs that God's kingdom had begun. John the Baptist sent his disciples to ask Jesus, "Are you he who is to come, [the Messiah] or shall we look for another?" Jesus replied, "Go and tell John what you hear and see: the blind receive their sight and the lame walk, lepers are cleansed and the deaf hear, and the dead are raised up, and the poor have good news preached to them" (Mt 11:3-5).

These three signs are definite indications of the presence of God's kingdom. In the Gospel of John, Jesus insists that even if people don't believe his words, they should believe in him because of his "works" (see Jn 10:24-25, 37-38). If Jesus had performed no miracles or mighty works, as some modern scholars claim, this reference in John's Gospel would make no sense.

We know that Jesus performed miracles. On Pentecost, Peter began his speech, addressed to those who had known Jesus and had witnessed his cruci-fixion, with these words: "Jesus of Nazareth, a man attested to you by God with mighty works and wonders and signs which God did through him in your midst, as you yourselves know..." (Acts 2:22). The power of Jesus' ministry was no secret; it was the growing jealousy and fear of the Jewish leaders concerning Jesus' evident power that finally led to his death.[12]

The reign of God is inaugurated with Jesus' public ministry. In Jesus himself the kingdom of God is present, at least in its initial form. This is what Jesus meant when he told the Pharisees, "The kingdom of God is not coming with signs to be observed; nor will they say, 'Lo here it is!' or 'There!' for behold, the kingdom of God is in the midst of you" (Lk 17:20-21). After Jesus ascended to the Father, he entrusted the message and the "keys" to the kingdom to his followers, especially to Peter (see Mt 16:19) and the twelve apostles (see Lk 22:29-30). The message and works of the kingdom of God continue to be proclaimed and carried out by the church through the leaders Jesus appointed (see CCC 551-53). However, the completion or fulfillment of God's kingdom, when his reign will be evident to all, will not occur until Jesus returns to earth in glory as its king and judge.

Jesus' Teaching

In addition to his mighty works, Jesus revealed the nature and truths of the kingdom of God in his teaching. Jesus taught in two modes: in parables and directly. Jesus' parables were original analogies and stories that challenged his hearers. The parables of Jesus covered a wide variety of topics, but all were in some way related to the kingdom of God. Some spoke about it directly: "The kingdom of heaven is like a grain of mustard seed..." (Mt 13:31). Other parables told of the kind of conduct required of those living under God's rule, such as the parable of the Good Samaritan (see Lk 10:25-37).

Jesus also taught directly, and much of this teaching, too, dealt with the kingdom of God. For example, Jesus' Beatitudes (see Mt 5:1-12; Lk 6:20-26) are a charter for living with God and his will fully ruling one's life. Prayer is essential for living under the reign of God, and Jesus taught his followers how to pray, how to relate to God. He instructs us in the proper motives and attitudes for prayer, and he even left us his own words of prayer by which we can address God as "our Father" (see Mt 6:9-13; Lk 11:2-4).

The wisdom and insight of Jesus' teaching is recognized by almost everyone. It is original, fresh, and marked by genius. It's also a message so radical and challenging that only with strong faith and the grace of God can anyone hope to put it into practice. Jesus promises this help to all who decide to take his teaching seriously, who are willing to leave everything to follow him.

Jesus Reveals God

One radical aspect of Jesus' teaching was his claim to know God in an intimate, personal way. Jesus addressed the omnipotent God as "Abba," the Aramaic equivalent of the English "dear Father" or "Papa." While Jews of that time would not even pronounce the proper name of God (YHWH), out of respect and reverence, Jesus called God his "dear Father." Not only did Jesus speak to God with this amazing intimacy and familiarity, but he taught his followers to address God in the same way. He instructed them to turn to the Father at all times in prayer, as he himself did.

What did Jesus teach about God, his Father? First, he taught that the Father loves Jesus' followers so much that he desires to care for them and to provide for them in all circumstances (for example, see the parable of the lilies of the field in Mt 6:25-34). In teaching us to address God as father, Jesus revealed that we are sons and daughters of God, and heirs of his kingdom—if we choose to allow God to rule over our lives. However, for those who choose to reject God and his kingdom and decide not to live as his sons and daughters, God is also a just Father who permits us to chart our own destiny freely. Sometimes it means that we must suffer the consequences of rebellion against him. Jesus, as God the Son, perfectly reflects his Father's joy over those who accept the kingdom of God (see Lk 15:3-7); his sorrow and grief over those who reject it or do not recognize it (see Lk 19:41-44); and his anger at those who prevent others from entering the kingdom by their hypocrisy, pride, or false teaching (see Mt 23).

Jesus revealed another essential fact about God's identity. Besides God being Father, with Jesus as his unique divine Son, Jesus also revealed that God is Holy Spirit. Jesus promised that he and the Father would send this Holy Spirit to his disciples in order to lead them into all truth (see Jn 14:15-17, 25-26; 16:7-15) and to fill them with the power of God (see Acts 1:8; 2). The Holy Spirit teaches us how to pray as we ought (see Rom 8:16, 26-27) and enables us to recognize that Jesus is Lord (see 1 Cor 12:3) and that God is our Father (see Rom 8:15; Gal 4:6).

The Way of Discipleship

Another radical aspect of Jesus' teaching was his expectations of those who believed in his message. "Disciple" literally means a student or follower. To be a follower of Jesus, it is necessary both to know what he says and to put it into practice. Jesus sternly warns his disciples of the dire consequences of failing to put his teaching into practice (see Mt 7:21-27).

Jesus' first concern in his public ministry was to invite people to follow after him. Why? So they could be formed, taught, and trained by Jesus in the ways of God and his reign. This demanded a radical and complete commitment. Simon, Andrew, James, and John immediately left their nets and fishing boats, and Matthew his tax booth, to follow Jesus (see Mt 4:18-22; 9:9). Jesus told a certain young man that in order to be perfect, he had to sell his possessions, give the proceeds to the poor, and follow him (see Lk 18:18-22).

Jesus continues even today to call us to discipleship. Being a Christian requires a radical commitment. Nothing in our lives can be more important than following Jesus and living according to his teaching. We may not necessarily have to leave our home or occupation to become a Christian, but it could involve that. Jesus warned: "Enter by the narrow gate; for the gate is wide and the way is easy, that leads to destruction, and those who enter by it are many. For the gate is narrow and the way is hard, that leads to life, and those who find it are few" (Mt 7:13-14). What is this "narrow way?" Jesus said, "I am the door; if anyone enters by me, he will be saved" (Jn 10:9).

What is the road or way that leads to eternal life? Jesus said, "I am the way, and the truth, and the life; no one comes to the Father, but by me" (Jn 14:6). The only sure way or road to eternal life is the way of discipleship in Jesus Christ.[13] As we shall see, discipleship involves both joy and suffering, glory and the cross. Christians are not perfect, but they are the people who have discovered the One who can save them from their sins and who shows them the true way of life—Jesus Christ. He is the "pearl of great value" (see Mt 13:44-46) that we must abandon all else to obtain.

It is important for us to realize that Jesus Christ is not just a figure of the past or a theological problem, but a living person who is calling each of us into a vital, intimate relationship with himself. Jesus wants each of us to come to know him and love him with all of our heart, so that his call to each of us to "Come, follow me" is not just a duty or a burden, but the greatest joy of our life.

The Jesus whom we read about in the Gospels, who profoundly touched and changed the lives of all who responded to his invitation, is the same Jesus who longs to touch each of us with his life, love, and power—if we will only let him! If we do, the affirmations that Jesus is Lord or Savior will be not just dry, doctrinal statements, but heartfelt professions of how we actually relate to and experience Jesus in our lives. As the *Catechism* teaches: "From this loving knowledge of Christ springs the desire to proclaim him, to 'evangelize,' and to lead others to the 'yes' of faith in Jesus Christ" (CCC 429).

Salvation Without Discipleship?

What about the salvation of those who do not know, believe in, or follow Jesus Christ? There is much theological speculation today about the salvation of non-Christians. Many people are very optimistic about the possibility of their salvation. Catholics do not claim to know the eternal destiny of any individual, but do affirm certain things.

1. We know that Jesus Christ is the only Savior. Acts 4:12 teaches, "there is salvation in no one else, for there is no other name under heaven given among men by which we must be saved."

2. The ordinary way for one to attain salvation through Jesus Christ is though faith, baptism, and a life of discipleship (that is, faithful obedience to Jesus and his teaching). Mark 16:15-16 records Jesus' words in a postresurrection appearance: "Go into all the world and preach the gospel to the whole creation. He who believes and is baptized will be saved; but he who does not believe will be condemned." We have already noted what Jesus says about those who hear his word, believe in it, and yet do not put it into practice. Obedience to Jesus, as well as faith and baptism, are normally necessary for salvation.

3. In God's mercy it is possible for those who are not Christians to be saved through the grace of Jesus Christ. There are certain biblical texts, such as the last judgment scene in Matthew 25 and Paul's Letter to the Romans, 2:12-16, that indicate that some will be saved by Christ on account of their charity, or through having followed the dictates of their conscience. The Second Vatican Council's "Dogmatic Constitution on the Church" affirms this:

> Those also can attain to everlasting salvation who through no fault of their own do not know the gospel of Christ or His church, yet sincerely seek God and, moved by grace, strive by their deeds to do His will as it is known to them through the dictates of conscience. Nor does divine Providence deny the help necessary for salvation to those who, without blame on their part, have not yet arrived at an explicit knowledge of God, but who strive to live a good life, thanks to His grace. Whatever goodness or truth is found among them is looked upon by the church as a preparation for the gospel.[14]

This passage refers to the possibility of salvation of those who have not accepted the gospel through no fault of their own, not to those who have consciously rejected and refused to believe in the Good News of Jesus Christ. It is also significant that the Catholic Church considers whatever goodness or truth possessed by non-Christians to be a "preparation for the gospel." There is no implication here that the gospel need not be preached to non-Christians. In fact, the closing paragraph of this section from the Second Vatican Council warns that those who have not accepted the gospel often fail to attain eternal life because of the deception of Satan or through falling into despair:

> But rather often men, deceived by the Evil One, have become caught up in futile reasoning and have exchanged the truth of God for a lie, serving the creature rather than the Creator (cf. Rom 1:21, 25). Or some there are who, living and dying in a world without God, are subject to utter hopelessness. Consequently, to promote the glory of God and procure the salvation of all such men, and mindful of the command of the Lord, "Preach the gospel to every creature" (Mk 16:15), the church painstakingly fosters her missionary work.[15]

We cannot assume that those who are not living as disciples of Jesus Christ will be saved. It is possible that they may receive the grace of Christ in an extraordinary way, but we cannot presume this. Jesus' commission to his disciples is clear: "Go therefore and make disciples of all nations, baptizing them in the name of the Father and of the Son and of the Holy Spirit" (Mt 28:19). We commend the destiny of those who have not heard or accepted the message of Jesus Christ to the plan and mercy of God, and continue to pray and work for their conversion to Jesus Christ, the one Savior of the world and only source of eternal life.

The Call To Discipleship

Jesus called everyone to follow him. All are called to be disciples of Jesus Christ. Although Jesus first called the Jews, "the lost sheep of the house of Israel" (Mt 15:24), he startled and scandalized his Jewish brethren by healing and delivering Gentiles, such as the Roman centurion's servant. Jesus praised the centurion for his faith in him, saying, "Truly, I say to you, not even in Israel have I found such faith. I tell you, many will come from the east and west and sit at table with Abraham, Isaac, and Jacob in the kingdom of heaven..." (Mt 8:10-11).

Jesus especially came "to preach good news to the poor" (Lk 4:18), but even the rich who were ready to renounce all for Jesus' sake could be saved, such as Zacchaeus in Luke 19.

Jesus' disciples included both men and women. Even though women had a limited social status in ancient society, Jesus personally invited a number of women to accept the Good News of the reign of God. Many of Jesus' miracles were healings and exorcisms of women. He made no distinction on the basis of gender in his basic call to discipleship.

Jesus' call to follow him is universal. It extends to all races, nations, peoples, and cultures. The key to discipleship is faith in Jesus Christ—faith that expresses itself in love, commitment, and obedience. As St. Paul wrote to the Galatians:

> For in Christ Jesus you are all sons of God, through faith. For as many of you as were baptized into Christ have put on Christ. There is neither Jew nor Greek, there is neither slave nor free, there is neither male nor female; for you are all one in Christ Jesus.
>
> GALATIANS 3:26-28

Catholics are called to "make disciples of all nations" by leading all people to salvation through faith in and discipleship to Jesus Christ. This is how we carry on Jesus' mission of proclaiming and establishing the reign of God in this world.

Discipleship and Jesus' Death

Discipleship can be very exciting. Jesus' disciples rejoiced as they witnessed his mighty works and heard his teaching (see Lk 10:17-20). The appearance of Jesus in splendor with Moses and Elijah at his side, the Transfiguration, was intended to strengthen his disciples' faith as Jesus prepared to undergo his Passion and death (see CCC 554-56).

At the heart of discipleship, however, is the cross. As his followers matured in faith, Jesus began to tell them of the suffering and painful death that awaited him and that also awaited many of them. "If any man would come after me, let him deny himself and take up his cross and follow me. For whoever would save his life will lose it; and whoever loses his life for my sake and the gospel's will save it" (Mk 8:34-35; also see Mt 16:24; Lk 9:23-24).

St. Paul prayed that he would never glory in anything but the cross of Christ, by which he was crucified to the world and its allurements (see Gal 6:14). The Scriptures make it clear that it is necessary to follow Jesus even when it means renouncing one's own preferences, opinions, comforts, and will—dying to oneself. Jesus did not live to please himself, but to obey the will of his Father. The Father's will for the redemption of the human race was that his Son, Jesus, would suffer and die:

And being found in human form he humbled himself and became obedient unto death, even death on a cross.

PHILIPPIANS 2:8

The death of Jesus can be a great obstacle to faith in him. St. Paul openly stated that, "we preach Christ crucified, a stumbling block to Jews and folly to Gentiles ..." (1 Cor 1:23). Indeed, the Jewish people of Jesus' time could not reconcile the image of the "suffering servant" of Isaiah 52:13–53:12 with their understanding of the triumphant Messiah who would set Israel free from oppression. The apostles proclaimed that God had made this "stumbling stone" (Isa 28:16; Rom 9:33) the cornerstone of the church (see 1 Pet 2:7-8). For

Christ is "the power of God and the wisdom of God. For the foolishness of God is wiser than men, and the weakness of God is stronger than men" (1 Cor 1:24-25).

Why did the Son of God have to die? Being God, he was not subject to death in his divine nature. In his human nature, being without sin, he did not *need* to die. Rather, he *chose* to die (see Mt 26:53-54). He chose to accept and to conquer death for the sake of mankind (see Heb 2:9-10; 7:27; 9:11-15; 1 Pet 3:18).

Jesus' death demonstrates the tremendous love that God has for us. As Jesus himself said, "Greater love has no man than this, that a man lay down his life for his friends" (Jn 15:13). Jesus laid down his life for the whole human race, to restore mankind to God's friendship—the friendship we had lost through the sin of Adam and our own personal sin. As St. Paul wrote:

> Why, one will hardly die for a righteous man—though perhaps for a good man one will dare even to die. But God shows his love for us in that while we were yet sinners Christ died for us.
>
> ROMANS 5:7-8

Jesus Christ died to prove God's love for us and to free us from the bondage of our sin. Jesus divested himself of the glory and majesty that was his as God to live among us and to die for us in order to save us from a second death.

Jesus' Passion and Death

The Paschal mystery—the passion, death, and resurrection of Jesus Christ—is the center of the Good News that Christians proclaim to the world. By this "once-for-all" sacrifice of himself on Calvary (Heb 9:26), Christ has conquered sin and death and reconciled the world to God (see CCC 571).

The church celebrates this Paschal mystery of the "pasch," or passover, of Jesus from life to death and back to life again annually during Holy Week. This week begins with Palm (or Passion) Sunday, commemorating Jesus' triumphal entry into Jerusalem amidst the waving of palm branches and shouts of "Hosanna to the Son of David!" fulfilling many prophecies (see CCC 559).

However, within less than a week, on Good Friday, these shouts of praise turned into a cry for Jesus death: "Crucify him!" (Jn 19:6).

Why this tragic turnabout? Certain Jewish leaders stirred up the people against Jesus, and accused him of blasphemy and false prophecy—religious crimes punishable by death in the Jewish law (see CCC 574). There were three things about Jesus and his teaching that instigated their wrath against him.

- *Jesus' interpretation of the Jewish Law and oral tradition,* including his apparent failure to submit to the whole Law (such as by healing on the Sabbath day);
- *Jesus' apparent challenge to the centrality of the Temple in Jerusalem* as a unique holy place where God must be worshiped;
- *Jesus' claim to know God as Father,* and to share in a unique way in the life and glory of God. (See CCC 576.)

In light of these things, when Jesus called for conversion and faith in his message, it is possible to understand why the Sanhedrin (the highest Jewish court) instead condemned Jesus as a blasphemer. The Scripture emphasizes that they acted out of "ignorance" and the "hardness" of their "unbelief" (CCC 591; see Lk 23:34; Acts 3:17-18; Mk 3:5; Rom 11:25, 20).

Jesus himself, at the point of death, cried out from the cross, "Father, forgive them; for they know not what they do" (Lk 23:34). This forgiveness included not only the Jewish leaders who condemned him, but the Roman authorities and soldiers who put him to death, and all those who reject and persecute Jesus and his church out of blindness and ignorance. For he came not to condemn the world, but to save it (see Jn 3:17).

The passion and death of Jesus remain one of the most terrible examples of the consequences of human sinfulness. Yet, the church also believes that this apparent tragedy was necessary for the salvation of the world. Acts 2:23 affirms that, "Jesus [was] delivered up according to the definite plan and foreknowledge of God." Jesus himself both predicted his passion and explained it after his resurrection. "Was it not necessary that the Christ should suffer these things and enter into his glory?" (Lk 24:26).

Why was this necessary? First, it was part of God's plan. St. Paul professes that "Christ died for our sins in accordance with the scriptures" (1 Cor 15:3);

that God "made him to be sin who knew no sin, so that in him we might become the righteousness of God" (2 Cor 5:21).

Second, Christ's sacrifice was the greatest expression of God's love. God showed his love for man by freely embracing the most terrible consequence of man's sin—death—in order to free us from sin and death. The greatness of God's love is revealed by the fact that Jesus died for sinners and those who rejected him, and not just for his "friends"—those who loved him and obeyed him (see Rom 5:8).

Despite the evident human fear and pain that Jesus faced as he approached the hour of his death (powerfully evidenced in his agony in the Garden of Gethsemane [see Mt 26:42; Lk 22:20]), he freely chose to accept his passion and death, "accepting in his human will that the Father's will be done" (CCC 612).

How Jesus' Death Saves Us

The New Testament states repeatedly that Jesus died for all people (see 2 Cor 5:13-15; Rom 5:18; 1 Thess 5:10). Jesus himself told his disciples at the Last Supper: "This is my blood of the covenant, which is poured out for many" (Mk 14:24). But what does it mean that "Christ died for all people?" How could the death of one man, Jesus Christ, affect the whole human race?

This question opens a whole field of Christian theology known as *soteriology*. It explores the question of how Jesus' death can be said to save (Greek: *soteria*) the human race. Many biblical scholars today conclude that it is impossible to determine exactly how Jesus' death saves us, but it is undeniable that it does. These are some approaches to understanding the saving value of Jesus' death that have arisen in Christian history:

1. *Jesus' death as a ransom to redeem sinners.* Jesus said of himself, "the Son of man also came not to be served but to serve, and to give his life as a ransom for many" (Mk 10:45). Jesus himself is the "suffering servant" prophesied in Isaiah 52 and 53. Jesus' suffering and death may be looked at as a ransom, the price that Jesus paid to redeem, or free, the human race from its slavery to the devil. In other words, Jesus offered his own priceless life as a ransom given by God in

exchange for the release of the human race from the bondage of Satan and sin. The effect of Jesus' death was to reconcile the human race with God (see 2 Cor 5:17-18).

2. Jesus' death as atonement or satisfaction for our sins. Mankind's sin is detestable and offensive to God. Jesus' death may be looked upon as a free *gift* offered to God to atone or make reparation for the sins of the human race. A later theology spoke about Jesus' death as satisfying the demand of justice: that this infinite offense against God's love and honor be corrected. Jesus' death satisfies God's just requirement that sin should be punished or repaired. One author says that, "Jesus made not only adequate but *superabundant* atonement and satisfaction because the measure of his love and obedience ... surpassed human egoism. In Jesus a power of love and truth was operative (and shown in his death) which surpassed all the forces of evil and falsehood." (cf. CCC 615, 616)[16]

3. Jesus as a "penal substitute" for us. Because of our sin, the human race deserved nothing but punishment and death. Jesus freely chose to accept, on behalf of the whole human race, the death penalty resulting from sin; he chose to substitute for each of us by accepting the penalty for sin in his suffering, abandonment, and terrible death on the cross. He represented, or substituted for, all of us as he carried the cross, was nailed to it, and died on it. "He himself bore our sins in his body on the tree, that we might die to sin and live to righteousness. By his wounds you have been healed" (1 Pet 2:24, cf. CCC 615).

4. Jesus' death as a sacrifice to expiate our sins. The notion of offering sacrifice to make amends for sin is rooted in the Old Testament. The Letter to the Hebrews particularly stresses the sacrificial dimension of Jesus' death, though it is also found in the Gospels and elsewhere in the New Testament.

In the Old Covenant, the high priest would offer the flesh and blood of animals to God as a sacrifice to plead for the forgiveness of the people's sins. Hebrews portrays Jesus as the great High Priest who offers to God, once for all, his own body and blood for the forgiveness and redemption of the whole human race. A spotless lamb was the Jewish people's Passover sacrifice, and John the Baptist recognized Jesus himself as "the Lamb of God, who takes away the sin of the world" (Jn 1:29). The Book of Revelation also highlights the image of Jesus as the Lamb who was slain as a perfect sacrifice to expiate (remove) the sins of the human race. Hence, Christ's death is the *sacrifice of the New Covenant,* with the "blood of the covenant, which was poured out for many for the forgiveness of sins" (Mt 26:28). This sacrifice of Christ is unique; it completes and surpasses all other sacrifices (cf Heb 10:10; cf. CCC 613, 614).

Ransom, atonement, penal substitute, sacrifice ... the magnitude and mystery of Jesus Christ's action in suffering and dying for the sins of the human race is so great that all of these aspects of his saving work can only begin to help us comprehend it. Our fitting response is to give praise and thanks to Jesus, the Son of God, for cleansing us from sin and reconciling us to God by his passion and death.

Jesus' Resurrection

"On the third day he arose again from the dead..." The climax of the Paschal mystery is the resurrection of Jesus: "by his death Christ liberates us from sin; by his Resurrection, he opens for us the way to a new life" (CCC 654). The bodily resurrection of Jesus Christ from the dead is at the center of the Gospel, the joyous "Good News" of our faith. The heart of the earliest *kerygma* or proclamation of Christianity is simply this: "Jesus the Nazorean, whom you crucified, God has raised from the dead" (see Acts 2:22; 3:13; 4:10; 1 Cor 15:3-5).

St. Paul boldly summarizes the implications of the Resurrection:

> If Christ has not been raised, your faith is futile and you are still in your sins. Then those also who have fallen asleep [died] in Christ have perished. If for this life only we have hoped in Christ, we are of all men most to be pitied.
>
> But in fact, Christ has been raised from the dead, the first fruits of those who have fallen asleep.... For as in Adam all die, so also in Christ shall all be made alive (1 Cor 15:17-20, 22).

"Christ's Resurrection—and the risen Christ himself, is the principle and source of our future resurrection" (CCC 655). The hope of Christians hinges on the reality of the resurrection of Jesus. The resurrection of Jesus is the act of God that reveals that death, sin, and Satan have been conquered. Jesus freely accepted death, but overcame death when he emerged from the tomb alive on the third day. The resurrection of Jesus fulfills the hopes of the Old Testament and the message of Jesus himself about the kingdom or reign of God. Indeed, the Nicene Creed declares that Christ was raised "in fulfillment of the Scriptures...."

As is true with the entire mission of the Son of God on earth, the resurrection of Jesus is a work of all three persons of the Trinity acting together as one. St. Peter attests, "This Jesus God [the Father] raised up ..." (Acts 2:32). He is raised by the power of the Holy Spirit (Rom 1:4). And yet, Jesus also speaks of his power to lay down his life and to take up it again (Jn 10:17-18; cf. CCC 648-50).

Christ's Burial and Descent Into Hell

The Apostle's Creed professes that Jesus, "was crucified, died, and was buried...." Jesus' death was a real death. It put an end to his earthly human existence, and his soul was separated from his body. While in the tomb, the divine person of the Son of God continued to possess both his body and his soul (though separated), and preserved the body of Jesus from corruption, in accordance with the Scripture (see Ps 16:9-10; Acts 13:37).

The Creed and Scripture both witness that the Son of God, while in the tomb, "descended into hell," that is, to the abode of the dead where all born from the beginning of the world awaited the Messiah (see Ps 6:5; Eph 4:8-9; Rv 1:18). There Jesus "preached to the spirits in prison" (1 Pet 3:19) and then ascended into heaven, leading "a host of captives" (Eph 4:8)—all those righteous and just people who had died and awaited their redemption. The doctrine of Christ's descent into hell is the extension of the saving message and mission of Jesus to all the righteous who ever lived before Christ (see CCC 634).

What Is the Resurrection?

What does it mean to say that Jesus was raised from the dead and that he rose? No one actually witnessed the resurrection (see CCC 467). Although there are variations among the four Gospel accounts of Easter Sunday morning, these all agree on two essential facts: (1) the tomb in which Jesus had been buried was found empty with the entrance stone rolled away; (2) Jesus appeared alive to his followers.

What was the risen Jesus like? The appearances of Jesus cannot be explained away as hallucinations, nor as the apostles' way of saying that even though Jesus was dead, he lived on in the hearts and minds of his followers.

The earliest New Testament writing that speaks of Jesus' postresurrection appearances is Paul's First Letter to the Corinthians, written in the early 50s A.D. Paul lists the witnesses who saw Jesus alive (including himself) and even mentions that on one occasion five hundred brothers saw Jesus, "most of whom are still alive, though some have fallen asleep" (1 Cor 15:6). The primary witnesses to the resurrection, though, remain Peter and the twelve, the "foundation stones" of Jesus' church, and the holy women who ministered to Jesus during his public life and who were the first witnesses to his resurrection.

If anyone questioned whether Jesus actually appeared alive after his resurrection, Paul provided a long list of eyewitnesses who were still alive at the writing of his letter, twenty years after the event. Is it possible that all of these people (including the apostles) were victims of the same hallucination? It is far more likely that these people, many of whom gave their lives for their beliefs about Jesus, actually did see him risen from the dead.[17]

What was Jesus' risen body like? There is an element of mystery in the Gospel accounts. Jesus could be touched and felt, but he could also appear, suddenly and unannounced, in locked rooms. According to some Gospel accounts, Jesus' own apostles and Mary Magdalene often did not immediately recognize him when he appeared (see Mt 28:17; Lk 24:16, 37-39; Jn 20:14; 21:12). The Gospel accounts imply that Jesus' risen body was the same as the body that was buried in the tomb, even if it was different in some ways. It bore the marks of the Passion, yet possessed "the new properties of a glorious body: not limited by space and time but able to be present how and when he wills" (CCC 645).

St. Paul described the risen body of both Jesus, and each of us: "What is sown [buried] is perishable, what is raised is imperishable. It is sown in dishonor, it is raised in glory. It is sown in weakness, it is raised in power. It is sown a physical body, it is raised a spiritual body" (1 Cor 15:42-44).

What will our own risen bodies be like? Like the body of Jesus: "Just as we have borne the image of the man of dust [Adam], we shall also bear the image of the man of heaven [Jesus]" (1 Cor 15:49). To the Philippians, Paul wrote that the Lord Jesus will "change our lowly body to be like his glorious body" (Phil 3:21).

This is the basis of Christian hope, to share in the resurrection of Jesus by having our own mortal bodies raised up, transformed, and glorified like the risen body of Jesus Christ (see 1 Cor 15:53-57).

Jesus' Ascension and Pentecost

The ascension of Jesus into heaven marks the conclusion of his appearances to his followers after his resurrection.[18] "So then the Lord Jesus, after he had spoken to them, was taken up into heaven, and sat down at the right hand of God" (Mk 16:19). The ascension means that Jesus returned in his glorified body, finally and irreversibly, to his Father in heaven.

Although he is the Second Person of God, Jesus forever retains this glorified human body. Jesus has gone before us to prepare a place for his faithful disciples with the Father. "Only Christ can open to man such access that we, his members, might have confidence that we too shall go where he, our Head and our Source, has preceded us" (CCC 661; see *RomM,* Preface of the Ascension).

The evangelist Luke, in both his Gospel and the Acts of the Apostles, places more emphasis than the other Gospels on the ascension, and specifies that it occurred forty days after the resurrection of Jesus (see Acts 1:1-11): "This Jesus, who was taken up from you into heaven, will come in the same way as you saw him go into heaven" (Acts 1:11).

In the Gospel of St. John, Jesus alludes to his ascension in his first appearance after his resurrection. He warns Mary Magdalene not to touch him because, "I have not yet ascended to the Father; but go to my brethren and say to them, I am ascending to my Father and your Father, to my God and your God" (Jn 20:17). John's Gospel also recounts Jesus' words: "And I, when I am lifted up from the earth, will draw all men to myself" (Jn 12:32). "The lifting up of Jesus on the cross signifies and announces his lifting up by his Ascension into heaven, and indeed begins it" (CCC 662).

After Jesus' ascension, he is, as the Creed proclaims, "seated at the right hand of the Father." That is, his glorified body has been honored and exalted with God the Father in the eternal kingdom. Thus the prophet Daniel's vision of the "Son of Man" is fulfilled (see CCC 664).

Although Jesus no longer dwells on earth bodily, nor appears in his glorified risen body, Jesus is still present to us in the sacraments, especially the Eucharist. He is present in his followers, his church, which St. Paul called "the body of Christ" (1 Cor 12:27). But Jesus is also present to us through his greatest gift to his followers: the Holy Spirit. In one of his postresurrection appearances, Jesus instructed his disciples "not to depart from Jerusalem, but to wait for the promise of the Father, which, he said, 'You heard from me, for John baptized with water, but before many days you shall be baptized with the Holy Spirit'" (Acts 1:4-5).

Jesus also spoke of this promise of the Father in John's Gospel:

> And I will pray the Father, and he will give you another Counselor, to be with you for ever, even the Spirit of truth....
>
> JOHN 14:16-17

The Gospel of John reports that Jesus' apostles first received the Holy Spirit on Easter Day (see Jn 20:19-23). Luke, in the Acts of the Apostles, recounts the first sending of the Holy Spirit as a gathering of Jesus' disciples in Jerusalem on the Jewish feast of Pentecost (see Acts 2:1-4).

Remember, the Gospel writers were primarily interested in the meaning of the sending of the Holy Spirit rather than in producing a consistent chronology of events. Luke's images of the coming of the Holy Spirit, including "a mighty wind" and "tongues as of fire" (Acts 2:2-3), are reminiscent of the fire and smoke of God's visitation to Moses on Mount Sinai, described in Exodus 19:16-19, when he delivered the Ten Commandments to Moses (see Ex 20:1-17).

This similarity is not merely coincidental. On Mount Sinai, God delivered the law of the Old Covenant, the Ten Commandments, to Moses and the chosen people, Israel. At Pentecost, God sent to his new people, the church of Jesus Christ, the law of the New Covenant, the Holy Spirit. The law of the Old Covenant was delivered to Moses on stone tablets, but the new law of the Spirit came as the prophet Jeremiah had announced concerning God's new Covenant: "I will put my law within them, and I will write it upon their hearts" (Jer 31:33; see also 2 Cor 3:3).

St. Paul explained that the law of the Old Covenant is "good and holy," because it reveals God's will and points out our sinfulness, but it contains no power enabling us to overcome sin (see Rom 7:7-11). In the New Covenant, God has given us a new law, the Holy Spirit, who not only convicts us of sin but empowers us to overcome it. St. Paul wrote that:

> We serve not under the old written code but in the new life of the Spirit.... For the law of the Spirit of life in Christ Jesus has set me free from the law of sin and death. For God has done what the law, weakened by the flesh, could not do: sending his own Son in the likeness of sinful flesh and for sin, he condemned sin in the flesh, in order that the just requirement of the law might be fulfilled in us, who walk not according to the flesh but according to the Spirit.
>
> ROMANS 7:6; 8:2-4

Jesus said that he hadn't come to abolish the law of the Old Covenant, but to fulfill it (see Mt 5:17-20). One aspect of this fulfillment is the sending of the Holy Spirit to empower Christians to fulfill the "just requirement of the law" and to live the radical new commandment of love and the Beatitudes that Jesus taught. Thus, the sending of the Holy Spirit at Pentecost fulfills Jesus' promise and completes the establishment of the New Covenant.

Jesus and the New Covenant

At the Last Supper, Jesus told his disciples, "This cup which is poured out for you is the new covenant in my blood" (Lk 22:20). With these words, Jesus began the final chapter of his life, fulfilling Jeremiah's prophecy that God would establish a New Covenant with Israel (see Jer 31:31-34).

Under the Old Covenant, the shedding of blood of sacrificial animals ratified a solemn covenant or agreement between God and man. Moses, in the Book of Exodus, ratified the covenant with God by pouring half of the sacrificial blood on the altar and the rest on the people, with the words, "Behold the blood of the covenant which the Lord has made with you in accordance with all these words" (Ex 24:8). The Letter to the Hebrews in the New Testament focuses on the far superior effect of the sacrifice of the blood of Jesus:

> He entered once for all into the Holy Place, taking not the blood of goats and calves but his own blood, thus securing an eternal redemption.... Therefore he is the mediator of a new covenant.... He has appeared once for all at the end of the age to put away sin by the sacrifice of himself.
>
> HEBREWS 9:12, 15, 26

There are numerous biblical images for Jesus that are related to his sealing of the covenant and removal of our sins through the shedding of blood. Hebrews also speaks of Jesus as the great High Priest who offered himself and his own blood as a perfect and eternal sacrifice for humanity's sins (see Heb 2:17; 5:5-10; 7:3ff, 26-27).

The lamb is another image of this type, originating from the Passover lamb that the Jewish people slaughtered before fleeing Egypt, sprinkling the blood of the lamb on the lintels of their doorposts to protect them from the angel of death. The prophet Isaiah said the suffering servant of YHWH was "like a lamb that is led to the slaughter,... so he opened not his mouth" (Isa 53:7).

Jesus is called "the Lamb of God, who takes away the sin of the world" (Jn 1:29) by John the Baptist, and the Book of Revelation also pictures Jesus as "a Lamb standing, as though it had been slain" (Rev 5:6). The Christian martyrs had "washed their robes and made them white in the blood of the Lamb" (Rev 7:14). Peter reminds us in his first letter that, "you were ransomed from the futile ways inherited from your fathers, not with perishable things such as silver or gold, but with the precious blood of Christ, like that of a lamb without blemish or spot. He was destined [for this] before the foundation of the world..." (1 Pet 1:18-20). Jesus is the spotless Lamb whose sacrifice of himself has cleansed the world of its sin and established a New Covenant, a new relationship between God and man. This New Covenant in his blood was *announced* by Jesus at the Last Supper, *sealed* by the shedding of his blood on the cross of Calvary, and *completed* in the revealing of the new way of life made possible for God's New Covenant people through the sending of the Holy Spirit on Pentecost. In the Eucharist, the New Covenant in Jesus' blood and in the Holy Spirit is continually celebrated and renewed.

Christ Will Come Again

Christians profess in the Apostles' Creed that "from thence [the Father's 'right hand'] he will come to judge the living and the dead." The story of Jesus is not complete with his ascension to the Father or with the sending of the Holy Spirit at Pentecost.

Recall the angelic messenger who announced at Jesus' ascension that Jesus "will come in the same way as you saw him go into heaven" (Acts 1:11). This is referring to the second coming of Christ or the *Parousia*. Jesus came a first time as a spotless Lamb, sacrificed on the cross to take away the sins of the world; Jesus "will appear a second time, not to deal with sin but to save those who are eagerly waiting for him" (Heb 9:28).

During his ministry on earth, Jesus spoke of a "Son of Man" who would come to the earth in splendor and majesty to judge humanity. Jesus was certainly referring to the Son of Man described in the Book of Daniel who appeared before God to receive an eternal kingdom and who would come to earth on the clouds of heaven (see Dan 7:13-14). Undoubtedly, this "Son of Man" is Jesus himself. Christians believe that Jesus will return in his glorified body with all the unimaginable splendor of the king of the universe.

Pilate, at Jesus' trial, asked him if he were a king. Jesus replied that he was, but that his kingdom was not of this world. When Jesus returns, the kingdom of God will be fully established on earth, and his glorious kingship will be revealed: "the kingdom of the world has become the kingdom of our Lord and of his Christ, and he shall reign for ever and ever" (Rev 11:15). Jesus Christ is Lord! He is "far above all rule and authority and power and dominion," for the Father "has put all things under his feet" (Eph 1:21-22). Christ is Lord of the cosmos and of history. In him human history and all creation will find their fulfillment (see Eph 1:10; CCC 668).

This is but a glimpse of what will be appropriately discussed in a later chapter of this catechism. Now we live in the era between the first and the second comings of Jesus in which the reign of God has been established on earth by Jesus, but not yet brought to completion. This is the era of God's people of the New Covenant, the church. "As Lord, Christ is also head of the Church, which is his Body (cf. Eph 1:22). Taken up to heaven and glorified after he had thus fully accomplished his mission, Christ dwells on earth in his Church. The redemption is the source of authority that Christ, by virtue of the Holy Spirit, exercises over the Church" (CCC 669).

CHAPTER 5

The Holy Spirit and the Church

"I believe in the Holy Spirit, the holy, catholic church...." In almost the same breath Christians profess their faith in the Holy Spirit—who is God, the Third Person of the blessed Trinity—and in the holy, catholic church, God's people of the New Covenant. While the difference between a Person of God (the Holy Spirit) and the human society founded by God (the church) appears to be great and even infinite, they do have some things in common, which is the *basis* for their close relationship.

Both the church and the Holy Spirit are intimately joined to Jesus Christ and continue his mission of establishing the kingdom of God on earth. They are joined as "body and soul": the church is the "body of Christ" (see Eph 1:22, 23; Col 1:18), and the Holy Spirit is the "soul" of the church. St. Augustine taught, "What the soul is to the human body, the Holy Spirit is to the Body of Christ, which is the Church."[1]

The Person of the Holy Spirit

Who is the Holy Spirit? Many find it more difficult to understand the divine Person of the Holy Spirit than to understand the Father and the Son. One evident reason is that we have natural human images of "Father" and "Son," but none of "Holy Spirit." Also, the Holy Spirit reveals and exalts the Father and the Son, in a humble "divine self-effacement," rather than speaking of himself (CCC 687). For example, the Bible teaches: "No one can say, 'Jesus is Lord' except by the Holy Spirit" (1 Cor 12:3), and "God has sent the Spirit of his Son into our hearts, crying, 'Abba! Father!'" (Gal 4:6; see CCC 683). The Holy Spirit alone enables us to know God through faith: "to be in touch with Christ, we must first have been touched by the Holy Spirit" (CCC 683).

Yet, the Holy Spirit is not completely unknown and hidden, though he is the last Person of the blessed Trinity to be "unveiled" by God. The Father and the Son exalt and honor each other, and also reveal their greatest gift to each other and to humanity, the Holy Spirit. In the Gospel of John, Jesus explains to the apostles: "I tell you the truth: it is to your advantage that I go away, for if I do not go away, the Counselor will not come to you; but if I go, I will send him to you" (Jn 16:7). Jesus also promises:

> If you love me, you will keep my commandments. And I will pray the Father, and he will give you another Counselor, to be with you for ever, even the Spirit of truth, whom the world cannot receive, because it neither sees him nor knows him; you know him, for he dwells with you, and will be in you.
>
> JOHN 14:15-17[2]

Christians "know" the Holy Spirit because the Father and the Son have sent him to us, to dwell within us, as in a temple (see Rom 8:9-11; 1 Cor 6:19). Further, Christians can know the Holy Spirit through his action and presence:

- in the sacred Scripture and tradition that he has inspired;
- in his "voice," speaking through the church's prayer, prophetic words, and in her official teaching;
- in the liturgy and the sacraments, which are his work;
- in the charisms and ministries by which he builds up the church;
- in the witness of missionaries and saints through whom he spreads the gospel to all people and manifests his holiness (see CCC 688).

There is no reason that a Christian should fail to know and recognize the Holy Spirit. The *Catechism* summarizes the teaching of John's Gospel: "The Holy Spirit will come and we shall know him; he will be with us forever; he will remain with us" (CCC 729). So, then, what does the church know about the Holy Spirit, from these sources?

The term "spirit" itself derives from the Hebrew "ruah," which means breath, air, or wind. There are a wealth of biblical images or symbols of the Holy Spirit, such as water, oil (anointing), fire, cloud and light, the seal, imposition of hands, God's "finger," and the dove (see CCC 694-701). Each of these reveals some aspect of the Holy Spirit's identity or work.

However, one shortcoming of these symbols is that they are all impersonal. Although the Holy Spirit is a Person of God, it is easy to think of "spirit" as an impersonal power or force. The Bible also reveals the *personal names* or titles of the Holy Spirit. Jesus calls him the "Paraclete," which literally means, "he who is called to one's side" (*ad-vocatus* in Latin). Other translations of "paraclete" are consoler, counselor, our "defense-attorney"—the legal form of "advocate" (see Jn 14:16; 15:26; 16:7; CCC 691, 692). Jesus also calls the Holy Spirit the "Spirit of truth" (Jn 16:13; CCC 691, 692).[3]

St. Luke emphasizes the Holy Spirit as a person, not by titles, as in John's Gospel, but by describing the personal activity of the Holy Spirit in the church: the Holy Spirit can be lied to and tested (see Acts 5:3, 9); he is busy in the church, speaking (see Acts 10:19), consoling (see Acts 9:31), sending people forth (see Acts 13:4), deciding (see Acts 15:28), warning (see Acts 20:23), prompting (see Acts 21:4), and even snatching Philip from one place to another (see Acts 8:39)! He prevents Paul and Timothy from preaching the message in the province of Asia: "When they had come opposite Mysia, they attempted to go into Bithynia, but the Spirit of Jesus did not allow them" (Acts 16:7, NAB). In the Acts of the Apostles, as elsewhere in the New Testament, the Holy Spirit is presented as a person who is in an active, personal relationship with the disciples of Jesus.

The Scripture also records the unfolding revelation of the Holy Spirit, beginning with the "breath" of God through which life was first imparted at creation. The restoration of the glory of God in man, the fulfillment of God's promises through his covenants, and the planting of God's kingdom on earth are all joint missions or works of the Son and the Holy Spirit. The Holy Spirit was present under the Old Covenant, but his action was limited. The clouds, or "shekinah glory," which appeared at important moments in the Old Testament are a symbol of the Holy Spirit's presence (see Ex 24, 33, 40; CCC 697). The Holy Spirit has "spoken through the prophets" of the Old Testament (Nicene Creed), especially in prophecies of the coming of the Messiah, and of the new Law that would be marked by the sending of a new spirit, the Holy Spirit.

However, until Jesus the Messiah removed original sin through his Passion and conquered death through his resurrection, the Holy Spirit could not *remain* in any person or in God's people, Israel, as a "permanent resident." Yes, the Spirit could come to rest on one anointed as king (see 1 Sam 10:6, 10; 16:13), could inspire and speak through prophets (see Isa 61:1; Ezek 2:2; 3:12; Zech 4:6), and could do other mighty works. However, the "living water" of the Spirit flowing from *within* people's hearts had not yet "been given, because Jesus was not yet glorified" (Jn 7:38-39).

For John, the "glorification" of Jesus is his victory over sin on the cross. Only after that liberation from original sin could the Holy Spirit be poured out (see Acts 2:17; CCC 713), and make the church (see Eph 2:19-22) and each Christian his "temple," his dwelling place (see 1 Cor 3:16; 6:19).

The Scripture testifies that this Holy Spirit who has been "poured out" is:

- God's greatest *gift* to the church (see Lk 11:13; Jn 16:7; Acts 1:4-5; 2:38-39)
- the giver of gifts (see Isa 11:2-3; 1 Cor 12:4-11)
- the source of new life (see Rom 7:6; 8:1-17; Gal 5:16-25)
- the Spirit of truth, leading the church into all truth (see Jn 16:12-15; CCC 729)
- the great master and teacher of prayer (see Mt 4:1-2; Lk 10:21-22; Rom 8:26-27; 1 Cor 14:15; Eph 6:18)
- God's love "poured into our hearts" (Rom 5:5).

Because Christians have the Holy Spirit—the love of God poured into our hearts—our sins are forgiven and the likeness of God (lost through sin) is restored (see CCC 734); we possess the very life and love of the Holy Trinity as a "pledge" or "first-fruits" of eternal life (see CCC 735); we have the power from the Holy Spirit to love as "God [has] loved us" (1 Jn 4:11-12; see CCC 735); and we bear the "fruit of the Spirit ... love, joy, peace, patience, kindness, goodness, faithfulness, gentleness, self-control" (Gal 5:22-23; see CCC 736). St. Basil the Great taught:

Through the Holy Spirit we are restored to paradise, led back to the Kingdom of heaven, and adopted as children, given confidence to call God "Father" and to share in Christ's grace, called children of light and given a share in eternal glory.[4]

The Witness of Tradition

Christian tradition provides another point of departure for exploring the question, "Who is the Holy Spirit?" From it we learn that the Holy Spirit is a Person of God, the third Person of the blessed Trinity.

In A.D. 325 the church stated its belief in the Holy Spirit in the Nicene Creed. In A.D. 381 at the Council of Constantinople, a council whose authority is almost universally recognized (by Catholics, Orthodox, and many Protestant and other Christians), the bishops of the church expanded this creed.

This council provided a response to a controversy that had arisen in the church of the fourth century about whether the Holy Spirit was fully God and really equal with the Father and the Son. In response to these questions, some great works on the Holy Spirit had been written in the Greek-speaking East by fathers of the church such as St. Basil the Great, St. Athanasius, St. Gregory of Nyssa, and St. Gregory of Nazianzus. The result was the Council of Constantinople's affirmation of the full divinity of the Holy Spirit; it added a section to the Nicene Creed which Catholics and many Christians profess today:

We believe in the Holy Spirit, the Lord, the giver of life, who proceeds from the Father [and the Son]. With the Father and the Son he is worshipped and glorified. He has spoken through the prophets.

Clearly the early church recognized the Holy Spirit as a person whom we may address as "Lord" and whom we worship and glorify along with the Father and the Son.

The tradition also indicates that Christians ought to have an intimate personal relationship with the Holy Spirit. The *Catechism* says simply: "The Holy Spirit will come and we shall know him..." (CCC 729). As St. Cyril of Jerusalem taught, "The Spirit comes with the tenderness of a true friend and protector to save, to heal, to teach, to counsel, to strengthen, to console."[5]

This image also summarizes what we know of the Spirit through revelation as the Paraclete who is sent by the Father and the Son to make his home within us in order to lead, strengthen, and guide us. He is truly the divine friend who is closest to our hearts. The *Catechism* describes the Holy Spirit as "the interior Master of life according to Christ, a gentle guest and friend who inspires, guides, corrects and strengthens this life" (CCC 1697).

Jesus and the Holy Spirit

The name of Jesus has been and will ever be connected in Christian tradition with the title, "Christ," which is the Greek form of the Hebrew, "Messiah," meaning "the anointed one." And how is Jesus anointed? With the Holy Spirit!

The entire mission of the Son and the Holy Spirit, in the fullness of time, is contained in this: that the Son is the one anointed by the Father's Spirit since his Incarnation—Jesus is the Christ, the Messiah ... Christ's whole work is in fact a joint mission of the Son and the Holy Spirit. (CCC 727)

Everything that Jesus does is guided and empowered by the Holy Spirit. The *climax* of Jesus' mission, after his suffering, death, and resurrection, is to fully reveal the Holy Spirit, and to pour him out upon his disciples: to "baptize" (immerse) them in the Holy Spirit, as all four Gospels explicitly state (see Mt 3:11; Mk 1:8; Lk 3:16; Jn 1:33).

At the Last Supper in the Gospel of John, Jesus tells the apostles that his departure is for their good, for unless he goes he cannot send them the Counselor, the Holy Spirit, "but if I go, I will send him to you" (Jn 16:7). The promise is fulfilled on the day of Pentecost, when the disciples, with Mary, receive the gift of the Holy Spirit, and Peter announces to the gathered crowds:

Repent, and be baptized every one of you in the name of Jesus Christ for the forgiveness of your sins; and you shall receive the gift of the Holy Spirit. For the promise is to you and to your children and to all that are far off, every one whom the Lord our God calls to him.

ACTS 2:38-39

This great promise of forgiveness of sins and the gift of the Holy Spirit is fulfilled for Christians in the sacraments of baptism, reconciliation or penance, and confirmation, as well as in other sacraments of the church, and through prayer and openness to God. Through baptism, God first comes to live in us and we begin to be empowered and guided by the Spirit to carry out Jesus' mission of proclaiming and establishing God's kingdom. We receive the same Holy Spirit who rested on Jesus at his Baptism (see Mt 3:16; Mk 1:10; Lk 3:22) and empowered and guided him in his life and ministry. Luke's Gospel describes Jesus' return to Nazareth at the beginning of his public ministry and his announcement that in him the prophecy of Isaiah is fulfilled in their hearing:

> The Spirit of the Lord is upon me,
> because he has anointed me to preach
> good news to the poor.
> He has sent me to proclaim release to the captives
> and recovering of sight to the blind,
> to set at liberty those who are oppressed,
> to proclaim the acceptable year of the Lord.
>
> LUKE 4:18-19[6]

Through the anointing of the Holy Spirit, Jesus carried out the mission that the Father had prepared for him. Likewise, it is only through the anointing of the Holy Spirit that each Christian can follow Jesus and carry out the particular mission and ministry that the Father has prepared for each of us.

What is the relationship of the Holy Spirit to the followers of Christ? In summary, Scripture teaches us that the Holy Spirit will come and we shall know him; he will be with us forever (see Jn 14:15-17). The Spirit will teach us everything, remind us of all that Jesus said to us, and bear witness to him (see Jn 14:26; 15:26). The Holy Spirit will lead us into all truth and will glorify Christ (see Jn 16:13-15). He will convict us of our sin, proving the world wrong about sin, righteousness, and judgment (see Jn 16:7-8; CCC 724).

Mary and the Holy Spirit

The greatest example and model of the Christian anointed and guided by the Holy Spirit is Mary. The *Catechism* calls her, "the masterwork of the mission of the Son and the Spirit in the fullness of time" (CCC 721). Mary was "full of grace," sinless from the moment of her conception, by a special gift of the Holy Spirit (see CCC 722). By the same Spirit, the Virgin Mary conceived and gave birth to the Son of God (see CCC 723): "Filled with the Holy Spirit she makes the Word visible in the humility of his flesh" (CCC 724).

Throughout Mary's life, the Holy Spirit acted in her to bring people (especially the humble) into communion with Christ, her Son: from the shepherds and Magi, to the bride and groom at Cana, to Jesus' first disciples (see CCC 725). At the end of his life, Jesus declared Mary to be the spiritual mother of all his disciples (see Jn 19:25-27). She is the "new Eve," the mother of all who would find new life in him (CCC 726). The Holy Spirit was given for the first time to *all* Jesus' disciples at Pentecost, after they had waited in prayer with Mary (see Acts 1:12-14; 2:1-4; CCC 726). Mary's unique and intimate union with the Spirit is reflected in her title "Spouse of the Holy Spirit."

The Holy Spirit and the Church

The church that Jesus founded begins, grows, carries out its mission, and reaches its fulfillment through the action of the Holy Spirit. The church was first manifested or revealed to the world on the morning of Pentecost, with the sending of the Holy Spirit on all Jesus' followers (see CCC 726).

Traditionally, Pentecost is called "the birthday of the church." As with human birth, the church's period of hidden formation ended at Pentecost. On that day the disciples of Jesus received the great gift of the Holy Spirit, who would bring to mind all that Jesus taught them and send them out in power as fearless witnesses to Jesus' cross and resurrection. Truly at Pentecost the church was born: "out of the womb" of the Upper Room, and "into the world,"[7] continuing Jesus' mission of proclaiming and establishing God's kingdom on earth.

The Holy Spirit continually enables the church to grow, by drawing people, by his grace, to Christ. It is the Holy Spirit who enables people to recognize and to profess that Jesus is Lord (see 1 Cor 12:3). The Holy Spirit draws them to the waters of baptism, where he cleanses them of sin and gives them the new life of grace. Then the Spirit continues to reveal Jesus' presence in the Word of God, in the Eucharist, and in the other sacraments, by which they are nourished and come into communion with God that they may "bear much fruit" (see CCC 737; Jn 15:8, 16).

Jesus pours out the gift of the Holy Spirit on his followers as a source of blessing for them. The Spirit nourishes and heals them, and gives them a variety of spiritual gifts ("charisms") both for themselves and for the good of the church.

The Spirit enables them to pray with real knowledge of Jesus and the Father; and gives them love, joy, and other "fruit" of the Spirit. All this reveals the distinctiveness of new life in Christ, which is also life "in" or "according to" the Spirit. We will explore the different dimensions of the Holy Spirit's work in the church at greater length later in this catechism when we discuss prayer, charisms, the sacraments, and Christian moral life (see CCC 738-41).

The Meaning of the Church

We have seen that Jesus proclaimed the coming of the reign or kingdom of God and promised to send the Holy Spirit after his return to his Father. Where were the reign of God and the Spirit of God to be found after Jesus' death, resurrection, and ascension? They were found in the community of Jesus' followers, who called themselves the church.

What is the church? First, it is the plan of God the Father for the reconciliation of humanity to himself. It is the people gathered together into communion with God the Father after the upheaval of the angels' fall and man's sin, "displaying all the power of his arm and the whole measure of the love he wanted to give the world" (CCC 760). Thus God willed the church from the very beginning as "the goal of all things,"[8] for all things are to be gathered back to God, and find their fulfillment in him.

Though it originates in the mind of the Father, the church cannot be understood apart from Christ and the Holy Spirit. The church is the continuing presence of Jesus on earth. The most authoritative modern presentation of the nature of the church is the Second Vatican Council's "Dogmatic Constitution on the Church" (*Lumen Gentium*), which begins:

> Christ is the light of humanity (*lumen gentium*); and it is ... the heart-felt desire of this sacred Council ... that by proclaiming his Gospel to every creature it may bring to all men that light of Christ which shines out visibly from the church.[9]

The only "light" of the church is Christ, who is "the light of the world" (Jn 9:5). After centuries of preparation for the church in the people of Israel, Jesus the Son of God was sent by the Father to establish his people of the New Covenant. The Lord Jesus inaugurated his church by preaching the Good News of the reign of God which is "already present in mystery"[10] in the church. Jesus' life was one of total self-giving, culminating in the gift of himself in the Eucharist and on the cross of Calvary. "The origin and growth of the Church are symbolized by the blood and water which flowed from the open side of the crucified Jesus."[11]

Catholic tradition speaks of the church emerging from the pierced heart of Jesus on the cross, as Eve was formed from the sleeping Adam's side (CCC 766).[12] It is evident that the origin and the life of the church is found entirely in Jesus, in fact, so inseparably that St. Paul could call the church "the body of Christ" (Rom 12:5; 1 Cor 12:27; Eph 1:22).

The church is also inseparable from the Holy Spirit, and is the living "temple" of the Spirit, the place where the Spirit lives among men. The Holy Spirit, the Sanctifier, is the source of the church's holiness. He is the provider of the *power* and the various *gifts* ("hierarchical and charismatic") needed for the church to fulfill her "mission of proclaiming and establishing among all peoples the Kingdom of Christ and of God."[13]

Despite the necessity of the church in God's plan of salvation and her present union with God, the church in this world is imperfect, comprised of sinners, and continues on a pilgrimage of faith that is fraught with struggles and trials. "Here below she knows that she is in exile far from the Lord, and longs for the full coming of the Kingdom, when she will be 'united in glory with her king.'"[14] Only then, when Jesus returns in glory at the end of time, will the full glory of the church be realized and revealed and "all the just from the time of Adam, 'from Abel, the just one, to the last of the elect,'… be gathered together in the universal Church in the Father's presence."[15]

Names and Images of the Church

In English, we use the word "church" to refer either to a people or to a building where the people gather to worship. The English word "church" is used to translate three distinct ancient words: *qahal* (or *kehal*) in Hebrew, and *ekklesia* (Latin: *ecclesia*) and *kyriake* in Greek. The concept of *church* originated with the

Jewish term *qahal,* meaning an assembly or gathering. The *qahal* (or *kehal)* YHWH was a phrase often used in the Old Testament for the assembling, or assembly, of God's chosen people, especially "their assembly on Mount Sinai where Israel received the Law and was established by God as his holy people" (CCC 751; see Ex 19).

The Greek term *ekklesia* (Latin, *ecclesia*), which we also translate into English as *church,* likewise means to assemble or "call forth" a people. This indicates that the first community of Christian believers recognized itself as the heir or continuation of the Jewish assembly, but "called forth" by God from all the ends of the earth to be his people and to do his will. "For as many of you as were baptized into Christ have put on Christ. There is neither Jew nor Greek, there is neither slave nor free, there is neither male nor female; for you are all one in Christ Jesus. And if you are Christ's, then you are Abraham's offspring, heirs according to the promise" (Gal 3:27-29). They are the ones who believe that Jesus is truly the Messiah, the Son of God, and who have been formed by God into a people with a distinctive way of life.

It should be noted that the term *ekklesia,* or church, is used to designate either the universal community of believers (see 1 Cor 15:9), the local communities (such as "the church in Corinth"; 1 Cor 1:2), or those assembled to worship the Lord (see 1 Cor 11:18; 14:19, 28, 34-35). The local "churches" (see 1 Cor 16:1), however, understood themselves as manifestations or "branches" of the one universal church of Jesus Christ, not as independent bodies.

Finally, the English word *church* and the German *Kirche* are also derived from another Greek word, *kyriake,* which literally means "what belongs to the Lord." In this usage, *church* may refer to the people in a particular locality who "belong to God," or to the building where they worship. The primary meaning of *church* in the New Testament (*ekklesia*) is the "assembly of God's people."

Besides the name *church,* the sacred Scripture is rich in images and names referring to God's people. These images include: a sheepfold (see Jn 10:1-10); a cultivated field (see 1 Cor 3:9); the building, house, or temple of God (see 1 Cor 3:9; Eph 2:19, 22; 1 Pet 2:5; Rev 21:3); and "Jerusalem above," which is "our mother" (Gal 4:26).

The biblical images that perhaps are most important for understanding the church today are the "bride of Christ" (Eph 5:25-28; Rev 21:2), the "body of

Christ" (Rom 12:5; 1 Cor 12:12; Eph 1:22-23), and the "temple" or "people" of God (2 Cor 6:16; 1 Pet 2:9-10). In 1943, Pope Pius XII wrote an encyclical letter on "The Mystical Body of Christ," which made this the primary focus of the church's reflection, until the fathers of the Second Vatican Council chose the "people of God" as the primary guiding image for the church today as the "pilgrim" people of God.

The Mystery of the Church

The rich variety of biblical images of the church reminds us that the church is an inexhaustible mystery, sharing in the mystery of Christ. A mystery cannot be defined, only described. It is a mystery that "the Church is in history, but at the same time she transcends it" (CCC 770). The church is a human society, having typical human social structures and dynamics governing her life, and yet at the same time she is a spiritual community, "the mystical body of Christ."[16] These two dimensions of the church cannot be separated or divided, any more than we can divide the divine and human natures of Christ. Hence, the full truth about the church can only be known through faith, which recognizes both her humanity and her divine foundation and mission.

The union of Jesus Christ, the "bridegroom," with his "bride," the church, is also a great mystery, as St. Paul says (see Eph 5:21-33), and is the source and model of Christian marriage. The object of this union is that the church is made holy by Christ, her spouse, and is progressively transformed into his image. "Christ loved the church and gave himself up for her, that he might sanctify her" (Eph 5:25-26).

Finally, the mystery of the church is seen in the fact that the church is a *sacrament* of Christ: she makes Jesus and his grace visible and present in the world. The church is the instrument or vehicle by which Jesus shows the Father's love to the world and draws all people to him (CCC 776). The church is a sacrament, that is, both a *sign* and an *instrument* or means of the human race coming into union with God, and of all people coming into true unity with one another. "In her, this unity is already begun, since she gathers men 'from every nation, from all tribes and peoples and tongues' (Rev 7:9); and at the same time, the Church is the 'sign and instrument' of the full realization of the unity yet to come" (CCC 775).

In other words, as a sacrament, the church makes Jesus present in the world to draw all people to God, and in God, to union with each other.

The church foreshadows the completion of God's plan, because her members already experience, even though imperfectly, the holiness, the union with God, and the union with others in Christ that will be attained fully in heaven. (This is part of the "eschatological" dimension of the church—how the church participates in and points to the "eschaton," the end of human history.) "The Church ... will receive its perfection only in the glory of heaven."[17] After great trials and struggles, at the time of Christ's second coming, "all the just from the time of Adam, 'from Abel, the just one, to the last of the elect,' ... [will] be gathered together in the universal Church in the Father's presence."[18] Only then will the church cease to be a mystery, when it is no longer a sign and a precursor of God's kingdom ("... the Kingdom of Christ—now present in mystery ..."),[19] but the full realization and revelation of God's reign. Then all will recognize Christ as "the head over all things for the church, which is his body, the fullness of him who fills all in all" (Eph 1:22-23; see 1 Cor 15:28).

The Body of Christ

St. Joan of Arc said, "About Jesus Christ and his Church I simply know that they are just one thing, and we shouldn't complicate the matter."[20] St. Paul expresses this mystery by speaking of the church as the "body of Christ" (1 Cor 12:27; see Eph 1:22-23; 4:12; Col 1:18). Jesus brought about his conversion by appearing to him and asking, "Saul, Saul, why do you persecute me?" (Acts 9:4). Paul understood that in persecuting Christians, he had been persecuting Christ.

Jesus makes the church his body through the Holy Spirit and baptism (see 1 Cor 12:13). Christ is the head of the body (see Col 1:18), and each person who belongs to the church is a unique "member" of the body, having particular gifts (or "charisms") and graces for its "building up" or edification (see Rom 12:6ff; 1 Cor 14:26). The union of Christians to Christ makes us belong to each other, "so we, though many, are one body in Christ, and individually members one of another" (Rom 12:5). Because of this, "If one member suffers, all suffer together; if one member is honored, all rejoice together" (1 Cor 12:26; see also Rom 12:15). In short, the Christian is not isolated, but through the church he is a part of Christ and of his fellow Christians, and has been given unique gifts to love and serve Jesus and the other members of his body, the church. "Christ and his Church thus together make up the 'whole Christ' *(Christus totus)*. The Church is one with Christ" (CCC 795).

The Bride of Christ

The bond of marriage is the closest human bond. Not surprisingly, marriage is only a reflection of and a sharing in the perfect unity we have just described, the union of Jesus and his church. In this ideal union, Jesus, "the bridegroom," takes the initiative to make the church one with himself and to share his divine life with her (see Eph 5:26-27, 29-32). Each person, to become part of Christ's bride, the church, must respond personally to Jesus' love calling each of us to himself to share his life in a true marriage.

The Temple of the Holy Spirit

St. Augustine said, "What the soul is to the human body, the Holy Spirit is to the Body of Christ, which is the Church."[21] Thus the Holy Spirit is the soul of the church and the church is the temple, or "dwelling place," of the Holy Spirit (see Eph 2:19-22). It is impossible to separate the Holy Spirit from the church, because Jesus and the Father sent the Holy Spirit to the church to be her source of life. St. Irenaeus said:

> Indeed, it is to the Church herself that the "Gift of God" has been entrusted.... For where the Church is, there is also God's Spirit; where God's Spirit is, there is the church and every grace.[22]

Further, the Holy Spirit is "the principle of every vital and truly saving action in each part of the Body."[23] There are many ways that the Holy Spirit comes to build up the church in God's love (see Eph 4:16): by God's Word (see Acts

20:32), by baptism (see 1 Cor 12:13) and the other sacraments, by the charism of apostleship and other leaders,[24] by the virtues he bestows on the church, and by the many special graces (called *charisms*), "by which he makes the faithful fit and ready to undertake various tasks and offices for the renewal and building up of the Church"[25] (see CCC 798).

What are these "charisms"? They are graces of the Holy Spirit which directly or indirectly benefit the church (see Rom 12:4-8; 1 Cor 12-14; Eph 4:7-13). They are ordered to her "building up," since the church is a work of God and not a merely human project. Therefore:

> Charisms are to be accepted with gratitude by the person who receives them and by all members of the Church as well. They are a wonderfully rich grace for the apostolic vitality and for the holiness of the entire Body of Christ, provided they really are genuine gifts of the Holy Spirit and are used in full conformity with authentic promptings of this same Spirit, that is, in keeping with charity, the true measure of all charisms.[26]

These charisms, or gifts of the Holy Spirit, must be tested (discerned) and ordered so that the various gifts of the church's members may work together harmoniously to strengthen the church. This task of discernnment and ordering of God's gifts is yet another charism that belongs especially to the bishops and other pastors of the church. As Vatican II put it: "their office [is] not indeed to extinguish the Spirit, but to test all things and hold fast to what is good."[27]

The People of God

The primary image that the Second Vatican Council chose to teach about the church is the "People of God":

> You are a chosen race, a royal priesthood, a holy nation, *God's own people,* that you may declare the wonderful deeds of him who called you out of darkness into his marvelous light.
>
> 1 PETER 2:9 (emphasis added)

This biblical image is, of course, rooted in the Old Testament, which speaks of God's call to and formation of his first covenant people. The church is God's people of the New Covenant. It is clear that God's plan for the salvation of the human race—his plan to reconcile all people to himself—is to form them into a people set apart to know, love, and serve him. As the Second Vatican Council explained, God has

> willed to make men holy and save them, not as individuals without any bond or link between them, but rather to make them into a people who might acknowledge him and serve him in holiness. He therefore chose the Israelite race to be his own people and established a covenant with it. He gradually instructed this people.... All these things, however, happened as a preparation for and figure of that new and perfect covenant which was to be ratified in Christ ... the new covenant in his blood (1 Cor 11:35); he called together a race made up of Jews and Gentiles which would be one, not according to the flesh, but in the Spirit.[28]

Having already spoken of the deep spiritual union of believers to each other in the body of Christ, we should not be surprised by this teaching. However, the idea that God wills to make us holy and to save us not as separated individuals, but *as a people,* contradicts so much of what comes to us from the world's "creed of individualism." It even differs from the view of many Christians who focus on the salvation of individuals, with the church necessary primarily to help the individuals to find Christ. Instead, Catholics recognize that the fullness of Christ's life comes to us in the life of the church. What are the attributes of the church as God's people?

> That messianic people has as its *head* Christ.... The *state* of this people is that of the dignity and freedom of the sons of God, in whose hearts the Holy Spirit dwells as in a temple. Its *law* is the new commandment to love as Christ loved us (cf. Jn 13:34). [This is the "new" law of the Holy Spirit. Rom 8:2; Gal 5:25; CCC 782]. Its *mission* is to be salt of the earth and light of the world (cf. Mt 5:13-16). Its *destiny,* finally, "is the kingdom of God which has been begun by God himself on earth, and which must be further extended until it is brought to perfection by him at the end of time...."[29]

The people of God of the New Covenant is dignified in sharing in the identity and ministry of Jesus Christ, "whom the Father anointed with the Holy Spirit and established as priest, prophet, and king" (CCC 783).

A Priestly, Prophetic, and Kingly People

By joining himself to us so that we can share in his sacrifice of himself on Calvary, Jesus has "made us into a kingdom, priests for his God and Father" (Rev 1:6, NAB). Through baptism, all Christians become "a holy priesthood, to offer spiritual sacrifices acceptable to God through Jesus Christ" (1 Pet 2:5). Joining our lives to Christ, the church responds to St. Paul's appeal "to present your bodies as a living sacrifice, holy and acceptable to God, which is your spiritual worship" (Rom 12:1).

In other words, the sacrifice that the church is called to make as Christ's holy priesthood is for each member to offer his or her whole life to God, as Jesus offered his life for us to the Father. In this way, the church and all her members share in Christ's priesthood.

It is in the holy sacrifice of the Mass that Jesus' sacrifice is made present in sacramental form, and the church solemnly offers her sacrifice to the Father in union with the unsurpassable, once-for-all sacrifice of Jesus on Calvary.

Jesus was also the greatest prophet, who embodied and spoke the fullness of God's truth. "I am the way, and the truth, and the life" (Jn 14:6). Jesus promised to guide his followers into all truth by the Holy Spirit (see Jn 16:13), and so the *whole* people of God has received a "sense of the faith" (*sensus fidei*) which enables it to know the truth when it "unfailingly adheres to this faith ... once for all delivered to the saints."[30]

The royal or kingly mission of Jesus was expressed in his guidance and care for the church as "the Good Shepherd" of his flock (Jn 10:11). Christ the King drew all people to himself by a life of sacrificial service that reached its climax in his death for all people, and in his Resurrection and Ascension, in which his kingly glory was revealed.

The church is called to imitate and carry on Jesus' prophetic mission of proclaiming this saving truth to the world, both in speech and in action. We also share the ministry of Jesus by seeking to establish kingship or rule of Jesus in our own lives, in the church, and in the world. Practically, this means leading ourselves and others to acknowledge God, his will, and his laws as the ultimate authorities that guide us, and to live accordingly. As the *Catechism* states: "The People of God fulfills its royal dignity by a life in keeping with its vocation to serve with Christ" (CCC 786).

Marks of the Church: Unity

Another way that Christians traditionally have sought to understand the church is by reflecting upon the four "marks" or characteristics of the church that we profess in the Nicene Creed: "We believe in one holy, catholic, and apostolic church." These characteristics of the church are important in understanding what the church is. They are also biblical characteristics of the church.

For example, the Creed states that "the church is one." The source and model of this unity is the unity of God the Father, Son, and Holy Spirit in the blessed Trinity (see CCC 813). Jesus died on the cross to reconcile all people to God, and to gather them into the unity of the church. Jesus himself prayed to his Father, "that they [the believers in Jesus] may be one even as we are one ... that they may become perfectly one, so that the world may know that thou hast sent me" (Jn 17:22-23). He taught that, "there shall be one flock then, one shepherd" (Jn 10:16). The Holy Spirit is the "soul" and continuing source of unity of the church, "who brings about that wonderful communion of the faithful and joins them together so intimately in Christ that he is the principle of the Church's unity."[31]

Indeed, the Letter to the Ephesians urges Christians to "maintain the unity of the Spirit in the bond of peace" (Eph 4:3), and St. Paul entreats the Christians at Philippi to "complete my joy by being of the same mind, having the same love, being in full accord and of one mind" (Phil 2:2).

Paul himself, as well as the other apostles, strove to maintain unity in the early church, realizing that there is only one body of Christ, which should not be divided. When crises emerged that threatened to divide the church of Jesus Christ, the apostles acted decisively to preserve unity. The Acts of the Apostles records two of these crises: the potential division between the Hebrew and Hellenistic Jewish Christians in Jerusalem in Acts 6:1-7 and the even more widespread dispute over the circumcision of Gentiles, which was resolved by the Council of Jerusalem (see Acts 15). This meeting, or council, of the apostles and elders preserved the unity of the church by its binding decisions that one need not undergo the Jewish rites of initiation in order to become a Christian.

Unity and Diversity

The unity of the church does not contradict the "great *diversity* which comes from both the variety of God's gifts and the diversity of those who receive them. Within the unity of the People of God, a multiplicity of peoples and cultures is gathered together. Among the Church's members, there are different gifts, offices, conditions, and ways of life" (CCC 814).

It is also important to note that the Catholic Church consists of a number of different *rites*,[32] and within these rites are particular churches that retain their own distinctive traditions of liturgy, discipline, prayer, and ordering of Christian life.[33] All of the rites of the Catholic Church are of equal rank and dignity,[34] and exemplify the rich diversity of the Catholic Church.

Amidst this diversity, what are the bonds of unity that characterize the church Jesus founded? What must the church have in common to be authentically *one?*

The fundamental basis of unity is *charity*, which "binds everything together in perfect harmony" (Col 3:14). Also, Catholics recognize the *visible* bonds of unity—common doctrine and creeds, common sacraments and liturgy, and common leaders through apostolic succession—as assuring the unity of the pilgrim church.[35]

The Catholic understanding of apostolic succession includes the oversight and governance of the church by the successor of St. Peter, the pope, and by the bishops (the successors of the apostles) in communion with him (see CCC 816).

The Division of the Church and Ecumenism

It is a tragedy that in spite of the clear teaching of Jesus and the New Testament, the one church of Jesus Christ has been divided. Catholics recognize this as an objectively sinful situation, violating the will of God. The "Decree on Ecumenism" (UR) of the Second Vatican Council addresses this situation:

> Without doubt, this discord openly contradicts the will of Christ, provides a stumbling block to the world, and inflicts damage on the most holy cause of proclaiming the good news to every creature.[36]

This decree also presents God's solution to this situation—the ecumenical movement:

> ... there increases from day to day a movement, fostered by the grace of the Holy Spirit, for the restoration of unity among all Christians. Taking part in this movement, which is called ecumenical, are those who invoke the Triune God and confess Jesus as Lord and Savior.[37]

The *Catechism* notes that, "The desire to recover the unity of all Christians is a gift of Christ and a call of the Holy Spirit" (CCC 820; cf. UR 1).

The Catholic Church believes she has a special role to play in the reunification of the church of Christ, by virtue of the special gift of unity that she has received from the Lord: "Christ bestowed unity on his Church from the beginning. This unity, we believe, subsists in the Catholic Church as something she can never lose, and we hope that it will continue to increase until the end of time."[38] "Christ always gives his Church the gift of unity, but the Church must always pray and work to maintain, reinforce, and perfect the unity that Christ wills for her" (CCC 820). Hence, Catholics are urged to take the initiative in efforts for Christian unity, "making the first approaches toward them [our separated brethren]," rather than waiting for them to approach us.[39]

This ecumenical imperative was underscored by Pope John Paul II in his encyclical letter "That They May Be One" (*Ut Unum Sint*, 1995). He stressed that concern for ecumenism was part of the very nature of the church, not an optional activity for some Catholics. Ecumenism flows from the first mark of the church—the church is one.

The "Decree on Ecumenism" presents clear guidance on how Catholics should look upon other Christians and how we are to pray and work for the reunification of the church of Jesus Christ. Note that the ecumenical movement, or ecumenism, is concerned with the restoration of unity among *Christians*. Jews, Muslims, Buddhists, and other non-Christians are not, properly speaking, the object of *ecumenical* activity or concern. The Second Vatican Council devotes another decree, the "Declaration on the Relationship of the Church to Non-Christian Religions" (*Nostra Aetate*), to the approach of the Catholic Church to non-Christians.

How are Catholics to approach other Christians and promote the restoration of the unity of the church of Jesus Christ? A few guidelines, taken from the "Decree on Ecumenism," will be summarized here.[40]

1. *Catholics bear a share of the blame for the division among Christians and ask forgiveness of God and of our fellow Christians for this sin.* Catholics readily forgive fellow Christians for their offenses against us and do not hold those born today into other Christian churches responsible for any sin of separation in the past.[41]

2. *The primary duty of Catholics in promoting ecumenism is to seek the renewal of the Catholic Church,* so that its life may be a clearer witness to its teachings: "Let all Christ's faithful remember that the more purely they strive to live according to the gospel, the more they are fostering and even practicing Christian unity."[42]

3. *Catholics consider that all those who are baptized and believe in the Trinity and in Jesus Christ as Lord and Savior "have a right to be honored by the title of Christian,* and are properly regarded as brothers in the Lord by the sons of the Catholic Church." Thus, the Catholic Church considers other Christians as "separated brothers and sisters" in Christ, not as heretics or schismatics.[43]

4. *The Catholic Church recognizes other bodies of Christians as churches or ecclesiastical communities that "the Spirit of Christ ... has not refrained from using as means of salvation. ..."* In other words, Christians in other churches or ecclesiastical communities may be saved through the grace available in their churches, although "the fullness of grace and truth (is) entrusted to the Catholic Church."[44]

5. *Catholics can genuinely learn and receive support from other Christians.* In fact, Catholics are encouraged both to study the beliefs and backgrounds of other

Christian churches in order to understand them better and to meet individually or in groups to pray with other Christians. Catholics may attend the worship services of other Christians, but normally may not participate in their communion services because of different understandings of the Eucharist, and a difference in the reality of Christ's presence.[45]

6. In discussing our beliefs with other Christians, Catholics should state the teachings of the Catholic Church clearly and nondefensively. As the "Decree on Ecumenism" instructs, when presenting Catholic belief, Catholics should avoid a "false conciliatory approach, which harms the purity of Catholic doctrine and obscures its assured genuine meaning." This decree also encourages Catholics to explain their beliefs "profoundly and precisely, in ways and in terminology which our separated brethren too can really understand."[46]

7. Finally, Catholics are encouraged to join with all Christians in professing to the whole world our "faith in God, one and three, in the incarnate Son of God, our Redeemer and Lord." The Decree reminds us that cooperation in matters of common social concern is essential.[47] We must always bear in mind that what unites us as Christians—our common faith, hope, and mutual love—is far greater that what divides us. It is Satan who desires the continuance of divisions among Christians. God desires our reconciliation, so that his church may be truly one, as we profess it to be in the Creed.

What will the unity that God desires for Christians look like? Exactly how will it come about? The Catholic Church knows that this is ultimately in God's hands and that it will come about only as Christians constantly imitate and pray to our Savior, Jesus Christ. It is in him that we will find our true unity. As the "Decree on Ecumenism" declares:

This most sacred Synod urgently desires that the initiatives of the sons of the Catholic Church, joined with those of the separated brethren, go forward without obstructing the ways of divine Providence and without prejudging the future inspiration of the Holy Spirit. Further, this Synod declares its realization that the holy task of reconciling all Christians in the unity of the one and only church of Christ transcends human energies and abilities. It therefore places its hope entirely in the prayer of Christ for the church, in the love of the Father for us, and in the power of the Holy Spirit. "And hope does not disappoint, because the charity of God is poured forth in our hearts by the Holy Spirit Who has been given to us" (Rom 5:5).[48]

The Church Is Catholic

"Catholic," as used in the Nicene Creed, means "universal" or "all-embracing"—always referring to the totality or the whole which is embraced. Catholic, as a mark or characteristic of the church, has different dimensions.

First, "catholic church" can simply mean the whole or total church. This is what St. Ignatius of Antioch meant when he said (in A.D. 110), "where Christ Jesus is, there is the catholic church."[49] The whole church is present where Jesus is, since the church is the "body of Christ" in its completeness.

Secondly, "catholic" refers to the fact that the church Jesus founded reaches out to include all peoples, cultures, and times. It is truly "universal," as St. Paul indicates when he teaches that all are one in Jesus Christ, whether Jew or Greek, woman or man, free person or slave (see Gal 3:27-28). The *Catechism* states, "the Church is catholic because she has been sent out by Christ on a mission to the whole of the human race" (CCC 831).[50]

The third dimension of "catholic" is that the church includes all, the totality, of what Jesus has entrusted to her. The fullness of Jesus Christ is present (subsists) in the church—a catholicity which began on the day of Pentecost[51] and will extend until the day of Parousia (see CCC 830).

If the whole church is "catholic," what about local or particular churches, such as St. Paul refers to when he wrote to "the church of the Thessalonians" (2 Thess 1:1) or to "the churches of Galatia" (Gal 1:2)? Today we call these "particular churches" dioceses (or eparchies). As long as they are in full communion with the church throughout the world (possessing the same faith, sacraments, and bishops ordained in apostolic succession), they, too, are "catholic," because they express the fullness of the universal church in a particular locality.

In the early centuries of Christianity, many saints and church fathers saw the union of particular churches with the Church of Rome, "which presides in charity,"[52] as a necessary sign of true "catholicity." In fact, the term *catholic* eventually came to be used as a *title* for that universal church, established by Jesus, which included all the "particular churches" (CCC 833, 834) fully united with each other and with the church of Rome. This distinguished it from certain 'breakaway' (heretical or schismatic) groups of Christians such as the Montanists (second century) or the Arians (fourth century). Hence, St. Monica prayed that her son, St. Augustine, would become a "Catholic Christian" before he died.[53]

The name "Roman Catholic Church" highlights the importance of the unity of the Catholic Church with the successor of St. Peter, the bishop of Rome.[54] Particular churches are fully catholic through their communion with the Church of Rome, "which presides in charity."[55] "For with this church, by reason of its pre-eminence, the whole Church, that is the faithful everywhere, must necessarily be in accord."[56] Indeed, "from the incarnate Word's descent to us, all Christian churches everywhere have held and hold the great Church that is here [at Rome] to be their only basis and foundation since, according to the Savior's promise, the gates of hell have never prevailed against her."[57]

Who Belongs to the Catholic Church?

The "Dogmatic Constitution on the Church" states that: "This Church [the unique Church of Christ which in the Creed we avow as one, holy, catholic, and apostolic] subsists in the Catholic Church, which is governed by the successor of Peter and by the bishops in union with that successor...."[58] The Vatican's Congregation for the Doctrine of the Faith explained that, "Catholics are bound to profess that ... they belong to that Church which Christ founded and which is governed by the successors of Peter...."[59]

What about those Christian churches and groups who do not recognize the universal teaching and governing authority of the pope? What is their relationship to the Catholic Church? The Second Vatican Council makes the distinction between those who are "fully incorporated into the Church"—the Catholic faithful—and those Christian churches and groups who possess "many elements of sanctification and of truth,... but who do not however profess the Catholic faith in its entirety or have not preserved unity or communion under the successor of Peter."[60]

Catholics look upon the fullness of "means of salvation" that the Catholic

Church has received from Christ and has preserved over the centuries as a tremendous unmerited blessing from God, but also as a grave responsibility. The first responsibility for Catholics is to accept and live according to the graces they themselves have received, for they will be judged according to how well they have used them. "Even though incorporated into the Church, one who does not however persevere in charity is not saved. He remains indeed in the bosom of the Church, but 'in body' not 'in heart.'"[61]

Secondly, Catholics are called to recognize that the Catholic Church, "is joined in many ways to the baptized who are honored by the name of Christian."[62] Catholics are to accept "them with respect and affection as brothers," since those "who believe in Christ and have been properly baptized are put in a certain, although imperfect communion with the Catholic Church."[63] With the Orthodox churches, this communion is so profound, "that it lacks little to attain the fullness that would permit a common celebration of the Lord's Eucharist."[64]

In short, by virtue of our faith in Christ, common baptism, and many other shared Christian endowments, Catholics are joined with other Christian churches and ecclesial communities in the People of God. "For the Spirit of Christ has not refrained from using them as means of salvation which derive their efficacy from the very fullness of grace and truth entrusted to the Catholic Church."[65]

The Church and Non-Christians

Though non-Christians do not belong in any direct sense to the church, the People of God of the New Covenant, "Those who have not yet received the Gospel are related to the People of God in various ways."[66]

The Jewish people have a unique place in God's plan of salvation, being "the first to hear the Word of God"[67] and to respond to it, thus entering into a covenant relationship with God (the Old Covenant) (see CCC 839). St. Paul teaches that the Jewish people remain dear to God (see Rom 11:28-29). Because of our common spiritual heritage, the Catholic Church, "wishes to encourage and further mutual understanding and appreciation" between Christians and Jews, and, "deplores all hatreds, persecutions, displays of anti-semitism leveled at anytime or from any source against the Jews."[68]

Likewise, the church demonstrates her "catholicity" by respecting whatever is "true and holy" in other non-Christian religions, whose precepts and doctrines "often reflect a ray of that truth which enlightens all men."[69] By these bonds of truth and holiness, these religions are already related to the Catholic Church in some way. However, the statement above from the Second Vatican Council's "Declaration on the Relation of the Church to Non-Christian Religions" (*Nostra Aetate*) continues with these words concerning the mission of the church to non-Christians: "Yet she proclaims and is in duty bound to proclaim without fail, Christ who is the way, the truth and the life (Jn 14:6). In him, in whom God reconciled all things to himself (2 Cor 5:18-19), men find the fullness of their religious life."[70]

Because Jesus Christ continues his saving presence in this world through his body, the church, we believe what St. Cyprian taught in the third century: that the church Jesus founded is necessary for salvation. If those who do not yet believe in Christ are saved through God's mercy and mysterious design, it is because they receive that saving grace through Christ and his church (CCC 846). Those people who *know*, or who *come to know*, that the Catholic Church was founded by God through Jesus Christ as necessary for salvation must remain in her, or enter her, if they are to be saved.[71] The goal of the church's missionary activity is "catholic"—to bring *all people* to share in the *fullness* of spiritual life and salvation that is found only in Jesus Christ and in his church.

The Church Is Holy

What does it mean that the church is holy? Many people equate holiness with sinlessness and say that a holy church must be a perfect church, or at least a church well on the way to perfection.

The holiness of the church, however, does not refer primarily to the merits and virtues of its individual members. Something is holy because it is chosen or set apart by God for his purposes and service. God has chosen and set apart a people, the church, for his purposes and service, and has made it holy: "But you are a chosen race, a royal priesthood, a holy nation, God's own people ..." (1 Pet 2:9). Thus, her members are called "saints" or "holy ones" (Acts 9:13; 1 Cor 6:1; 16:1).

The church is holy, not because of its own merits, but because Jesus Christ died to win forgiveness for this people and to cleanse it of its sin:

> Christ loved the church and gave himself up for her, that he might sanctify her, having cleansed her by the washing of water with the word, that he might present the church to himself in splendor, without spot or wrinkle or any such thing, that she might be holy and without blemish.
>
> EPHESIANS 5:25-27

Jesus also "joined her to himself as his body and endowed her with the gift of the Holy Spirit for the glory of God."[72]

The church, being sanctified or made holy by Christ, is able to sanctify others. One joins the holy church in order to be made holy, and so the members of the church, "are called by the Lord to that perfection of sanctity by which the Father himself is perfect."[73] "Charity is the soul of the holiness to which all are called" (CCC 826).

Nevertheless, the holiness of the church on earth reflects the present status of the kingdom of God in this world: already present, but not yet brought to completion. Holiness is a gift of God, and perhaps it is to remind us of this truth that God has blessed, chosen, and set apart a people who still struggle with sin. As St. Paul taught, "we have this treasure in earthen vessels, to show that the transcendent power belongs to God and not to us" (2 Cor 4:7).

There is no contradiction when Catholics claim that the church is holy, but is for sinners. Jesus came to call sinners (see Mt 9:13). "All members of the Church, including her ministers, must acknowledge that they are sinners (cf. 1 Jn 1:8-10).... Hence the Church gathers sinners already caught up in Christ's salvation but still on the way to holiness" (CCC 827).

Sin is overcome in the church as its members repent and incessantly turn to God for his mercy and forgiveness. In response, God sends the Holy Spirit to renew the church and sanctify its members, transforming them "into his likeness from one degree of glory to another" (2 Cor 3:18). The church *canonizes* some of the faithful after their death (i.e., declares them to be saints who are now in the glory of heaven). This reminds and encourages us that it is possible to attain holiness and a great degree of freedom from sin even in this life.

The saints serve us as models of holiness and as intercessors, and "have always been the source and origin of renewal in the most difficult moments in the church's history."[74] Mary is the ultimate model of holiness: "in her, the Church is already the 'all holy'" (CCC 829).

In conclusion, Vatican II's "Dogmatic Constitution on the Church" teaches, "while Christ, holy, innocent, undefiled (Heb 7:26) knew nothing of sin (2 Cor 5:21), but came to expiate only the sins of the people (cf. Heb 2:17), the church, embracing sinners in her bosom, is at the same time holy, and always in need of being purified and incessantly pursues the path of penance and renewal."[75]

This understanding of the holiness of the church has many practical implications. For example, some people (past and present) have claimed that the Catholic Church cannot be called holy because of the personal sinfulness of its members and leaders.

Some individuals and groups have broken away from the Catholic Church because of this, desiring to found or join a "truly holy," sinless church. The irony of this is that those who condemn or leave the Catholic Church because of its sinful members or leaders soon discover, if they are honest, that there is no sinless, perfect church or group of Christians. Sooner or later, every group of human beings reveals the fallen, sinful nature of man, and must cry out to God for mercy and forgiveness. The Catholic Church claims to be holy because God has called it to be a people set apart for him and his purposes. The church trusts in him for pardon and the renewing grace of the Holy Spirit.

The Church Is Apostolic

The church is apostolic because she is "built upon the foundation of the apostles and prophets, Christ Jesus himself being the cornerstone" (Eph 2:20). The primary meaning of this "mark," or characteristic, of the church is simply that "she was and remains built on 'the foundation of the Apostles,' (Eph 2:20; Rev 21:14) the witnesses chosen ... by Christ himself" (cf. Mt 28:16-20; Acts 1:8; 1 Cor 9:1; 15:7-8; Gal 1:1; etc.) (CCC 857).

Secondly, the church is apostolic because she announces and defends the true teaching of the apostles. Acts 2:42 states, "they devoted themselves to the apostles' teaching...."

Finally, the church is apostolic because the ministry or office of the apostles is continued in the church in unbroken succession to this day. Where? In the "college" (body) of bishops, "assisted by priests in union with the successor of Peter, the church's supreme pastor."[76]

The word *apostle* means "one who is sent," an "emissary." Jesus was sent by the Father, and he in turn "called to him those whom he desired;... And he appointed twelve, [whom also he named apostles], to be with him, and to be sent out to preach" (Mk 3:13-14; see CCC 859). These apostles learned from Jesus and received from the Father. Jesus' apostles knew that they were called by God as "ministers of a new covenant," "servants of God," "ambassadors for Christ," "servants of Christ and stewards of the mysteries of God" (1 Cor 4:1; 2 Cor 3:6; 5:20; 6:4), and that apart from him they could do nothing (see Jn 15:5).

Only the twelve were "the chosen witnesses of the Lord's Resurrection and so the foundation stones of the Church. But their office also has a permanent aspect" (CCC 860). When the original twelve apostles died, they were not replaced by a new set of apostles. Who, then, continued the teaching and ministry of the apostles after they died? The Pastoral Epistles of the New Testament (1 and 2 Timothy, Titus), probably authored by the apostle Paul, clearly indicate that the bishops (Greek, *episcopoi*) assumed the ministry and office of the apostles in the early church. They were the primary teachers in the early churches: "he [the bishop] must hold firm to the sure word [of the gospel] as taught, so that he may be able to give instruction in sound doctrine and also to confute those who contradict it" (Titus 1:9; see also 1 Tim 3:2).

The bishops also were the primary shepherds and leaders of the local churches, representing the Chief Shepherd, Jesus Christ, in their care for the churches. Many early Christian writings exhorted the local Christian churches to honor and respect their bishop as they would Jesus Christ, since they represented him just as the apostles had. The letters of Ignatius of Antioch, who was martyred for his faith in about A.D. 110, are particularly clear and powerful in presenting the importance of the bishops as the representatives of Jesus and successors of the apostles in their churches.

The bishops of the local churches also recognized their responsibility for the entire church of Jesus Christ. Like the apostles they succeeded, the bishops viewed themselves as a body of men who were commissioned by the Lord to spread the gospel and lead the church in unity. The bishops of the early church expressed their unity by correspondence about the important matters affecting the whole church, working together to develop creeds that expressed accurately the faith of Christians, and meeting together in regional or worldwide (ecumenical) councils or synods where they sought the Lord's guidance on important matters of Christian belief and practice.

The prototype of these councils of bishops was the Council of Jerusalem described in Acts 15. There, the apostles and elders reached a decision concerning Gentile circumcision and observance of the Jewish law that affected the whole church. In the letter they drafted as a result to the council, they stated, "For it has seemed good to the Holy Spirit and to us to lay upon you no greater burden than these necessary things…" (Acts 15:28). Later councils of bishops also believed that when they met as a body of elders representing the whole church, their decisions were assuredly guided by the Holy Spirit and thereby binding upon the whole church. The Catholic Church recognizes the apostolic authority of twenty-one such worldwide, or ecumenical, councils of bishops that have been held from the time of the early church until today. Through these ecumenical councils, Catholics believe that the Holy Spirit continues to guide the church through the apostolic authority of the bishops.

The Apostolic Mission

In speaking of the "apostolic mission" of the church, we cannot neglect mentioning the specifically missionary apostolate and activity of the church. The church is missionary by her very nature,[77] motivated by the love of God to spread the gospel to the world with the same zeal shown by the apostles and their early successors.

God wills the salvation of everyone through the knowledge of the truth. Salvation is found in the truth. Those who obey the prompting of the Spirit of truth are already on the way of salvation. But the Church, to whom this truth has been entrusted, must go out to meet their desire, so as to bring them the truth. Because she believes in God's universal plan of salvation, the Church must be missionary. (CCC 851)

The Holy Spirit is "the principal agent of the whole of the Church's mission,"[78] who leads the church on her missionary paths:

The Church, urged on by the Spirit of Christ, must walk the road Christ himself walked, a way of poverty and obedience, of service and self-sacrifice even to death, a death from which he emerged victorious by his resurrection.[79]

Truly the most powerful apostolic missionaries are the *martyrs*, who have witnessed to Jesus Christ even to the point of accepting death for his sake.

Vocations in the Church

Among the people of God there is a wonderful variety of callings (vocations) and gifts. This should not surprise us, since God's creation is beautifully diverse. There are many ways that Christians reflect the image of Jesus and respond to his call. St. Paul compares the diversity of call and gift in the church with the many parts of the human body, which are all different, yet all important for the body to function properly (see 1 Cor 12).

Through baptism, all the members of the church have an equal dignity (CCC 872). Each person, regardless of gifts or vocation, is precious to the Lord. Each person is unique in his or her particular way of sharing in the life and ministry of Jesus (CCC 871). Yet, the church distinguishes three general types of vocations—three ways the faithful share in the office of Jesus as priest, prophet, and king.

Some are set apart by the sacrament of Holy Orders to serve God's people as bishops, priests, and deacons—the hierarchy of the church. Others share in Jesus' threefold ministry in the midst of the world as lay people—the laity. Finally, some from among the hierarchy and the laity consecrate their lives to God and dedicate themselves to serve the mission of the church through vowed profession of the "evangelical counsels" of poverty, chaste celibacy, and obedience. Those whose lives are so consecrated are called "religious" (CCC 873).

The Hierarchy of the Church

Many people today have a negative reaction to the word or concept of *hierarchy*. To some the idea of people in offices of authority in the church seems "unspiritual," too prone to abuse, or too similar to purely human institutions. Some note that Jesus often was critical of the leaders of Judaism in his time.

Nonetheless, Jesus himself established the hierarchy of the church. He chose "the twelve"; specifically trained them to understand his message and continue his ministry; and gave them power and authority to heal, expel demons, and proclaim the Good News of God's kingdom. Those members of the church who receive this call and gift today, through the sacrament of Holy Orders, exercise their ministry in the name of, and by the authority of, Jesus Christ.

From him, bishops and priests receive the mission and faculty ("the sacred power") to act *in persona Christi Capitis* (in the person of Christ the head); deacons receive the strength to serve the people of God in the *diaconia* (service) of liturgy, word, and charity (CCC 875).

One reason for aversion to authority is the idea or practice of authority as power or control over others. Jesus vigorously rejected this notion, and defined authority in terms of service. Far from "lording it over" others (Mk 10:42), Jesus told his apostles: "whoever would be great among you must be your servant, and whoever would be first among you must be slave of all. For the Son of Man also came not to be served but to serve, and to give his life as a ransom for many" (Mk 10:43-45; see CCC 876).

The hierarchy of the Catholic Church has been pictured as a pyramid, with those of greater authority (e.g., the pope and the bishops) at the top of the pyramid; priests, deacons, and religious in the middle; and the laity at the bottom. Because the laity are not just *ruled* by the hierarchy, but are *served* by them, perhaps the pyramid could be inverted to remind us that the hierarchy are *servants* of the rest of the church, with the pope being the "Chief Servant."

Pope Gregory the Great (A.D. 590-604) called himself the "Servant of the Servants of God," and this has become a favorite title of the popes. St. Paul wrote about how the apostles, the first members of the hierarchy, were treated as the "world's rubbish" (1 Cor 4:13, NAB; see 4:9-13), and proclaimed, "For what we preach is not ourselves, but Jesus Christ as Lord, with ourselves as your servants for Jesus' sake" (2 Cor 4:5).

The Episcopacy or Office of Bishop

Catholics believe that the bishops who govern and guide the Catholic Church today are true successors to the apostles of Jesus. The principal duty of the bishop is to preach the gospel of Jesus Christ (CCC 888). This is most frequently done in the context of the Mass or other liturgies, which the bishop celebrates as one who possesses the fullness of the priesthood of Jesus Christ that is conferred upon him in his episcopal consecration. As *Lumen Gentium* explains:

> By the imposition of hands and through the words of consecration, the grace of the Holy Spirit is given and the sacred character is impressed in such wise that bishops in a resplendent and visible manner take the place of Christ himself, teacher, shepherd and priest, and act as his representative.[80]

Also, the bishop has full apostolic authority within his local church to guide and govern its members in the name of Christ. "The Good Shepherd ought to be the model and 'form' of the bishop's pastoral office" (CCC 896).

Each bishop, at his consecration, is given a particular jurisdiction (usually a geographical area) in which he is empowered to shepherd and guide God's people with the same authority that Jesus conferred on his apostles. "The faithful," in turn, "should be closely attached to the bishops as the Church is to Jesus Christ, and as Jesus Christ is to the Father."[81]

Even though the bishops of the Catholic Church have distinct ministries and jurisdictions, the Second Vatican Council emphasized that the bishops are to see themselves and to function as fellow members of a college or body of bishops. Just as the apostles were a body who worked together for the sake of Jesus and his kingdom, the bishops as a body are the successors of the apostles and are called to work together for the good of God's people, the church. Practically, this means that each bishop has a pastoral concern and care for the whole church, as well as for his particular diocese or jurisdiction.[82]

Christ's ministers act in communion with one another. They also act according to personal conviction as pastors, always obedient to the teaching of Christ and the law of the church. Each one is called personally: "Follow me" (Jn 21:22), in order to be a personal witness within the common mission, to bear personal responsibility before him who gives the mission—Jesus himself.

The collegiality of the bishop is expressed most visibly when groups of bishops meet together for synods or councils, where they pray and confer about God's direction for the church. In fact, Catholics believe that when the bishops representing the entire world meet together for an ecumenical or worldwide council, the Holy Spirit is present in a special way.

The solemn doctrinal definitions of ecumenical councils are believed by Catholics to be infallibly true, since we firmly believe that God would not allow Satan to deceive the whole body of bishops who have been called by God to teach and govern the church. Jesus' promise to his apostles that he would send the Holy Spirit to guide the church into all truth (see Jn 16:12-15) is certainly fulfilled when the bishops concur on a matter of faith or morals. Even though an individual bishop may err, the whole college of bishops will not when they formally define a doctrine of faith or morals. As *Lumen Gentium* states:

> Although the individual bishops do not enjoy the prerogative of infallibility, they can nevertheless proclaim Christ's doctrine infallibly. This is so, even when they are dispersed around the world, provided that while maintaining the bond of unity among themselves and with Peter's successor, and while teaching authentically on a matter of faith or morals, they concur in a single viewpoint as the one which must be held conclusively. This authority is even more clearly verified when, gathered together in an ecumenical council, they are teachers and judges of faith and morals for the universal Church. Their definitions must then be adhered to with the submission of faith.[83]

Through the apostolic succession of the bishops, God has provided the Catholic Church an unbroken ministry of teaching, governance, and sacramental life for almost two thousand years. We must be aware that other Christians do not share the Catholic belief in the apostolic succession of bishops. Many of them believe that the expression, "the church is apostolic," means that the church faithfully preserves the teaching of the apostles, or simply that the church is missionary. They do not consider the unbroken historic succession of bishops from the apostles to be essential to the apostolic ministry, but consider this ministry as a work of the Holy Spirit that could be conferred on any person at any time. Catholics observe that from New Testament times onward the apostles' role was assumed by the bishops, and that these bishops conferred this office on other men through prayer and the "laying on of hands." In precisely this way have bishops been recognized and consecrated for their ministry in the Catholic Church from apostolic times to the present day.

Priests and Deacons

The bishop is assisted in his role of teaching, shepherding, and leading the church in worship by other ordained elders: priests and deacons. These three groups of ordained leaders together comprise the hierarchy of the church.

The orders of priest and deacon originated in the early church. The Greek word *presbyteros,* meaning "elder," is often used in the New Testament to designate one of the leaders of the local church. At first, there was apparently no sharp distinction (in at least some local churches) between the different types of elders—all were called presbyters. But by the time of the writing of the Pastoral Epistles (between A.D. 60 and 90), bishops and deacons are spoken of as distinct classes of elders.

Actually, the office of deacon (from the Greek *diakonos,* meaning "servant") was one of the first distinct leadership roles in the church, tracing its origins back to the selection of the seven men in the Jerusalem church to oversee the distribution of food to the widows (see Acts 6). This service freed the apostles to devote themselves "to prayer and to the ministry of the word" (Acts 6:4). Deacons became the "right hands" of the bishops of the early church and the diaconate continued to be a key office of the church into the Middle Ages.

Although the office of deacon fell into disuse in the Catholic Church, becoming a stage in preparation for priestly ordination, the Second Vatican Council has called for the restoration of the permanent diaconate according to the model of the early church.[84]

The presbyter or elder gradually assumed a distinct role or office in the early church, subordinate to the bishop but carrying on many of the same tasks. The letters of Ignatius of Antioch in the beginning of the second century inform us that the churches to which he wrote all had a distinctive three-tiered leadership structure comprised of a single bishop, assisted by presbyters and deacons. This structure of ministry was universally accepted in the church by the middle of the second century and has been preserved in the Catholic Church to this day in the ordained ministries of a single bishop presiding over each local church, assisted by priests and deacons.

The Role of the Pope

The chief representative, or vicar, of Jesus Christ and the spiritual head of the Roman Catholic Church under Christ is the pope, the bishop of Rome. While Catholics understand the college or body of bishops to be the legitimate successors to the college of the apostles, the pope is viewed as the successor to the specific apostle singled out by Jesus to be leader and shepherd of the whole church, St. Peter.

"The Lord made Simon alone, whom he named Peter, the 'rock' of his Church. He gave him the keys of his Church and instituted him shepherd of the whole flock" (CCC 881; see Mt 16:18-19; Jn 21:15-17).

Furthermore, the Acts of the Apostles and the other New Testament writings clearly indicate that Peter was the preeminent elder of the New Testament church, in spite of his human failings and weaknesses. Peter was the first to proclaim the good news of Jesus at Pentecost (see Acts 2:14-40), the first to preach to and baptize Gentile converts (see Acts 10:46-48), and is consistently portrayed as the spokesman or leader of the twelve (see Mt 18:21; Mk 8:29; Lk 9:20; 12:41; Acts 3:6-7, 12-16; 4:8-12; 5:3-9, 29-32; 8:20-23; 10:34-43; 11:4-18; 15:7-11). In fact, it would be unlikely that the Gospels of Matthew and John (written around A.D. 80 and 90-100, respectively) would have spoken so definitely about Peter's leadership if he had not actually served in the church as they indicate.

"The *Pope*, Bishop of Rome and Peter's successor, 'is the perpetual and visible source and foundation of the unity both of the bishops and of the whole company of the faithful.'"[85] How did this come to pass?

The other bishops and Christians of the early church looked regularly to the bishop of Rome to provide decisive guidance and direction for the church. This made sense, since the bishop of Rome was the bishop succeeding Peter and Paul, who both gave up their lives witnessing to their faith in Rome. The great bishop of the early church, Irenaeus of Lyon, testified to this in his defense of the tradition of the Catholic Church in his work *Against Heresies*, written in the late second century:

I can, by pointing out the tradition which that very great, oldest, and well-known church, founded and established at Rome by those two most glorious apostles, Peter and Paul, received from the apostles, and its faith known among men, which comes down to us through successions of bishops, put to shame all of those who ... gather as they should not. For every church must be in harmony with this church [the church in Rome] because of its outstanding pre-eminence, that is, the faithful from everywhere, since the apostolic tradition is preserved in it by those from everywhere."[86]

Irenaeus goes on to trace the successors of Peter as bishop of Rome from the first, Linus, to the twelfth, Eleutherus, who was bishop of Rome at the time of his document's composition. His point is that the see of Rome and its bishops have special authority—preeminence, as he says—because of their direct link to the apostles, Peter and Paul.

By the middle of the fourth century, the bishop of Rome was first called pope, a title referring to his special care for the entire church as a "papa" or "father" to them. As a father of the church, the pope was often called upon to arbitrate disputes within the church, to be a final judge in matters of Christian doctrine, and even to defend the church against the incursions of secular rulers or invaders. Although the full authority of the office of pope was not exercised immediately in the early church, Catholic Christians recognize that its emergence, and the recognition of the bishop of Rome as the successor of Peter, is a work of the Holy Spirit intended to strengthen the church and lead it into the fullness of truth, as Jesus promised (see Jn 16:13).

"For the Roman Pontiff, by reason of his office as Vicar of Christ, and as pastor of the entire Church has full, supreme, and universal power over the whole Church, a power which he can always exercise unhindered."[87]

The Gift of Infallibility

Jesus promised to be with the church until the end of time (see Mt 28:20), and to send the Holy Spirit to guide it into the fullness of the truth and reveal the things to come. This belief that the church cannot be led astray from the truth when it believes and defines a doctrine under the guidance of the Holy Spirit is called infallibility.

Catholics believe that infallibility in belief may be expressed in three ways. First, the church as a whole is infallible when it recognizes and agrees upon a truth in the sphere of faith and morals. As *Lumen Gentium* pronounced:

> The body of the faithful as a whole, anointed as they are by the Holy One (cf. 1 Jn 2:20, 27), cannot err in matters of belief. Thanks to a supernatural sense of the faith ("sensus fidei") which characterizes the people as a whole, it manifests this unerring quality when "from the bishops down to the last member of the laity," it shows universal agreement on matters of faith and morals.[88]

Of course, it is difficult to determine what all the faithful in the world believe. The Catholic Church also teaches that Christian truth can be stated infallibly by the bishops of the church, in union with the pope. Their authority is comparable to a statement of faith by the apostles with Peter, since the bishops and the pope are their genuine successors.

Finally, Catholics believe that the pope alone, in specific circumstances, can speak with the gift of infallibility that Jesus has given to his church.

> The Roman Pontiff, head of the college of bishops, enjoys this infallibility in virtue of his office, when, as supreme pastor and teacher of all the faithful— who confirms his brethren in faith—he proclaims by a definitive act a doctrine pertaining to faith or morals.[89]

Although the doctrine of papal infallibility was not formally defined by the Catholic Church until 1870 (in the decree *Pastor Aeternus* of the First Vatican Council), Catholics had long understood that the pope possessed this gift. The First Vatican Council defined more specifically when and how the pope spoke with the charism of infallibility.

Concerning the faithful's reception of infallible statements, when the church through its supreme Magisterium proposes a doctrine, "for belief as being divinely revealed,"[90] and as the teaching of Christ, the definitions "must be adhered to with the obedience of faith."[91]

However, most of the teaching of the church's Magisterium, now and throughout the centuries, has not been in the form of infallible definitions of faith or morals. The *Catechism* explains that this teaching of the "ordinary magisterium" of the church is to be received with "religious assent" or "religious submission of will and of mind,"[92] but not necessarily with the "obedience (or assent) of faith" that is required for infallibly defined doctrines. This teaching in the mode of the ordinary magisterium is valuable because it "leads to better understanding of Revelation in matters of faith and morals" (CCC 892).

The Laity

When Catholics hear the phrase, "the church," what comes to mind? In the past, it was common for Catholics to think of the pope, bishops, clergy, or religious as "the church." Some even thought of the church building. The Second Vatican Council has emphasized that the church is the whole People of God. Most members of this people are not ordained and have not devoted their lives to a religious state through special vows of poverty, chastity, and obedience.

The church is mainly comprised of baptized believers who follow the call of Christ to live his gospel in the midst of the secular world, with occupations often not directly related to the church. The people who respond to this call, either in the married or single state of life, are the laity. Pope Pius XII spoke eloquently of the importance of the laity:

> Lay believers are in the front line of Church life; for them the Church is the animating principle of human society. Therefore, they in particular ought to have an ever-clearer consciousness not only of belonging to the Church, but of being the Church, that is to say, the Community of the faithful on earth under the leadership of the Pope, the common Head, and of the bishops in communion with him. They are the Church.[93]

A great breakthrough of Vatican II led Catholics to realize that to be a lay person was a genuine vocation—a call of the Lord to serve him in the church and the world in a unique way. As the "Dogmatic Constitution on the Church" states:

> The laity, by their very vocation, seek the kingdom of God by engaging in temporal affairs, and by ordering them according to the plan of God.... They

are called there by God so that by exercising their proper function and being led by the spirit of the Gospel they can work for the sanctification of the world from within, in the manner of leaven.[94]

This document proceeds to explain how lay people carry on the priestly, prophetic, and kingly ministry of Jesus Christ in a way that is different than clergy or religious, but equally important in God's plan for the salvation of the world.

While lay people certainly must use their talents and gifts within the church, they are also commissioned by Christ himself to represent him and bring the Good News of salvation in the daily affairs and ordinary circumstances of human society: "Through their baptism and confirmation, all are commissioned to that apostolate by the Lord Himself."[95] While the clergy's ministry is specifically to the church, building up the body of Christ, the lay person's ministry is specifically to the world—to extend the body of Christ and bring the influence of the church and the gospel to bear upon the world's affairs. There is no reason, then, for any lay Catholic to think of him or herself as "just a lay person." Not only have the laity been commissioned by Jesus himself to the apostolate of bringing the gospel to the world, they have been equipped for this apostolate by the gifts (charisms) of the Holy Spirit, which are given to each Christian for the upbuilding of the church and for the service and evangelization of the world. Vatican II's "Decree on the Apostolate of the Laity" (*Apostolicam actuositatem*) specifies that:

> From the reception of these charisms or gifts ... there arise for each believer the right and duty to use them in the Church and in the world for the good of mankind and for the upbuilding of the Church. In doing so, believers need to enjoy the freedom of the Holy Spirit who "breathes where He wills" (Jn 3:8). At the same time, they must act in communion with their pastors. The latter must make a judgment about the true nature and proper use of these gifts, not in order to extinguish the Spirit, but to test all things and hold fast to what is good (cf. 1 Thess 5:12, 19, 21).[96]

This decree states repeatedly that lay people are called and equipped to be active in service and leadership in the church, working in willing cooperation with the church's ordained pastors. Any notion of competition—clergy versus laity—is excluded, since we are brothers and sisters working together as God's family for the cause of Christ and his kingdom.

One of the most significant statements of the Second Vatican Council expressing the importance and equality of all members of the church—regardless of their vocation or state of life—was the fifth chapter of *Lumen Gentium*, entitled, "The Call of the Whole Church of Holiness." Regardless of whether one is a priest, married person, religious, single man or woman, or the pope— *all* are equally called by God to holiness or Christian perfection. *Lumen Gentium* states:

> The Lord Jesus, the divine Teacher and Model of all perfection, preached holiness of life to each and every one of His disciples, regardless of their situation: "You therefore are to be perfect, as your heavenly Father is perfect" (Mt 5:48).... Thus it is evident to everyone that all the faithful of Christ of whatever rank or status are called to the fullness of the Christian life and to the perfection of charity.[97]

Of course, Christians must pursue holiness and perfection in Christ according to their state in life and particular calling from the Lord. A married woman with small children, for example, will seek holiness in a different way than would a cloistered contemplative nun. Yet both are equally called to holiness and equally able to attain it, though in different ways.[98]

A key to holiness for all Christians is prayer and "living union with Christ" in everyday life. This is also the source of fruitfulness and success of the person's apostolate, as Vatican II's "Decree on the Apostolate of the Laity" affirms:

> Since Christ in His mission from the Father is the fountain and source of the whole apostolate of the Church, the success of the lay apostolate depends on the laity's living union with Christ. For the Lord has said, "He who abides in Me, and I in him, he bears much fruit, for without Me you can do nothing" (Jn 15:5). This life of intimate union with Christ in the Church is nourished by spiritual aids which are common to all the faithful, especially active participation in the sacred liturgy....[99]

The Priestly, Prophetic, and Kingly Ministries of the Laity

The Second Vatican Council enriched our understanding of the lay apostolate and opened the way for lay persons to share more fully in the threefold ministry of Jesus as priest, prophet, and king (or teacher, priest, and pastor).

The laity exercise their "royal priesthood" (1 Pet 2:9) in Christ in a general way by offering their whole lives as a spiritual sacrifice to the Father:

Hence the laity, dedicated as they are to Christ and anointed by the Holy Spirit, are marvelously called and prepared so that even richer fruits of the Spirit may be produced in them. For all their works, prayers, and apostolic undertakings, family and married life, daily work, relaxation of mind and body, if they are accomplished in the Spirit—indeed even the hardships of life if patiently born—all these become spiritual sacrifices acceptable to God through Jesus Christ. In the celebration of the Eucharist these may most fittingly be offered to the Father along with the body of the Lord. And so, worshipping everywhere by their holy actions, the laity consecrate the world itself to God.[100]

The laity may also serve the Lord and the church in specific liturgical ministries, either in permanent ministries of lector and acolyte, or "when the necessity of the Church warrants it and when ministers are lacking," as readers, prayer leaders, to distribute Holy Communion "in accord with prescriptions of [Church] law," or to baptize (see CCC 903).

Regarding the prophetic mission of the laity, lay people are all called to teach the faith and to evangelize. St. Thomas Aquinas taught, "To teach in order to lead others to faith is the task of every preacher and of each believer."[101]

Lay people also fulfill their prophetic mission by evangelization, "that is, the proclamation of Christ by word and the testimony of life." For lay people, "this evangelization ... acquires a specific property and peculiar efficacy because it is accomplished in the ordinary circumstances of the world."[102]

Specific tasks of spreading the faith may include many things. "Lay people who are capable and trained may also collaborate in catechetical formation, in teaching the sacred sciences, and in use of the communications media" (CCC 906; cf. CIC, cann. 229; 774; 776; 780; 823 § 1).

Finally, lay persons at times are called to speak a "prophetic word" to the church by letting their pastors and other Christians know, in a proper and respectful manner, "their opinion on matters which pertain to the good of the Church...."[103]

The laity strive to establish the reign or kingship of Jesus Christ first in their own lives (see CCC 908), and then by implanting the values of the kingdom of God in the world in which they live and work.[104] There are also specific ways that lay persons may share in the governance of the church according to canon law, such as by serving on a parish pastoral council or on a diocesan committee.[105]

The mission of lay people in the church and the world today has been set forth clearly in Pope John Paul II's stirring apostolic letter *Christifideles Laici* ("The Lay Members of Christ's Faithful People," 1988). This teaching expands the vision for the lay apostolate which was set forth at the Second Vatican Council. It speaks of "a new era of group endeavors of the lay faithful,"[106] calls for a renewed effort of evangelization,[107] and a "re-evangelization" of the formerly Christian cultures of the West,[108] and speaks of the laity being equipped for this task by the power of the gospel and a new outpouring of the "charisms," or gifts, of the Holy Spirit in our day.[109] The document also speaks of the central role of the family and of women in the mission of the church today.[110] Truly, this time in the Catholic Church is often rightly referred to as "the age of the laity"!

The Consecrated of Religious Life

Jesus Christ calls all his followers to live in perfect charity, and to embrace his "evangelical counsels" of poverty, chastity, and obedience. However, "it is the *profession* of these counsels, within a permanent state of life recognized by the Church, that characterizes the life consecrated to God" (CCC 915; cf. LG 42-43; PC 1), which is also known as the "religious" state of life.

"Religious," whose lives are marked by the profession of the vows of poverty, chaste celibacy for the sake of God's kingdom, and obedience, include both lay (unordained) religious and religious orders of priests. Over the course of centuries, many types of consecrated life have emerged in the church, which have been compared to a great tree with many branches.[111] Among these varieties of consecrated or religious life are:

- the "eremitic life"—the life of solitude as a hermit (see CCC 920, 921);
- women who live in the ecclesial order of consecrated virginity (see CCC 922-24);
- religious life, distinguished by "its liturgical character, public profession of the evangelical counsels, fraternal life led in common ..." (CCC 925; cf. CIC, cann. 607; 573; UR 15);
- secular institutes, "in which the Christian faithful living in the world strive for the perfection of charity and work for the sanctification of the world especially from within"[112]; and
- societies of apostolic life, "whose members without religious vows pursue the particular apostolic purpose of their society..." (CCC 930; cf. CIC, can. 731 §§ 1 and 2).

The history of the church, and indeed of the whole world, has been profoundly influenced and shaped by those who have consecrated themselves to God through religious vows and community.

Consider the impact of the ascetic or monastic movement in the early church (many following the monastic rules of St. Basil, St. Benedict, or St. Augustine), or the later religious communities founded by St. Francis and St. Clare, St. Dominic, St. Ignatius of Loyola, St. Jeanne François de Chantal, and others, and continuing with new forms of consecrated life and religious communities emerging right up through the twentieth century.

The consecrated life certainly is a great resource and gift to the church. These men and women have responded decisively to Jesus' call to Christian perfection: "If you would be perfect, go sell what you possess and give to the poor, and you will have treasure in heaven; and come, follow me" (Mt 19:21). Their response to this through living the evangelical counsels is a sign to the world and to the church of the reality and primacy of God's kingdom. "The religious state reveals in a unique way that the kingdom of God and its overmastering necessities are superior to all earthly considerations. Finally, to all men it shows wonderfully at work within the Church the surpassing greatness of the force of Christ the King and the boundless power of the Holy Spirit."[113]

Besides including a chapter on religious in the "Dogmatic Constitution on the Church," the Second Vatican Council also devoted an entire conciliar decree to the "Appropriate Renewal of Religious Life" (*Perfectae Caritatis*). This decree has been the charter for the proper changes and renewal of religious life since the Second Vatican Council. Pope John Paul II's apostolic letter on the consecrated life (*Vita Consecrata*, 1996) renews the vision for consecrated life in our time and underscores its lasting value.

Some people claim that the era of religious life has passed. "Modern man," the argument goes, no longer understands or respects people who pledge themselves to observe poverty, celibacy, and obedience. People who follow this path are perceived as foolish, or at least quaint and irrelevant to the modern world.

Those perceptions only highlight the power and the necessity of lives consecrated to God through the evangelical counsels. Yes, in societies which place tremendous value on consumerism and material wealth, free sexual expression, and autonomy from authority (except where absolutely necessary), voluntary vows of poverty, chastity, and obedience appear repulsive and absurd. The fact is that the evangelical counsels directly contradict the most cherished values of the modern, hedonistic, consumer societies. Hence they are more effective and necessary than ever as signs that there is a society with radically different values—the kingdom or reign of God—which is visibly present in the world as the church of Jesus Christ.

"We Believe in the Communion of Saints ..."

These words of the Apostles' Creed highlight an essential aspect of Christian faith. But what is the "communion of saints"? It is the church (see CCC 946). It is not only the church on earth that, as we have seen, is comprised of clergy, laity, and religious, but it is the church that stretches through time and history and embraces all the holy persons (*sancti*) who finally are united in Christ and the Holy Spirit, and who are bound together through sharing communion "in holy things" (see CCC 948).

The "holy things" that unite this communion are seen as early as the first community of Christians in Jerusalem, in which the disciples "devoted themselves to the apostles' teaching and fellowship, to the breaking of bread and the prayers" (Acts 2:42, see CCC 949). The *Catechism* finds in this description a communion in *faith* (CCC 949), in the *sacraments* (CCC 950), in the *charisms,* the special gifts of the Holy Spirit for building up the church (CCC 951), and in *charity* (CCC 953).

One way charity is expressed is in the communion of *money and goods* through generosity, as evidenced in Acts 2:44-45: "All who believed were together and had all things in common; and they sold their possessions and goods and distributed them to all, as any had need" (see CCC 952). Although this charity may be expressed in different ways, it has always been normative for Christians to be generous in sharing their material possessions with each other, and especially with the poor.[114]

The description of the primitive church in the Acts of the Apostles shows us that the church is by nature a communion, a community. From the very beginning of Christianity, it is clear that there were no solitary Christians. Becoming a follower of Jesus through faith and baptism meant becoming part of his body, the church. Life in the church is a shared life in which we receive our beliefs from the elders (the apostles' teaching); we receive spiritual nourishment from the Eucharist (the breaking of the bread) and prayer (both personal and communal); and we give and receive personal and material support (fellowship, or community, and sharing of possessions). These elements of the church's life have been evident and essential from its very beginning.

The Communion of Saints

Reflecting on this, someone might say that the church sounds like a family. It is! The church is God's family (see CCC 959). This is not just a metaphor but a reality. Jesus revealed that God is our Father, and the members of the church are his adopted sons and daughters. We are brothers and sisters of the Son of God, Jesus Christ, who taught, "For whoever does the will of my Father in heaven is my brother, and sister, and mother" (Mt 12:50). This implies that all members of the church, whether living or dead, are related to each other as brothers and sisters in Jesus Christ and as sons and daughters of God, our Father.

Catholic theology calls this concept of the church as God's family "the communion of saints." As God's family, all members of the church, whom the apostle Paul called saints, are in communion or fellowship with one another. "When the Lord comes in glory, and all his angels with him, death will be no more and all things will be subject to him. But at the present time some of his disciples are pilgrims on earth. Others have died and are being purified, while still others are in glory, contemplating 'in full light, God himself triune and one, exactly as he is.'"[115]

It is important to grasp this broader vision of the church. First, it is necessary to view the church as a united family of believers, committed to loving and serving one another because of our common recognition of God as our Father and our brotherhood in Jesus Christ and the Holy Spirit.

The church should not be viewed primarily as just another human organization with functional goals. The ultimate goal of the church is to reflect the life of God by our faith and unity. Jesus said, "By this all men will know that you are my disciples, if you have love for one another'" (Jn 13:35).

Second, the membership of the church is not limited to those who are presently alive on earth. Jesus said, "Now he is not God of the dead, but of the living; for all live to him" (Lk 20:38). The Book of Revelation presents some marvelous images of the saints and martyrs who have passed from this life gathered around God's throne, praising him forever (see Rev 14:1-5; 19:1-8). Christians have believed since the time of the early church that it is possible for us here on earth to have fellowship or communion with these glorified saints through our prayer. In the same way that we ask fellow Christians on earth to pray for us and for our needs, we can ask the saints in heaven to pray and intercede for us before the throne of God.

We are united to these saints in heaven as brothers and sisters in Jesus Christ in just as real a way as we are united to our fellow "saints" on earth. We do not worship the saints in heaven or pray to them as we pray to God, since worship (Latin, *latria*), or adoration, is due to God alone. But we may honor and venerate these saints as examples of Christian virtue; imitate their faith, love, and other qualities; and ask them to pray for us. The Bible nowhere prohibits such prayer, which has been practiced by Christians for centuries (see the writings of Saint Jerome and Saint Augustine).

The intercession of the saints and Mary on our behalf does not detract from the unique mediation of Jesus. All Christian prayer, whether of the saints, of Mary, or our own, is directed to the Father through Jesus Christ, who is the "one mediator between God and men" (1 Tim 2:5).[116]

Purgatory and Prayer for the Dead

There are some members of the church who have died and yet have not entered the glory of God's presence because of some unrepented sin or the effects of sin still remaining at the time of their death. Catholics have believed since the time of the early church that God, in his mercy, purifies these people and purges them of this sin and its effects so that they may worthily enter the presence of the all-holy God, before whom "nothing unclean shall enter" (Rev 21:27). This final act of God, freeing his people from any remaining bondage of sin, is called purgatory.[117]

Just as the Lord purified the unclean lips of the prophet Isaiah with a burning coal (see Isa 6:5-7), so all those who have been basically faithful to God's call and grace in this life will be cleansed of their sin in purgatory. Many Catholics hold that the section of Paul's First Letter to the Corinthians (see 1 Cor 3:11-15) that refers to the testing of each person's work by fire is a reference to purgatory: "If any man's work is burned up, he will suffer loss, though he himself will be saved, but only as through fire" (1 Cor 3:15). Since this purgation by fire is painful, just as it is often painful when God breaks us from patterns of sin in this life, Christians have had a long tradition of praying for those who have died. We ask God's mercy on them, praying that any purification necessary for them to enter the full glory of heaven will soon be completed. Many leaders of the early church encouraged Christians to pray for the dead for this reason, and the Second Vatican Council taught:

> Very much aware of the bonds linking the whole Mystical Body of Jesus Christ, the pilgrim church from the very first ages of the Christian religion has cultivated with great piety the memory of the dead. Because it is "a holy and wholesome thought to pray for the dead that they may be loosed from sin" (2 Macc 12:46), she has also offered prayers for them.[118]

So it appears that the church, the communion of saints, is truly God's family, with all the members having a mutual love and care for each other. Like an iceberg, only the tip of the church, those living in the church now on earth, is visible to us without the eyes of faith. With faith, we recognize that the church includes also those who now stand before God's throne in glory and all who are awaiting full entry into God's presence as he cleanses them of sin and its effects.

The concept of the communion of saints, the church as God's family, should be a great encouragement to us. We are not alone, but part of a vast multitude of believers that spans the ages. As the Letter to the Hebrews exhorts us:

> Therefore, since we are surrounded by so great a cloud of witnesses, let us also lay aside every weight, and sin which clings so closely, and let us run with perseverance the race that is set before us, looking to Jesus the pioneer and perfecter of our faith, who for the joy that was set before him endured the cross, despising the shame, and is seated at the right hand of the throne of God.
>
> HEBREWS 12:1-2

Mary as Mother and Model of the Church

As we speak of the church as a family, we should call to mind that God has given this family a mother. From the cross, Jesus told John, "Behold, your mother," as he had told Mary, "Woman, behold your son" (Jn 19:26-27). The early Christians understood this event as a powerful symbol: Jesus gave Mary to be the mother of all his disciples. Mary, in this sense, is "the Mother of the Church."[119]

Although chapter eleven of this catechism is devoted to Mary and her role in God's plan, it is important to include here a brief discussion of Mary's relationship to the Church. The bishops at the Second Vatican Council reserved their final chapter of "The Dogmatic Constitution on the Church" (*Lumen Gentium*) to a discussion of Mary. Why? In addition to being the mother of the Church, Mary summarizes in her person all that the church is and all that she aspires to be.

It is because Mary was such an exemplary follower of Jesus that she is seen by Catholics as a model or type of the church. However, Mary is also a member of the church, redeemed by the grace of Jesus Christ, and called to imitate and follow him. Mary models or typifies all the virtues that should characterize the church. She was totally submitted to the will of God, as is seen in her response to Gabriel's announcement that she was to be the mother of God: "Behold, I am the handmaid of the Lord; let it be done to me according to your word" (Lk 1:38). She realized that any goodness or glory that she had came from God, as her *Magnificat* in Luke 1:46-55 illustrates. She acted in faith at all times, which led to Jesus' first miracle in John's Gospel, at the wedding feast at Cana (see Jn 2:1-11). She served Jesus in humility even when she did not fully understand what his mission was (see Lk 2:41-50). She followed him humbly throughout his public ministry, even up to his death on the cross, where she remained with him when most of his disciples had fled. Finally, Mary was among the first disciples to receive the Holy Spirit, as she prayed with the disciples in the Upper Room at Pentecost, receiving once again the same Spirit that had overshadowed her to conceive Jesus in her womb (see Acts 1:14; Mt 1:18). In her unmatched purity of heart and steadfast following of Jesus, Mary is a model of what the church is meant to be and to do. Mary is the woman of faith whom God has given to the church as its mother and as a model for its life.

Now that Mary has been assumed into heaven and has been united forever with her Son, her motherhood of the church assumes even greater meaning and power. "Taken up to heaven she did not lay aside this saving office but by her manifold intercession continues to bring us the gifts of eternal salvation.... Therefore the Blessed Virgin is invoked in the Church under the titles of Advocate, Helper, Benefactress, and Mediatrix."[120]

In heaven, Mary also stands as a sign of what the church hopes to become at the end of her journey on earth—she is the eschatological icon or image of the church. "The Mother of Jesus, in the glory which she possesses in body and soul in heaven, is the image and beginning of the Church as it is to be perfected in the world to come. Likewise she shines forth on earth, until the day of the Lord shall come, a sign of certain hope and comfort to the pilgrim People of God."[121]

In chapter eleven we will discuss more fully devotion to Mary, and her role in God's plan of salvation. Since the church is primarily a people set apart to serve and to worship God, in the next chapter we will explore the church's life of prayer.

CHAPTER 6

Christian Prayer and the Liturgy:
Part 1: The Nature and Types of Prayer

I n the last chapter we spoke of the nature of the church, whose love for God is expressed in obedience and service, as well as worship and adoration. In this chapter we will reflect upon the worship and adoration of God by his people, the church.

The church is, above all, a worshiping community, a community that exists to adore, praise, and glorify God. This is the only "work" of the church that will never end. "Prayer" is the name Christians give to the worship of God that embraces every dimension or way of relating to him. Prayer is the essence of "a vital and personal relationship with the living and true God" (CCC 2558).

Prayer as God's Gift

"*Humility* is the foundation of prayer" (CCC 2559) because we can't do it on our own: "we do not know how to pray as we ought" (Rom 8:26, NAB). Fortunately, God comes to aid us in our weakness, coming to us in the person of the Holy Spirit, who enables us to pray, "with sighs too deep for words" (Rom 8:26). Hence, the Holy Spirit "is the interior Master of Christian prayer." For while it is true that there are as many ways to pray as there are people who pray, "it is the same Spirit acting in all and with all" (CCC 2672).

Prayer is a gift of God, a work of the Holy Spirit in us. As Pope John Paul II testifies in his book, *Crossing the Threshold of Hope:* "How does the Pope pray? You would have to ask the Holy Spirit! The Pope prays as the Holy Spirit permits him to pray."[1]

Prayer is a gift because it is God who takes the initiative and invites us to pray—invites us into an intimate personal relationship with himself. God approaches us, as Jesus did the Samaritan woman at the well (see Jn 4). The "thirst" of God for our salvation meets the unspoken and hidden "thirst" of the woman (and of each of us) for God (see CCC 2560).

Prayer From the Heart

Prayer is not only an action of God, the Holy Spirit praying within us. It is also a human act, flowing from the "heart," that hidden center in each person known only to the Spirit of God (see CCC 2563).

The Bible speaks of the "heart" more than a thousand times. "According to Scripture, it is the *heart* that prays. If our heart is far from God, the words of prayer are in vain" (CCC 2562).

Prayer Is Communion With God

Prayer brings us into the unity of communion with God. What is "communion"? It is the living, personal relationship that God's children have with their all-good Father, and with the Son and the Holy Spirit. It is fostered and deepened by the habit of coming into the presence of God and of speaking and listening to him (see CCC 2565).

Prayer in the Old Testament

"Prayer is bound up with human history, for it is the relationship with God in historical events." (CCC 2568)

We tend to emphasize man's search for God, but in reality it is God who always takes the initiative (see CCC 2567). The history of God's revelation of himself to the human race, especially through his chosen people, is a "covenant drama" of God's call and the human response of prayer.

The *Catechism of the Catholic Church* traces the development of prayer in history beginning with the Book of Genesis (Cain and Abel, Noah, Abraham, and Jacob), and continuing with focus on the prayers of Moses, David, and Elijah.

According to the *Catechism*, the Psalms form the core of the official liturgical daily prayer of the church—the "Liturgy of the Hours," or the "Divine Office." The Psalms are also called "the Praises," and the recurrent response of *Hallelu-Yah!* ("Alleluia"), "Praise the Lord!" resounds throughout their pages (see CCC 2589). The Psalms are "the masterwork of prayer in the Old Testament," and represent the prayer of both the individual and of the community (see CCC 2596).

Prayer and the Gospels

In the Gospels, Jesus showed us how to pray in an intimate, personal way—as the beloved children of our Father in heaven (CCC 2599). While he was on earth, Jesus prayed constantly and stayed in constant communion with the Father.

The New Testament, especially the Gospel of St. Luke, recounts specific aspects of Jesus' prayer: how he prayed before decisive moments of his ministry (CCC 2600); in solitude for the needs of all men (CCC 2601); and with spontaneous thanksgiving (e.g. Lk 10:21-22), on some occasions thanking his Father even *before* his prayer was answered.

Jesus' prayer was particularly poignant when it expressed the agony of suffering, including his own suffering during his passion, and his mental anguish over those who had rejected God and his plan (CCC 2605). These prayers offered by the Son of God, "with loud cries and tears," not only "perfected" the Son in his humanity, but "became the source of eternal salvation to all who obey him" (Heb 5:7-9; cf. CCC 2606). By his own example, and through both direct instruction and parables, Jesus taught his followers to pray—and, through them, he continues to teach us (CCC 2607).

Following the example of Jesus and the apostles, we find that a proper attitude and conversion of our heart is essential to prayer. We need to be reconciled with one another (see Mt 5:23-24), to love and pray for our enemies and persecutors (see Mt 5:44-45), and to pray in secret and in humility, not for "show" (see Mt 6:5-8). We are to pray with watchfulness and persistence, and especially to pray in *faith* with the boldness and confidence of God's beloved children, always disposed in our hearts to accept and to do the Father's will (CCC 2608-13).

When we pray to the Father in Jesus' name (see Jn 14:13), we discover the power of that name. As so many stories in the Gospels and Acts of the Apostles reveal, Jesus himself hears and answers those who cry out to him in faith (CCC 2616).

Mary, the mother of Jesus, also is a Gospel model of Christian prayer. In chapter eleven we will look at the prayer of Mary as a model and inspiration for the prayer of the church.

Forms of Prayer in the Spirit

"The Holy Spirit is the living water ... in the heart that prays." (CCC 2652)

With the sending of the Holy Spirit, the church was fully formed, instructed, and empowered to pray as Jesus taught us (CCC 2623). Henceforth, the Holy Spirit would keep "the memory of Christ alive in his Church at prayer," and inspire new formulations of prayer, "developed in the great liturgical and spiritual traditions" (CCC 2625).

The *Catechism* describes certain forms of prayer that "remain normative for Christian prayer":

1. *Blessing and Adoration*—Through the Holy Spirit, we "bless God" for having blessed us. We adore God, exalting in the greatness of the Lord who made us (CCC 2626-28).

2. *Petition*—Acknowledging and asking forgiveness for our sins, we humbly turn to God, praying first for his kingdom to come, and then for our own needs (CCC 2629-33).

3. *Intercession*—We join with and participate in the intercession of Jesus and the Holy Spirit for the needs of others, calling on the mercy of God (CCC 2634-36).

4. *Thanksgiving*—We thank God for his many blessings, past and present, both to us personally and to all of God's people (CCC 2637, 2638).

5. *Praise*—In praise, God's people give him glory not because of what he has done or will do, "but simply because HE IS.... Praise embraces the other forms of prayer and carries them toward him who is its source and goal: the 'one God,

the Father, from whom are all things and for whom we exist'" (1 Cor 8:6; CCC 2639). The Eucharist, above all, is *the* "sacrifice of praise" (CCC 2643).

These elements are essential for all Christian prayer, as acknowledging in prayer the three Persons of the one God. We pray to God our Father, as Jesus did and has taught us to do. We pray to God the Son in the name he has taken for eternity: Jesus. We pray to the Holy Spirit, who "with the Father and the Son ... is worshipped and glorified" (Nicene Creed). In the liturgy of the church our prayer is often addressed to the Father, through the Son, and in the Holy Spirit.

Christians sometimes have difficulty knowing how to address and pray to the Holy Spirit, though he is a *Person* of God, just as the Father and the Son are. We can ask the Father and the Son to give us the Holy Spirit (see Lk 11:13), but we may also address him directly: "Come, Holy Spirit" (see CCC 2671). The Holy Spirit is "the interior Master of Christian prayer ... the artisan of the living tradition of prayer" (CCC 2672), who prays within us with "sighs too deep for words" (Rom 8:26).

The Holy Spirit leads us to the great teacher of prayer, *Jesus Christ,* and to the "wellsprings," where Christ awaits us to enable us to drink of the Holy Spirit (see CCC 2652). These "wellsprings" that nourish Christian prayer are the Word of God (see CCC 2653, 2654), the liturgy of the church (CCC 2655), and the theological virtues of faith, hope, and love.

As Christians, we enter prayer through faith and persevere in prayer through hope. But the source of prayer is love: God's love, which has been poured into our hearts through the Holy Spirit (see Rom 5:5; CCC 2656-58).

Christians have another rich prayer resource in the lives and writings of the saints, who teach us to pray and guide us in prayer through the spiritualities they have developed. "In their rich diversity ... [these spiritualities] are refractions of the one pure light of the Holy Spirit" (CCC 2684). One thinks of the contemplative prayer of the monastic life, the active meditation using the imagination developed by St. Ignatius of Loyola, the mystical spirituality of St. Teresa of Avila and St. John of the Cross, and the practical spiritualities for lay people exemplified by Sts. Philip Neri, Francis de Sales, and Thérèse of Lisieux.

With these spiritual riches at our disposal, all Christians must learn to pray. This process begins in childhood, within the context of family.

Education in Prayer

"The *Christian family* is the first place of education in prayer" (CCC 2685). It is in the family, the "domestic sanctuary of the church,"[2] that children learn to pray and to persevere in prayer. "For young children in particular, daily family prayer is the first witness of the Church's living memory as awakened patiently by the Holy Spirit" (CCC 2685).

Catholics are also instructed and guided in prayer by sources outside the family: through ordained ministers of the church (CCC 2686) and religious (CCC 2687), through catechesis (CCC 2688), in prayer groups ("one of the driving forces of renewal of prayer in the Church," CCC 2689), and by spiritual directors with "gifts of wisdom, faith and discernment" (CCC 2690).

The Ways to Pray

For our relationship with God to deepen or grow, we must be faithful to prayer, and regular in it. Just as married persons should normally speak with their spouses every day, hopefully in a significant and mutual way, so Christians should set aside a time every day to speak with God. After all, he is the one we are called to know, love, and serve with our whole heart, mind, soul, and strength (see Deut 6:5). If we want to grow closer to God, we need to spend at least a few minutes every day speaking to him in prayer, and listening to him speak to us through the Bible as well as other Christian literature.

How are we to pray to God? According to the *Catechism*, "Christian Tradition has retained three major expressions of prayer: vocal, meditative and contemplative. They have one basic trait in common: composure of heart" (CCC 2699).

Vocal prayers are prayers said aloud, with our heart "engaged." This is a most human and natural way to pray, either alone or with others. Jesus taught us to pray the "Our Father" (see Mt 6:9-13; Lk 11:2-4). Scripture records that Jesus joined in the liturgical prayers of the synagogue, but also that he prayed aloud in his own personal prayer: "from exultant blessing of the Father to the agony of Gethsemani [see Mt 11:25-26; Mk 14:36]" (CCC 2701).

It is important that each Christian grow in a deeper understanding of prayer and of the ways to pray. St. Paul encouraged us to "pray at all times" (Eph 6:18; 1 Thess 5:17), and, indeed, "his Spirit is offered us at all times, in the events of *each day*, to make prayer spring up from us" (CCC 2659).

However, "we cannot pray 'at all times' if we do not pray at specific times, consciously willing it" (CCC 2697). Christians must set aside time each day for "personal prayer"—a time to be alone to communicate with God.

Prayer is two-way communication: we speak with God, and he speaks to us. We speak to God in the quiet of our hearts: spontaneously and through prayers we learn or read. We may also speak to God aloud in vocal prayer. In meditation and contemplation, however, our focus becomes listening to God rather than speaking to him.

Meditation is active reflection in which the mind seeks to understand the truth of God and how to respond in faith to what the Lord is asking (see CCC 2705). A few minutes of quiet, perhaps reflecting on God's Word in a Scripture reading or just being quiet in his presence, gives God an opportunity to speak to us.

God speaks to us in a variety of ways: through the thoughts and gentle urgings that the Holy Spirit stirs up in our minds and hearts, through his Word in Scripture, and through the writings of saints or of holy men and women. Meditation is often aided by reflection on books (such as the Bible, liturgical texts, or spiritual writings); holy icons and art; and the "books" of creation, history, and of our own lives and times.

Reading and reflecting on these sources may be done along with the daily prayer time, or at a different time during the day. In the process of pondering these things, we discern what God is teaching us through them and what he wants us to do. We meditate on the life of Christ, using sacred Scripture, the rosary, or spiritual reading, and aspire above all "to the knowledge and love of the Lord Jesus, to union with him" (CCC 2708).

Contemplative prayer, according to St. Teresa of Avila, is "a close sharing between friends; it means taking time frequently to be alone with him who we know loves us."[3] In this prayer, our gaze is fixed on Jesus: "I look at him and he looks at me" (CCC 2715). It is a gift, a grace in which we approach God with a recollected attentiveness to him and to his Word, watching and waiting upon him in silent love.

When two persons come to know each other fairly well, sometimes they can communicate their love without words or activities. Just being together is enough. Similarly, as we grow closer to the Lord through prayer, the nature of our communication with him deepens. Often God begins to draw a person to simply be present to God, without speaking or actively meditating on him, allowing God to speak and act as he wills.

The Catholic mystical tradition, which includes such great saints as Teresa of Avila and John of the Cross, teaches about this gift of prayer and describes different types or stages of contemplative prayer. In this type of prayer many people experience God as fully as is possible in this life. This may involve unity with Christ in his cross and suffering through the experience of "dark nights," as described by St. John of the Cross, or it may take the form of the unspeakable joy and peace of knowing God's presence, like a "mystical marriage" with Christ.

The Catholic Church has always cautioned against seeking spiritual experiences for their own sake. The primary focus of Christian prayer is not what we can get out of it or what stage of perfection we can attain. True prayer is a selfless seeking to love, worship, and serve God simply because he is worthy of all love, praise, and adoration. The best measure of the success of personal prayer is not how we feel while we pray or what consolations we receive, but how faithful we are to prayer, regardless of how we feel. The true test of prayer is how fully we seek to worship God and give over our lives entirely to him and his will, whatever his will may be for us.

The Battle of Prayer

"Resist the devil, and he will flee from you. Draw near to God, and he will draw near to you."

JAMES 4:7-8, NAB

God wants each Christian to draw near to him through prayer. Jesus said, "Behold, I stand at the door and knock. If anyone hears my voice and opens the door, [then] I will enter his house and dine with him, and he with me" (Rev 3:20, NAB).

As St. James admonishes us to "resist the devil," Christians are reminded that prayer is a battle. First, it is a battle against our own "flesh"—the laziness (sloth), busy-ness, or distractions that keep us from praying. It is a battle against the lies of the "world," which generally views prayer as an unproductive waste of time (except, perhaps, for the therapeutic value of silence). Both the modern world and the devil also call into question the very existence of God or the efficacy of prayer.

In reality, prayer is one of the most important investments in time that we can make. Yet, it can also be a difficult discipline to acquire because we must battle against numerous distractions, some from outside ourselves, some from within. Prayer is a battle when we confront failure or disappointment, or when we seem to be losing faith in God or falling into *acedia,* "a form of depression due to lax ascetical practice, decreasing vigilance, carelessness of heart" (CCC 2733).

Still other Christians succumb to presumption, forgetting the Lord's words that "Without me you can do *nothing*" (Jn 15:5, NAB). However, "the humble are not to be surprised by their distress; it leads them to trust more, to hold fast in constancy" (CCC 2733).

Understanding the nature of prayer through God's revelation can help us to overcome some of these obstacles. Sometimes we lack faith, or ask with a "divided heart," or ask for things to satisfy our own passions or desires (see Jas 4:3-4). If anyone wonders why we pray at all if God already knows our needs, they fail to understand that God awaits our petition because the dignity of the children of God lies in their *freedom* (see CCC 2736). We must freely choose to pray and then trust God as his beloved sons and daughters that he will answer our prayers as he knows is best. However, we must *persevere* in prayer, like the importunate widow (see Lk 18:1-8) and the friend in need (see Lk 11:5-8), and pray without ceasing (see Eph 6:18). "This tireless fervor can only come from love. Against our dullness and laziness, the battle of prayer is that of humble, trusting, and persevering *love*" (CCC 2742).

The *Catechism* concludes its discussion of "the battle of prayer" with three essential "facts of faith" about prayer:

1. It is always possible to pray, regardless of where you are or what you are doing (see CCC 2743);

2. Prayer is a vital necessity: "... If we do not allow the Spirit to lead us we fall back into the slavery of sin (cf. Gal 5:16-25)." St. Alphonsus Liguori said: "Those who pray are certainly saved, those who do not pray are certainly damned" (see CCC 2744);

3. And, the bottom line: "Prayer and *Christian life* are *inseparable*" (CCC 2745).

Part 2: Communal and Liturgical Prayer

God relates to us and saves us not as isolated individuals, but as members of his people.[4] For this reason, praying with other Christians and with the church in communal prayer is as necessary for spiritual health and growth as having a personal prayer time. Both types of prayer are important.

Personal prayer is a Christian's lifeline to God, but it is also a preparation for prayer with the community of God's people, the church. If we do not have a personal relationship with God and a regular individual time of prayer, we will probably find that prayer with other Christians has little impact on our lives. Personal prayer is the foundation of meaningful communal prayer, while communal prayer can and does enrich personal prayer.

As we cultivate a daily time of personal prayer, we are drawn more fully into our identity and life as God's people. God has created human beings to be social, and the most important society to which he calls all men to belong is the church of Jesus Christ. As the Second Vatican Council stated:

> All men are called to belong to the new People of God. It was for this reason that God sent His Son, whom He appointed heir of all things, (cf. Heb 1:2), that He might be Teacher, King and Priest of all, the Head of the new and universal people of the sons of God.[5]

And what is this People of God created to do? Our highest calling is to worship God. After all, this is the eternal, eschatological destiny of the church—to be united to God forever in praise and worship.[6] That eternal destiny begins even now, as Jesus taught us to pray to the Father: "Thy will be done, on earth as it is in heaven" (Mt 6:10).

In communal prayer, we come together as God's people to fulfill our most exalted task—to worship and praise our Creator. All of our individual works, activities, intentions, and needs are gathered together and brought to God when his people join to worship as a united body.

The Lord's Prayer

There is perhaps no greater example of communal prayer than the model that Jesus gave to his apostles, the Lord's Prayer (or the "Our Father"), in which Jesus taught them to address God as "Our Father" (see CCC 2768). Jesus' priestly prayer at the Last Supper is a summary of the Lord's Prayer in glorifying the Father's name, seeking his kingdom, and dedicating himself to the accomplishment of his will and of our deliverance from evil (see CCC 2750).

Tertullian called the "Lord's Prayer" (or the "Our Father") "the summary of the whole gospel"[7]. St. Augustine claimed that no biblical prayer was missing from the Lord's Prayer (see CCC 2763). The earliest Christian communities prayed the Lord's Prayer three times a day.[8] The Lord's Prayer is an essential part of Catholic teaching; the *Catechism* comments upon each petition of this prayer, and summarizes its importance as follows:

> In the Our Father, the object of the first three petitions is the glory of the Father: the sanctification of his name, the coming of the kingdom, and the fulfillment of his will. The four others present our wants to him: they ask that our lives be nourished, healed of sin, and made victorious in the struggle of good over evil. (CCC 2857)

According to the apostolic tradition, the Lord's Prayer is an essential part of the liturgy. It is prayed in the Mass, present in all the major hours of the Divine Office and in the sacraments of Christian initiation (see CCC 2768, 2776).

What Is Liturgy?

Liturgy is the official communal prayer of the whole church. The word "liturgy" literally means the "work" or "service" of the people, reminding us that the primary work or service of God's people is to worship together as a body, the body of Christ. The "Constitution on the Sacred Liturgy" taught that:

> The liturgy is the summit toward which the activity of the Church is directed; at the same time it is the fountain from which all her power flows. For the

goal of apostolic works is that all who are made sons of God by faith and baptism should come together to praise God in the midst of His Church, to take part in her sacrifice, and to eat the Lord's supper.[9]

Liturgical worship, although carried out by man, is first a work of God. It is God *blessing* his people. The *Catechism* reminds us that, "the whole of God's work is a *blessing* ... the plan of salvation [is] one vast divine blessing ... [and] ... in the Church's liturgy the divine blessing is fully revealed and communicated" (CCC 1079, 1082).

How is this so? The liturgy is an expression of *sacramental* dimension (or "economy") of the church. When the Word of God took on our humanity, a new era in God's dealings with humanity began. God chose to reveal himself and to communicate his blessing and grace through perceptible signs accessible to our human nature (see CCC 1084). Certain of these signs that Jesus blessed or instituted are recognized by the church as "sacraments." So the liturgy, the formal prayer of the church, centers on the celebration of these sacraments.

In the church's liturgy, Jesus principally signifies and makes present his own passion, death, and resurrection—the Paschal mystery. This was the central event of Christ's life, and it is unlike any other event in history:

All other historical events happen once, and then they pass away, swallowed up in the past. The Paschal mystery of Christ, by contrast, cannot remain only in the past, because by his death he destroyed death, and all that Christ is—all that he did and suffered for all men—participates in the divine eternity, and so transcends all times while being made present in them all. The event of the Cross and Resurrection *abides* and draws everything toward life. (CCC 1085)

The Catholic Mass: A Perfect Prayer

The central liturgical celebration of the church is the Mass. The "once-for-all" sacrifice of Jesus Christ on Calvary and his glorious resurrection from the dead are not only commemorated in the Mass, but are actually *made present* in sacramental form—in the Holy Eucharist, as well as in the person of the *priest*, who acts in Jesus' name and by his authority.

Christ is also present in his Word, "since it is he himself who speaks when the holy Scriptures are read," in *other sacraments* that are celebrated, and in the *song and prayer* of the people of God, for he promised "where two or three are gathered together in my name, there am I in the midst of them" (Mt 18:20).[10]

Thus, the liturgy is a work of Jesus Christ, "in which God is perfectly glorified and men are sanctified."[11] In the liturgy God "lifts us up" and gives us a foretaste of the heavenly liturgy which is eternally celebrated by the angels and saints,[12] where signs are no longer needed and "celebration is wholly communion and feast" (CCC 1136). However, we also know that the liturgy "is an 'action' of the *whole Christ*" (CCC 1136), which means it is an action of *all* the members of the church, the body of Christ, united with Jesus, their head. Through baptism, Christians are consecrated to be "a spiritual house" and "a holy priesthood" (1 Pet 2:4-5), and so they all participate in offering the liturgy to God. As the Second Vatican Council exhorts us:

> Mother Church earnestly desires that all the faithful should be led to that full, conscious, and active participation in liturgical celebrations which is demanded by the very nature of the liturgy, and to which the Christian people, "a chosen race, a royal priesthood, a holy nation, a redeemed people," have a right and an obligation by reason of their Baptism.[13]

Called to Serve

The whole *community* of the church, united with its head, celebrates the liturgy (see CCC 1140). Yet, St. Paul reminds us that "all the parts do not have the same function" (Rom 12:4, NAB).

Only those who have been consecrated for this ministry by the sacrament of Holy Orders may *preside* over the celebration of the sacraments (CCC 1142). Other particular ministries, such as servers, readers, commentators, extraordinary Eucharistic ministers, and members of the choir, may be exercised as determined by the bishops, careful to "carry out *all* and *only* those parts which pertain to his office...."[14] In all this, the church seeks to have each member of the congregation join together to worship God attentively, with reverence, and in the "unity of the Spirit" who acts in all (see CCC 1144).

The History of the Mass

As we have seen, the Mass is the center of Catholic liturgical prayer, because it recalls and perpetuates the greatest event of history and of Christian faith: the Paschal mystery—the passion, death, resurrection, and ascension of our Lord and Savior Jesus Christ. The Mass perpetuates or re-presents—makes present again in the midst of God's people—the one eternal sacrifice of Jesus Christ, who gave up his human life on the cross of Calvary so that all might be saved from sin and eternal death.

This sacrifice of Christ is foreshadowed in many places in the Old Testament, especially in the sacrifice of the spotless lamb at the Israelite's exodus from Egypt. The blood of that lamb, sprinkled on the doorposts of the Hebrew people, signaled the angel of death to "pass over" their houses, as the firstborn of every Egyptian household was killed in the final plague (see Ex 12:29-30). This final plague convinced Pharaoh to allow the Israelites to "pass over" from slavery in Egypt to freedom.

The New Testament, especially the Letter to the Hebrews, explains how the Christian people are saved from destruction and eternal death by the blood of the spotless Lamb of God, Jesus Christ (see Heb 9:11-15, 23-26). Jesus enables us by his sacrifice on Calvary to "pass over" from the slavery of sin and Satan into the freedom of the sons and daughters of God. The "Christian Passover," or Paschal mystery—the death, resurrection, and ascension of Jesus—is made present to us in the sacrament every time Catholics celebrate the Mass.

Even though the form of the Mass has developed over the course of centuries, it has always been the center of communal Christian prayer. The Acts of the Apostles notes that those who were converted at Pentecost, "devoted themselves ... to the breaking of bread and the prayers" (Acts 2:42). The apostle Paul admonished the church in Corinth, instructing them to purify the way they were conducting the Lord's Supper (see 1 Cor 11:17-35), which he recognizes as a central part of their community life.

The Structure of the Mass

Some of the earliest Christian writings, such as the *Didache*, or the "Teaching of the Twelve Apostles," chapters 9-10 (late first and early second century), and the *First Apology* of Justin Martyr, chapters 65-67 (about A.D. 155), describe the primitive form of the Mass and its prayers in a way that bears striking resemblance to the basic format of the Mass today. In fact, the main elements of St. Justin's description of the Mass are almost identical to the form Catholics now employ.

This should not surprise us; the Catholic Church has sought to preserve in the Mass the basic form of the communal worship of primitive Christianity, adding or adapting prayers only after careful discernment.

In its structure, the Mass has always included two basic parts: readings from the sacred Scriptures (the Liturgy of the Word), and the breaking of the bread and the offering and sharing of the cup of the Lord (the Liturgy of the Eucharist). It is through both God's Word proclaimed and Jesus Christ, the Bread of Life, received in the sacrament of the Eucharist, that God's people are nourished spiritually. As Vatican II put it: "The Church has always venerated the divine Scriptures as she venerated the Body of the Lord, in so far as she never ceases, particularly in the sacred liturgy, to partake of the bread of life and to offer it to the faithful from the one table of the Word of God and the Body of Christ."[15]

The Liturgy of the Word begins with a time of repentance from sin and of preparation to hear God's Word and to receive him in the Eucharist. The penitential rite is followed by a brief time of worship, including on Sundays or special feast days the "Gloria," a hymn of glory to God.

The Word of God is then proclaimed. First is a reading from the Old or New Testament (other than the Gospels), or both, followed by responsorial verses (usually from one of the psalms), and then a reading from one of the four Gospels. These readings are selected by the Catholic Church as part of a cycle, so that readings from the whole Bible will be proclaimed on Sundays over a three-year period, and on weekdays over a two-year period. A sermon or homily on the readings is then given. The Second Vatican Council taught:

The sermon ... should draw its content mainly from scriptural and liturgical sources. Its character should be that of a proclamation of God's wonderful works in the history of salvation, that is, the mystery of Christ, which is ever made present and active within us, especially in the celebration of the liturgy.[16]

In the early church, catechumens (those preparing for entry into the church) withdrew from Mass at this point of the service. They had not yet been initiated through baptism into the great mystery of faith that is the heart of the second part of the Mass, the Eucharist. On Sundays and special feast days we profess the Nicene Creed, a profession of our faith first written by the Catholic Church at the Council of Nicea in A.D. 325 and completed at the First Council of Constantinople in A.D. 381. It is important to reaffirm and profess each week the common faith that is the foundation of Christianity (see Eph 4:5-6, 13). The Prayer of the Faithful, following the homily or Nicene Creed, presents to God the prayers and petitions of the gathered community, so that they may be offered to God the Father in union with Jesus Christ, who constantly intercedes for us to the Father (see Heb 7:25).

In the Offertory of the Mass, the priest offers to God the prayers of the community, and the bread and wine which we pray will become the Body and Blood of Christ. It is important to realize that at this point all the participants also offer themselves to God, both as a community and as individuals. Catholics gathered at Mass offer to God all that they are and all that they have done in the past day or week, humbly asking him to accept and purify this offering, and to unite it with the eternal offering of Jesus himself.

From this point on, the Mass moves to the great Eucharistic Prayer during which the solemn Consecration of the bread and wine takes place. First, the celebrant prays that the Holy Spirit will make this offering of bread and wine acceptable, an offering "in spirit and truth" (Jn 4:23, 24). This is called the *epiclesis,* or invocation of the Holy Spirit.

Following this are the words of consecration, the words of Jesus himself, "This is my body ... this is my blood ..."(Mt 26:26, 28, NAB) and "Do this in remembrance of me ..."(Lk 22:19). Catholics believe that because the priest speaks *in persona Christi* (in the person of Christ), at this point the bread and wine truly become the Body and Blood of Jesus Christ. At this climactic moment of the Mass the whole congregation reflects on the mystery of God's coming among us, and worships him in our midst.

After the Consecration, the saving death and resurrection of Christ is commemorated explicitly, and another *epiclesis* is offered, this time calling down the Holy Spirit on the congregation, that, through receiving the Body of the Lord, it might become more fully the body of Christ. Then prayers are offered for the whole church, the pope and bishops, and all the church's members, living and deceased. At this time we express our hope that we will also one day share the joy of eternal life united with God and his angels and saints. This time of worship and petition ends with another elevation of the host, Christ's Body and the chalice of his Blood, at which time the priest declares, "Through him, with him, and in him, in the unity of the Holy Spirit, all honor and glory are yours almighty Father, forever and ever," and all the people respond with the great "Amen!"

In immediate preparation for receiving the Body and Blood of Jesus Christ, the congregation prays the Lord's Prayer together and usually at this point greet one another with a sign or kiss of peace, to express unity, peace, and reconciliation with each other (see Mt 5:23-24) and with the Lord. All Catholics who are not living in a state of serious unrepented sin then are encouraged to approach the altar to receive the Lord's Body and Blood in Holy Communion. What a tremendous, precious time when Jesus Christ approaches us personally, and individually enters each person's heart through the sacramental reality of his own Body and Blood! At least a few moments are devoted to prayer and reflection after Communion, a time in which the Lord lives within us in the most personal, intimate way that is possible in this life.

The Mass draws to a conclusion with the final prayers, dismissal, and sometimes a closing hymn. The word *Mass* originates in the Latin words of dismissal, *Ite missa est.* "Go, the Mass is ended" literally means, "Go, you are dismissed," or, better, "Go, you are sent forth"—sent forth into the world to live out what has been celebrated and received in the liturgy.

Liturgical Renewal and Vatican II

The "Constitution on the Sacred Liturgy" of the Second Vatican Council called for the restoration of the Catholic liturgy, distinguishing between the "unchangeable elements divinely instituted, and elements subject to change."[17] The goal of this restoration was to be that "both texts and rites be drawn up so that they express more clearly the holy things which they signify. Christian people, as far as possible, should be able to understand them with ease and to take part in them fully, actively, and as befits a community."[18]

A better translation of the phrase "active participation," which is so often found in the liturgy document, is "actual" or "real" participation. The emphasis is not primarily on how much we sing or respond, but on the depth and quality of our prayer and participation in the liturgy.

The renewal of the liturgy was one of the primary tasks and most visible fruit of the Second Vatican Council. In the "Constitution on the Sacred Liturgy" (*Sacrosanctum Concilium*) the Council fathers stated the key principle for this renewal:

> In the restoration and promotion of the sacred liturgy the full and active participation by all the people is the aim to be considered before all else; for it is the primary and indispensable source from which the faithful are to derive the true Christian spirit.[19]

Participation in the liturgy, particularly the Mass, is what brings Catholics together and is the heart of our common life.

There are many aspects of the renewal or restoration of the liturgy begun by Vatican II. Among these are the increased emphasis on the place of sacred Scripture in the liturgy, and on the proclamation of God's Word in the homily.[20]

The council declared that nothing essential to the liturgy[21] may be changed. However, they also directed that "The rites should be distinguished by a noble simplicity. They should be short, clear, and free from useless repetitions. They should be within the people's powers of comprehension, and normally should not require much explanation."[22] This was intended to enhance the understanding and participation of the faithful.

Other Forms of Communal Prayer

Just as there are various forms of personal prayer, there are different forms of communal prayer. In addition to the highest form of communal prayer, the Mass, there are also more informal types of shared prayer. Examples of other kinds of communal prayer include prayer meetings, fellowship groups, prayer breakfasts, and rosaries and novenas prayed together.

In addition to participating in the Mass and receiving the Lord in Holy

Communion, Catholics also express the eucharistic focus of their worship by adoration of the Lord in the Blessed Sacrament. The consecrated eucharistic bread, the Body of Christ, is kept in the tabernacle of every Catholic Church, usually marked by a vigil candle. Catholics believe that there the Lord is truly present, and so speak of the "real presence" of Jesus in the Eucharist.

Another expression of communal prayer is joining with Jesus in his prayer for unity, which has an honored place among Catholics. Jesus, in his great high priestly prayer at the Last Supper (see Jn 14-17), prayed fervently for his followers, "so that they may all be one, as you, Father, are in me and I in you, that the world may believe that you sent me" (Jn 17:21, NAB). The whole of Jesus' priestly prayer is a prayer of unity (see CCC 2748).

Some gatherings of communal prayer may be ecumenical or interdenominational, and could be led by lay people or even ministers or laity from other Christian churches. They may include the use of some of the gifts of the Holy Spirit about which St. Paul speaks (see 1 Cor 12; Eph 4). Vatican II's "Decree on Ecumenism" teaches that:

> It is allowable, indeed desirable, that Catholics should join in prayer with their separated brethren. Such prayers in common are certainly a very effective means for petitioning for the grace of unity, and they are a genuine expression of the ties which even now bind Catholics to their separated brethren. "For where two or three are gathered together for My sake, there am I in the midst of them" (Mt 18:20).[23]

Catholics may also join in prayer with other Christians in their services of liturgical or communal worship, as long as Catholics do not receive Holy Communion (*communicatio in sacris*) at these services. The practice of intercommunion (receiving Holy Communion together) must be approved by the Catholic bishop and is normally not allowed since the Catholic Church is not yet in full communion with these churches, and our churches may even disagree with each other on the meaning of the Eucharist itself. We pray for the day when full ecclesial unity may be restored and we then may come to the table of the Lord together as an expression of that full unity.

The Second Vatican Council, as well as both Paul VI and John Paul II, has approved and encouraged Catholics to exercise the charismatic gifts in personal and communal prayer. They also reaffirm St. Paul's advice about the need for spiritual discernment of these gifts, and the need to avoid pride and ostentation in exercising them (see 1 Cor 12; 14; 1 Thess 5:12, 19-21).

Living in Union With God: Helps to Union

Prayer, the sacraments, and the study of God's Word in the Bible and authentic Christian tradition are the basic ways that God has given humanity to grow in union with him. However, God has also provided many helps to assist us in living a fuller, richer Christian life. Let us look at some of these helps to deeper union with the Lord.

The Liturgical Year

Catholics understand that time is one of God's greatest gifts, and seek ways to consecrate time to God. The Catholic Church sets aside special times to offer God praise and worship and to commemorate his mighty works and those people who have been powerful instruments of his work in the world.

The time in which we live is traditionally designated "A.D."—Anno Domini, or "Year of the Lord." Each year, the Catholic Church joins with many Christians to celebrate the major events of our redemption in Jesus Christ. The liturgical year begins with the first Sunday of Advent, a season which prepares us for the coming, or advent, of Jesus Christ among us. This season reaches its climax in the feast of the birth of Christ, Christmas.

The day of Christmas had been observed by Gentiles in the Roman Empire as the feast of *Sol Invictus,* the unconquered sun, which begins to shine for a longer time every day after the winter solstice, which begins around December 21. By replacing this pagan feast with a celebration of the true "unconquered Son"—the Son of God and light of the world, Jesus Christ—Christians began to reclaim time for God.

The early church established other Christian feasts as well, to replace former pagan customs.[24] The Christmas season continues with the feast of Mary, Mother of God, on January 1, consecrating the entire new year to her prayers, followed by Epiphany, the feast of the manifestation of Christ to the nations, celebrated on January 6, or on the Sunday nearest that date. The Christmas season concludes with the feast of the Baptism of the Lord.

The next major liturgical observance for Catholics is Lent, followed by Easter, the Ascension, and Pentecost. Lent began as a period for the instruction and preparation of catechumens (those who would enter the church at Easter) and became a time of penance and renewal for the whole church. The forty days of Lent emulate Jesus' forty days of temptation in the desert, or the wandering of Israel for forty years in the Sinai Desert.

The Catholic Church in the United States observes Lent by abstaining from meat every Friday (for those between the ages of fourteen and sixty-nine), and also fasting (eating solid foods only at one full meal and two smaller meals, maximum) and abstinence from meat for those between the ages of twenty-one and fifty-nine on Ash Wednesday and Good Friday. These are minimal sacrifices observed by all, but the faithful are urged by church teaching to seek other ways during Lent to prepare their hearts for the great feast that lies ahead.

The last week of Lent, known as Holy Week, commemorates the events of Jesus' life from the time of his triumphal entry into Jerusalem (Palm Sunday) until his resurrection on Easter morning (preceded by Holy Thursday, commemorating Jesus' Last Supper, and Good Friday, recalling Jesus' suffering and death at the hands of men).

The joyous feast of Christ's resurrection, Easter Sunday, is the greatest Christian feast and the climax of the liturgical year. Its vigil St. Augustine called the "mother of all vigils." It is the Christian Passover of Jesus Christ from death to life, and with this passing over of God's people from the bondage of sin to the freedom of God's sons and daughters through the resurrection of Jesus. Therefore, *Easter* is not simply one feast among others, but the "Feast of feasts," the "Solemnity of solemnities" (see CCC 1168, 1169).

The Catholic Church continues to celebrate the Easter season with the feast of the ascension of Jesus into heaven on Ascension Thursday, forty days after Easter.

The third great Christian feast of the liturgical year is Pentecost, from the Greek word for fifty since it occurs fifty days after Easter. This feast commemorates the sending of the Holy Spirit on the apostles and the birth of the church. After this, there is a long period of ordinary time in which the Catholic Church remembers the events and teaching of Jesus' public ministry, culminating in his teaching on the end of time and on his second coming, as the liturgical year draws to a close.

Within this framework of the major events of Christ's life and the coming of the Holy Spirit, feasts of the saints (holy men and women who have served God in an exemplary way) are interspersed throughout the year. Some of these feasts honor Mary, the Mother of God, such as the feasts of the Annunciation (March 25), the Visitation (May 31), the Immaculate Conception (December 8), and the Assumption of Mary into heaven (August 15). The church celebrates these feasts of Mary because of our love for her as our mother, and because of the fact that she is inseparably linked with the saving work of her Son. Because she is the perfect image of the church, we also celebrate in Mary what we hope to become, now and in the glory of God's kingdom.[25]

The liturgical year, based upon the events of Jesus Christ's life and readings from the sacred Scriptures, is an important way that Catholics continually are enabled to reflect upon and live out the mysteries of our salvation in Jesus Christ.

The Lord's Day
The day which the Church traditionally has set apart for prayer and celebration of the Paschal mystery is called the Lord's Day, or Sunday. This day of Christ's resurrection is both the first day of the week, the memorial of the first day of creation, and the "eighth day," or the beginning of the eternal day which Jesus inaugurated by his resurrection.

Christians from the time of the most primitive era of the church have gathered every Sunday to worship God in the liturgical assembly, "to listen to the word of God and take part in the Eucharist, thus calling to mind the Passion, Resurrection, and glory of the Lord Jesus, and giving thanks to God...."[26] As St. Jerome wrote:

> The Lord's day, the day of the Resurrection, the day of Christians, is our day. It is called the Lord's day because on it the Lord rose victorious to the Father. If pagans call it the "day of the sun," we willingly agree, for today the light of the world is raised, today is revealed the sun of justice with healing in his rays.[27]

The Catholic understanding of Sunday in the liturgical year is beautifully summarized by Vatican II:

The Lord's day is the original feast day, and it should be proposed to the faithful and taught to them so that it may become in fact a day of joy and of freedom from work. Other celebrations, unless they be truly of the greatest importance, shall not have precedence over Sunday, which is the foundation and kernel of the whole liturgical year.[28]

The Liturgy of the Hours

Not only is every day dedicated to God, but in the Catholic tradition certain hours of the day are set aside for prayer and reflection on God's Word. The Liturgy of the Hours, or the Divine Office, is the official daily liturgical prayer of the whole Catholic Church. In response to St. Paul's exhortation to "pray constantly" (1 Thess 5:17), the Liturgy of the Hours is, "so devised that the whole course of the day and night is made holy by the praise of God...."[29] This prayer developed first from the regular prayers said by all Christians at certain times of the day (see the *Didache*, St. Hippolytus, Tertullian) and was fostered and developed further by the founders and leaders of the monastic movement.

In its present form, the Liturgy of the Hours consists of: (1) an office of readings for the day, which may be said at any time; (2) morning prayer; (3) midday prayer; (4) vespers, or evening prayer; and (5) a brief night prayer (compline). It is comprised mainly of the recitation of psalms, readings from the Bible, and some selections from distinguished church fathers and conciliar statements. Those who have received the sacrament of Holy Orders and those who are vowed to religious life usually are required to pray the Liturgy of the Hours daily, but lay persons are also invited to pray it.

The liturgical renewal that has taken firm hold in the church since the Second Vatican Council urges parishes to have public recitation of morning and evening prayer, especially on Sunday, so that lay people can attend. Even though the Liturgy of the Hours may be prayed alone, it was originally designed to be sung, chanted, or recited together by groups of Christians, whether in monastery, rectory, convent, or parish. It does not exclude, but complements and calls forth other devotions in the church, especially adoration and worship of the Blessed Sacrament (see CCC 1178).

Prayer and Devotion to Mary and the Saints

The previous chapter on the church introduced us to the concept of the communion of saints. Through our baptismal covenant, Catholics enter into a living, committed relationship not only with God but also with all of God's people in the church of Jesus Christ. It is a great mystery, yet a truth, that the church consists of all those who have died in union with Jesus Christ, as well as the living.

The Letter to the Hebrews exhorts us that since we are "surrounded by so great a cloud of witnesses," from Abel to the present, we should lay aside every burden and sin and "run with perseverance the race that is set before us" (Heb 12:1). The Book of Revelation recounts John's inspired vision of a great multitude of people in white robes, the martyrs, standing before the throne of God, worshiping (see Rev 7:9-17) with their prayers rising like incense up to God's throne (see Rev 8:3-4).

An important aspect of both the Jewish and Christian tradition has been to honor and praise the godly men and women who have gone before us (see Sir 44). One reason for this, as the Letter to the Hebrews relates, is to receive encouragement from their example and to imitate their virtues. Another reason that the Catholic tradition insists upon this is that we may receive help from their prayers as they remember our particular needs before the throne of God.

Because of the faith and obedience of these saints, Catholics believe that Mary and the other saints are particularly close to God, God's special friends. Just as we might ask a friend here on earth (especially holy or godly persons) to pray for us and our needs, the Catholic Church teaches that it is proper and good to ask those recognized by the church as saints to pray for us and for our needs. (The process by which the Catholic Church formally recognizes a deceased person as a saint is called "canonization.") We are all part of God's family, whether we are living here on earth or living with the Lord, and even the death of our bodies does not divide our unity in Jesus Christ. We continue to support each other.

Thus, another help for growing in union with God is our relationship with Mary and the saints. We can both imitate their lives and ask them to pray to the Lord for us and for our intentions. As the Second Vatican Council taught:

The Church has always believed that the apostles, and Christ's martyrs who had given the supreme witness of faith and charity by the shedding of their blood, are quite closely joined with us in Christ. She has always venerated them with special devotion, together with the Blessed Virgin Mary and the holy angels. The Church too has devoutly implored the aid of their intercession.[30]

The Catholic Church cautions that the honor given the saints and Mary and their intercession for us in no way contradicts or detracts from the adoration given to God alone. We must always approach God with our needs through Jesus Christ, "the one mediator between God and men" (1 Tim 2:5), in the power of the Holy Spirit.[31]

Devotion and Devotions

The Catholic tradition recognizes that there is a proper devotion that a Christian may have to one of the saints, to Mary, or to a certain mystery of faith. Praying and reflecting on any of these may inspire a person and draw him or her closer to God. Often Catholics are led to seek the prayers of a particular saint before God's throne. Just as in a family there are special bonds between certain members, in God's family there often develop special bonds of spiritual unity and friendship among members of the church. It should not surprise us, then, that nearly every Catholic has an attraction, bond, or devotion to some saint or mystery of our faith. The message of the gospel is so rich that it touches different people in different ways, and leads us each to discern a saint or Christian symbol that especially embodies the gospel and brings it alive for us. Some people may identify with

- the poverty and joy of St. Francis of Assisi and St. Clare;
- the zeal for God of St. Ignatius of Loyola or St. Catherine of Siena;
- the wisdom of St. Thomas Aquinas or St. Augustine;
- the mystical prayer of St. Teresa of Avila;
- the missionary fervor of St. Paul, St. Dominic, St. Thérèse of Lisieux, St. Francis Xavier, and countless others;
- the holiness of St. Benedict, St. Frances de Sales, or St. Jeanne de Chantal;
- the brilliance and steadfastness of St. Thomas More;
- the joy and humor of St. Philip Neri;

- the zeal for reform of St. Charles Borromeo; or
- the love of the poor of St. Vincent de Paul and many others.

The diversity of these canonized saints, who represent all of the saints in heaven, indicates the richness of God's work in the church and calls us forth to follow and imitate Christ, as they did. The lives of all the saints echo the words of St. Paul: "Imitate me as I imitate Christ" (see 1 Cor 11:1).

Our devotion to Mary, to the saints, or to mysteries such as the Cross of Christ or the Sacred Heart of Jesus gives rise to special prayers or devotions directed to them. It is beyond the scope of this short catechism to present the wide variety of Catholic devotions. They include prayers such as consecration and novenas to Our Lady; the rosary; and a plethora of prayers to the saints, to Mary, and to Jesus and the Holy Spirit under various titles.

Sacramentals

Sacramentals are another type of help to growing in union with God. As their name implies, sacramentals usually are related to one of the seven sacraments. Like the sacraments, sacramentals make use of material objects to remind us of God and to put us into contact with him through our senses. They differ from the sacraments in that their effectiveness in drawing us closer to God depends more on our personal faith and devotion, whereas Christ acts in the sacraments in a more sovereign way, even when the faith of some people approaching the sacrament may be weak or lacking.

Sacramentals include such things as blessed (or holy) oil, water, or salt, that Catholics can use in prayer and blessing every day. Some sacramentals are objects connected with the sacraments, such as the altar, the baptismal font, the crucifix or cross, and the paten and ciborium used at Mass. They remind us of God and of his presence in the sacraments. The use of some of these sacramentals are reserved to the ordained ministers or to extraordinary ministers of the sacraments, because their use is primarily or exclusively within the sacraments.

Other sacramentals are related to devotion, such as the rosary, the scapular, medals, pictures, and statues of Mary and the saints. The Eastern Christian use of icons or sacred images is an ancient and venerable form of sacramental. Sacramentals are signs that point to God and remind Catholics of his presence. They help us to proclaim the richness of the mystery of Jesus Christ, who desires to use all things he has created to lead us to recognize him and to praise him for his glory revealed in them.

Fasting and Abstinence

Another means to union with God is self-denial. Catholics deny themselves food, drink, sleep, or comfort not because the body is evil or demands punishment, but: (1) as a form of prayer of petition to God; (2) to remind us of God's goodness and of our utter dependence on him; and (3) to detach ourselves temporarily from some good things of the world in order to focus more fully on God and to hear him speak to us more clearly.

Jesus himself said that his followers would fast after he (the bridegroom) was no longer with them on earth (see Mk 2:18-20). Fasting was observed in the primitive church (see Acts 13:2; 14:23; 2 Cor 11:27), and one of the earliest Christian writings outside the Bible, the *Didache*,[32] records that the early Christians fasted on Wednesdays and Fridays. In later times, special periods of fasting and abstinence from food and drink were established by the church, in both the East and the West, especially the penitential season of Lent preceding Easter.

The Catholic Church has always taught the importance of penance and self-denial, even though it has established different specific guidelines at times. Although the requirements of fasting and abstinence for Catholics are not as rigorous today as in the past, this is intended to allow us to be more responsible in this area, undertaking penances voluntarily. Pope Paul VI's "Apostolic Constitution on Fast and Abstinence" (February 17, 1966) reaffirms that penance is essential to Christianity, for all Christians are called by Jesus to take up the cross daily to follow him (see Mt 16:24; Mk 8:34; Lk 14:27). As the Constitution states: "By divine law all the faithful are required to do penance."[33]

Penance not only involves fasting and abstinence, but also prayer and charity, especially giving alms, or money, to those in need. Pope Paul VI emphasized that this ancient Jewish triad of prayer, fasting, and almsgiving, also recognized by Christianity, is the fundamental way that the Catholic Church teaches its members to deny themselves in order to grow in love for the Lord and others.

Indulgences

The Catholic understanding of indulgences has been clouded by certain abuses in the past, such as the selling of indulgences, which was rightly denounced by Martin Luther in the sixteenth century. Probably it is best today to keep the understanding of indulgences fairly simple: prayer and penance call down the mercy of God; the Catholic Church simply recognizes the value of certain prayers and acts of penance in calling down God's mercy when it designates them indulgences. The Catholic Church designates certain indulgences as "plenary" (removing all effects of sin that result in God's just punishment) or "partial" (removing part, but not all, of these consequences of sin).

In studying carefully the Catholic Church's teaching on indulgences, it is inspiring to discover that at its root is the redeeming work of Jesus Christ and the body of Christ in action. Christians are called to pray for themselves and for others, even for those departed from life on earth, that the infinite merits of Jesus Christ and of all the saints united with him would free us from the bondage of sin and all its effects.[34]

Elements That Enhance Liturgical Prayer

Because the church is the assembly of faithful, "living stones" gathered to be "built into a spiritual house" (1 Pet 2:4-5), Christian worship is not tied exclusively to any one place (see CCC 1179) or to any one cultural expression (see CCC 1204).

However, since God has become man and comes to us in visible, human ways, the church recognizes that its worship is not purely spiritual but is expressed in tangible ways. For example, the church building is a "house of prayer ... [which] ought to be in good taste and a worthy place for prayer and sacred ceremonial."[35]

The church building is truly a "sacred space," which should invite those who enter it to enter into prayer in God's presence. Within the church building are various places, furnishings, and objects that are signs of God's presence and work in the liturgy (see CCC 1182-85). The most central of these focus attention on the Eucharistic meal, sacrifice, and presence of Jesus (altar and tabernacle), and on the Word of God (lectern or "ambo," also see CCC 1154).

Following the "incarnational principle," Catholics believe that the presence of Christ and his saints may be represented by holy images (statues or icons). St. John Damascene wrote:

Previously God, who has neither a body nor a face, absolutely could not be represented by an image. But now that he has made himself visible in the flesh and has lived with men, I can make an image of what I have seen of God ... and contemplate the glory of the Lord, his face unveiled.[36]

In the eighth century (at the Second Ecumenical Council of Nicea) the Catholic Church *condemned* the view that it is idolatry to use icons or sacred images in Christian worship. (This view was held by the iconoclasts.) Thus, Catholics *may* use sacred images or icons in prayer. We do not worship images, but the God whom they represent in the person of Jesus Christ, who is the perfect image of the Father. Images of saints remind us of those we honor or venerate because they reflect Christ by the holiness of their lives. As the *Catechism* explains:

All the signs in the liturgical celebrations are related to Christ: as are sacred images of the holy Mother of God and of the saints as well. They truly signify Christ, who is glorified in them. They make manifest the "cloud of witnesses" (Heb 12:1) who continue to participate in the salvation of the world and to whom we are united, above all in sacramental celebrations. (CCC 1161)

Music and Singing

There are other special signs that are part of the liturgical worship of the church, and among these singing and music have a special place. The musical tradition of the universal church is a treasure of inestimable value, greater even than that of any other art.[37] In the Old Testament, the psalms were sung, often accompanied by musical instruments. The church continued and developed this tradition: In the New Testament, St. Paul urges Christians to "address ... one another in psalms and hymns and inspired songs. Sing praise to the Lord with all your hearts" (see Eph 5:19). St. Augustine taught that "He who sings prays twice."[38]

Music in the liturgy not only gives God glory, but also lifts the mind and heart to God. Catholics know that worship of God involves the whole person, the "heart" (including the emotions), as well as the intellect. Music certainly can move the heart to worship God. As St. Augustine remarked in his *Confessions:*

> How I wept, deeply moved by your hymns, songs, and the voices that echoed through your Church! What emotion I experienced in them! Those sounds flowed into my ears, distilling the truth in my heart. A feeling of devotion surged within me, and tears streamed down my face—tears that did me good.[39]

In the Catholic Church today, all in the assembly of worship are encouraged to participate in song at the designated moments (see CCC 1157, 1191). How beautiful it is when voices of the faithful are heard, joined in singing songs and hymns drawn from sacred Scripture and liturgical sources![40]

Liturgy and Culture

Music joins in harmony with the other signs in the liturgy to express the *cultural richness* of those who are celebrating (see CCC 1158). "The mystery celebrated in the liturgy is one, but the forms of its celebration are diverse" (CCC 1200). This diversity includes both the various *ancient* liturgical families or "rites" recognized by the church,[41] and the liturgies of other cultures where the gospel has been more recently planted through the church's missionary activity. Without threatening the *unity* of the faith or changing the *immutable* (unchangeable) *part* of the liturgy, the mystery of Christ must be expressed, proclaimed, celebrated, and lived in all cultures in such a way that the culture is redeemed and finds fulfillment through this mystery (see CCC 1204). Pope John Paul II has been a leader in affirming, in his travels, the diverse cultural expressions of the church's liturgy.

Part 3: The Work of the Holy Spirit

The Spirit in the Liturgy and Sacraments

Now that we have considered some aspects of Catholic worship and devotion, the final section of this chapter will be devoted to the source and foundation of all Christian prayer: God's work in us through the Holy Spirit. The Catholic Church teaches that it is impossible to pray or have a life of true devotion without the Holy Spirit. Jesus said that true worshipers must worship "in spirit and truth" (Jn 4:23, 24).

The *Catechism* presents a powerful and comprehensive teaching on the work of the Holy Spirit in the liturgy and the sacraments (CCC 1091-1112). It states:

> In the liturgy the Holy Spirit is teacher of the faith of the People of God and artisan of "God's masterpieces," the sacraments of the New Covenant. The desire and work of the Spirit in the heart of the Church is that we may live from the life of the risen Christ. When the Spirit encounters in us the response of faith which he has aroused in us, he brings about genuine cooperation. Through it, the liturgy becomes the common work of the Holy Spirit and the Church. (CCC 1091)

There are four distinct ways that the Holy Spirit makes the liturgy of the church possible and effective.

First, *the Holy Spirit prepares for the reception of Christ* (see CCC 1093-98). He has already done this in history by inspiring the prophets and the authors of the Old Testament writings to foretell the coming of Christ and by preparing God's Old Covenant people for the Messiah's coming through prayer, repentance, and faith. Likewise, the Holy Spirit prepares God's people today to encounter and receive Jesus in the liturgy. "The grace of the Holy Spirit seeks to awaken faith, conversion of heart, and adherence to the Father's will" (CCC 1098).

Second, *the Holy Spirit recalls the mystery of Christ.* The Holy Spirit, who is "the Church's living memory," calls Christ to mind by making the Word of God in

Scripture "come alive" for us, giving us a spiritual understanding of his Word so that we are drawn into a living relationship with Christ (see CCC 1100-1101). Specifically, in awakening our memory of all that the Lord has done for us (*anamnesis*), especially in Jesus Christ, the Holy Spirit leads us to give thanks and praise to God (*doxology*; see CCC 1103).

Third, *the Holy Spirit makes present the mystery of Christ.* The Holy Spirit not only prepares us for Christ in the liturgy and recalls what he has done for us. The priest, at the *epiclesis* (invocation of the Holy Spirit), entreats the Father to send the Holy Spirit so that the offerings of bread and wine may become the Body and Blood of Jesus, and the congregation also becomes a pleasing sacrifice to God. Thus the *epiclesis,* along with the *anamnesis,* is at the heart of the celebration of the Eucharist and of the other sacraments (see CCC 1105). As St. John Damascene wrote:

> You ask how the bread becomes the Body of Christ, and the wine ... the Blood of Christ. I shall tell you: the Holy Spirit comes upon them and accomplishes what surpasses every word and thought.... Let it be enough for you to understand that it is by the Holy Spirit, just as it was of the Holy Virgin and by the Holy Spirit that the Lord, through and in himself, took flesh."[42]

Fourth, *the Holy Spirit works in the liturgy to bring us into communion with Christ.* The *Catechism* states that "the most intimate cooperation of the Holy Spirit and the Church is achieved in the liturgy" (CCC 1108), and hence the Holy Spirit is "the Spirit of communion," who works in the liturgy to bring the church into communion with God and with one another in the unity of the church. This is summarized by St. Paul's benediction: "The grace of the Lord Jesus Christ, and the love of God, and the fellowship of the Holy Spirit be with you all!" (see 2 Cor 13:13).

The liturgy, through the action of the Holy Spirit, can and must lead the church into the true and lived communion with the Holy Trinity and with one another (see CCC 1155).

The Work of the Holy Spirit Outside the Liturgy and Sacraments

The work of the Holy Spirit is not limited to the sacraments and liturgy. As the Second Vatican Council taught:

> It is not only through the sacraments and Church ministries that the Holy Spirit sanctifies and leads the people of God and enriches it with virtues. Allotting His gifts "to everyone according as he will" (1 Cor 12:11), He distributes special graces among the faithful of every rank. By these gifts He makes them fit and ready to undertake the various tasks and offices advantageous for the renewal and upbuilding of the Church, according to the words of the Apostle: "The manifestation of the Spirit is given to everyone for profit" (1 Cor 12:7). These charismatic gifts, whether they be the most outstanding or the more simple and widely diffused, are to be received with thanksgiving and consolation, for they are exceedingly suitable and useful for the needs of the Church.[43]

What are these charismatic gifts, or manifestations, of the Holy Spirit, of which the Second Vatican Council speaks? They may be divided into three general categories, although the activity of the Holy Spirit in the lives of Christians is not limited to these. They are the "Isaian gifts" of the Holy Spirit, the "Pauline gifts," and the "fruit of the Spirit."

The prophet Isaiah listed seven gifts that properly belong to the Messiah, and which are now shared by God's messianic people, the church: "The spirit of the Lord shall rest upon him: a spirit of wisdom and of understanding, A spirit of counsel and of strength, a spirit of knowledge and of fear of the Lord, and his delight shall be the fear of the Lord" (Isa 11:2-3, NAB).

These seven gifts—wisdom, understanding, counsel, knowledge, fortitude, piety, and fear of the Lord—have traditionally been recognized by Catholics as manifestations of the Holy Spirit's indwelling in the believer: gifts of the Holy Spirit.

St. Paul presents another set of gifts of the Spirit, most fully set forth in 1 Corinthians 12:4-11 (NAB):

There are different kinds of spiritual gifts but the same Spirit; there are different forms of service but the same Lord; there are different workings but the same God who produces all of them in everyone. To each individual the manifestation of the Spirit is given for some benefit. To one is given through the Spirit the expression of wisdom; to another the expression of knowledge according to the same Spirit; to another faith by the same Spirit; to another gifts of healing by the one Spirit; to another mighty deeds; to another prophecy; to another discernment of spirits; to another varieties of tongues; to another interpretation of tongues. But one and the same Spirit produces all of these, distributing them individually to each person as he wishes.

This is the list of the gifts of the Spirit (see also Eph 4) that the "Dogmatic Constitution on the Church" states, "are to be received with thanksgiving and consolation, for they are exceedingly suitable and useful for the needs of the Church."[44] St. Thomas Aquinas called these gifts the "graces freely given" (*gratia gratis datae*) by God to the church. The designation of these as "extraordinary" gifts is later terminology.

Paul's lists of these workings of the Holy Spirit are not complete or exclusive; there may be other charisms of the Spirit in addition to these. The *Catechism of the Catholic Church* describes these Pauline charisms and their proper use in worship and in other ways in which they are necessary to build up the body of Christ (see CCC 799-801).

Finally, St. Paul also describes the "fruit of the Spirit" in his letter to the Galatians. This "fruit" is the sign of the Holy Spirit's working in a person's character, as God transforms each of us to his likeness in our thoughts, attitudes, and actions. Paul writes:

> The fruit of the Spirit is love, joy, peace, patience, kindness, generosity, faithfulness, gentleness, self-control. Against such there is no law.
>
> GALATIANS 5:22-23, NAB

The value of all these workings of the Spirit is always determined by the way they are used and their end, or purpose. They must be used in love, or else they are worthless (see 1 Cor 13), and their highest purpose is the "common good" (1 Cor 12:7), or "building up the body of Christ" (Eph 4:11-12). They are never to be considered personal property or causes for boasting. They are free gifts of God.

The Holy Spirit's presence in our lives is not limited to these gifts and fruits. Christians are called to relate to the Holy Spirit as a person—the person of God who guides us (see Acts 16:6-8); speaks to us (see Acts 10:19; 13:2; 21:11; 28:25); consoles us (see Acts 9:31); sends us forth (see Acts 13:4); warns us (see Acts 20:23); prompts us (see Acts 21:4), and teaches us the truth (see Jn 16:13). As Catholics grow in personal relationships with the Holy Spirit, they will realize the importance of being led by the Holy Spirit in all decisions and actions. "Since we live by the spirit, let us follow the spirit's lead" (see Gal 5:25).

Another important working of the Holy Spirit is in creating and safeguarding the unity of Christians and the church. After St. Paul listed the various gifts of the Holy Spirit (see 1 Cor 12:4-11), he proceeded to describe the church as a body with many parts or members, each member having its own particular gift and place in the body (see 1 Cor 12:12-27). Each Christian has a particular gift and place in the church. Many of the problems in the church in Corinth, and in the church of Jesus Christ today, stem from Christians not understanding or accepting their particular gift and role in the body of Christ. They may have an individualistic perspective, not understanding that in God's eyes and plan they are not just individuals, but part of a whole church, a people, for whom they should have personal concern. The gifts of the Spirit are given as they are, so "that there may be no division in the body, but that the parts may have the same concern for one another" (1 Cor 12:25, NAB). The Holy Spirit calls Catholics to consider our lives and our gifts as belonging first to God, and then to each other in the church.

In this view of the church, there is to be no contention between those who are called by God to serve as leaders in the church, especially the ordained, and those who have other gifts and callings. There is not a hierarchical church (the ordained) opposed to or set apart from a charismatic church (those not ordained who possess certain gifts). There is only one church of Jesus Christ, whose members all are charismatic, possessing gifts of the Holy Spirit of various types for the common good.[45] God has sent the Holy Spirit to his people in power and with an abundant variety of gifts and manifestations. Catholics seek the presence of the Spirit and all of his gifts to serve one another for the glory of God!

The Holy Spirit in Catholic Renewal

The charismatic renewal, or "pentecostal movement," has called attention to the action of the Holy Spirit outside of the framework of the liturgy and sacraments, focusing on the experience of a "release" or "baptism" in the Holy Spirit, often accompanied by charisms. Many Catholics see this as God's response to Pope John XXIII's prayer at the council for the Holy Spirit to renew his wonders in our time, as by a "new Pentecost." Pope Paul VI and Pope John Paul II have both recognized and endorsed the Catholic charismatic renewal as a genuine work of the Holy Spirit.

This subject merits discussion in a catechism because many baptized and confirmed Catholics have felt a need to pray for a fuller release or empowerment of the Holy Spirit in their lives that they might love, serve, and witness to Christ more effectively. They desire Christ and the Holy Spirit to come alive in them as a reality, rather than just a concept or doctrine. In response to this prayer to be "baptized in the Holy Spirit," millions of Christians have claimed that the Holy Spirit has come into their lives in a new way, bringing gifts, graces, deeper virtue, and the love of God.

How is this extrasacramental working of the Holy Spirit to be understood theologically by Catholics? Some theologians have explained that being "baptized in the Holy Spirit" with the reception of certain "charisms" or gifts of the Holy Spirit has been recognized as an integral aspect of the sacraments of Christian initiation from the earliest days of the church. A "release," or new "baptism," in the power and gifts of the Holy Spirit should be seen as an "unfolding," or "coming to awareness," of the graces conferred in these sacraments, especially baptism and confirmation.[46]

Taking a somewhat different approach, St. Thomas Aquinas spoke of a new sending or sendings of the Holy Spirit in the lives of Christians in addition to the visible sendings of the Holy Spirit in the sacraments. St. Thomas wrote in his *Summa Theologia:*

> There is an invisible sending (of the Holy Spirit) also with respect to an advance in virtue or an increase of grace....
>
> Such an invisible sending is especially to be seen in that kind of increase of grace whereby a person moves forward into some new act or new state of

grace: as, for instance, when a person moves forward into the grace of working miracles, or of prophecy, or out of the burning love of God offers his life as a martyr, or renounces all of his possessions, or undertakes some other such arduous thing.[47]

One interpreter of Aquinas explains that this new sending of the Holy Spirit is more than the conferral of a new gift (or gifts) of the Spirit, but "a new way of the Spirit's indwelling in the soul, a real innovation (making new) of the person's relationship with the indwelling Spirit."[48]

There are different theological understandings of what is commonly termed being "baptized in the Holy Spirit," or the "release of the Spirit." One thing is clear. Far from being only a Protestant or Pentecostal phenomenon, the Second Vatican Council and recent popes have affirmed the validity and importance of this manifestation of the Holy Spirit as a renewal and deepening of Christian prayer. They also point out the perennial presence and necessity of the charisms or gifts of the Spirit in the church's life.

Conclusion

Prayer is at the heart of the Catholic life, the life of a people united with God in worship and praise. Liturgical prayer, the prayer of the church, has a central place in the church as its source of life, power, and unity. Liturgy has many elements. It always incorporates the sacred Scripture, which is "of paramount importance,"[49] and often includes music, art, and other supportive elements. However, the indispensable aspect of liturgical prayer is the presence and active participation of the people of God, joined to worship God "in spirit and truth" (Jn 4:23-24), according to the rites and forms determined by the church.

Some people object that liturgical prayer is too formal because most of its prayers are determined. However, one aspect of the beauty of the liturgy is its universality, that it is the common prayer of Catholics throughout the world. That is why no one, not even an ordained minister, is free to change it to suit his own taste or theology.[50] Yet, Catholic liturgy can never be totally uniform or rigid, because within the liturgy there is room for legitimate variation, for the unique insights and styles of different preachers and celebrants, and for appropriate cultural adaptation. Liturgical worship is rich, because it is the worship of God's people that has developed in the church for nearly two thousand years, and is brought to life again each day through the enlivening presence of God himself in our midst. If liturgical prayer is ever "deadening," it is not because *it* is dead, but because *we* have not fully come alive to God or to what we are doing when we worship together as his people. Christians must always ask the Holy Spirit to enliven our prayer, whether personal or communal, so that it might strengthen us and be truly pleasing to God who is the object of our love and worship. Jesus himself taught that "God is spirit and those who worship him must worship in spirit and truth" (Jn 4:24). As the "Constitution on the Sacred Liturgy" reiterates, the liturgy can manifest the body of Christ to others:

> For it is through the liturgy, especially the divine Eucharistic Sacrifice, that "the work of our redemption is exercised." The liturgy is thus the outstanding means by which the faithful can express in their lives, and manifest to others, the mystery of Christ and the real nature of the true Church.[51]

CHAPTER 7

The Sacraments

Catholics approach God, as Jesus did, both in personal prayer and in communal worship. The center of Catholic communal worship is our sacramental life, especially the Eucharist. Why do Catholics value the sacraments so highly? Why not just have personal or nonliturgical prayer? The major reason is that Catholics believe that God himself has given sacraments to the church to be privileged channels of his grace, his life, and his power.

Where do the sacraments come from? How has God given them to the church? Catholics believe that all of the sacraments flow from the life and ministry of Jesus himself as recorded in the New Testament. Jesus himself instituted all of the sacraments (CCC 1114), either by explicit command or by his work or teaching. Another name for sacrament (Latin: *sacramentum*) is "mystery" (Greek: *mysterion*), which reminds us of the mystery of Christ's presence and action in each of these signs that he instituted. As Pope St. Leo the Great said, "what was visible in our Savior has passed over into his mysteries."[1]

The sacraments are Jesus continuing his ministry among his people after his resurrection and ascension. Jesus promised to remain with his people, "until the end of the age" (Mt 28:20, NAB). One way that Jesus fulfills this promise is through the sacraments; through them he continues to walk among us and minister to us: "it is he who baptizes, he who acts in his sacraments in order to communicate the grace that each sacrament signifies" (CCC 1127).

Sacraments of the Church

The sacraments are, thus, sacraments of Christ: the continuation of the ministry of Jesus. They are also sacraments of Christ's church, for it is through the church that Jesus ministers his sacraments today. There is also a sense in which the whole church of Christ may be called a sacrament. When Jesus departed the earth at his ascension, he left behind not just his spiritual presence, but a visible body of faithful believers—his church. Through this church, subsequent generations of people could come into contact with Jesus Christ and believe in him through its preaching and example. As the Catholic bishops at the Second Vatican Council declared in the "Dogmatic Constitution on the Church": "By her relationship with Christ, the church is a kind of *sacrament* of intimate union with God, and of the unity of all mankind, that is, she is a *sign* and *instrument* of such union and unity...."[2]

The church of Jesus Christ is the universal sacrament. It is a sign, spread throughout the world, of the presence of God through Jesus Christ. *Lumen Gentium* also states:

Christ ... through his Spirit, has established His body, the Church, as the universal sacrament of salvation. Sitting at the right hand of the Father, He is continually active in the world, leading men to the Church, and through her joining them more closely to Himself.[3]

It is this visible church that carries on the work of Jesus Christ and makes him present through its preaching, its actions, and through the particular saving sacraments that Jesus himself established and left for us within the church.

The Father always hears the prayer of his Son's Church which, in the epiclesis of each sacrament, expresses her faith in the power of the Spirit. As fire transforms into itself everything it touches, so the Holy Spirit transforms into the divine life whatever is subjected to his power. (CCC 1127)

As we see here, the sacraments are also a work of the Holy Spirit. "They are actions of the Holy Spirit at work in his Body, the Church. They are 'the masterworks of God' in the new and everlasting covenant" (CCC 1116).

Origin of the Sacraments

The sacraments are an essential part of God's plan to communicate his grace and life to us in Jesus Christ. As we have seen, the word "sacrament" comes from a Latin translation of the Greek "mysterion," or "mystery" (see Eph 1:9ff), which refers to the mystery of God's salvation coming to us in visible form.

This mystery is first seen in the Incarnation. It unfolds through God's continuing presence among us in the body of Christ, the church. It is further seen in the visible signs of God's presence among us in the church—the sacraments. "Mystery," or "sacrament," is a fitting word to describe this incomprehensible miracle of God coming to mankind in visible form, whether in Jesus, in his church, or in the individual sacraments of Christ and the church.

Sacraments have a twofold nature: one visible and the other hidden. The visible aspect of the sacraments are the part experienced through our senses (bread, holy oil, words of absolution, etc.) These are signs that point to the presence of God among his people. The hidden aspect of the sacraments is the special grace they impart and their effects in the life of those who receive them. In this aspect, the sacraments are called "efficacious signs"—that is, they bring about or effect what they signify. "They are *efficacious* because in them Christ himself is at work..." (CCC 1127).

Catholics believe that God wills to make himself present and to confer his grace upon us in a particular way whenever a sacrament is properly enacted within the church.

> This is the meaning of the Church's affirmation[4] that the sacraments act *ex opere operato* (literally: "by the very fact of the action's being performed"), i.e., by virtue of the saving work of Christ, accomplished once for all.... From the moment that a sacrament is celebrated in accordance with the intention of the Church, the power of Christ and his Spirit acts in and through it, independently of the personal holiness of the minister. Nevertheless, the fruits of the sacraments also depend on the disposition of the one who receives them. (CCC 1128)

Indeed, to obtain the full benefits and grace that God wishes to confer through the sacraments, it is important that we come to them with the proper dispositions.[5] The suitable attitudes that Catholics should have in approaching any sacrament are, first, *faith* (believing in God and in the particular way that he has chosen to come to us and bless us through the sacrament), and, second, *reverence* before the mystery of God and his presence in the sacrament.

The sacraments are not magic. We can neither conjure up God nor control him. It is God who chooses to be present and to grant his graces and blessings through the sacraments, out of his infinite love and mercy. God is to be embraced there by the faith and love of his people.

Sacraments of Faith

The *Catechism* emphasizes that all of the sacraments are "sacraments of faith." This is so, first, because faith is necessary in order to receive and assent to the sacrament. This presumes that the sacrament has been presented and prepared for by the proclamation of the Word of God. Vatican II's "Decree on the Ministry and Life of Priests" explains:

> The People of God is formed into one in the first place by the Word of the living God.... The preaching of the Word is required for the sacramental ministry itself, since the sacraments are sacraments of faith, drawing their origin and nourishment from the Word.[6]

Secondly, the sacraments nourish, strengthen, and express faith: "because they are signs they also instruct. They not only presuppose faith, but by words and objects they also nourish, strengthen, and express it. That is why they are called 'sacraments *of faith*.'"[7]

The faith of the individual believer is preceded by and based upon the faith of the church. As a Catholic, my faith in God's work in the sacraments, as well as my understanding of them, must be rooted in the church's faith and understanding, since the sacraments have been handed on to me by and within the church. The sacraments have been handed on in the context of the prayer and worship of the church, whence comes the ancient saying, "The law of prayer is the law of faith" (*lex orandi, lex credendi*): the church believes as she prays (see CCC 1124). This is why the rites of the liturgy and the sacraments may not be changed arbitrarily, even by the highest authorities of the church. The church is bound to protect and defend what has been handed down to her by the Lord and in the prayer and practice of the early church (see CCC 1125).

This means, first, that the proper outward, visible signs or actions of each sacrament (such as water, bread, wine, oil, the laying of hands, etc.) must be used, and the authorized liturgical prayers should be employed, since these are handed on within the church.

Likewise, only those sacraments performed and presided over by the correct and authorized *minister* of the church merit our faith. Since sacraments are based on words and actions of Jesus himself, most sacraments are administered by those in the church who have been set apart to represent Christ and to carry on this ministry in the church in a special way. These are the bishops and priests, and sometimes deacons.

All the "priestly people" of God celebrate or participate in the liturgy and the sacraments (see CCC 1119), but the ordained or ministerial priesthood has a special role "at the service of the baptismal priesthood."[8] They, as successors of the apostles, represent Jesus Christ in a particular way. They receive the Spirit of Jesus to act in his name and in his person in leading the community of the church in worship and in the celebration of the sacraments (see Mt 28:18-20; Lk 24:47; Jn 20:21-23).

Historical Development of the Sacraments

From a historical perspective, the term "sacrament" was used more loosely in the early church than it is today. The church fathers of the first six centuries used *sacramentum* (Latin) or *mysterion* (Greek) to refer to many aspects of church life. Gradually, in the Middle Ages, "sacrament" came to have a more precise meaning, and it became necessary to determine which of the church's ancient practices fit the more exact definition.

In the twelfth and thirteenth centuries, Catholic theologians and bishops began to reach an agreement on the meaning of "sacrament," and came to recognize seven sacraments. The Council of Trent in the sixteenth century officially confirmed that there were seven, and only seven, sacraments of the church. This idea that the church could identify or define the number of sacraments is not new: the church had done the same in defining the official list of inspired books (the "canon") of the Bible, as well as other doctrines of faith. This was done through the guidance of the Holy Spirit, whom Jesus promised to guide the church into all truth (see Jn 16:13). Although it took time for the church's formal understanding and enumeration of sacraments to emerge, the important fact is that the actual practice of these seven sacraments was a vital part of Christian life and worship from the first century onward (see CCC 1117).

Saving Power of the Sacraments

Having received these seven sacraments as gifts from the Lord, instituted by Jesus Christ, "the Church affirms that for believers the sacraments of the New Covenant are *necessary for salvation.*⁹ 'Sacramental grace' is the grace of the Holy Spirit, given by Christ and proper to each sacrament. The Spirit heals and transforms those who receive him by conforming them to the Son of God. The fruit of the sacramental life is that the Spirit of adoption makes the faithful partakers in the divine nature (cf. 2 Pet 1:4) by uniting them in a living union with the only Son, the Savior" (CCC 1129).

In this, the sacraments give us on earth a foretaste and a share of eternal life with God, causing us to cry out to God for the completion and the fullness of our inheritance: "Maranatha! Come, Lord Jesus!" (see 1 Cor 16:22; Rev 22:17, 20).

Jesus Christ as the Center and Source of the Sacraments

The Catholic Church proclaims that the greatest sacramental expression of God's love for us is the humanity of Jesus Christ. Jesus, being the incarnate Son of God, is the ultimate visible sign of God's presence among us. He is the unsurpassable means by which the fullness of God's grace and love came into the world to restore the human race to right relationship with him. The First Letter of John begins:

That which was from the beginning, which we have heard, which we have seen with our eyes, which we have looked upon and touched with our hands, concerning the word of life—the life was made manifest, and we saw it, and testify to it, and proclaim to you the eternal life which was with the Father and was made manifest to us....

1 JOHN 1:1-2

This Word of Life is, of course, Jesus Christ. Through the ultimate sacrament of God, the sacred humanity of Jesus Christ, we are brought into fellowship or communion with God the Father. Catholics understand that the seven sacraments recognized by the Catholic Church are vital because they embody nearly every aspect of Jesus' ministry while he was on earth.

Catholics do not glorify the material things used in the sacraments (such as water, bread, wine, and oil), nor do we "divinize" the ministers of the sacraments, nor exalt merely human rituals. Again, Catholics use these material things, and respect the authority of the ministers of the church, only because Jesus himself used such things, and commanded his apostles to carry on his ministry with his authority.

The seven sacraments are not ends in themselves; they possess no power in themselves. They are simply channels of God's grace and mercy coming to the human race. The fathers of the church described them as flowing from the pierced side of Christ on the cross. The grace and life of God, won for us through the cross of Christ, flows down to us within the church, century after century, through these channels.[10]

Finally, our recognition and acceptance of the sacraments as channels of God's grace is based on faith. Faith is the foundation of a mature Christian's relationship with God. Some Christians reject the sacraments because they claim that they don't experience anything or feel any different when receiving them. However, grace—God's life—is not something that can be accurately detected or measured by human experience or feelings.

Catholics recognize the sacraments because we believe that they have been instituted by Jesus Christ, through his word or example, as a primary means of receiving his life and grace, not because we necessarily feel different when we receive them. On the other hand, it is true that a Catholic's experience or perception of God's presence in the sacraments can grow, especially over the course of time.

For example, in receiving the Sacrament of Reconciliation regularly, Catholics should begin to see the power of God at work in their lives, liberating them from sin. Catholics who receive the Eucharist frequently should expect to see the fruit of this in their lives over the course of weeks or years, such as a deepening in prayer or a growth in virtue and charity. The sacraments cannot be evaluated simply on the basis of experience, but they do have power. Catholics should grow in expectant faith that God desires to strengthen, restore, and refresh us as we receive the sacraments in faith.

The Sacrament of Baptism

Baptism, the Holy Eucharist, and confirmation are known as the "sacraments of initiation" because they enable a person to enter into the full Christian life. Baptism is the foundational Christian sacrament, the basis of the whole Christian life.

Because baptism is the beginning of our life in Christ, in the Spirit, and in the church, it is required before reception of the other sacraments. The effects of baptism are the cleansing of all sin, including original sin, which is passed on to us from our first parents at our conception; the coming of the triune God to dwell within us; and our becoming living members or parts of Christ's body, the church, and sharing in her mission (see CCC 1213).

"To baptize" literally means to "to plunge," or "to immerse"; "the 'plunge' into the water symbolizes the catechumen's burial into Christ's death, from which he rises up by resurrection with him, as 'a new creature'" (2 Cor 5:17; Gal 6:15; see Rom 6:3-4; Col 2:12) (CCC 1214).

Baptism is called "the washing of regeneration and renewal by the Holy Spirit" (Titus 3:5). In the Gospel of St. John, Jesus explains to Nicodemus that to be baptized is to be "born anew," "born again," or "born from above" (in the various English translations of Jn 3:3, 7), and insists that "unless one is born of water and the Spirit, he cannot enter the kingdom of God" (Jn 3:5). The early church called baptism "enlightenment," or "illumination," because in baptism we receive Jesus Christ, "the true light that enlightens every man" (Jn 1:9; CCC 1216; see also Eph 5:8; 1 Thess 5:5; Heb 10:32).

Water, the primary sign of baptism, symbolizes both refreshment and *life*, pointing to eternal life through the resurrection of Jesus, and death by water, reminding us of our communion with Christ's death on the cross. Baptism by immersion in water (the preferred form) is a powerful visible sign that through baptism we die and rise with Jesus Christ (see Rom 6:3-4).

At the Easter Vigil, a beautiful prayer recounting the symbolism of water in God's saving acts in the Old Covenant accompanies the blessing of the baptismal water (see CCC 1217-22). These symbols find their fulfillment in Christ, who humbly submitted to be baptized in the Jordan River by St. John the Baptist at the beginning of his public ministry. In this act of humility, Jesus was revealed as the one upon whom the Holy Spirit rested, and as the "beloved Son" of God the Father (Mt 3:13-17).

At the end of his public ministry, Jesus experienced another "baptism": the baptism of suffering on the cross (Mk 10:38; see Lk 12:50). By enduring this horrible death, Jesus fulfilled the plan of God for the salvation of the human race, conquering sin and death, and pouring out new, eternal life that we receive through baptism. As St. Ambrose wrote:

> See where you are baptized, see where Baptism comes from, if not from the cross of Christ, from his death. There is the whole mystery: he died for you. In him you are redeemed, in him you are saved.[11]

Now the central mission of Jesus and his church was made clear: to offer all people freedom from sin, the gift of the Holy Spirit, and the new life of grace through faith in Jesus Christ and baptism. After his resurrection Christ gives this mission to his apostles: "Go therefore and make disciples of all nations, baptizing them in the name of the Father and of the Son and of the Holy Spirit, teaching them to observe all that I have commanded you" (Mt 28:19-20; see CCC 1223; Mk 16:15-16).

This mission began to be carried out on the day of Pentecost, when St. Peter proclaimed to those who believed in Jesus and asked what to do:

> Repent and be baptized, every one of you, in the name of Jesus Christ for the forgiveness of your sins; and you will receive the gift of the holy Spirit.
>
> ACTS 2:38, NAB

Throughout the Acts of the Apostles, baptism accompanied by faith is described as the first step in becoming a Christian (see Acts 2:38; 8:12-13, 37-38; 9:18; 10:47; 16:15; 19:5).

The Effects of Baptism

There are three major effects of baptism. The first is that *our sins are forgiven* (see Acts 2:38) *and we receive Jesus Christ and his saving grace.* Original sin and all other sins are forgiven and "washed away" by the waters of baptism (see CCC 1263). The visible "washing" with water is a sign of a total, spiritual cleansing. St. Paul explains that Christians must consider themselves "dead to sin and living for God in Christ Jesus" (Rom 6:11, NAB). It is through baptism that we first die to sin and become "alive for God" (see Rom 6:3-4). Through baptism we receive what Catholic theology calls "sanctifying grace"—the grace that makes us holy, like God.

Baptism gives us an entirely new relationship with God, as his sons and daughters through our "new birth." St. Paul also speaks of baptism as "putting on Christ" (see Gal 3:27), with the result that the baptized person has an entirely new life "in Christ." "Therefore, if any one is in Christ, he is a new creation: the old has passed away, behold, the new has come" (2 Cor 5:17; see CCC 1265).

The second result of baptism is that *the Christian first receives the greatest gift of the Father and the Son: the Holy Spirit.* In baptism, Jesus sends us the Holy Spirit to dwell within us, making us "temples of the Holy Spirit" (see 1 Cor 6:19). Because of original sin, the Spirit of God could not dwell in any person in the Old Covenant. But since Jesus' death, the cleansing from original sin that Christians receive in baptism makes it possible for the Holy Spirit to make his home in us as his temples. The new life in Christ is also life in the Spirit.

Third, *the baptized person becomes part of the fellowship of the church, the body of Christ.* "For by one Spirit we were all baptized into one body ..." (1 Cor 12:13). Baptism is the first "sacrament of initiation," and the newly baptized (neophytes) are initiated into both the life of Christ and the life of his body or people, the church (see CCC 1267-70).

Baptism forms a "sacramental bond of unity" among all who have been baptized, even among those who belong to different churches.[12] The *Catechism* calls baptism "the foundation of communion among all Christians" (CCC 1271). "For men who believe in Christ and have been properly baptized are put in some, though imperfect, communion with the Catholic Church. Justified by faith in Baptism, [they] are incorporated into Christ; they therefore have a right to be called Christians, and with good reason are accepted as brothers by the children of the Catholic Church."[13]

Christian Initiation

Although the full process of initiation into Jesus Christ and his church has developed over time, it has always consisted of some stages of preparation and instruction, known as the catechumenate, culminating in the sacraments of initiation. The essential elements in this initiation process include: proclamation of the Word; acceptance of the gospel, entailing conversion; profession of faith; baptism itself; the outpouring of the Holy Spirit (confirmation); and admission to Eucharistic Communion (see CCC 1229).

In the early church, the proclamation of the Word led to the conversion of mainly adult converts. The period of instruction (catechumenate) extended over many months, even years in some cases. Baptism normally occurred at the Easter Vigil, when the catechumens finally tasted the reality of the "mysteries" of Christ's death and resurrection. After being baptized and confirmed, the neophytes (those newly baptized) were led into the assembly of the believers, where they celebrated and received the Eucharist for the first time with the local church. Upon receiving these three sacraments, they became new, full-fledged members of the church. They experienced the "first fruits" of their salvation through the Holy Spirit entering their lives through baptism (see Rom 8:23). The neophytes, as the newly baptized were called, were clothed in white robes, symbolizing their rebirth as new creations in Jesus Christ.

The Second Vatican Council calls for the restoration of the catechumenate for adults for the Latin rite church, known as the "Rite of Christian Initiation of Adults" (RCIA). This, and every form of the catechumenate, is to be "a formation in the whole Christian life ... during which the disciples will be joined to Christ their teacher. The catechumens should be properly initiated into the mystery of salvation and the practice of the evangelical virtues, and they should be introduced into the life of faith, liturgy, and charity of the People of God by successive sacred rites."[14] Through their desire and intention to be baptized, catechumens already are considered to be joined to the church and to Christ.

Infant Baptism

As the church spread, the practice of the baptism of infants and young children became more common. In fact, it is an immemorial tradition of the church that has been explicitly mentioned in Christian writings from the second century onward. It is very probable that from the beginning of the apostolic preaching, when whole households received baptism, that infants were among those baptized (see Acts 16:15, 33; 18:8; 1 Cor 1:16; CCC 1152). Christian parents baptized their children because they desired their salvation, which came through sharing in the new life in Christ conferred in this sacrament.

A common question about infant baptism today is how an infant or child can be baptized, or saved, without a personal and mature faith in God. Is faith no longer the foundation of a genuine relationship with God?

The first factor to consider in answering this question is God's desire to save and share his life with people of all ages. Jesus never refused to bless or heal anyone on account of his or her age. He even spoke of little children as those who would inherit the kingdom of God on account of their utter dependence on God and simple trust in him. This underscores that salvation is a free gift of God. When someone baptizes, it is Christ who baptizes.[15] He is the one who saves us all, out of his sheer love and mercy. Infant baptism reminds us that we cannot "earn" or "merit" salvation, even through our faith. "The sheer gratuitousness of the grace of salvation is particularly manifest in infant Baptism" (CCC 1250).

Second, even in infant baptism, there is someone capable of believing in God and thus receiving his gift of divine life. The parents or godparents, as well as the witnessing church community, believe in God and accept his gift of new life on behalf of the child when he or she is baptized. This faith of the church is present and sufficient when an infant or child is baptized.

Consider how, in the Gospels, Jesus healed children, exorcised them, and even raised them from the dead when their parents approached Jesus in faith and asked for those things. How much more would Jesus desire to free an infant or child from the bondage of sin and eternal death when the parents and the Christian community present the child to be baptized!

The *Catechism* is even more adamant in stating the duty of Catholic parents to baptize their children: "The Church and the parents would deny a child the priceless grace of becoming a child of God were they not to confer Baptism shortly after birth[16] ... Christian parents will recognize that this practice also accords with their role as nurturers of the life that God has entrusted to them"[17] (CCC 1250, 1251).

Third, it must be understood that the Catholic Church recognizes that baptism is only the *beginning* of a life of faith. Baptism does not require a perfect or mature faith, but a beginning of faith that must develop. All Christians must grow in faith after baptism, expressed by the renewal of baptismal promises each year at the Easter Vigil (see CCC 1253, 1254).

For faith to grow, the newly baptized require the prayers and support of parents, godparents, and the whole ecclesial community (CCC 1255).

Is Baptism Necessary for Salvation?

How does one baptize? The basic form, or rite, of baptism is to pour water over a person's head three times (or immerse the person in water three times), while saying "(Name), I baptize you in the name of the Father, and of the Son, and of the Holy Spirit." Although the clergy (bishops, priests, or deacons) are the normal ministers of baptism, any Catholic (or even a non-Christian who has the intention of baptizing according to the belief of the Catholic Church) may baptize, and should be prepared to baptize in case of an emergency (see CCC 1256).

One reason for the simplicity of the baptismal rite and the possibility of anyone administering it is that baptism is normally necessary for salvation (see Jn 3:5; CCC 1257). "Normally" refers to the fact that the Lord Jesus commanded baptism, but there are ways known only to God that the grace of salvation may reach even the unbaptized, for *"God has bound salvation to the sacrament of Baptism, but he himself is not bound by his sacraments"* (CCC 1257).

For example, those who are martyred for faith in Christ without having received baptism will be saved by the shedding of their blood (see CCC 1258). Catechumens who die before their baptism may be saved (see CCC 1259), and even the person who, through no fault of his own, does not know Jesus Christ, "but seeks truth and does the will of God in accordance with his understanding of it, can be saved. It may be supposed that such persons would have *desired*

Baptism explicitly if they had known its necessity" (CCC 1260).

This teaching is based on our belief in a God who is just (i.e., who would not condemn people for what they, through no fault of their own, neglected to do), and a God who desires the salvation of every person (see 1 Tim 2:4).

The church entrusts *children who have died without baptism* to the mercy of God. The church's hope in their salvation is inspired by the revelation of Jesus' tenderness toward children, which caused him to say: "Let the children come to me; do not prevent them" (Mk 10:14, NAB). Based on this, the church is urgent in her call not to hinder little children from coming to Christ in the sacrament of baptism—infants should be baptized without undue delay (see CCC 1261).

What about Catholics who have fallen away from the practice of their faith, but who later desire to be rebaptized to express their return to the Lord and his church? "Rebaptism" neglects the fact that baptism (along with the sacraments of confirmation and Holy Orders) confers an "indelible character," that is, it changes the person in a way that is permanent and irrevocable. "Baptism seals the Christian with the indelible spiritual mark (*character*) of his belonging to Christ. No sin can erase this mark, even if sin prevents Baptism from bearing the fruits of salvation.[18] Given once for all, Baptism cannot be repeated" (CCC 1272).

Like the prodigal son in Jesus' parable, any baptized Catholic who desires to return to full participation in the church after falling away should simply repent and seek forgiveness in the Sacrament of Reconciliation in order to renew and refresh the grace first received at baptism. In the Catholic Church's view, the person who goes astray remains a member of God's family. He or she need only turn away from sin and return to the church to be joyfully welcomed back with full family status, as the father in Jesus' parable of the prodigal son rejoiced at his son's return (see Lk 15:11-32).

Likewise, anyone who has been baptized validly (i.e., with proper form and intention) outside the Catholic Church may be instructed and received into the Catholic Church by means of a profession of faith. The person may not be "rebaptized," though he or she may be baptized "conditionally," if it is uncertain whether the person had been given a valid Christian baptism.

Responsibilities and Privileges of the Baptized

As the foundational Christian sacrament, baptism gives people a share in the life and mission of Jesus Christ. The baptized no longer belong to themselves, but to God (see CCC 1269; 1 Cor 6:19; 2 Cor 5:15). They are called, like Christ, to be servants and to "obey and submit" to the church's leaders (see Heb 13:17). They are called to profess their faith actively, and to share in the church's mission to establish God's kingdom on earth.[19]

Many people mistakenly think that baptism in the Catholic Church is a "ticket to heaven"—a guarantee of salvation. Actually, it is the first step in a life-long journey of discipleship—following and obeying Jesus Christ. Both St. Paul (see 1 Cor 9:24-27; Phil 3:12-15) and Jesus himself emphasize the need to per-severe until the end of life in faith and love in order to obtain eternal salvation: "He who endures to the end will be saved" (Mk 13:13). Vatican II reiterated St. Augustine's teaching that one can be a member of the church "in the body" but not "in the heart." The distinction is love: "one who does not persevere in charity is not saved."[20]

While baptism confers these great responsibilities, "the baptized person also enjoys rights within the Church: to receive the sacraments, to be nourished with the Word of God and to be sustained by the other spiritual helps of the Church."[21]

The Sacrament of Confirmation

To equip and strengthen each baptized person to follow Jesus faithfully and to carry out the responsibilities of being a Christian, the Father and the Son send the Holy Spirit in a special way in the sacrament of confirmation. Confirmation continues and is a necessary completion of the mission of the Holy Spirit that was begun in baptism, making the person able to assume greater responsibilities in love and service of God and of his people (see CCC 1287).

Jesus promised to send the same Holy Spirit who had rested on him as the Messiah (see Isa 11:2; 61:1; Lk 4:16-22) upon all of his followers (see Lk 24:49; Jn 16; Acts 1:4-8). He fulfilled this promise on Easter Sunday and at Pentecost (see CCC 1287; Jn 20:22; Acts 2:1-4).

With the sending of the Spirit, the apostles sought to fulfill God's will and promise that the Spirit be poured out on all flesh (see Joel 2:28-32; Acts 2:17-21). Through the laying on of hands, they imparted to the newly baptized the gift of the Spirit that completes the grace of Baptism (see CCC 1288). This "laying on of hands" is the original sign of the sacrament of confirmation, which "perpetuates the grace of Pentecost in the Church."[22] To this, an anointing with oil (*chrism*) was added, highlighting the truth of the name "Christian," which means "anointed," named after *the* Christ whom God anointed with the Holy Spirit (see Acts 10:38).[23]

Two traditions emerged in the early church about how and when baptized Christians received this sacrament. In the Eastern Christian tradition, "chrismation" (anointing with chrism) was always done immediately after baptism by the bishop or priest who baptized. The Western Christian tradition wished confirmation always to be conferred by the bishop, which meant that it was separated from the baptismal rite (which priests generally began to administer as the church grew).

A centuries-old Latin custom set the "age of discretion" as the reference point for receiving confirmation, though children in danger of death may be confirmed earlier (CCC 1307). Confirmation is sometimes called the "sacrament of Christian maturity." However, maturity of faith must not be confused or identified with chronological age: even children may be spiritually mature, as in the case of child martyrs.[24]

In the Latin rite the bishop is the ordinary minister of confirmation. This is both for historical reasons and because confirmation administered by the bishop shows the unity of those confirmed with the church. However, the bishop may grant the faculty of administering confirmation to his priests, if the need arises (see CCC 1313).

To be confirmed, a person also should: (1) be in the state of grace; (2) have prepared spiritually for the sacrament by instruction, intense prayer, and the sacrament of penance; (3) have chosen a sponsor, often a godparent, to support him spiritually; and (4) have chosen the name of a saint who is a special patron and intercessor for the person to be confirmed.

The Purpose and Effects of Confirmation

The primary effect of confirmation is simple: the special outpouring of the Holy Spirit, as he was given to the apostles at Pentecost (see CCC 1302). We know with assurance that this prayer of the church will be answered, for Jesus himself taught: "For every one who asks receives, and he who seeks finds, and to him who knocks it will be opened.... If you then, who are evil, know how to give good gifts to your children, how much more will the heavenly Father give the Holy Spirit to those who ask him!" (Lk 11:10, 13).

The Acts of the Apostles records instances in which baptized persons were not aware of the presence or power of the Holy Spirit in their lives (see Acts 8:15-17; 19:6). On these occasions, the apostles laid their hands on and prayed over these people, and they received the Holy Spirit in a way clearly evidenced by gifts of the Spirit. This first occurred on a large scale at Pentecost, when the disciples of Jesus and others received the Holy Spirit with power. At that time, they received from the Spirit spiritual gifts that equipped them to live as Christians and to proclaim the Good News of Jesus Christ with new boldness.

Regardless of whether there are any outward signs or manifestations of the Spirit's coming, Catholics rely on Jesus' promise and know in faith that God grants through confirmation the gift of the Spirit that he so desires to give. The *Catechism* notes that:

> Confirmation brings an increase and deepening of baptismal grace: it roots us more deeply in the divine filiation which makes us cry, "Abba! Father!" (Rom 8:15); it unites us more firmly to Christ; it increases the gifts of the Holy Spirit in us; it renders our bond with the Church more perfect (cf. LG 11); it gives us a special strength of the Holy Spirit to spread and defend the faith by word and action as true witnesses of Christ, to confess the name of Christ boldly, and never to be ashamed of the Cross.[25] (CCC 1303)

Confirmation is another sacrament that changes a person in such a profound way that it can be received only once (see CCC 1121, 1304). In confirmation, God confers a new character, marks a person as his witness in a way that can never be effaced (see CCC 1304-1305).

Of course, the "character" and grace received in the sacrament of confirmation can be, and should be, renewed and "reawakened." Many Catholics today have experienced a powerful renewal of the grace of their baptism and confirmation through being "baptized in the Holy Spirit," often (though not always) in the context of the charismatic renewal movement in the church.

As in all the sacraments, the full benefits of the sacrament of confirmation are realized only when it is approached with a clear understanding of its meaning, and with expectant faith in what God wishes to do through the sacrament. Today, many Catholics are discovering how much God wishes to confer his power and the gifts of the Holy Spirit through this sacrament, and are preparing people for confirmation with this in mind. According to the *Catechism,*

> *Preparation* for Confirmation should aim at leading the Christian toward a more intimate union with Christ and a more lively familiarity with the Holy Spirit—his actions, his gifts, and his biddings—in order to be more capable of assuming the apostolic responsibilities of Christian life. (CCC 1309)

It also aims at leading the Christian to identify more deeply with the needs and mission of the universal church.

The Sacrament of the Eucharist

The Holy Eucharist is the final "sacrament of initiation" into Jesus Christ and his church (see CCC 1322). It is "the source and summit of the Christian life."[26] What is the Eucharist and why is it so important? Vatican II's "Constitution on the Sacred Liturgy" explains:

> At the Last Supper, on the night he was betrayed, our Savior instituted the Eucharistic sacrifice of his Body and Blood. This he did in order to perpetuate the sacrifice of the cross throughout the ages until he should come again, and so to entrust to his beloved Spouse, the Church, a memorial of his death and resurrection: a sacrament of love, a sign of unity, a bond of charity, a Paschal banquet "in which Christ is consumed, the mind is filled with grace, and a pledge of future glory is given to us."[27]

To understand the Eucharist, we must go back to Jesus' Last Supper with his apostles, and to his death on Calvary the following day. These historical events, completed by Jesus' resurrection from the dead on the third day, comprise the single greatest "mystery" of the Christian faith—the passover of Jesus from life to death, to new, glorified life—the "Paschal mystery."

This final drama of Jesus' earthly life began when he gathered his apostles together to celebrate the Jewish feast of Passover, which was now to become the celebration of the new passover of Christ from death to life. The words of institution, which are found in the three Synoptic Gospels (Mt 26:26-29; Mk 14:22-25; Lk 22:19-21; see CCC 1338) also reveal the meaning and purpose of Jesus' death: "This is my body, which will be given for you" (Lk 22:19, NAB); "Drink of it, all of you; for this is my blood of the covenant, which is poured out for many for the forgiveness of sins" (Mt 26:27-28).

How are we to understand these words of Jesus? Was Jesus speaking symbolically, indicating that the bread and wine of the Lord's Supper represent his body and blood, but that there was not to be an actual change in these elements? Or was it a call to receive Christ through faith, or indirectly, through the action of the Holy Spirit, who is offered to us through the sacrifice of Jesus' body and the shedding of his blood? How do we understand and receive Jesus as "the living bread that came down from heaven" (Jn 6:51, NAB)?

Catholics believe that God himself provided commentaries on the "words of institution" of the Eucharist in the last Gospel to be written (the Gospel of John) and in the letters of St. Paul. Other important insights from Christian tradition are to be found in the writings on the Eucharist from the early church.

John's Gospel (6:48-70) indicates that Christ himself elaborated on the fact that the eucharistic bread and wine were truly the body and blood of Jesus. This belief had apparently become a source of scandal to the Jews and others who were considering becoming Christians. John emphasizes that Jesus really meant that he expected his followers to eat his flesh and drink his blood (see Jn 6:51-57) and that he predicted that many people would be scandalized and fall away from him because of this teaching (see Jn 6:60-66).

When Jesus said, "unless you eat the flesh of the Son of Man and drink his blood, you do not have life within you" (Jn 6:53, NAB), he was speaking about them receiving his body and blood in the form of the bread and wine of the Lord's Supper or Eucharist. This was no symbolic reception, according to John, but meant that in the Eucharist one literally eats the body of Christ and drinks his blood, even if these still appear to our senses as bread and wine.

This teaching is as much of a challenge to the faith of Christians today as it was to the readers of John's Gospel. Catholic Christians accept this challenging teaching at its face value, and believe that when we receive the bread and wine of the Eucharist, we are actually partaking in the body and blood of Jesus Christ.

This understanding is also affirmed by the apostle Paul, who wrote: "The cup of blessing which we bless, is it not a participation in the blood of Christ? The bread which we break, is it not a participation in the body of Christ? Because there is one bread, we who are many are one body, for we all partake of the one bread" (1 Cor 10:16-17). Further on in this letter, after restating Jesus' words of institution, Paul concludes: "Whoever, therefore, eats the bread or drinks the cup of the Lord in an unworthy manner will be guilty of profaning the body and blood of the Lord. Let a man examine himself, and so eat of the bread and drink of the cup. For any one who eats and drinks without discerning the body eats and drinks judgment upon himself" (1 Cor 11:27-29). The most straightforward interpretation of these passages is that Paul considered the eucharistic bread and wine to be literally the body and blood of Christ.

The Early Church's Understanding of the Eucharist

How did the early Christians understand the Bible's teaching about the Eucharist? To summarize a vast amount of literature, nearly every notable writing of the early church that mentions the Eucharist either implies or directly states that the bread and wine of the Lord's Supper are truly the body and blood of Jesus Christ. These include the writings of Ignatius of Antioch:

They hold aloof from the Eucharist and from services of prayer because they refuse to admit that the Eucharist is the flesh of our savior, Jesus Christ...;[28]

Justin Martyr:

For we do not receive these things as common bread or common drink; but as Jesus Christ our Savior being incarnate by God's Word took flesh and blood for our salvation, so also we have been taught that the food consecrated by the word of prayer that comes from Him ... is the flesh and blood of that incarnate Jesus...;[29]

Irenaeus of Lyon:

He [Jesus] declares that the cup, [taken] from the creation is His own blood ... and He has firmly assured us that the bread, [taken] from the creation, is His own body.... For when the mixed cup and the bread that has been prepared receive the Word of God, and become the Eucharist, the body and blood of Christ,... by these our flesh grows and is confirmed...;[30]

Cyril of Jerusalem, [31] Saint Augustine, [32] and many others. It appears that every reliable early Christian writer who wrote on the subject believed that the bread and wine of the Eucharist are the body and blood of Christ. The Catholic understanding of the Eucharist as truly the body and blood of Christ appears to be firmly supported by both the New Testament and the early Christian church.

The Real Presence, Transubstantiation, and Eucharistic Adoration

For these reasons, Catholics speak of the "real presence" of Jesus Christ in the Eucharist (CCC 1374). This presence of Jesus can only be accepted in faith, since the outward appearance of the bread and wine does not change. Medieval Catholic theologians and the Council of Trent used the term "transubstantiation" to describe the mystery by which the inner reality, or "essence," of the bread and wine is transformed into the Body and Blood of Jesus, while the outward appearance, or "accidents," remains the same (see CCC 1376). (Today we would say that there is no change in the molecular structure of the bread and wine of the Eucharist.)

This doctrine is not intended to explain *how* this happens, as if to reduce this mystery of faith to something totally comprehensible to the human mind. It simply affirms, in faith, that Jesus' words are literally true: the bread and wine offered to God in the Eucharist become his Body and Blood. This explains why

Catholic Christians have great reverence for the eucharistic bread and wine, since they believe that the Word of God is present there just as fully as he was present in the physical body of Jesus. Catholics do not worship a piece of bread or a cup of wine, but worship Jesus Christ, whom they discern by faith to be present, "body and blood, soul and divinity," under the appearance of bread and wine.[33]

Flowing from this belief, the Catholic Church fosters and encourages various forms of "Eucharistic adoration." As Pope Paul VI taught in his encyclical letter *Mysterium Fidei:*

> The Catholic Church has always offered and still offers to the sacrament of the Eucharist the cult of adoration, not only during Mass, but also outside of it, reserving the consecrated hosts with the utmost care, exposing them to the solemn veneration of the faithful, and carrying them in procession.[34]

The Eucharistic body of Jesus, which is known as the "Blessed Sacrament," is reserved for adoration and prayer in each Catholic church. A tabernacle "in an especially worthy place" is marked by a lighted vigil candle whenever the Blessed Sacrament is present there (see CCC 1379).

Understanding the Eucharist

For Catholics, the heart of the Mass and the center of Christian worship is the Eucharist. "Eucharist" means "thanksgiving." In the ancient Jewish tradition, the term "eucharist" referred to the thanksgiving to God that the head of the household pronounced before the Passover meal or other Jewish festive meals over the third cup of wine, the cup of blessing (see 1 Cor 10:16), for all the benefits God had given them. Therefore, in the Christian tradition, we give thanks for the great gift and sacrifice of God's Son, Jesus. By the beginning of the second century, Christians were using the word "eucharist" to designate their coming together to commemorate and reenact this great event, the Lord's Last Supper (see CCC 1328).

This central mystery of the Christian faith is known by many other titles, each of which highlights a dimension of its meaning. It is known as "the Lord's

Supper" (see 1 Cor 11:20; Rev 19:9); the "breaking of bread" (see Mt 14:19; 15:36; 26:26; Mk 8:6, 19; Lk 24:13-35; Acts 2:42, 46; 20:7, 11; 1 Cor 10:16-17; 1 Cor 11:24); the Eucharistic assembly; and the memorial of the Lord's Passion and Resurrection (see CCC 1329). Because the Eucharist is a holy sacrifice, in the Latin West we use the terms "holy sacrifice of the Mass," "sacrifice of praise," "spiritual sacrifice," or simply "the Mass" (*Missa*). This reminds us of the sending forth (*missio*) of the faithful to fulfill God's will in their daily lives (see CCC 1332, 1330). The Eastern rite Catholic churches tend to focus on the *mystery* of the Eucharistic celebration, and speak of it as the Holy and Divine Liturgy, or the Sacred Mysteries (see CCC 1330).

However, what is really important is not the name, but the meaning of the sacrament. This cannot be expressed in just a few words, because it is, in a sacramental way, the realization and summation of the entire Christian mystery of salvation. The meaning of the Eucharist is multidimensional, like a priceless diamond. A major error of some past theology has been to artificially separate the various dimensions of the Eucharist, or even to deny the validity of some aspects. Let us briefly examine some of the dimensions of the Eucharist.

1. The Eucharist as covenant. The Hebrew people understand their entire relationship with God to be based on a covenant with Him—a solemn agreement involving mutual commitment. Moses sealed the first covenant with God with the shed blood of sacrificial animals. The blood that sealed the new and final covenant of God with man is the blood of Jesus, the Son of God. Jesus declared at the Last Supper: "This cup which is poured out for you is the new covenant in my blood" (Lk 22:20). The Letter to the Hebrews (9:11-28; 10:19-31) proclaims the surpassing power of the blood of Christ in purifying and liberating God's people of the New Covenant.

2. The Eucharist as praise, thanksgiving, and sacrifice. At the Last Supper, Jesus led the traditional Jewish table prayers that focused on praise and thanksgiving (*berakhah*) to God (see Lk 22:17-20). The early Christians called their celebration of the Last Supper "the Eucharist," the thanksgiving to God the Father for his greatest gift, his Son, Jesus Christ (see CCC 1358-61).

The Old Testament often speaks of a sacrifice of thanksgiving, or praise (see Ps 50:14, 23; 116:17; 119:108). The concepts of thanksgiving and sacrifice, seen in the Jewish sacrificial meal of the Passover, are closely connected. The sacrifice most pleasing to God is the offering of our entire being to him in thanksgiving and praise (see Ps 40). Jesus himself offered the most perfect thanksgiving to God by offering his life as a sacrifice, according to his Father's will (see Heb 10:10, 12, 14), to atone for the sins of humanity.

Some Christians object that it is blasphemous to call the Mass a sacrifice, because Jesus offered the perfect sacrifice of thanksgiving once for all when he died on Calvary (see Heb 9:11, 25-28). They think Catholics believe that Jesus is sacrificed again every time that the Eucharist is celebrated. Catholics actually believe that in the Mass Christ's one sacrifice on Calvary is re-presented (made present once again) or perpetuated.[35] Christ's death on the cross is both a historical and a "transhistorical" event. It is as real and powerful today as it first was nearly two thousand years ago. Catholics believe that God, in his love and mercy, desires to make the one, eternal sacrifice of Christ present to his people in the sacrament of the Eucharist, so that we may enter ever more deeply into its saving power.[36]

3. The Eucharist as a memorial in which Jesus is continually made present. After Jesus offered his apostles the bread of his body and the cup of his blood, he commissioned them to: "Do this in remembrance of me" (Lk 22:19; 1 Cor 11:24-25). The Eucharist is also an *anamnesis,* a remembrance or memorial, of what Jesus did at the Last Supper, of his whole life and ministry, and in a particular way of his sacrificial death on the cross.

The Semitic, biblical concept of memorial meant more than merely remembering something mentally, or commemorating it symbolically. It meant making something from the *past* actually *present* once more. Thus, Catholic Christians have always understood the Eucharist as memorial to mean that the reality of Jesus' Body and Blood (*offered* to us at the Last Supper and *sacrificed* once and for all for us on Calvary) is truly made present in the sacrament, under the appearances of bread and wine. As described earlier, Catholics speak of the real presence of Jesus Christ in the Eucharist, which ultimately results from Jesus' commission to his apostles to reenact the first Eucharist "in remembrance of me" (Lk 22:19; see CCC 1362-64).

4. The Eucharist as the Paschal banquet. The Mass is at the same time a memorial and perpetuation of the sacrifice of the cross, and the Paschal banquet of communion with the Lord's Body and Blood.[37] Likewise, the altar of the Mass represents both the altar of the sacrifice and the table of the Lord. "This is all the more so since the Christian altar is the symbol of Christ himself, present in the midst of the assembly of his faithful, both as the victim offered for our reconciliation and as food from heaven who is giving himself to us" (CCC 1383).

Indeed, the Eucharist is spiritual nourishment for our lives. In the Gospel of John, Jesus calls himself the "true bread from heaven" (Jn 6:32), and tells his followers: "I am the bread of life; he who comes to me shall not hunger, and he who believes in me shall never thirst ... he who eats my flesh and drinks my blood has eternal life, and I will raise him up at the last day. For my flesh is food indeed, and my blood is drink indeed" (Jn 6:35, 54-55).

We receive this nourishment and life when we approach the Eucharist in faith, truly discerning that this is the Body and Blood of the Lord (see 1 Cor 11:27-29), for we are nourished by Jesus himself, who becomes our spiritual food.

5. The Eucharist as communion. The *Catechism* emphasizes that the goal of the Eucharist is to bring us into union, or communion, with Christ (see CCC 1383). The Lord himself exhorts us, "Truly, I say to you, unless you eat the flesh of the Son of man and drink his blood, you have no life in you" (Jn 6:53).

The Catholic Church teaches "that the faithful, if they have the required dispositions (cf. CIC, can 916), [ought to] *receive communion when* they participate in the Mass" (CCC 1388; cf. CIC, can. 917), and obliges them to go to Mass on Sundays and feast days (commonly called "holy days of obligation"). Prepared by the sacrament of Reconciliation, Catholics are required to receive the Eucharist at least once a year, if possible during the Easter season. However, this is only a minimum; Catholics are encouraged to celebrate Mass and receive the Eucharist often, even daily (see CCC 1389).[38]

There are many "fruits" of receiving Jesus in Holy Communion. This sacrament deepens our union with Jesus (see CCC 1391); helps us to overcome and avoid sin (see CCC 1393, 1395); removes venial sins (see CCC 1394); unifies the church and promotes the unity of Christians (see CCC 1396, 1398); and unites us with the poor (see CCC 1398).

We can also reflect on the Eucharist in terms of the covenant relationship it establishes between God and his people: "this cup which is poured out for you is the new covenant in my blood" (Lk 22:20; see 1 Cor 11:25).

In the Eucharist, we affirm our covenant relationship with God, sealed by the blood of Jesus. Any Catholic who has broken this covenant with God through serious sin must seek forgiveness and be reconciled with God through the sacrament of reconciliation before receiving the Lord's Body and Blood (see 1 Cor 11:27-29). Catholics must also prepare to receive Communion worthily by keeping the required fast, and by coming to receive Communion with bodily demeanor and clothing that reflect the "respect, solemnity and joy of this moment when Christ becomes our guest" (CCC 1387).

Through the Eucharist we also reaffirm our covenant with one another in the church. "The bread which we break, is it not a participation in the body of Christ? Because there is one bread, we who are many are one body, for we all partake of the one bread" (1 Cor 10:16-17; see CCC 1396). Participation in the Eucharist expresses our unity. If there is anything serious dividing Christians, it should be settled before approaching the altar (see Mt 5:23-24). The kiss of peace at the Mass is not just a ritual, but a visible sign of our unity in Christ.

For this reason, the Catholic Church does not (except in very specific circumstances) allow intercommunion—that is, Christians of different denominations and traditions receiving Holy Communion together (see CCC 1399-1401). For Catholics, the Eucharist is the highest, most primary sign of the reality of our communion with God and our unity with one another. If there is a serious disagreement among Christians that results in division into different denominations or churches, the Catholic Church believes that reconciliation must first occur before we can approach the altar of the Lord together for Communion. The unity of the altar is the goal of ecumenism and not a means of ecumenical endeavor.

Fortunately, some significant steps toward Christian unity have been made through the ecumenical movement. We must continue to pray and work for the day when the church's unity is fully restored and all Christians will be able to approach the table of the Lord together in full communion of mind and heart. "The more painful the experience of the divisions in the Church which break the common participation in the table of the Lord, the more urgent are our prayers to the Lord that the time of complete unity among all who believe in him may return" (CCC 1398).

6. The Eucharist as a work of the Holy Spirit, anticipating the age to come. Just as the Holy Spirit guided Jesus throughout his life and led him to his final sacrifice on the cross, the Holy Spirit leads Christians to the Eucharist and enables them to recognize Jesus Christ truly present there. The eucharistic prayer in the liturgy begins with the *epiclesis*, the invocation or calling down of the Holy Spirit. The Spirit is invoked to bless the bread and wine, preparing it to become the Body and Blood of Christ. We also call upon him to bless the community gathered, that by receiving the Body of the Lord, we ourselves might become more profoundly the body of the Lord, lifting up our hearts and minds to God in praise and thanksgiving.

The Holy Spirit also points toward the future, when the sacramental presence of Christ will be replaced by seeing him face to face. Truly the Eucharist is also an anticipation of this heavenly glory.

An ancient prayer of the church acclaims the mystery of the Eucharist: "O sacred banquet in which Christ is received as food, the memory of his Passion is renewed, the soul is filled with grace and a pledge of the life to come is given to us."[39]

As St. Paul taught, "For as often as you eat this bread and drink the cup, you proclaim the death of the Lord until he comes" (1 Cor 11:26, NAB). The Holy Spirit stirs up in the hearts of believers the reality of the eucharistic response: "Christ has died! Christ has risen! Christ will come again!" Indeed, "The Spirit and the Bride [the church] say, 'Come!'" (Rev 22:17). "Amen. Come, Lord Jesus!" (Rev 22:20).

> There is no surer pledge or clearer sign of this great hope in the new heavens and new earth "in which righteousness dwells" (2 Pet 3:1) than the Eucharist. Every time this mystery is celebrated, "the work of our redemption is carried on" and we "break that one bread that provides the medicine of immortality, the antidote for death, and the food that makes us live for ever in Jesus Christ."[40]

In conclusion, it is in the Eucharist that Jesus manifests himself and gives himself to his church most fully. Likewise, the church is a eucharistic community, a community which exists to give thanks and praise to God. This happens most perfectly when the church unites its prayers and offerings with the perfect offering of Jesus himself on Calvary.

The Sacrament of Reconciliation

The sacrament of reconciliation (also known as the sacrament of penance, of conversion, of forgiveness, or simply as "confession") is one of the two "sacraments of healing," for it heals Christians of the greatest sickness, *sin,* which corrupts our true humanity and separates us from God and from each other (see CCC 1440).

The origin of this sacrament is our Lord Jesus Christ, "physician of our souls and bodies, who forgave the sins of the paralytic and restored him to bodily health" (CCC 1421; see Mk 2:1-12).

Jesus' ministry was clearly one of reconciliation and forgiveness. He forgave the woman caught in the act of adultery (see Jn 8:1-11); forgave Peter, who denied Christ three times (see Jn 21:15-19); and even forgave those who crucified him (see Lk 23:34).

As the Son of God incarnate, he alone had the authority within himself to forgive sins. However, reconciliation and forgiveness did not end with Jesus; this has become the ministry of the church. "Christ reconciled us to himself and gave us the ministry of reconciliation.... So we are ambassadors for Christ, God making his appeal through us. We beseech you on behalf of Christ, be reconciled to God" (2 Cor 5:18-20).

Jesus Christ conferred special authority to forgive sins in God's name upon the apostles. Certainly all Christians are expected to forgive those who sin against us, as we pray in the Lord's Prayer (see Mt 6:14; 18:21-23; Lk 17:3-4). However, Jesus shared with his apostles the unique authority that he possessed to forgive the sins of all persons, even those guilty of grave offenses against God and man. To Peter he said, "whatever you declare bound on earth shall be bound in heaven; whatever you declare loosed on earth shall be loosed in heaven" (see Mt 16:18-19). Later he told the apostles the same thing (see Mt 18:18). Even more directly, in John's Gospel, Jesus appeared to the apostles on Easter and said, "Receive the Holy Spirit. If you forgive the sins of any, they are forgiven; if you retain the sins of any, they are retained" (Jn 20:22-23).

In the early church, the apostles and their successors, the bishops, exercised this authority given them by Christ. The church's official act of forgiveness, sometimes called absolution, was reserved for those who had committed very serious sin, such as murder, adultery, or apostasy (denying one's faith), and it was accompanied by a long period of severe public penance. A person could normally receive absolution for these sins only once in a lifetime. The early Christians took seriously the teaching of Paul about becoming a new creation when baptized. It was expected that a baptized person had the grace to avoid serious sin.

Because the formal forgiveness of serious sin in the church was restricted and involved severe penances, many converts to Christianity began to delay being baptized until late in their lives. They feared falling into serious sin after baptism, and the rigors of public penance.

A change in the understanding of this sacrament took place in the sixth and seventh centuries. Irish monks, probably in the context of spiritual direction, developed the practice of forgiving sins in Jesus' name as a part of a more frequent private confession that included less serious sins. This eventually became the standard form of the sacrament (see CCC 1447).

In the Latin rite today, the sacrament of reconciliation normally begins with a greeting and blessing from the priest, often followed by a short reading from the Word of God to illuminate the conscience and elicit contrition, and an exhortation to repentance. Then the penitent confesses his or her sins to the priest. The priest may offer some counsel, and then must give a penance, which must be acknowledged and accepted by the penitent, who then must express sorrow for his or her sins and ask God's forgiveness. (This may be done using an "act of contrition," or in one's own words). The priest absolves the person of sin in Jesus' name (called *absolution*), and the confession may end with a prayer of thanksgiving and praise, and dismissal with the blessing of the priest (see CCC 1480). Penitents may confess their sins to a priest either face to face or using a screen. Other specific directives, such as concerning communal celebration of this sacrament, are listed in the *Catechism* (CCC 1481-85).

Ongoing Conversion

One may ask why the church needs a sacrament of forgiveness after baptism cleanses us of all sins and makes us a "new creation" (2 Cor 5:17). The *Catechism* explains what every Christian knows from his or her own experience that "the new life received in Christian initiation has not abolished the frailty and weakness of human nature, nor the inclination to sin that tradition calls *con-cupiscence,* which remains in the baptized..." (CCC 1426). The Christian life is, therefore, a life of ongoing repentance and conversion. "Christ's call to conversion continues to resound in the lives of Christians. This *second conversion* [continual conversion after baptism] is an uninterrupted task for the whole Church who, 'clasping sinners to her bosom, [is] at once holy and always in need of purification, [and] follows constantly the path of penance and renewal.'"[41]

This conversion is first and primarily a *"conversion of the heart, interior conversion"* (CCC 1430), a decision to reject sin and to turn back to God. This interior conversion expresses itself in works and gestures of penance, such as fasting, prayer, and almsgiving (see CCC 1434), as well as in other actions or attitudes. These may include seeking reconciliation, concern for the poor, the exercise and defense of justice and right (see Isa 1:17; Am 5:24), the admission of faults to one's brethren, fraternal correction, change of life, examination of conscience, spiritual direction, acceptance of suffering, and enduring persecution for the sake of righteousness (see CCC 1435). "Taking up one's cross each day and following Jesus is the surest way of penance" (CCC 1435; see Lk 9:23).

In the Sacrament of Reconciliation, the confessor assigns a particular "penance" as an expression of the penitent's sorrow or contrition for sin. It is also an act of reparation to God, and sometimes to others, for the injury and offense caused by the sin. The *Catechism* explains:

> Absolution takes away sin, but it does not remedy all the disorders sin has caused.[42] Raised up from sin, the sinner must still recover his full spiritual health by doing something more to make amends for the sin: he must "make satisfaction for" or "expiate" his sins. This satisfaction is also called "penance." (CCC 1459)

The *penance* the confessor imposes must take into account the penitent's personal situation and must seek his spiritual good. It must correspond as far as possible with the gravity and nature of the sins committed. It can consist of prayer, an offering, works of mercy, service of neighbor, voluntary self-denial, sacrifices, and above all the patient acceptance of the cross we must bear. Such penances help configure us to Christ, who alone expiated our sins once for all. They allow us to become co-heirs with the risen Christ, "provided we suffer with him" (Rom 3:25; Rom 8:17; 1 Jn 21-22) (CCC 1460; cf. Council of Trent (1551): DS 1690).

We must not forget, though, that the essential and most remarkable aspect of reconciliation is not the penance, but the conversion of heart—the desire and the will to turn back to God—which is a work of grace.

God must give man a new heart (cf. Ezek 36:26-27). Conversion is first of all a work of the grace of God, who makes our hearts return to him: "Restore us to thyself, O LORD, that we may be restored!" (Lam 5:21). God gives us the strength to begin anew. It is in discovering the greatness of God's love that our heart is shaken by the horror and weight of sin and begins to fear offending God by sin and being separated from him. The human heart is converted by looking upon him whom our sins have pierced (see Jn 19:37; Zech 12:10). (CCC 1432)

Yet, in many traditionally Catholic countries, the confessionals stand empty: few people, it seems, desire to avail themselves of the forgiving, healing, and liberating grace of the Sacrament of Reconciliation. Why? Perhaps it is a sign of a great loss of faith in God, or in the "institutional church" as God's instrument of forgiveness. Or it may be a loss of the sense or meaning of sin as an offense against God, or against anyone.

In 1946, Pope Pius XII had already declared that "the sin of the century is the loss of the sense of sin." This loss goes hand in hand with the "loss of the sense of God."[43] Indeed, true or "perfect" contrition (sorrow for sin) "arises from a love by which God is loved above all" (CCC 1452) and sorrow stems from the realization of the horror of ever offending the all-loving and all-merciful God. Even "imperfect contrition" (sorrow for sin because of the ugliness of sin or from fear of punishment) is "a gift of God, a prompting of the Holy Spirit" (CCC 1453) that many people lack today.

If only the world could become aware of the reality of God and the depth of his love! This love led God to humbly take on our humanity and then to suffer and die a horrible, shameful death. He did this for the sole purpose of freeing humanity from the bondage and consequences of sin, and, through forgiveness, to reconcile us with God and with each other. It is clear that the Holy Spirit, who convicts the world of sin (see Jn 16:8-9), "is also the Consoler who gives the human heart grace for repentance and conversion" (see Jn 15:26; Acts 2:36-38) (CCC 1433; John Paul II, DeV 27-48).

Why Confession? The Role of the Church

We have seen the stages of repentance and reconciliation: the Holy Spirit reveals and *convicts or convinces* a person of sin. This leads (by God's grace) to *conversion* of heart and *confession* of this sin, along with acts of *penance* to express sorrow for sin and to seek to make reparation or satisfaction for the offense or injury done to God and others.

Yet the question often is asked: Why is this sacrament necessary? Why not confess your sins directly to God, instead of to another human being?

Catholics believe that it is appropriate and even essential to repent directly before God for one's sins. When Catholics participate in this sacrament they are primarily expressing their repentance and sorrow for sin to God, and seeking to be reconciled to him. However, Catholics believe that Jesus had a purpose in granting particular persons the authority to forgive sins in God's name.

In this sacrament, as in all the others, the priest acts *in persona Christi,* "in the person of Christ." That is, the priest acts as a special representative of Christ by virtue of his ordination, and exercises the authority of Jesus Christ in his sacramental ministry. In the Sacrament of Reconciliation, it is not the priest who grants forgiveness of sins, but God, who uses the priest as an instrument and sign of his mercy. When our sins are forgiven by one who has been set apart by the church to represent Jesus Christ in a special way, we can experience the mercy of Jesus himself through that person and his ministry. Thus, the Catholic Church teaches that it is necessary to confess all mortal or deadly sins in the Sacrament of Reconciliation, "even if they are most secret"[44] and interior, and it is strongly recommended to confess everyday faults (venial sins). The regular confession of our venial sins helps us form our conscience, fight against evil tendencies, let ourselves be healed by Christ, and progress in the life of the Spirit (see CCC 1455).[45]

Confessing sins to a person reminds one of the social dimension of sin. When someone sins, that person not only offends God; his or her sin also has an effect, either direct or indirect, on other people. The effect of this sacrament is to reconcile the penitent with the church. In the sacrament, Jesus heals the negative social effect of sin and restores the person to the communion of the church, which revitalizes the church's life (see CCC 1469). Note that in this healing sacrament the priest who grants God's forgiveness not only represents Jesus Christ, but also the whole Christian community, the church.

Finally, the priest or minister is often able to counsel and encourage the penitent, or even pray with the penitent for healing of some area of sin or brokenness in the person's life. Jesus often uses his representative, the priest, to minister to the needs of people in remarkable ways through the Sacrament of Reconciliation.

There is power in this sacrament. Along with its primary power of reconciling us with God and restoring the sinner to His grace and friendship, the Sacrament of Reconciliation has power to reconcile and restore relationships among people, to heal the wounds and other effects of sin, and to give the Christian the spiritual strength and courage to avoid sin and to overcome temptation. Little wonder that "the Fathers of the Church present this sacrament as the 'second plank [of salvation] after the shipwreck which is the loss of grace'"[46] (CCC 1446). Thanks be to God for this marvelous gift of God's mercy!

The Anointing of the Sick

Like the Sacrament of Reconciliation, the anointing of the sick is another healing sacrament of the church, carrying on Jesus' own ministry of healing. While the Sacrament of Reconciliation focuses on healing sin and the effects of sin, this sacrament calls on God's healing for those physically or psychologically ill.

The scriptural roots of the sacrament of anointing of the sick are clear. Jesus healed the sick and commanded and empowered his disciples to do the same: "And they cast out many demons, and anointed with oil many that were sick and healed them" (Mk 6:13). The elders or priests in the early church continued this practice: "Is any among you sick? Let him call for the elders [priests] of the church, and let them pray over him, anointing him with oil in the name of the Lord; and the prayer of faith will save the sick man, and the Lord will raise him up; and if he has committed sins, he will be forgiven" (Jas 5:14-15).

The Bible explicitly teaches that the "presbyters" of the church should be called to pray over the sick and anoint them with oil for healing and forgiveness. Therefore, the only ministers of this sacrament are priests (i.e., bishops and presbyters; see CCC 1516). In the rite of the sacrament, the priest lays hands on the sick, prays over them (see Jas 5:15), and then anoints them with oil (usually blessed by the bishop; see CCC 1519).

When does one participate in this sacrament? It may be conferred whenever any one of the faithful begins to be in danger of death from sickness or old age, or just prior to a serious operation. The sacrament may be repeated if a person recovers and then falls into another grave illness, or during the same illness if a person's condition becomes more serious (see CCC 1514-15).

This sacrament has been practiced since the earliest days of the church, but its focus has shifted at times. Until recently, the emphasis was on preparation for death, but the Second Vatican Council restored an emphasis on prayer for physical and spiritual healing for all seriously ill persons.

While the ministering of this sacrament is reserved for priests, this does not preclude the practice of individual Christians praying for the sick. The *Catechism* states that "The Holy Spirit gives to some a special charism of healing[47] so as to make manifest the power of the grace of the risen Lord" (CCC 1508). The sacrament of the Anointing of the Sick simply acknowledges Jesus' command to his apostles to anoint and heal the sick, and recognizes the power that has always been at work through their ministry and through that of the elders who succeeded them.

Healing and the Sacrament of the Anointing of the Sick

Because the church believes in the life-giving presence of Christ, the physician of souls and bodies, she responds in faith to his command to "Heal the sick!" (Mt 10:8; see CCC 1509). The Catholic Church believes that the sacrament of the Anointing of the Sick can be a means of the Lord healing a person physically.

However, this sacrament does not guarantee that every sick person will be healed in a particular way. The *Catechism* notes that "even the most intense prayers do not always obtain the healing of all illnesses" (CCC 1508). St. Paul learned from the Lord that "my grace is sufficient for you, for my power is made perfect in weakness" (2 Cor 12:9), and gained insight into the mystery of the redemptive value of his suffering through his union with Jesus: "In my flesh I complete what is lacking in Christ's afflictions for the sake of his Body, that is, the Church" (Col 1:24).

Catholics understand "that suffering can also have a redemptive meaning for the sins of others" (CCC 1502; cf. Isa 53:11), when it is united with the suffering of Jesus, our redeemer. Suffering is never easy, but the burden may be lighter when we realize that suffering configures us to him—makes us like Jesus, unites us with him in his suffering and death, and may be offered for the forgiveness and expiation of others' sins (see CCC 1505).

Our God is a healing God, and he often responds to the prayer of Christians and works through the sacrament of the Anointing of the Sick to restore to health those who are suffering. Catholics will see the power of God manifest as they pray for the sick with expectant faith and call upon his healing power through this sacrament. There are certain graces that always accompany the celebration of this sacrament:

1. "The first grace of this sacrament is one of strengthening. Through this sacrament the infirm find peace and courage to overcome the difficulties that go with the condition of serious illness or the frailty of old age. This assistance from the Lord by the power of his Spirit is meant to lead the sick person to healing of the soul, but also of the body, if such is God's will.[48] Furthermore, 'if he has committed sins, he will be forgiven'" (Jas 5:15) (CCC 1520, emphasis added; cf. Council of Trent (1551): DS 1717).

2. The second grace unites the sick person to the passion of Christ, for his own good and that of the whole church. God's ways are above our ways, and often God will allow sickness or suffering to continue, yet will work on a deeper level in the person. Many texts in the New Testament exhort Christians to rejoice in their sufferings, and to consider them a sharing in the suffering of Christ (see Rom 8:16-17; 2 Cor 4:16-18; Col 1:24; 2 Tim 1:11-12; 1 Pet 4:13).

3. The third grace is found in "the preparation for passing over to eternal life" (see CCC 1532). The grace found in the Anointing of the Sick is a gift of the Holy

Spirit, who renews trust and faith in God and strengthens the believer against the temptations of the evil one, particularly the temptation to discouragement and anguish in the face of death (see Heb 2:15).

Along with the Anointing of the Sick, the priest will offer the seriously ill person the Eucharist. Holy Communion received near the point of death is known as "viaticum," which refers to the "passing over" from life in this world to eternal life (see CCC 1524). Thus, "the sacraments of Christian initiation" (baptism, confirmation, and the Eucharist) are "mirrored" by the sacraments of the end of life that prepare us for our homeland of heaven (penance, the Anointing of the Sick, and the Eucharist as viaticum) (CCC 1524).

Special Sacraments of Christian Vocation

God invites each person into relationship and union with himself by calling the person to a particular state of life or vocation, which means "calling." It is through or by means of this vocation that the person will attain the Christian perfection or holiness that is required of all followers of Jesus Christ, as is emphasized in Vatican II's "Dogmatic Constitution on the Church," chapter five, on "The Universal Call to Holiness."

It is important that each Christian pray fervently and seek counsel to discern the vocation that would best enable him or her to know, love, and serve God fully. God has a plan for each of our lives. Respecting the freedom that he has given us, God allows us to choose freely the path we are to follow. However, if we seek the guidance of the Holy Spirit in choosing our vocation, and do our best to obey what God appears to be speaking, we can have confidence that we will find the state in life which will enable us to mature as Christians, grow in holiness, and advance the kingdom of God.

Two Christian vocations are consecrated to God in a special way through sacraments of the church: ordination to the ministerial priesthood, and marriage. The sacrament of marriage is considered by the Catholic Church to be indissoluble in this life. The effect of Holy Orders is eternal. Jesus himself taught about marriage, "What therefore God has joined together, let no man put asunder" (Mt 19:6), and of priesthood, the Old Testament says, "You are a priest forever, according to the order of Melchizedek" (see Ps 110:4).

The sacraments of Matrimony and Holy Orders are directed toward to salvation of others and the building up of the church. Hence they are called "sacraments in service of communion." Through them, members of the church are set apart or consecrated for their special ministry of service to God and his people (see CCC 1535).

Holy Orders—The Call to Christ's Ministerial Priesthood

Jesus Christ entrusted a mission to his apostles that will continue to be carried out in the church until the end of time. "Holy Orders" is the sacrament that confers this special apostolic ministry and mission that Jesus gave to his apostles. It includes three degrees: episcopate, presbyterate, and diaconate (see CCC 1536).

All Catholics are members of the royal priesthood (see 1 Pet 2:9) of Jesus Christ, and share in his threefold ministry of priest, prophet, and king. However, Jesus selected certain men from among his followers to share in his ministry in a particular way. (This is the origin of the "ministerial priesthood," as distinguished from the common priesthood of all the baptized.)

Jesus chose twelve men, his apostles, and set them apart to lead his people after his death, resurrection, and ascension. The synoptic Gospels record that on the night before he died, Jesus shared the bread, his body, and the cup of wine, his blood, with them and commissioned them to "Do this in remembrance of me" (Lk 22:19). John's Gospel recounts that when he appeared to these same men three days later, after his resurrection, he said:

> "Peace be with you. As the Father has sent me, even so I send you." And when he said this, he breathed on them, and said to them, "Receive the Holy Spirit. If you forgive the sins of any, they are forgiven; if you retain the sins of any, they are retained."
>
> JOHN 20:21-23

Thus, the apostles were empowered by Jesus Christ to lead and teach his followers, celebrate the Eucharist, and forgive sins. The bishops later carried on the mission of the apostles. Bishops in early Christianity normally were set apart for this ministry through a ceremony of the laying on of hands, an anointing with blessed oil, and prayer by other bishops (see 1 Tim 4:14; 2 Tim 1:6-7). This later became known as episcopal consecration. The consecration of a bishop, or *episcopos,* was recognized by the Catholic Church as the fullness of the sacrament of Holy Orders.[49] The Second Vatican Council teaches:

> ...that bishops, in an eminent and visible manner, take the place of Christ himself, teacher, and shepherd, and priest, and act as his representative....[50] By virtue, therefore, of the Holy Spirit who has been given to them, bishops have been constituted true and authentic teachers of the faith and have been made pontiffs and pastors.[51]

The bishop is the chief shepherd and representative of Jesus Christ within his own diocese or jurisdiction. As we have seen, in the Latin rite of the Catholic Church the bishop is the normal minister of the sacraments of confirmation and Holy Orders. He is the chief teacher of the Catholic faith in his diocese. The bishop, in exercising his ministry, must also act in communion or unity with the pope and the other bishops, fellow members of the "college of bishops," or "episcopal college," that succeeds the "college" or body of apostles in each age.

One expression of this "collegiality," which began in the early church, is the practice of several bishops participating in the consecration of a new bishop (see CCC 1559). This is also expressed by the action and concern of each bishop for all the churches—the entire church—as well as for the particular church entrusted to his pastoral care (see CCC 1560).

The bishop also builds unity or communion with the "college" or body of priests and deacons who serve God's people with him, as well as building the unity in the true faith of all members of the local church entrusted to his care. This is expressed in a special way when the bishop presides at a eucharistic gathering of the people entrusted to his care by Christ and the church (see CCC 1561).

The Ministerial Priesthood

In the early church, presbyters (priests) and deacons received through their ordination a share in Christ's authority to teach, govern, and make holy God's people in a particular region in union with and under the authority of the bishop of that territory. This is summarized well by the "Dogmatic Constitution on the Church" of the Second Vatican Council:

> Christ, whom the Father sanctified and sent into the world (Jn 10:36) has, through His apostles, made their successors, the bishops, partakers of his consecration and his mission. These in their turn have legitimately handed on to different individuals in the church various degrees of participation in this ministry.
>
> Thus the divinely established ecclesiastical ministry is exercised in different levels by those who from antiquity have been called bishops, priests, and deacons. Although priests do not possess the highest degree of priesthood, and although they are dependent on the bishops in the exercise of their power, they are nevertheless united with the bishops in sacerdotal dignity. By the power of the sacrament of orders, and in the image of Christ the eternal High Priest (Heb 5:1-10; 7:24; 9:11-28), they are consecrated to preach the gospel, shepherd the faithful, and celebrate divine worship as true priests of the New Testament.[52]

Just as Jesus called and set apart the apostles to lead and minister to God's people, God continues to call men today to serve his people in the ordained priesthood of Jesus Christ. The mission of the priest or bishop continues to be: (1) to proclaim, teach, and guard the Word of God found in Scripture and authentic Catholic tradition with the authority of Christ; (2) to carry on the priestly ministry of Jesus by presiding over the Eucharist, or Lord's Supper, while acting in the person of Christ, and serving as the normal minister of the other sacraments; (3) to shepherd and govern God's people according to the example of Jesus, the Good Shepherd (see Jn 10), and according to his Word and teaching. Those ordained, "have taken up the service of the (Church) Community, presiding in the place of God over the flock whose shepherds they are, as teachers of doctrine, priests of sacred worship, and officers of good order."[53]

As with lay people, the ordained ministers of the church, "grow in love for God and neighbor through the daily exercise of their duty."[54] Like Christian marriage, the sacrament of Holy Orders also provides a special grace which enables the priest to carry out his vocation faithfully and successfully. The Second Vatican Council's "Decree on the Ministry and Life of Priests" affirms that:

> Since every priest in his own way represents the person of Christ himself, he is also enriched with special grace.... Consecrated by the anointing of the Holy Spirit and sent by Christ, priests mortify in themselves the deeds of the flesh and devote themselves entirely to the service of men. Thus, they can grow in the sanctity with which they are endowed in Christ, to the point of perfect manhood.[55]

The Order of Deacon

The third ministerial order is that of deacon, which literally means "servant." The origin of this order was the need for men to assist the apostles in the practical affairs of the church so that they could devote themselves to "prayer and to the ministry of the word" (Acts 6:4, NAB). Seven men were thus chosen and ordained to be "servants" (deacons) through prayer and the laying on of hands (see Acts 6:5-6). St. Stephen, the church's first martyr, was one of these deacons.

The office of deacon is frequently mentioned in the Pauline letters of the New Testament (see Rom 16:1; Phil 1:1; 1 Tim 3:8-13). Hence, the *Catechism* teaches that deacons are ordained, "not unto the priesthood, but unto the ministry [of service],"[56] and that:

> The sacrament of Holy Orders marks them with an *imprint* ("character") which cannot be removed and which configures them to Christ, who made himself the "deacon" or servant of all. (Cf. Mk 10:45; Lk 22:27; St. Polycarp, *Ad Phil.* 5, 2: SCh 10, 182) (CCC 1570)

The specific tasks of deacons are numerous and varied. They assist the bishop and priests in the celebration of the divine mysteries, above all the

Eucharist, in the distribution of Holy Communion, in blessing marriages, in the proclamation of the Gospel and preaching, in presiding over funerals, and in dedicating themselves to the various ministries of charity.[57]

One of the major contributions to the renewal of the church by the Second Vatican Council was the restoration (in the Latin Church) of the diaconate "as a proper and permanent rank of the hierarchy"[58]—the *permanent diaconate*. This order, which always has existed in the Eastern churches, can be conferred on married men, as well as on those vowed to the celibate life. As the name *diaconate* implies, this holy order of service is tremendously beneficial to the church in fulfilling the mission Jesus has given her (see CCC 1571).

The Demands and Graces of Holy Orders

Each "degree" of this sacrament is conferred through the laying on of hands by a validly ordained bishop (or bishops), usually on Sunday within the eucharistic liturgy (see CCC 1572-74). No one has a *right* to receive the sacrament of Holy Orders. Indeed, no one claims this office for himself; he is called to it by God (see Heb 5:4; CCC 1578). It is for the bishops of the church (and, in the case of episcopal consecration, the pope, as head of the college of bishops) to discern whom God is calling to receive this sacrament.

There are some basic requirements. First, by virtue of the Lord Jesus' own choice of only men to represent him in the ministerial priesthood, "'Only a baptized man (*vir*) validly receives sacred ordination'[59] ... the ordination of women is not possible"[60] (CCC 1577).

Secondly, "all the ordained ministers of the Latin Church, with the exception of permanent deacons, are normally chosen from among men of faith who live a celibate life and who intend to remain celibate 'for the sake of the kingdom of heaven' (Mt 19:12). Called to consecrate themselves with undivided heart to the Lord and to 'the affairs of the Lord' (1 Cor 7:32), they give themselves entirely to God and to men" (CCC 1579).

For nearly two thousand years, many Christian men and women have heard this call to renounce the good of marriage for the sake of the kingdom of God. Although celibacy is not a doctrinal requirement for priesthood, it is a discipline of the Latin rite of the Roman Catholic Church that has clear biblical precedent and has borne much good fruit over the centuries. This may be seen in the evident holiness and freedom of service of so many celibate Catholic priests, bishops, and deacons. Again, if God calls a man to this vocation, he will provide the grace and strength for it to be faithfully carried out.

The centuries-old practice of the Eastern churches has been that while bishops are chosen from among those clergy who have vowed themselves to the celibate life, refraining from marriage for the sake of God's kingdom, married men can be ordained as deacons and priests.

In the East, a man who has already received the sacrament of Holy Orders can no longer marry if he is celibate or if his wife dies after his ordination. The same is true of a married permanent deacon in the Latin West. These are signs that celibacy for priests and deacons is highly honored in the Latin and in the Eastern rites, as well as among Orthodox Christians (see CCC 1580).

Celibacy is a sign of this new life to the service of which the Church's minister is consecrated; accepted with a joyous heart celibacy radiantly proclaims the Reign of God.[61]

While the sacrament of Holy Orders has many demands, it also has an abundance of graces attached to it. As in the case of baptism and confirmation, this share in Christ's priestly office confers an indelible spiritual character, and therefore it cannot be repeated (see CCC 1582). No matter how sinful or unworthy the priest, Jesus himself acts and effects salvation through the ordained minister (see CCC 1584). However, it must be emphasized that the ordained minister, by sharing in Christ's priesthood or ministry, receives a special grace of the Holy Spirit to configure the man to Jesus Christ as priest, teacher, and pastor (see CCC 1585). As St. John Vianney said, "The priest continues the work of redemption on earth.... If we really understood the priest on earth, we would die not of fright but of love.... The priesthood is the love of the heart of Jesus."[62]

Therefore, Catholics in the West should not fear the decline in the number of vocations to the priesthood.[63] We are called to faith and hope in God, that He will issue resoundingly the call to priesthood to many men, and that they will heed this call in faith and trust. Like married men today, the priesthood needs support from priests banding together to pray, support, and encourage each other, and from lay people and religious continuing to pray for priests and to support them in their vital ministry.

The Sacrament of Matrimony

Love is the fundamental vocation of every human being. We are created in the image and likeness of God, who is himself love (see Gen 1:27; 1 Jn 4:8,16). There is a special mutual love between a man and a woman that, with God's sacramental blessing, becomes an image of the absolute and unfailing love with which God loves man. Little wonder that this love is good, very good, in the Creator's eyes. This love is also very good because it is *fruitful*, begetting new life, and *responsible*, watching over creation (especially the new life it has brought forth) and caring for it: "And God blessed them, and God said to them: 'Be fruitful and multiply, and fill the earth and subdue it'" (Gen 1:28; see Gen 1:31, CCC 1604).

God calls most Christians to marriage. Why? The Book of Genesis tells us that God said, "It is not good for the man to be alone" (Gen 2:18, NAB), and so made man and woman to come together and "become one body" (Gen 2:24, NAB). They were to bring forth children and mutually support each other on the road to holiness. The Catholic Church today continues to recognize procreation and conjugal love (that is, faithful mutual love and support within the marriage covenant) as the two greatest benefits of marriage.

Marriage existed long before Christianity, because of the natural laws of human attraction and the natural recognition of the importance of fidelity and stability within human families. It was Jesus Christ who raised marriage to a new level, basing its existence and conduct clearly on the law of God (see Mt 19:3-9). Jesus showed his blessing on married love at the wedding feast at Cana (see Jn 2:1-11). The Letter to the Ephesians recognizes marriage as a sacrament when it describes the love of husband and wife as a visible sign of the "great mystery": the love of Christ for his church (Eph 5:21-33). With this understanding, marriage cannot be viewed merely as a human agreement or even as only a civil or religious contract. The relationship of a married couple is a *covenant*, a solemn promise involving the man, the woman, and God himself at the center. This covenant is modeled upon the New Covenant between Jesus Christ and the church, sealed by the blood of Christ.

> "For this reason a man shall leave his father and mother and be joined to his wife, and the two shall become one." This is a great mystery, and I mean in reference to Christ and the church....
>
> EPHESIANS 5:31-32

What Makes a Christian Marriage?

Many marriages today, even Christian marriages, end in divorce. The teaching of the Catholic Church (in fidelity to Jesus' teaching in Mark 10:11-12) is that a divorced spouse cannot remarry if the church recognizes the validity of the original marriage bond (see CCC 1650).

The church, through a judicial process, may judge that a marriage was not valid—was never an actual marriage—and grant an annulment (see CCC 1629). However, the focus of the church's ministry is to prepare the faithful for marriages that will last and truly reflect the love of Christ for his church.

A first and essential step is simply for both the man and the woman to know, to believe in, and to commit themselves to living what is required for a marriage in Christ and in his church. Among these requirements are:

1. *Marriage takes place between "a baptized man and woman, free to contract marriage, and who freely express their consent"* (see CCC 1646-49);[64]

2. *Spouses vow themselves to be totally faithful to each other as long as each one lives* (see CCC 1646-49);

3. *The marriage is indissoluble—it cannot be ended or dissolved except by the death of one of the spouses* (see CCC 1644-45). As Jesus said, "What therefore God has joined together, let not man put asunder" (Mk 10:9; see Mt 19:6);

4. *The couple vows to "accept children lovingly from God,"* since, "by its very nature ... marriage ... is ordered to the procreation and education of the off-

spring and it is in them that it finds its crowning glory."[65]

Many marriages fail, or are doomed to fail from the beginning, because one or both of the spouses do not commit themselves to God's plan for marriage as expressed in the teaching of the church.

Those who are ready to accept these responsibilities and are called to marriage are married, in the Latin rite, usually during Holy Mass, by "mutually confer[ring] upon each other the sacrament of Matrimony by expressing their consent before the Church" (CCC 1623; at least a priest and two witnesses are required).[66] As we have seen, "The consent by which the spouses mutually give and receive one another is sealed by God himself" (cf. Mk 10:9) (CCC 1639).

Thus *the marriage bond* has been established by God himself in such a way that a marriage concluded and consummated between baptized persons can never be dissolved. This bond, which results from the free human act of the spouses and their consummation of the marriage, is a reality, henceforth irrevocable, and gives rise to a covenant guaranteed by God's fidelity. (CCC 1640)

When his disciples first heard Jesus prohibit divorce, their response was incredulous. "If such is the case of a man with his wife, it is not expedient to marry!" (Mt 19:10). Jesus did not soften his command, knowing that for those who would marry under the New Covenant, a new grace would be available to them to live out their marital covenant. *And Jesus Christ is the source of this grace.* "Just as of old God encountered his people with a covenant of love and fidelity, so our Savior, the spouse of the Church, now encounters Christian spouses through the sacrament of Matrimony."[67]

How does Jesus help married couples? He gives them the strength to take up their crosses and so follow him, and to rise again after they have fallen. He enables couples to forgive one another, to bear each other's burdens, share each other's joys, and to "be subordinate to one another out of reverence for Christ" (Eph 5:21, NAB; see Gal 6:2). Jesus gives married couples the power to love one another with supernatural, tender, and fruitful love. In the joys of their love and family life he gives them here on earth a foretaste of the wedding feast of the Lamb (see CCC 1642). The church father Tertullian wrote:

How can I ever express the happiness of a marriage joined by the Church, strengthened by an offering, sealed by a blessing, announced by angels, and ratified by the Father?... How wonderful the bond between two believers, now one in hope, one in desire, one in discipline, one in the same service! They are both children of one Father and servants of the same Master, undivided in spirit and flesh, truly two in one flesh. Where the flesh is one, one also is the spirit.[68]

Married couples must often call upon Jesus and invoke "the grace of the sacrament" to enable them to persevere in living their vocation. God is faithful to his covenant, and will always be present to strengthen them. Thus, the man and the woman who make this covenant receive special graces from this sacrament to remain faithful to the covenant and to carry out the duties of this state of life with the spirit of Christ.[69] Besides the duty of faithful, mutual love and support of each other, the couple may also receive the blessing of children, whom they have the duty to raise in the faith of the church and for the service of God.

As part of their marriage covenant, Catholic couples vow to receive children lovingly from God. By the gift of children there emerges a new social unit, the family, which Vatican II and the *Catechism* refer to as "the domestic church" (see CCC 1655-58). We recall that Christ himself, "chose to be born and grow up in the bosom of the holy family of Joseph and Mary" (CCC 1655).

In our own time, in a world often alien and even hostile to faith, believing families are of primary importance as centers of living, radiant faith. It is in the bosom of the family that parents are "by word and example ... the first heralds of the faith with regard to their children."[70] Parents should encourage each child to seek God's call for the direction of his life. They are especially to foster any religious vocation in their children.

The family is the normal and precious fruit of Christian marriage, unless the couple is unable to conceive children. In the face of much confusion in society today, Catholics must be clear that the call to marriage is a call to accept the responsibility and joy of children and family life. The Catholic Church has always highly valued the family and has done everything in its power to protect it and preserve its integrity. The "Pastoral Constitution on the Church in the Modern World" calls the family "the foundation of society,"[71] and teaches about the vital responsibilities of both the husband and the wife, working together, in making this foundation strong:

> The family is a kind of school of deeper humanity. But if it is to achieve the full flowering of its life and mission, it needs the kindly communion of minds and the joint deliberation of spouses, as well as the painstaking cooperation of parents in the education of their children. The active presence of the father is highly beneficial to their formation. The children, especially the younger among them, need the care of their mother at home. This domestic role of hers must be safely preserved, though the legitimate social progress of women should not be underrated on that account.[72]

The call to be married in Christ is a high one, and today one that challenges Catholic married couples and families to be the "salt of the earth" (Mt 5:13) and the "light of the world" (Mt 5:14) in the midst of an increasingly insipid and dark society. Catholic married couples are to proclaim the value and gift of *life*, against the swelling tide of artificial contraception, abortion, and infanticide; the value and gift of *fidelity*, where infidelity, separation, and divorce are rampant; and the value and gift of *Christian family life*, against the inroads and attacks of radical feminism, materialism, selfish individualism, pornography, and the anti-Christian values proclaimed in music and in the media.[73] Christians can advance in hope and confidence, knowing that God's grace offered in the sacrament of marriage is sufficient to overcome any obstacle to Christian marriage and family life, if we only turn to him continually in faith and ask for that grace: "for he who is in you is greater than he who is in the world" (1 Jn 4:4).

Catholic married couples and families can also support one another in their marriage and family lives, promoting and instilling Christian values and a Christian way of life. Christian communities, vibrant Christian parishes, and other associations are ways that Christian families can come together to support each other. Only through such means of unity and mutual support can Catholic families today hope to build a truly Christian culture in the midst of secular society. Those in other states of life and vocations—priests, religious, and single people—can also strengthen and support Catholic marriages and family life in diverse ways.

CHAPTER 8

Life in Christ and the Holy Spirit

All the faithful of Christ of whatever rank or status are called to the fullness of the Christian life and to the perfection of charity.[1]

This brief statement summarizes what Christian life and Christian morality are all about. Whether one is married or single, ordained or professing religious vows—*all* are called to the same holiness of life and the perfect charity that comes from following Jesus Christ.

The Christian way of life is a sharing in God's own life: the life of the Father, the Son, and the Holy Spirit. The third part of the *Catechism* refers to this as "Life in Christ," or "Life in the Spirit" (see CCC 1691-99). It is also a life in God's grace, "for by grace you have been saved through faith; and this is not your own doing, it is the gift of God" (Eph 2:8; see CCC 1697).

Our Lord Jesus, who perfectly modeled the way God created us to live, called each of his disciples, regardless of their situation, to holiness and moral perfection: "So be perfect, just as your heavenly Father is perfect" (Mt 5:48, NAB).

While we cannot live a life of perfect holiness and charity on our own, the "spirit of holiness," the Holy Spirit, has been sent to help us (see Lk 11:9-13). The Holy Spirit is "the interior Master of life according to Christ, a gentle guest and friend who inspires, guides, corrects and strengthens this life" (CCC 1697). He inspires us to love God with our whole heart, soul, mind, and strength (see Mk 12:30) and to love one another as Christ has loved us (see Jn 13:34; 15:12).

264 / *The Essential Catholic Catechism*

Jesus Christ as the Model
and Source of the Christian Life

All Catholic moral teaching can be summarized in just five words: to be like Jesus Christ. As followers of Jesus Christ, we learn to live like him, act like him, think like him, love like him. We must become truly Christlike.

Who is Jesus? Jesus Christ is the incarnate Word of God, God himself in human form. He is God come among us to show what life is all about and how to live. He has also come to share the very life of God with us. All we need to do to receive this new, divine life that will enable us to live like Jesus Christ is to turn to him and ask for it. "Behold, I stand at the door and knock; if any one hears my voice and opens the door, I will come in to him and eat with him, and he with me" (Rev 3:20).

Jesus taught in such a simple way how we are to live: "You shall love the Lord your God with all your heart, and with all your soul, and with all your mind. This is the great and first commandment. And a second is like it, You shall love your neighbor as yourself" (Mt 22:37-39). In the Gospel of John Jesus added, "love one another as I have loved you" (Jn 15:12).

This is so simple, and yet so difficult! It is difficult because it requires us to die to ourselves—our selfishness and our sin. "The way of perfection passes by way of the Cross. There is no holiness without renunciation and spiritual battle (cf. 2 Tim 4). Spiritual progress entails the ascesis and mortification that gradually lead to living in the peace and joy of the Beatitudes" (CCC 2015).

It is important to begin a chapter on Christian morality in this way because too often Christians lose sight of the goal or ask the wrong questions. We often begin by asking what God's law is—what we can and can't do. This is to miss the whole point of the Christian life. The call of Jesus Christ is basically a positive one: a call to love, a call to true freedom. It is primarily a call to become like Jesus Christ, not just to avoid sin or vice, or even just to practice certain virtues. As we set our eyes on Christ and pray earnestly for his grace, we will see ourselves freed from sin and increasing in virtue because we will grow to be more like him. The goal of the Christian life is "to grow up in every way into him who is the head, into Christ..." (Eph 4:15).

The Catholic bishops of the United States have taught:

Christian morality defines a way of living worthy of a human being and of an adopted son of God. It is a positive response to God, by growing in the new life given through Jesus Christ. It is supported and guided by the grace and gifts of the Holy Spirit.... (cf. Rom 5:5)

Sustained by faith, man is to live a life of love of God and of his fellow men. This is his greatest responsibility, and the source of his greatest dignity. A man's holiness, whatever his vocation or state of life may be, is the perfection of love of God (cf. LG 39-42).[2]

All are called to holiness, and holiness means the perfection of our love of God and of our neighbor.

Freedom From Sin

Why can't we love God, others, and ourselves as we would like? Sin is the reason. Sin not only injures and disfigures us, but it offends God, our good, all-loving Father. The horror and stupidity of sin is this: instead of accepting God's love and favor, we turn our backs on him and cut ourselves off from the source of life and mercy.

Sin deeply offends God (see CCC 1850). To make this more graphic, some have said sin is like slapping Jesus in the face, or driving nails further into his pierced hands. Christians must detest sin, realizing what it really is and what it does to us, and to others. Our own sin turns us in upon ourselves, inhibiting our ability to love others and to reach out to God.

Sin promises happiness, but its fleeting pleasure leaves behind either emptiness or an unsatisfied craving for something more. It harms other people and society, in ways that we know of, but also in invisible, hidden, or indirect ways. Scripture teaches that the ultimate result or "wages" of sin is death (see Rom 6:23).

The second chapter of this catechism described the original sin of the first man and woman, which resulted in the separation or alienation of the entire human race from God and his love. The state of original sin led to personal sin: individual acts done knowingly and deliberately that violate God's will and law. This is sometimes called formal sin. The Catholic Church has long recognized seven capital or "deadly" sins that are at the heart of most personal sin. These capital sins are: pride, greed, lust, anger, gluttony, envy, and sloth (laziness) (see CCC 1866). All personal, or formal, sin offends God and harms our relationship with him. However, Scripture and the Catholic Church recognize an important distinction. Personal sin that is very serious, called "mortal" or "deadly" sin (see 1 Jn 5:16-17), separates one from the friendship of God or deepens one's alienation from God.[3] "Venial sins" are less serious offenses against God that injure our relationship with him but do not totally sever it (see CCC 1855, 1862). In human relations, too, we understand that we can offend or hurt others in ways that either damage our relationship with another person or bring it to an end.

The good news for the human race is that God has not left us trapped in the bondage of sin. He has forgiven our sin and reconciled mankind to himself through his Son, Jesus Christ. As the *Catechism* declares: "By his Passion, Christ delivered us from Satan and from sin. He merited for us the new life in the Holy Spirit. His grace restores what sin had damaged in us" (CCC 1708).

Since the coming of Christ, God has offered this forgiveness and reconciliation to each person living on earth. If there remains a breach in the relationship between God and any person, God is not responsible for it. God has done his utmost to bring each of us back to his friendship by becoming a man and dying a shameful, painful death on a cross. The Lord did this in order to conquer sin and to give us the gift of life with him—for eternity! (See Rom 8:3; 2 Cor 5:21.) God invites every person, each of us, back into loving union with him, a communion that begins now and lasts forever.

With the coming of Christ, two "ways" have been set before each person: the way of life (obedience to God; accepting his invitation to friendship) and the way of death (rebellion against God; refusing to accept his love or to enter into friendship with him) (see CCC 1696). This distinction is found in the earliest Christian writings of the first and second century (the *Didache,* the *Epistle of Barnabas,* and others). It is even found in the Old Testament:

I call heaven and earth to witness against you this day, that I have set before you life and death, blessing and curse; therefore choose life, that you and your descendants may live, loving the Lord your God, obeying his voice, and cleaving to him; for that means life to you and length of days...

Deuteronomy 30:19-20; see also Deut 30:15-19

This Old Testament passage reveals that from God's earliest dealings with his people, Israel, he set forth the same choice: to love and obey him and find life, or to rebel against him and die. In Jesus Christ, the choice is made clearer, for Jesus himself is "the way, and the truth, and the life" (Jn 14:6; see CCC 1698); the person who believes in him and faithfully follows him will enjoy eternal life and happiness with God (see Jn 14:1-6, 23-24).

Yet it is possible to choose to reject Christ and God's ways.

Mortal sin is a radical possibility of human freedom, as is love itself. It results in the loss of charity and the privation of sanctifying grace, that is, of the state of grace. If it is not redeemed by repentance and God's forgiveness, it causes exclusion from Christ's kingdom and the eternal death of hell, for our freedom has the power to make choices for ever, with no turning back. (CCC 1861)[4]

Venial sin, "does not deprive the sinner of sanctifying grace, friendship with God, charity, and consequently eternal happiness."[5] Nonetheless these sins diminish our charity and are punished either through trials in this life or in purgatory. Moreover, "deliberate and unrepented venial sin disposes us little by little to commit mortal sin" (CCC 1863). Christians cannot take venial sin lightly. It should be confessed in the Sacrament of Reconciliation.

Finally, there is one sin, blasphemy against the Holy Spirit, which Scripture says cannot be forgiven (see Mt 12:31; Mk 3:29; Lk 12:10). While there are no limits to God's mercy, a person may deliberately reject his mercy by refusing to repent when the Holy Spirit convicts the person of sin and offers the grace of salvation in Jesus. This "hardness of heart" that opposes the work of the Holy Spirit and God's mercy can ultimately lead to eternal separation from God.[6]

The Enemies of God:
The World, the Flesh, and the Devil

Despite Christ's definitive victory over sin on Calvary, there still remain enemies to God's salvation that seek to lure people away from the way of life in Christ. Catholic theology has traditionally identified the three greatest enemies of

God's salvation as the "world," the "flesh," and the devil.

The "world" in this sense is not the created order that the Bible proclaims to be "very good" (Gen 1:31), nor is it the world which God loved so much that he came to save (see Jn 3:16). Rather, it is a biblical term for that world or world-system of human ideas and values that are opposed to God and his rule (see Jn 17:9; 1 Jn 2:15).

The "world" here can refer to false values or ideologies in human society, or to idolatrous, inordinate attraction or attachment to things or ideas in the world, even though these things may be good in themselves. Especially in Western society, the greatest manifestation of the world is materialism, the ceaseless pursuit of material things and the insatiable desire for more. The world lures us to desire power, money, possessions, status, and success for their own sake and not for the glory of God or for the advancement of his kingdom.

The "flesh" is not our physical flesh or bodies, which are good because they are created by God, but flesh in the Pauline sense of the allurements of our fallen human nature. As Paul wrote to the church in Galatia:

> Now the works of the flesh are plain: immorality, impurity, licentiousness, idolatry, sorcery, enmity, strife, jealousy, anger, selfishness, dissension, party spirit, envy, drunkenness, carousing, and the like. I warn you, as I warned you before, that those who do such things shall not inherit the kingdom of God … those who belong to Christ Jesus have crucified the flesh with its passions and desires.
>
> GALATIANS 5:19-21, 24

As Jesus taught: "If any man would come after me, let him deny himself and take up his cross and follow me" (Mt 16:24). Christians must learn to recognize, renounce, and break from attractions and passions of the flesh and instead follow Jesus by submitting our emotions and passions to his rule.

Not all passions are evil, however. "There are many passions. The most fundamental passion is love, aroused by the attraction of the good" (CCC 1765). Passions, in themselves, are neither good nor evil (see CCC 1767). They are "natural components of the human psyche," that connect "the life of the senses and the life of the mind" (CCC 1764). The moral content of our passions is determined by what we do with them: they are morally good when they contribute to a good action, evil in the opposite case. It is the person's *will* that either orders the passions and desires of our senses to the good (forming virtues), or fails to do so and succumbs to disordered passions (creating vice; see CCC 1768).

Some mistakenly think that passions, emotions, or "feelings" are to be shunned as opposed to the dignity of man as a rational being. The *Catechism* insists that "the passions be governed by reason"[7] (CCC 1767), not annihilated or replaced by reason. The passions are part of our humanity that Christ has assumed and redeemed. They are made to glorify God. Observe how the Holy Spirit works in Jesus' life to order every interior movement, even "sorrows, fears and sadness, as is visible in the Lord's agony and passion. In Christ human feelings are able to reach their consummation in charity and divine beatitude" (CCC 1769). Jesus was angry with sin and hypocrisy, and sometimes expressed that anger in word and in action (see Mt 23; Mk 11:15-17; Jn 2:13-17). In Jesus, too, the words of the psalmist are fulfilled: "My heart and flesh sing for joy to the living God" (Ps 84:2; see CCC 1770).

The final enemy of Christians is the devil, or Satan, "the ancient serpent ... who deceived the whole world" (Rev 12:9, NAB), the fallen angel, Lucifer, who first rebelled against God. He now lives only to lure all other rational creatures into the same eternal misery of rebellion and separation from God. Jesus confronted the devil himself (see Mt 4:1-11; Mk 1:12-13; Lk 4:1-13) and the hosts of demons and evil spirits, until Satan put it into the heart of Judas Iscariot to deliver Jesus up to death (see Lk 22:3; Jn 13:27). Although Satan was defeated and all his power broken by Jesus' death and resurrection, in the mystery of God's plan Satan and other evil spiritual powers are still allowed to tempt humanity until Christ's glorious second coming (see Rev 20).

For this reason, Christ and the apostles Peter, James, and Paul call Christians to prayer, watchfulness, and spiritual warfare. Jesus prayed for his followers that the Father would "keep them from the evil one" (Jn 17:15, NAB). Peter warned: "Be sober, be watchful. Your adversary the devil prowls around like a roaring lion, seeking some one to devour. Resist him, firm in your faith ..." (1 Pet 5:8-9). James confirms: "Resist the devil and he will flee from you. Draw near to God and he will draw near to you" (Jas 4:7-8). Finally, Paul instructs:

Be strong in the Lord and in the strength of his might. Put on the whole armor of God, that you may be able to stand against the wiles of the devil. For we are not contending against flesh and blood, but against the principalities, against the powers, against the world rulers of this present darkness, against the spiritual hosts of wickedness in the heavenly places. Therefore, take the whole armor of God....

EPHESIANS 6:10-13

The devil is real, but Christians who are aware of his presence have no reason to fear him or evil spirits. Jesus Christ has overcome all evil, and we need only draw near to Christ in prayer and faith, and daily put on the "whole armor of God" (truth, righteousness, the gospel of peace, faith, the Word of God, and prayer—see Eph 6:14-18) to find protection from Satan and the spiritual powers of evil. Catholics also rely on the intercession of Mary ("her seed" has been sent to crush the head of Satan [see Gen 3:15]), of St. Michael the Archangel, and of all the angels and saints to protect us in our battle against Satan and his demons.

Some theologians prefer to think of the biblical teaching about Satan and evil spirits as mythical—a story that personified evil in the world. Primitive people, they say, may have accepted this personification of evil as literally true, but modern man understands that Satan, demons, and other spiritual realities spoken of in the Bible are merely symbolic. In the twentieth century, biblical scholar Rudolph Bultmann led the way in this task of "demythologizing" the Bible.

Recent popes such as Paul VI, however, and great Christian thinkers like C.S. Lewis, have strongly reaffirmed and illustrated the reality of Satan and evil spirits.[8] Lewis argues that Satan's most effective strategy today in luring people to damnation is to make people believe that he doesn't exist, or exists only as a comical figure with horns and hoofs.[9]

Ironically, at the same time that some people are denying the existence of Satan and evil spirits, fascination with the occult has become widespread and often popular in Western society. The Catholic teaching and tradition on the occult or any form of spiritism (including astrology) is clear: avoid it; have nothing to do with it. Even seemingly harmless or entertaining forms of the occult, such as Ouija boards or seances, are ways that Satan and evil spirits open people to their influence. Christians have no need for such dangerous diversions or "entertainment." Why live in the twilight, in possible danger of deception? Christ, our Light, has come to dispel all darkness!

The Freedom and Dignity of the Human Person

Christians must acknowledge the ever-present danger of sin and its harmful effects. The "world," the "flesh," and Satan also threaten to turn the Christian away from God and the way of salvation. Yet Christians remain free. No one can say, "the devil *made* me do it," or, "I just *had* to yield to his passion." Catholic moral teaching today always begins with a consideration of the dignity and freedom of the person.

> The human person participates in the light and power of the divine Spirit. By his reason, he is capable of understanding the order of things established by the Creator. By free will, he is capable of directing himself toward his true good. He finds his perfection "in seeking and loving what is true and good."[10]

Sin has weakened human freedom, but Jesus Christ has restored it: "For freedom Christ has set us free" (Gal 5:1) by his sacrificial death and glorious resurrection. Jesus came to reveal the "truth that makes us free" (Jn 8:32), and to give us his own spirit, the Holy Spirit, who frees us from sin. As the apostle Paul teaches, "Where the Spirit of the Lord is, there is freedom" (2 Cor 3:17). Already we glory in the "liberty of the children of God" (Rom 8:21; see CCC 1741).

We know that the grace of Christ does not interfere with human freedom, but brings it to perfection by assisting us in reaching our true good. Indeed, the more responsive we are to the grace of God, the more interiorly free and confident we become in facing the pressures and trials of modern life. By our obedience to God's grace, "the Holy Spirit educates us in spiritual freedom in order to make us free collaborators in his work in the Church and in the world" (CCC 1742).

Claiming Our Freedom: Repentance and Conversion

How do we accept God's offer of forgiveness and the free gift of his grace? The first step is to renounce sin and all evil and turn toward God, which is called repentance. The word is taken from the Greek *metanoia,* which literally means to "change your mind" about the way you are living and to accept God's judgment and will.

Some people fear that God will not forgive their sins, the serious wrongdoing of their past life. The Bible, both the New and the Old Testaments, confirms that our turning away from sin is God's deepest desire. He is eager, even longing, to forgive us. The prophet Isaiah says, "though your sins are like scarlet, they shall be as white as snow" (Isa 1:18), and Psalm 103 reminds us that "as far as the east is from the west, so far does he remove our transgressions from us" (v. 12). Jesus told the parable of the lost sheep and concluded that there is more joy in heaven over one repentant sinner than over ninety-nine who have no need of repentance (see Lk 15:3-7). Through the power of the Holy Spirit we share in Christ's passion by dying to sin, and in his resurrection by receiving his new life of grace (see CCC 1988).

Some people view repentance as a negative or painful experience. On the contrary, it is sin that is negative. Repentance is joyful, because we know we have a loving Father, ready to forgive us and receive us back into his love whenever we repent, no matter how serious the sin or how many times we fall. The parable of the prodigal son beautifully illustrates this (see Lk 15:11-32). Jesus told Peter that his forgiveness was to be unlimited—"seventy times seven" (Mt 18:22). Is Peter to be more forgiving than God himself? The only sin beyond God's mercy is the sin "against the Holy Spirit" (Mk 3:28-29), which means attributing God's work to Satan, thus refusing to believe that there is a loving God who desires to love, heal, and forgive us (see CCC 1864).

Along with repentance comes conversion. "The first work of the grace of the Holy Spirit is *conversion,* effecting justification in accordance with Jesus' proclamation at the beginning of the Gospel: 'Repent, for the kingdom of heaven is at hand' (Mt 4:17). Moved by grace, man turns toward God and away from sin, thus accepting forgiveness and righteousness from on high" (CCC 1989). As we turn away from sin, we must turn toward God in Jesus Christ by believing in him and submitting our lives to him and to his plan for us. By turning to God in faith Christians receive the great gift of "justification."[11] The *Catechism* explains:

> Justification is the *most excellent work of God's love* made manifest in Christ Jesus and granted by the Holy Spirit. It is the opinion of St. Augustine that "the justification of the wicked is a greater work than the creation of heaven and earth," because "heaven and earth will pass away but the salvation and justification of the elect ... will not pass away."[12] He holds also that the justification of sinners surpasses the creation of the angels in justice, in that it bears witness to a greater mercy. (CCC 1994)

Conversion to God, which results in justification of the sinner, may occur in different ways. Some people tell of a sudden conversion experience in which they radically turned away from sin and turned to God in a single, momentous event. Conversion also may be more gradual, as a person breaks from the life of sin to God's life and his will in progressive stages.

Even for those who have had a radical conversion experience, conversion to Christ actually never ceases. Christians are always in need of deeper, ongoing conversion—turning our lives over to God more fully every day. Our minds and hearts need constantly to be conformed to the mind and heart of Jesus Christ. As Jesus himself taught: "If anyone wishes to come after me, he must deny himself and take up his cross daily and follow me. For whoever wishes to save his life will lose it, but whoever loses his life for my sake will save it" (Lk 9:23-24, NAB).

Conversion is a process of losing our lives for Jesus Christ more completely every day, that we may find our lives in him.

Christian Character and Virtues: The Theological Virtues

Christians are called to be "other Christs," to possess the same character and virtues that Jesus Christ had. The *Catechism* explains that: "A virtue is an habitual and firm disposition to do the good. It allows the person not only to perform good acts, but to give the best of himself" (CCC 1803). As St. Gregory of Nyssa said: "The goal of a virtuous life is to become like God" (see CCC 1803).

This is not something we can earn or achieve by our own unaided efforts. We must ask God in prayer to form his character in us, especially seeking the specific virtues we lack. We can cooperate with God's grace by seeking to assume the character and virtues of Christ through discipline and by our decisions to act or think in certain ways: "The moral virtues are acquired by human effort. They are the fruit and seed of morally good acts ..." (CCC 1804). All goodness and virtue come from God; it is his gifts that we must ask for and then act upon as his grace is offered to us.

Paul said that he considered everything else to be rubbish compared with the "supreme good of knowing Christ Jesus my Lord" (Phil 3:8, NAB). Of his own life he said, "the life I now live in the flesh I live by faith in the Son of God" (Gal 2:20).

At baptism, Christians receive the Holy Spirit, the gift of God's sanctifying grace, and also certain virtues essential to Christian life called "infused virtues." The most important of these infused virtues are faith, hope, and charity (or love). These are the so-called theological virtues that St. Paul says will remain after all other gifts of God pass away (see 1 Cor 13:13). These virtues are called "theological" because by them, and only by them, we attain God (*Theos*) directly.

As one author has put it, "**charity** is the source, center, and goal of every virtue, for every virtue centers in the loving orientation of man to God.... Charity perfects the virtues, gives them life, and directs them to God."[13] Charity is the greatest virtue (see 1 Cor 13:13), the virtue that is the heart of God's identity, for "God is love" (1 Jn 4:8). Through charity, we are enabled to love God above all things, and our neighbor as ourselves for the love of God (see CCC 1822). The practice of all the virtues is animated and inspired by charity, which "binds everything together in perfect harmony" (Col 3:14, see CCC 1827).

Faith is belief: belief in God and belief in all that God has revealed to us through sacred Scripture, through sacred tradition, and through the Holy Spirit continuing to guide the church into the fullness of truth (see Jn 16:13-14). We believe in God and in what he has revealed because he is truth itself. By faith, "man freely commits his entire self to God."[14]

Faith is another indispensable Christian virtue, because it is the only proper orientation toward God through which we are justified, considered righteous in God's sight (see Rom 4:24-25), and sanctified, that is, made holy or like God. As the Council of Trent of the Catholic Church taught:

> "Faith is the beginning of human salvation" (St. Fulgentius), the foundation and root of all justification; "without which it is impossible to please God" (Heb 11:6) and to enter the fellowship of His sons.[15]

Possessing the virtue of faith means not only "keeping the faith" and striving to live it; it also is manifested when we profess our belief, confidently bear witness to it, and spread it (see Mt 10:32-33; CCC 1816).

Finally, **hope** is trust in Christ's promises that we will gain our greatest desire: the kingdom of heaven and the joy of eternal life with God. This theological virtue enables us to rely not on our own strength, but on the help of the grace of the Holy Spirit. "Let us hold fast the confession of our hope without wavering, for he who promised is faithful." (Heb 10:23; see CCC 1817).

Hope is the firm confidence God gives to a person that he or she will persevere in faith and love and so attain eternal life and happiness with God. Hope is not only personal but also communal. It is the hope of the whole Christian people in Christ's desire to save us as a people, bringing all who are faithful to God and his grace to the glory of heaven. We also hope in God's mercy and blessings for his people in this life on earth, although this is not the ultimate goal of hope. St. Paul said, "If for this life only we have hoped in Christ, we are of all men most to be pitied" (1 Cor 15:19).

The Letter to the Hebrews expresses God's desire that "each one of you ... show the same earnestness in realizing the full assurance of hope until the end, so that you may not be sluggish, but imitators of those who through faith and patience inherit the promises" (Heb 6:11-12). St. Paul expresses confidence given to the Christian through hope, saying that, "we rejoice in our hope of sharing the glory of God" (Rom 5:2), and "For in this hope we were saved. Now hope that is seen is not hope. For who hopes for what he sees? But if we hope for what we do not see, we wait for it with patience" (Rom 8:24-25).

The Cardinal Virtues

Besides the virtues of faith, hope, and charity, there are other virtues that reflect aspects of these central virtues or that remove obstacles to love of God and others. Four of this type are known as the moral virtues, or "cardinal virtues": prudence, justice, fortitude, and temperance. "If any one loves righteousness, [Wisdom's] labors are virtues; for she teaches self-control and prudence, justice and courage" (Wis 8:7).

Prudence enables one to choose correctly how to best carry out the will of God; it "is the virtue that disposes practical reason to discern our true good in every circumstance and to choose the right means of achieving it; 'the prudent man looks where he is going'" (Prv 14:15; CCC 1806).[16]

Justice inclines us to give to others at all times what is due to them by right (see CCC 1807). There are many forms of justice—social, legal, distributive—that are specific applications of this same virtue in different circumstances. In all instances, justice must be balanced and expanded by charity.

Fortitude, or courage, enables the Christian to do what is right and required in the Christian life, whatever the cost or consequences. It enables us to resist temptations and to overcome obstacles in the moral life. "The virtue of fortitude enables one to conquer fear, even fear of death, and to face trials and persecutions. It disposes one even to renounce and sacrifice his life in defense of a just cause. 'The Lord is my strength and my song' (Ps 118:14). 'In the world you have tribulation; but be of good cheer, I have overcome the world'" (Jn 16:33; see CCC 1808).

Temperance, or self-control, is a virtue that enables us to control our bodily desires and appetites, especially our sexual powers and appetite for food and drink. Temperance is needed to channel properly all our passions and desires for good and godly purposes. The Old Testament instructs us: "Do not follow your base desires, but restrain your appetites" (Sir 18:30). In the New Testament, temperance is called "moderation," or "sobriety." We ought "to live sober, upright, and godly lives in this world" (Titus 2:12; see CCC 1809).

Other Characteristics of the Christian Moral Life

The church recognizes other important characteristics of the Christian life, given by God, such as the Beatitudes (see Mt 5:2-12) and the gifts and fruits of the Holy Spirit.

The gifts of the Holy Spirit, which sustain the moral life, are part of the Christian inheritance in baptism which make a person open and ready to follow the promptings of the Holy Spirit throughout one's life. The prophet Isaiah lists these messianic gifts (see Isa 11:1-2), and they have been traditionally listed as: wisdom, understanding, counsel, fortitude, knowledge, piety, and fear of the Lord (see CCC 1830-31).

The "fruit of the Spirit"—"love, joy, peace, patience, kindness, goodness, generosity, gentleness, faithfulness, modesty, self-control, chastity" (Gal 5:22-23), are called "fruit" because they are "perfections that the Holy Spirit forms in us as the first fruits of eternal glory" (CCC 1832). All of these are attributes of God himself that he wishes to instill in his people to make us more like him. These characteristics develop in the lives of Christians as they are practiced, until they become mature habits, intrinsic parts of the Christian character (see CCC 1810). If we lack any of these fruits, we should pray for them, receive the sacraments frequently, and seek to practice them in our daily lives. We must also cooperate with the Holy Spirit, and follow his call to love what is good and avoid every form of evil (see 1 Thess 5:21-22; CCC 1811).

Works of Mercy

Christian virtue expresses itself visibly in many ways. Traditional Catholic teaching has spoken of works of mercy which are concrete expressions of virtue. Some of these works serve the physical and practical needs of others (the "corporal works of mercy")—to feed the hungry; to give drink to the thirsty; to clothe the naked; to shelter the homeless; to visit the imprisoned; to care for the sick; and to bury the dead. Jesus spoke of the great reward for some of these works in his sermon on the last judgment (see Mt 25:31-36).

Likewise, there are also works of mercy that meet the spiritual needs of others (the "spiritual works of mercy"): to admonish the sinner; to instruct the ignorant; to advise the perplexed; to comfort the sorrowing; to bear wrongs patiently; to forgive all injuries; and to pray for the living and the dead. These works also are commanded or encouraged by the Bible in many places and hold a venerable place in Catholic moral tradition.

Grace

All Christian virtues and character flow from God and his grace. Through baptism and the other sacraments, we come to share the very life of God, which Catholics call "sanctifying grace."

Grace is a gift: the free gift of God's own life, infused by the Holy Spirit into our souls to heal them of sin and to sanctify them. The basic gift of God's own life, of God coming to dwell within us, is called *sanctifying* or *deifying* grace and is received in baptism (see CCC 1999). The Eastern Christian tradition refers to the grace of the indwelling of the Holy Spirit, sharing in God's own nature, as "divinization." As St. Athanasius wrote:

> [God] gave himself to us through his Spirit. By the participation of the Spirit, we become communicants in the divine nature.... For this reason, those in whom the Spirit dwells are divinized.[17]

Because of God's life within, the person "in the state of [sanctifying] grace" is inclined or disposed to do God's will ("habitual grace"). In addition, God offers us the power each day, at every moment of our lives, to avoid sin and to do his will in particular circumstances ("actual grace," see CCC 2000).

God's grace precedes every good thought or action, and even every inclination to the good ("prevenient grace"). "The *preparation of man* for the reception of grace is already a work of grace" (CCC 2001).

Finally, God offers the grace of final perseverance, the ability to continue to follow Jesus Christ to the end of our lives so we will be able to share eternal life with him in heaven. God freely offers all that is necessary for a life that is rich and fruitful—the grace that can transform each person into the image of Jesus Christ, forming his character within us (see CCC 2016). The *Catechism* explains other special graces—modes of God's work and presence that lead people to holiness and build up the church:

Grace is first and foremost the gift of the Spirit who justifies and sanctifies us. But grace also includes the gifts that the Spirit grants us to associate us with his work, to enable us to collaborate in the salvation of others and in the growth of the Body of Christ, the Church. There are *sacramental graces*, gifts proper to the different sacraments. There are furthermore *special graces*, also called *charisms* after the Greek term used by St. Paul and meaning "favor," "gratuitous gift," "benefit" (cf. LG 12). Whatever their character—sometimes it is extraordinary, such as the gift of miracles or of tongues—charisms are orientated toward sanctifying grace and are intended for the common good of the Church. They are at the service of charity which builds up the Church. (CCC 2003; see 1 Cor 12)

Having gifts that differ according to the grace given to us, let us use them: if prophecy, in proportion to our faith; if service, in our serving; he who teaches, in his teaching; he who exhorts, in his exhortation; he who contributes, in liberality; he who gives aid, with zeal; he who does acts of mercy, with cheerfulness. (Rom 12:6-8; see CCC 2004)

How do we know if grace is present in our lives? This cannot be known with certainty by experience or feelings, but only by faith. However, the Lord Jesus said that one could know who was doing the works of God (which are possible only through God's grace) by the "fruit" that was coming forth (see Mt 7:20). Hence the "fruit" and blessings that we observe in ourselves and others (including the saints), "offers us a guarantee that grace is at work in us and spurs us on to an ever greater faith ..." (CCC 2005).

Grace and Free Will

God's grace is never forced upon anyone. It must be sought after and freely accepted. When we do accept it and embrace it, we are able to do God's will and the Christian virtues flourish in our lives.

In view of this, one might ask whether any virtues or good works are due to our own human will or effort or whether they are entirely the work of God. The New Testament makes it clear that no Christian can boast of any good work as being his own doing (see 1 Cor 1:31; 2 Cor 10:17; Eph 2:8-10). God is the primary source and author of every virtue and good work. God's grace is essential. Jesus himself said, "apart from me you can do nothing" (Jn 15:5).

On the other hand, the active cooperation of the human will with God's grace is essential. When Jesus invites us to "Come, follow me," and commands us to love God and each other, there is a presupposition that people are free to choose whether to accept or reject Jesus' invitation, to obey him or not. As the *Catechism* puts it: "As long as freedom has not bound itself definitely to its ultimate good which is God, there is the possibility of *choosing between good and evil,* and thus of growing in perfection or of failing and sinning" (CCC 1732).

For this reason, human acts truly can deserve either praise or blame. Ultimately they merit either the eternal reward of life with God, which is heaven, or the eternal separation from God, hell. We can also conclude:

1. *"Freedom makes man* responsible *for his acts to the extent that they are voluntary"* (CCC 1734). The Catholic Church has always maintained the reality of free will that makes possible real human responsibility for our choices and actions. Without genuinely free will, the concept of Christian morality would be relatively meaningless, since no one would be responsible for his actions. "Every act directly willed is imputable to its author" (CCC 1736).

2. "Imputability *and responsibility for an action can be diminished or even nullified by ignorance, inadvertence, duress, fear, habit, inordinate attachments, and other psychological or social factors"* (CCC 1735). It is for this reason that only God can be the absolutely just judge of a person's responsibility or culpability for an action, since only God knows the "heart" of man and how these factors have affected the person's choices.

3. *"The more one does what is good, the freer one becomes. There is no true freedom except in the service of what is good and just"* (CCC 1733). Only grace makes true freedom possible, for only by grace can we choose and do what is good.

Freedom, for the Christian, is defined as that which we choose that perfects or fulfills our nature as created by God and with God as our final end. As we have seen in an earlier chapter, Jesus is the most free person who ever lived, because he possessed the fullness of grace (God's life) and did only the will of God, his Father, from the beginning to the end of his life.

Merit

Since every human good comes from the grace or free gift of God, can anyone be said to *merit* eternal life or any other blessing? To begin with, the goal of the Christian life is not to earn, or "merit," God's favor or blessings, but to love God for his own sake.[18] However, Jesus himself promises to bless those who use wisely the gifts or "talents" God has entrusted to them (see Mt 25:20-23; Lk 19:15-19).

"Merit" is receiving from God what one justly deserves through the use of human freedom. In one sense, any human "merit" is really the gift of God, who is the source of all good, and particularly the gift of Jesus Christ, who merited our redemption through his love, "even unto death" (see CCC 2009-11). In our own lives, the *initial* grace of conversion and forgiveness is a free, unmerited gift of God. *After* this, however, there is a sense in which a person can merit grace by the exercise of free will in response to God's grace and the promptings of the Holy Spirit. The *Catechism* teaches:

> Moved by the Holy Spirit and by charity *we can then merit* for ourselves and for others the graces needed for our sanctification, for the increase of grace and charity, and for the attainment of eternal life. Even temporal goods like health and friendship can be merited in accordance with God's wisdom. These graces and goods are the object of Christian prayer. (CCC 2010)

A large measure of our Christian and human dignity lies in this: that the exercise of our free will, in response to God's grace and the Holy Spirit's guidance, really does make a difference in the salvation and even the human welfare of ourselves and others, in the fulfillment of God's plan, and in the coming of his kingdom! It is too easy to slip into a lethargic or fatalistic attitude of "whatever will happen will happen," and fail to exercise our free will and make the choices that will save and help ourselves and others. God is generous and just, and he will act and render justice according to how we use our freedom in response to and in cooperation with his grace (see CCC 2009). St. Augustine pinpoints the mystery when he says, "Our merits are God's gifts."[19]

Conscience

Our actions must be conducted in accordance with the dictates of our conscience. Conscience is the core of a person's being, the faculty by which a person makes practical judgments about whether particular acts are morally right or wrong. The Christian desires to hear the voice of God in his or her conscience so that these judgments will be correct and in accordance with God's will. "When he listens to his conscience, the prudent man can hear God speaking" (CCC 1777).

The conscience listens and judges, and then the person's will acts, either according to what the conscience dictates or in opposition to it. Human freedom and moral sensitivity rest in the conscience, as the "Pastoral Constitution on the Church in the Modern World" beautifully expresses:

Deep within his conscience man discovers a law which he has not laid upon himself but which he must obey. Its voice, ever calling him to love and to do what is good and to avoid evil, tells him invariably at the right moment: do this, shun that ... his conscience is man's most secret core, his sanctuary. There he is alone with God whose voice echoes in his depths. By conscience, in a wonderful way, that law is made known which is fulfilled in the love of God and of one's neighbor ... Hence the more a correct conscience prevails, the more do persons and groups turn aside from blind choice and try to be guided by the objective standards of moral conduct.[20]

As this passage indicates, the dictates of a person's conscience must be obeyed, because it is the only internal source a person has to judge what is right and wrong (see CCC 1790). The Second Vatican Council's "Declaration on Religious Freedom" states that:

In all his activity, a man is bound to follow his conscience faithfully, in order that he may come to God, for whom he was created. It follows that he is not to be forced to act in a manner contrary to his conscience. Nor, on the other hand, is he to be restrained from acting in accordance with his conscience, especially in matters religious.[21]

Since each person is bound to follow the dictates of his conscience, whether correct or incorrect, it is essential that the conscience be properly formed and informed.

The education of the conscience is a lifelong task. From the earliest years, it awakens the child to the knowledge and practice of the interior law recognized by conscience. (CCC 1784)

In the formation of conscience the Word of God is the light for our path (cf. Ps 119:105), we must assimilate it in faith and prayer and put it into practice. We must also examine our conscience before the Lord's Cross. We are assisted by the gifts of the Holy Spirit, aided by the witness or advice of others and guided by the authoritative teaching of the Church.[22] (CCC 1785)

The individual's conscience may always err, but one is not guilty of negligence or sin if one has done his best to form his conscience according to God's will. However, if a person is ignorant or in error in a moral decision because of negligence in seeking the truth, God holds the person responsible for this. As the Second Vatican Council teaches:

Conscience frequently errs from invincible (unavoidable) ignorance without losing its dignity. The same cannot be said of a man who cares but little for truth and goodness, or of a conscience which by degrees grows practically sightless as a result of habitual sin.[23]

Even if a person errs through no fault of his own in following his or her conscience, the mistake or ignorance remains a disorder, an evil, that the person must diligently strive to correct (see CCC 1793).

How, then, is a person's conscience formed correctly? First, the Catholic Church believes that there are reliable, objective sources through which God reveals his will. They include divine revelation, natural law, official church teaching, and human law. These will be discussed in detail in the next section of this chapter.

The conscience cannot be formed properly if one is not genuinely open to the truth and to all the ways God has established to reveal the truth. Clearly, one must consult these sources, seek the advice of competent people, use right reason, and pray and "listen" for the guidance of the Holy Spirit. The practice of the Christian virtues and works of mercy also form the conscience in truth and incline the person to act according to God's will.

Other important principles that always must be followed include the "Golden Rule" ("Do unto others as you would have others do unto you" see Tob 4:15; Mt 7:12; Lk 6:31); the "new law" of charity (always respecting one's neighbor and his conscience; see Rom 14:21; 1 Cor 8:12); and the principle that one may never do evil that good may come of it (see CCC 1756, 1789).

Let us take a specific case in which a person must make an important moral decision and is unsure about what is right and wrong in the matter. Suppose a married person is deciding whether to use artificial contraceptives. How does the person properly form the conscience?

First, the person should pray earnestly for God's guidance, asking God to reveal his perfect will and praying for the desire and power to do only what would be most pleasing to him. All selfish desires and attitudes must be put aside. Then the person should consult the objective sources of God's revelation in order to find out what God desires. In most cases, there is something in the Bible, Christian tradition, the natural law, or the teaching of the church that relates to the decision being made. To be responsible in forming one's conscience entails being diligent in seeking out truth from these sources. This may require study and consultation with reliable sources.

For the issue of artificial contraception, Catholics have a long-standing tradition, based on natural law, of rejecting artificial means of contraception. This tradition was confirmed by Pope Paul VI in his encyclical letter, *Humanae Vitae*.

Finally, once the person has prayed for God's guidance and sought out God's truth from objective sources of revelation, the person is ready to think prayerfully about the right or best thing to do. In this reflection, Catholic theology has taught that the person must consider three aspects of the decision (see CCC 1750):

1. The object: Does the act itself conform to the moral law? Is the act good in itself according to God's revelation through objective sources? (see CCC 1751).

2. The end or purpose: Is the intention behind performing the act a genuinely good one? Does the act have a good end or purpose? (see CCC 1752-53).

3. Circumstances: Are there any relevant circumstances that may affect the degree of rightness or wrongness of the act? (see CCC 1754).

All three of these aspects must be positive for the act or decision to be assuredly a good one. "A *morally good* act requires the goodness of the object, of the end, and of the circumstances together" (CCC 1755).

A certain modern school of thought, often called "situation ethics," holds that the moral value of an act may be determined almost entirely by the situation or circumstances. Catholic teaching rejects this view. Even though circumstances may affect the decision or may lessen or increase the person's culpability for a wrong act, circumstances cannot make an act right which is wrong or evil in itself, or which is done with an evil or selfish intention (such as praying and fasting "in order to be seen by men" [Mt 6:1; 23:5]).

For example, a married person may consider using artificial contraceptives because of certain circumstances (e.g., having a large family already, with a low income). Yet, if the use of this means of birth regulation is wrong or objectionable in itself (as the Catholic Church teaches it is, based on the natural law), then it cannot be morally justified, regardless of the circumstances or the intentions (motives) of the persons involved.

It is therefore an error to judge the morality of human acts by considering only the intention that inspires them or the circumstances (environment, social pressure, duress or emergency, etc.) which supply their context. There are acts which, in and of themselves, independently of circumstances and intentions, are always gravely illicit by reason of their object, such as blasphemy and perjury, murder and adultery. One may not do evil so that good may result from it (CCC 1756).

So, in the case of artificial contraception, a Catholic couple who has sought to form their conscience according to the teaching and tradition of the Catholic Church would find no justification for using artificial contraceptives under any circumstances, regardless of their intention. This is so because the use of this artificial means of the regulation of conception always seeks to obstruct the God-given procreative aspect and purpose of the marital act, which is intrinsic to it by nature.

In conclusion, Catholics, and all Christians, are bound to do what their conscience dictates in this matter and in all decisions of right and wrong, but in forming their conscience they are obliged to seek God's will in prayer and to follow the will of God as it is revealed in the Bible, authentic Christian tradition, natural law, and church teaching.

God's Guidance in Moral Living

God has a clear plan for how we should live. In the "Declaration on Religious Freedom" of the Second Vatican Council, the Catholic Church teaches:

> that the highest norm of human life is the divine law—eternal, objective and universal—whereby God orders, directs, and governs the entire universe and all the ways of the human community, by a plan conceived in wisdom and love. Man has been made by God to participate in this law, with the result that, under the gentle disposition of divine Providence, he can come to perceive ever increasingly the unchanging truth.[24]

The Catholic Church always has taught that good and evil, right and wrong, are not arbitrary, subjective concepts, but are realities clearly determined by the Creator of all, God himself.[25]

Some people are offended by the idea that there is a God who establishes rules for human life and behavior. Should it surprise us that the God who created the human race would also determine, and then reveal, the ways by which we would find true fulfillment and happiness? Truly, God "desires all men to be saved and to come to the knowledge of the truth" (1 Tim 2:4), as Paul wrote to Timothy. The truth about morality, like all Christian truth, is a truth that liberates, a truth that sets us free (see Jn 8:32).

It is important for Catholics to realize that the moral guidance provided by the church and by the Scriptures is not to be viewed as a set of arbitrary restrictions, but as a gift of God. The church father Tertullian observed:

Alone among all animate beings, man can boast of having been counted worthy to receive a law from God: as an animal endowed with reason, capable of understanding and discernment, he is to govern his conduct by using his freedom and reason, in obedience to the One who has entrusted everything to him.[26]

Thanks be to God that he has chosen to reveal his will to his people, with clear guidance! Even when the demands of God's will are challenging and oppose our own selfish and sinful desires, we should rejoice. Should it surprise us that the demands of the moral teachings of the church are often as difficult and challenging as the demands and call of Jesus himself? This would only make sense, since the church's moral teachings and guidance are extensions and practical applications of Jesus' teaching. What most of us need to develop is a greater love for the law of God and a desire to form our conscience according to it. The longest of the psalms of the Old Testament, Psalm 119, is a psalm praising God's law and thanking him for giving it to us:

> Oh, how I love thy law! It is my meditation all the day. Thy commandment makes me wiser than my enemies for it is ever with me.... Thy word is a lamp to my feet and a light to my path.
>
> PSALM 119:97-98, 105

The laws of God are not just restrictions, but the source of true freedom and peace. Jesus said, "If you continue in my word, you are truly my disciples, and you will know the truth, and the truth will make you free" (Jn 8:31-32). Christian freedom, genuine freedom, is not found in doing whatever we want, but in doing God's will. Jesus was the most free person who has ever lived because he was most obedient to the will of his Father. Jesus himself is the fulfillment of the law, the "Way" of perfection (see CCC 1953). "For Christ is the end of the law, that every one who has faith may be justified" (Rom 10:4).

Our consciences will find their freedom and peace when they are formed according to God's law and will, as expressed in perfection and fullness in the life and teaching of Jesus Christ. Yet even before the coming of Christ, much of God's will for human action and decisions could be known. Let us consider now the sources of moral guidance that God has graciously provided.

Natural Law

It would be strange if God created people to live a moral life, then made it difficult or impossible for them to discover or to understand his will for their lives. Catholics believe that God reveals his plan and his will for human life in a variety of ways, so that no one can claim total ignorance of it.

There are certain objective sources of the knowledge of God's will for human living (moral norms) that are accessible to all people. The most basic and universal level of understanding God's plan for human life is through "natural law." Natural law refers not to laws of nature, such as gravity, but the ways God created man to act and interrelate that may be discovered or deduced from observing human nature itself. These are universal principles that apply to people of all times, places, cultures, and situations. Even sin, the rebellion of mankind against God, cannot totally obscure our recognition of the truths of natural law.

Like conscience, natural law is God's law inscribed in the human heart, informing the conscience of what is good and evil. The natural law is that "original moral sense" that guides human reason in distinguishing good from evil, the truth from falsehood (see CCC 1954). St. Thomas Aquinas stated:

> The natural law is nothing other than the light of understanding placed in us by God; through it we know what we must do and what we must avoid. God has given this light or law at the creation.[27]

C.S. Lewis lucidly illustrates the principle of natural law in the first section of *Mere Christianity,* where he describes the universal "law of fair play" that everyone naturally recognizes and wishes others to abide by, even when we would like to make exceptions for ourselves! Whenever we say, "that's not fair!" we assume the existence of a universal moral law. I would refer anyone interested to *Mere Christianity* for a simple, convincing explanation of natural law.

An example of natural law is the fact that men and women were created by God as two different sexes in order to procreate. This points to the natural purpose and meaning of sexuality and indicates that homosexual activities and masturbation are distortions of the natural law in this area. The apostle Paul commented on God's response to certain people who rejected the truth about God that was plain to them by nature:

For this reason God gave them up to dishonorable passions. Their women exchanged natural relations for unnatural, and the men likewise gave up natural relations with women and were consumed with passion for one another.... And since they did not see fit to acknowledge God, God gave them up to a base mind and to improper conduct.

ROMANS 1:26-28

On the other hand, Paul taught in the following chapter of Romans that non-Jews (or non-Christians) who sincerely seek God and live according to the natural law will be rewarded, even though they have not received the law of God revealed in the Old and New Testament:

When Gentiles who have not the law do by nature what the law requires, they are a law to themselves, even though they do not have the law. They show that what the law requires is written on their hearts, while their conscience also bears witness and their conflicting thoughts accuse or perhaps excuse them on that day when, according to my gospel, God judges the secrets of men by Christ Jesus.

ROMANS 2:14-16

The law of God, his will for human life and morality, is not totally unknown to anyone, for God has written on the human heart what his law requires. It is known to us through our conscience. However, the natural law presents us with God's plan only indirectly, like a shadow of the full reality. It would be easy to confuse or to miss the fullness of God's plan if all we had to rely on were the natural law.

The precepts of natural law are not perceived by everyone clearly and immediately. In the present situation sinful man needs grace and revelation so that moral and religious truths may be known, "by everyone with facility, with firm certainty and with no admixture of error."[28] (CCC 1960)

Divine Law

Through the inspired authors of the Bible, God has revealed more fully his plan for living. This is the divine law. To his people of the Old Covenant, Israel, God revealed the Decalogue, or the Ten Commandments (see Ex 20:2-17; Deut 5:6-22). A summary form of the Ten Commandments should be kept in memory by all Catholics; an explanation of the meaning of each of these commandments is very important, suited to the age or condition of the hearer.

An exposition of some of the main points of the Ten Commandments will be presented at the end of this chapter. There are many other laws conveyed by God in the Old Testament, but the Decalogue constitutes the essential commandments that are binding for all people at all times.

The New Law or the Law of the Gospel

Nevertheless, the Old Law remains a preparation for the gospel (see CCC 1964). The Law is holy, spiritual, and good (see Rom 7:12, 14, 16), yet it is still imperfect. St. Paul likens the Law to a tutor (see Gal 3:24), which shows what must be done, but doesn't provide the strength to fulfill it. Only the gift of the Holy Spirit, later sent by Christ, gives us the power to overcome sin. Hence the Law can denounce and *expose sin* (see Rom 7), but cannot remove it, and thus, "remains a law of bondage…. However, the Law remains the first stage on the way to the kingdom. It prepares and disposes the chosen people and each Christian for conversion and faith in the Savior God" (CCC 1963).

The Law, the "Ten Commandments," remains important for Christians. We recall that Jesus himself enjoined the rich young man to keep the commandments in order to attain eternal life (see Mt 19:16-19). He further explained that his mission was to fulfill the teaching of the law and the prophets, not to abolish it: "For truly, I say to you, till heaven and earth pass away, not an iota, not a dot, will pass from the law until all is accomplished" (Mt 5:18).

Jesus not only taught the Law of Moses, he fulfilled it by radicalizing it. Jesus explains that it is not enough to obey the commandments in our actions, but even our thoughts must be conformed to God's law or else we are sinning.

Jesus Christ himself is the fulfillment of the Law, the revealer and full revelation of God's will for human life. When asked what was the greatest commandment of the law, Jesus summarized God's law and his plan for our lives in two points:

> You shall love the Lord your God with all your heart, and with all your soul, and with all your mind. This is the great and first commandment. And a second is like it, You shall love your neighbor as yourself. (Mt 22:37-39; see Lev 19:18; Deut 6:4-5)

In the Gospel of John, Jesus radicalizes the second commandment, making it "new." "A new commandment I give to you, that you love one another; even as I have loved you, that you also love one another" (Jn 13:34). The Christian life is basically a life of love—love of God and love of every other human being. Jesus himself revealed this love fully by living it perfectly, not merely speaking about it. The real norm for human life is Jesus himself, because he is the fullness of God's revelation in the flesh—"the image of the invisible God" (Col 1:15).

> The New Law or the Law of the Gospel is the perfection here on earth of the divine law, natural and revealed. It is the work of Christ and is expressed particularly in the Sermon on the Mount. It is also the work of the Holy Spirit and through him it becomes the interior law of charity: "I will establish a New Covenant with the house of Israel. . . . I will put my laws into their minds, and write them on their hearts, and I will be their God, and they shall be my people." (Heb 8:8, 10; cf. Jer 31:31-34) (CCC 1965)

This promise was fulfilled on the day of Pentecost, when the Holy Spirit was sent as the "New Law" into the hearts of all Jesus' disciples gathered in the Upper Room in Jerusalem (see Jer 31:33-34; Ezek 36:26-27). The signs of wind and fire (see Acts 2:2-4) evoke the giving of the Old Law to Moses on Mount Sinai (see Ex 19:16–20:20). "The New Law is the *grace of the Holy Spirit* given to the faithful through faith in Christ" (CCC 1966). It is the law of God, "written on our hearts" (see Jer 31:33). It expresses itself, above all, through charity, since the Holy Spirit is the wellspring of "God's love ... poured into our hearts" (Rom 5:5). The meaning and effect of this "New Law" is expressed most fully by Jesus in his Sermon on the Mount, in which he tells us of the Beatitudes:

> Blessed are the poor in spirit, for theirs is the kingdom of heaven.
> Blessed are those who mourn, for they shall be comforted.
> Blessed are the meek, for they shall inherit the earth.
> Blessed are those who hunger and thirst for righteousness, for they shall be satisfied.
> Blessed are the merciful, for they shall obtain mercy.
> Blessed are the pure in heart, for they shall see God.
> Blessed are the peacemakers, for they shall be called sons of God.
> Blessed are those who are persecuted for righteousness' sake, for theirs is the kingdom of heaven.
>
> MATTHEW 5:3-10

These are not commandments, but promises for those who keep the commandments, follow Jesus, and open themselves to the promptings and grace of the Holy Spirit, especially through the sacraments (see CCC 1966). The Beatitudes are at the heart of Jesus' moral teaching, since they show us what it means to possess the kingdom of heaven that he came to announce and establish on this earth (see CCC 1716-17).

Along with Jesus' teaching of the "new commandment" of love and the Beatitudes, the sacred Scripture presents other dimensions of the moral teaching of the New Law of the gospel. Certain sections of the New Testament letters, such as the epistles of St. Paul and other Pauline writings (Rom 12–15, 1 Cor 12–13, Eph 4–5, Col 3–4, etc.), hand on the Lord's teaching through the Holy Spirit speaking through the apostles to guide and instruct the young church. For example, St. Paul exhorts the church in Rome: "Let charity be genuine ... love one another with brotherly affection.... Rejoice in your hope, be patient in tribulation, be constant in prayer. Contribute to the needs of the saints, practice hospitality" (Rom 12:9-13; see CCC 1971).

Jesus also presents some gospel or *evangelical counsels*—poverty, chastity, and obedience—that express a radical commitment to follow him and to live fully according to the values of God's kingdom and of perfect charity, "which is never satisfied with not giving more ..."(CCC 1974; see also CCC 1973).

Indeed, in his moral teaching, Jesus always wishes to call people on to the perfection of holiness and discipleship. He does not call people to meet certain minimum standards of conduct, but to perfection: "You, therefore, must be perfect, as your heavenly Father is perfect" (Mt 5:48). Perhaps one can be saved by avoiding sin, by keeping the commandments, but why stop there? "The young man said to him, 'All these [the commandments] I have observed; what do I still lack?' Jesus said to him, 'If you would be perfect, go, sell what you possess and give to the poor, and you will have treasure in heaven; and come, follow me'" (Mt 19:20-21).

Following Jesus is what Christianity is about; keeping the commandments is but one of the necessary and expected consequences of following Jesus. The "New Law," or the "Law of the Gospel," always calls us to more: greater growth in virtue and more radical discipleship.

The Decalogue, the Sermon on the Mount, and the apostolic catechesis describe for us the paths that lead to the Kingdom of heaven. Sustained by the grace of the Holy Spirit, we tread them, step by step, by everyday acts. By the working of the Word of Christ, we slowly bear fruit in the Church to the glory of God. (cf. Mt 13:3-23; CCC 1724)

The Teaching Office of the Church

It is to the church, "the pillar and bulwark of the truth" (1 Tim 3:15), that Jesus has entrusted the proclamation of the gospel, including its moral teaching (see CCC 2032).

Through preaching and catechesis the pastors of the church (with the help of theologians and spiritual writers) pass on and interpret the "deposit" of Christian moral teaching to the faithful of every age (see CCC 2033). The basis and source of authority of their moral teaching is *divine revelation* (the laws and moral truths that God has revealed (see CCC 2035), and the *natural law* (see CCC 2036), both of which need to be proclaimed and understood.

Hence, Catholics believe that God provides authoritative interpretation and application of the Bible, natural law, and authentic Christian tradition through the official teaching office (Magisterium) of the Catholic Church. This is a third objective source of moral guidance for Catholics. Even when the Bible does not explicitly address an issue, Catholics can ask, "What does the Christian tradition—such as the fathers of the church and other great Catholic thinkers—have to say about it?" and, "Have the popes or ecumenical councils of Catholic bishops ever taught definitively about this matter?"

On certain moral issues of current concern, there is a unanimous consensus of the Christian tradition from the early church until recent times. Abortion, for instance, has been universally rejected by Christians from the second through the twentieth centuries, until recently, when some Christians have questioned this tradition. Some disputed moral issues have been settled by the formal teaching of popes or ecumenical councils of bishops—for example, such acts as masturbation, fornication, adultery, homosexual acts, and other sexual vices. These throughout the centuries have been condemned by the ordinary teaching of the church and by formal judgments of the Magisterium.[29]

> The *ordinary* and universal *Magisterium* of the Pope and the bishops in communion with him teach the faithful the truth to believe, the charity to practice, the beatitude to hope for. (CCC 2034)

The teaching office of the church has the dual role of protecting the truth of revelation from error or distortion and of "developing a deeper understanding of revelation and applying this revelation to the various issues and situations of human life." These have been called the "protective aspect" and "creative aspect" of the church's teaching role in the area of morality.[30]

Besides the essential work of the pope, bishops, and priests in defending and interpreting the true Christian way of life, the church depends on the faithful teaching, dedication, and knowledge of religious, theologians, and informed lay persons to make her teaching more widely known and understood. Remembering the contribution of lay saints such as Francis of Assisi, Catholics recognize that, "the Holy Spirit can use the humblest to enlighten the learned and those in the highest positions" (CCC 2038).

Also, teachers and parents play a vital role in passing on this saving truth to others, especially to young people. Without parents and teachers actively understanding and explaining the Christian way of life and the church's teaching on specific moral questions, the work of the pope and the bishops would be in vain. Few would actually hear what the Magisterium and Tradition of the church has to say without parents, pastors, and teachers passing this on to others, especially to youth.

Many Catholics wonder whether there is a comprehensive list of Catholic teachings on moral issues, and what church teachings Catholics are bound to believe. Although there is no definitive list of official pronouncements on moral teaching, many of them are summarized in official documents of Vatican congregations, or from national bishops' conferences. The *Catechism of the Catholic Church* also provides the authoritative summary of the Catholic Church's moral teaching in many areas.

Church Teaching: Dissent or Acceptance?

What about the possibility of dissent from or disagreement with a teaching of the Catholic Church? It is important here to distinguish the different degrees of authority of a church teaching. In the Catholic tradition, some moral and religious teachings have been formally defined by dogmatic definitions of ecumenical councils or popes. These are to be accepted by Catholics as part of our Christian faith. Further, there are other teachings of the church which are considered matters of faith because they have been consistently believed by Christians from the time of the early church until recent times. These must be accepted as part of the faith of the church, even though they have not been formally defined by a pope or ecumenical council. Many moral teachings of the Catholic Church fall into this latter category, such as the condemnation of abortion, homosexual acts, and masturbation, as we have just discussed.

Some Catholics may go through a period of questioning and struggling with such teachings in order to fully understand them. The end result of this process of conscience formation should be for them to recognize and embrace personally the truth of the teaching presented by the Catholic Church as a dogmatic definition or a matter of faith.

Those who finally reject a matter of Christian belief considered essential by the Catholic Church are faced with a serious choice. They must decide whether they can submit their personal judgments to the church's teaching, or whether they must, in honesty, cease to consider themselves Catholic Christians. The Catholic Church has always strongly emphasized preserving the unity of its members based on a common faith, and has warned against false teaching (see Lk 10:16; Gal 1:6-9; Eph 4:5, 14-15; Phil 1:27; 1 Tim 6:3-5; 2 Tim 4:2-4; Titus 1:9–2:1; 2 Pet 2:1-3).

With regard to moral teaching, the Catholic has certain rights and duties. Put simply, the faithful have the *right* to receive correct (orthodox) teaching in moral matters (i.e., "the divine saving precepts," not theological opinion), and the *duty* to receive this teaching from the church and to observe it (even in disciplinary matters), by the help of God's grace (see CCC 2037).

What about the right and duty that each person has to follow one's conscience in moral matters? This is, indeed, a right, but it demands the active duty of the Catholic to form the conscience according to the truth, which certainly would include church teaching. The grace of baptism should incline us to desire the guidance of our mother, the church, through which we were reborn in Christ (see CCC 2040).

In seeking to form the conscience according to the mind of Christ and his church, each person must transcend his or her own individual concerns and desires and take into account God's will and the good of all as it is expressed in the moral law and in the church's authoritative teaching (Magisterium) on moral questions. In doing this, Catholics will avoid the error of seeing personal conscience and reason in opposition to the moral law or the Magisterium of the church (see CCC 2039).

The Catholic bishops of the United States have taught in the "Basic Teachings on Catholic Religious Education":

> The conscience of the Catholic Christian must pay respectful and obedient attention to the teaching authority of God's Church. It is the duty of this teaching authority, or Magisterium, to give guidance for applying the enduring norms and values of Christian morality to specific situations of everyday life.[31]

Lumen Gentium has taught that the ordinary teaching of the Magisterium of the church is to be heeded in forming one's conscience, even when it does not formally define a doctrine:

In matters of faith and morals, the bishops speak in the name of Christ and the faithful are to accept their teaching and adhere to it with a religious assent of soul. This religious submission of will and of mind must be shown in a special way to the authentic teaching authority of the Roman Pontiff, even when he is not speaking *ex cathedra.*[32]

It may be inferred from this that there is room for legitimate difference of opinion and a plurality of views within the Catholic Church in matters on which Scripture and the apostolic tradition are not clear in their teaching or on which the church's teaching office has not spoken; in certain practical applications of the moral law; or on issues not considered matters of faith or morals. Here we could apply the beautiful ancient Catholic dictum: "let there be unity in what is necessary, freedom in what is unsettled, and charity in everything.'"[33]

Human Law

A final source of moral guidance for Christians is human law, which includes both church law and civil law. Jesus himself respected civil law and civil authority, as long as it did not violate God's law (see Mt 22:17-21, 23:1-3). He also observed many of the laws and traditions of Judaism (church law), except where their observance had grown legalistic and had violated the supreme law of love (see Lk 13:10-17, 14:1-6).

Human law, especially church law, can actually be an aid to observing the law of God. Because of fallen man's inclination to sin, human law can curb our tendency to sin and help us to follow God's will and the guidance of the Holy Spirit. Church law applies the laws of God to specific areas of Christian and human life. We must beware of legalism and avoid this by being aware that the higher gospel values, such as charity, always direct, and sometimes supersede, the observance of human (even church) laws. Normally, though, "obedience to church laws gives us an opportunity in practical daily ways to obey the Lord and His church."[34]

The laws or precepts of the church are, "the very necessary minimum" required for Catholics to express their commitment to Jesus Christ through participation in the life of the church he founded—its worship and sacraments (see

CCC 2041). Here these precepts will simply be listed (see CCC 2042-43 for fuller commentary):

1. You shall attend Mass on Sunday and holy days of obligation, and rest from servile labor;[35]
2. You shall confess your sins at least once a year;
3. You shall receive the sacrament of the Eucharist at least during the Easter season;
4. You shall observe the prescribed days of fasting and abstinence established by the church;
5. You shall help to provide for the needs of the church.

Civil laws are necessary to protect the common good and to maintain essential aspects of the common good, such as justice and order. As long as they do not violate God's laws, Christians should observe civil laws as honestly and fully as possible. This is done out of respect to the authority of civil government, which comes from God, and in order to set a good example of obedience to others (see Rom 13:1-7).

We have seen that God makes known his will for human conduct in a variety of ways: through natural law, divine revelation, the teaching office of the church, and human law. When God's will, revealed through those channels, is consistently observed and followed, the result is the development in a person of Christian character and virtue—the character and virtue of Jesus Christ himself.

Living According to God's Will

Studying the principles of how to form our consciences and live according to God's will should lead us to consider the specific things we are to do and to avoid in our daily lives as Catholic Christians. The basic command of Jesus is our primary task each day: to love the Lord with our whole heart, mind, soul, and strength, and to love those around us, our neighbor, as Christ has loved us. We are called to love all people, but this love begins with those around us, especially those to whom we have a commitment through the sacraments and our common life in the body of Christ, the church.

There is an order to love. If we are married or living with our family, we are called to love our spouses, children, parents, brothers, and sisters with a committed love that is sealed by the sacrament of matrimony. We are also especially called to love the members of the new family that God has given us in Jesus Christ, the church. With regard to our love of members of the church, the New Testament teaches the vital place of the "love of the brethren" (*philadelphia*) in the Christian life. This refers to the love of those with whom we are united in Christ through baptism (see 1 Thess 4:9; Heb 13:1; 1 Pet 1:22; 3:8). As St. Paul instructed the Galatians: "let us do good to all men, and especially to those who are of the household of faith" (Gal 6:10). An important part of Christian witness to the world that Christ has come is the love we have for one another in the body of Christ. As Jesus told his apostles, "By this all men will know that you are my disciples, if you have love for one another" (Jn 13:35). "The witness of a Christian life and good works done in a supernatural spirit have great power to draw men to the faith and to God."[36]

These teachings remind us of the communal nature of Christianity, including Christian morality. No one can attain salvation or live the Christian life totally alone. God has formed us into a people, the church, so that we can learn how to love one another and extend that love to all men. We also cannot live a moral life according to God's will on our own. Not only do we need teaching and guidance from the leaders in the church to show us how to live, we also need support and encouragement, and sometimes correction and admonition, from other Christians to spur us on to live according to God's will each day.

Sin and grace are social and communal, as well as individual. If one member of the body of Christ is rebelling against God, or even on the borderline of sin, it affects other Christians. We need to pray for each other, for we all are sinners. We must also call one another back to righteousness and God's will when we fall: "Speaking the truth in love, we are to grow up in every way into him who is the head, into Christ..." (Eph 4:15). Likewise, when one member of the body of Christ accepts God's grace and grows in holiness, it strengthens and encourages other Christians, so that we can all imitate that example and grow more fully into the image of Christ.

We realize that "genuine Christian love ... demands the avoidance of particular kinds of behavior that are always wrong and the practice of other kinds of Christian behavior that are always right."[37] The Catholic bishops of the United

States have summarized some of our practical obligations of love toward God, neighbor, and ourselves:

Toward God, the Christian has a lifelong obligation of love and service. The Will of God must be put first in the scale of personal values, and must be kept there throughout life. One must have toward God the attitude of a son to an all-good, all-loving Father, and must never think or live as if independent of God. He must gladly give to God genuine worship and true prayer, both liturgical and private.

Man must not put anyone or anything in place of God. This is idolatry, which has its variations in superstition, witchcraft, occultism.... Honoring God, one is to show respect for persons, places, and things related specially to God. Atheism, heresy and schism are to be rejected in the light of man's duties to God.

Toward his fellow man, the Christian has specific obligations in love. Like Christ, he will show that love by concern for the rights of his fellow man—his freedom, his housing, his food, his health, his right to work, etc. The Christian is to show to all others the justice and charity of Christ—to reach out in the spirit of the beatitudes to help all others, to build up a better society in the local community and justice and peace throughout the world. His judgment and speech concerning others are to be ruled by the charity due all sons of God. He will respect and obey all lawful authority in the home, in civil society, and in the Church.

Many are the sins against neighbor. It is sinful to be selfishly apathetic towards others in their needs. It is sinful to violate the rights of others—to steal, deliberately damage another's good name or property, cheat, not to pay one's debts. Respecting God's gift of life, the Christian cannot be anti-life and must avoid sins of murder, abortion, euthanasia, genocide, indiscriminate acts of war. He must not use immoral methods of family limitation. Sins of lying, detraction and calumny are forbidden, as are anger, hatred, racism and discrimination. In the area of sexuality, the Christian is to be modest in behavior and dress. In a sex-saturated society, the follower of Christ must be different. For the Christian there can be no premarital sex, fornication, adultery, or other acts of impurity or scandal to others. He must remain chaste,

repelling lustful desires and temptations, self-abuse, pornography and inde-
cent entertainment of every description.

Towards self, the follower of Christ has certain duties. He must be another
Christ in the world of his own day, a living example of Christian goodness.
He must be humble and patient in the face of his own imperfections, as well
as those of others. He must show a Christlike simplicity towards material
things and the affluence of our society. The follower of Christ must be pure
in words and actions even in the midst of corruption.

To be guarded against is the capital sin of pride, with its many manifestations. So too with sloth—spiritual, intellectual and physical. The Christian
must resist envy of others' success and of their financial and material possessions. He is not to surrender self-control and abuse his bodily health by
intemperance in drugs, alcohol, food.

Obviously, this listing does not cover all morality or all immorality. But it
indicates the practical approach which will help the Christian to form a right
conscience, choose always what is right, avoid sin and the occasions of sin,
and live in this world according to the Spirit of Christ in love of God.[38]

CHAPTER 9

The Ten Commandments

The Decalogue ("ten words") or "Ten Commandments" are a summary of the revealed, divine moral law, which is also "a privileged expression of the natural law" (CCC 2070). Jesus himself affirmed, "If you would enter life, keep the commandments" (Mt 19:17).

Jesus "radicalized" the Ten Commandments and "showed the power of the Spirit at work in their letter" (CCC 2054). He taught that these commandments could be summarized in the two "great commandments" of love of God and love of neighbor (see Lev 19:18; Deut 6:5; Mt 22:37-40; CCC 2055). "The Ten Commandments state what is required in love of God and love of neighbor. The first three concern love of God, and the other seven love of neighbor" (CCC 2067).

The *Catechism* devotes an entire section (almost five hundred points) to a detailed exposition of the Ten Commandments as a summary of the moral life. It follows the traditional Catholic division of the commandments (also used by Lutherans) established by St. Augustine (see CCC 2066). In fact, "Ever since St. Augustine, the Ten Commandments have occupied a predominant place in the catechesis of baptismal candidates and the faithful.... The catechisms of the Church have often expounded Christian morality by following the order of the Ten Commandments" (CCC 2065).

Both the Council of Trent and the Second Vatican Council[1] reaffirm the obligation of all Christians to keep these commandments (see CCC 2068). They are, as part of the natural law, "engraved by God in the human heart" (CCC 2072; see Jer 31:33). Through the gift of the Holy Spirit it is possible to keep these commandments as Jesus interpreted them. Although a detailed exposition of the Ten Commandments is not possible in this book, I will summarize some major points that are made in the *Catechism of the Catholic Church*. (A summary of the ten commandments and where they are found in the Bible may be found in the *Catechism of the Catholic Church*, after 2051.)

The First Commandment

"I am the Lord your God;... You shall have no other gods before me" (Deut 5:6-7). It is written: "You shall worship the Lord your God and him only shall you serve" (Mt 4:10).

The first commandment calls us to recognize who God is (through faith), and to adore him.

> To adore God is to praise and exalt him and to humble oneself, as Mary did in the Magnificat, confessing with gratitude that he has done great things and holy is his name (cf. Lk 1:46-49). The worship of the one God sets man free from turning in on himself, from the slavery of sin and the idolatry of the world. (CCC 2097)

We adore God in prayer (see CCC 2098), in offering sacrifices to him (see CCC 2099-2100), and in making and keeping promises or vows to love and serve him.

For this commandment to be observed, the freedom to worship God (religious freedom) must be insured. This freedom also makes it possible for the church to fulfill its duty to proclaim the true God and "the one true religion which subsists in the Catholic and apostolic Church"[2] (CCC 2105).

The first commandment is kept by approaching God in faith, hope, and love—the theological virtues. Conversely, anything directly opposed to faith in God, hope in God, and love of God is a sin against God and a violation of this commandment. Sins against *faith* include doubt (see CCC 2088), incredulity, heresy, apostasy, and schism (see CCC 2089). Sins against *hope* are despair and presumption (see CCC 2091-92). There are many sins against *love* of God: indifference, ingratitude, lukewarmness, spiritual laziness (*acedia*), and hatred of God, which comes from pride.

The command "You shall have no other gods before me," calls for a rejection of any false gods (idolatry) and false spiritual ways (superstition, divination, and magic, the occult) and also a rejection of irreligion, atheism, and agnosticism (see CCC 2110-28).

Finally, another possible "strange god" would be the worship of a "graven image" (Deut 4:15-16) instead of God. In the eighth century a controversy arose in the Christian East over the veneration of icons of Christ, Mary, and the angels and saints. Is this a rejection of the first commandment? The Second Council of Nicea (the Seventh Ecumenical Council) determined that veneration of icons or statues was not worship of strange gods. St. Basil the Great taught that, "the honor rendered to an image passes to its prototype."[3] The doctrinal definition of the Second Ecumenical Council of Nicea declared that, "whoever venerates an image venerates the person portrayed in it."[4]

The Second Commandment

"You shall not take the name of the Lord your God in vain" (Deut 5:11).

God has done an amazing thing in revealing his name and his identity to us. Since the Lord's name is holy, no one should use the name of God except to bless, praise, and glorify it (see CCC 2143). Likewise the names of Mary and the saints are to be honored and not abused. "Respect for his [God's] name is an expression of the respect owed to the mystery of God himself and to the whole sacred reality ..." (CCC 2144).

It is acceptable to make solemn promises or to take oaths (administered by legitimate authority) in God's name (see CCC 2147, 2154-55). However, false oaths, oaths that misuse God's name, and magical use of the divine name are to be rejected. Speaking words of hatred or defiance against God, speaking ill of God, failing to respect God's name, or misusing it is the sin of blasphemy, which Scripture condemns (see Jas 2:7; CCC 2148). Perjury, which is lying under oath or taking an oath with no intention of keeping it, is also contrary to the second commandment.

Christians not only respect the name of God, but also the names of other people, since the name of a person represents the person. The person's name deserves respect as a sign of respect for the dignity of that person (see CCC 2158).

The Third Commandment

"Remember to keep holy the Lord's Day" (Deut 5:12).

"The seventh day is a sabbath of solemn rest, holy to the Lord" (Ex 31:15).

The Sabbath, which Israel kept in commemoration of God's rest on the seventh day of creation (see Ex 20:11) and of his covenant and saving actions on behalf of Israel, has been continued and fulfilled by observance of "the Lord's Day," Sunday—the day of Jesus Christ's resurrection from the dead. St. Justin Martyr wrote in the second century:

> We all gather on the day of the sun, for it is the first day [after the Jewish Sabbath, but also the first day] when God, separating matter from darkness, made the world; and on this same day Jesus Christ our Savior rose from the dead.[5]

St. Justin alludes to the fact that from the beginning of the church, Christians gathered to worship God and celebrate his Eucharist on Sunday, the Lord's Day (see CCC 2177-78). If you are a Christian, you join with the church on Sunday to worship God. This is the first precept of the church, and one of its most ancient practices. Sunday is thus, "the original feast day and it should be proposed to the faithful and taught to them so that it may become a day of joy and of freedom from work."[6] Jesus himself observed the Jewish Sabbath law, but was ready to do good works when the needs of others demanded it. He noted, "the sabbath was made for man, not man for the sabbath" (Mk 2:27).

Man needs a day each week set apart to worship God, for relaxation, and for the leisure to visit others and perform works of mercy that cannot easily be done on other days. *The Catechism of the Catholic Church* gives some guidelines and practical directives with regard to observance of the Lord's Day (in addition to the obligation to attend Mass on Sunday and all holy days of obligation). For example, Christians are to refrain from work and other activities on Sundays and holy days of obligation that would prevent or hinder the worship due to God, the performance of the works of mercy, and appropriate relaxation in a spirit of joy (see CCC 2185). On these days, Christians traditionally devote time and care to their families and relatives, which may be difficult to do on other days. They are also encouraged to take additional time for reflection, prayer, cultivation of the mind, and silence (see CCC 2186).

Christians may need to take action together to see to it that people are not required to work unnecessarily on Sundays and holy days or on schedules that conflict with divine worship. Christians must see that leisure activities and entertainment, especially on these days, avoid excesses and violence (see CCC 2187). This may require courage and decisive action against generally accepted norms and practices in some cultures. I would recommend study of Pope John Paul II's apostolic letter "On Keeping the Lord's Day Holy" (*Dies Domini,* May 31, 1998).

The Fourth Commandment

"Honor your father and your mother" (Deut 5:16).

This commandment, stated in positive terms (see CCC 2198), directly concerns duties of children to their parents, as Jesus was obedient to Mary and Joseph (see Lk 2:51). In the Bible, this is the only commandment with a promise for those who obey it: "that your days may be prolonged, and that it may go well with you in the land which the Lord your God gives you" (Deut 5:16; see also Ex 20:12; Eph 6:1-3).

This universal parent-child relationship also indicates the duties of all toward elders and those who are in authority over us: "Pay all of them their dues, taxes to whom taxes are due, revenue to whom revenue is due, respect to whom respect is due, honor to whom honor is due" (Rom 13:7). This commandment presupposes and includes the duties owed and the proper respect due to all those who exercise legitimate authority over us: parents, instructors, teachers, leaders, magistrates and law enforcement officials, those who govern, and so on (see CCC 2199).

The primary duty enjoined by this commandment is honor and respect, which in some way is due to every person in recognition of God as the Creator and Father of each one of us, and flowing from Jesus' great commandment: "Love one another ... as I have loved you" (Jn 13:34). Honor and respect are an expression of that love. After God himself, we should honor our parents, to whom we owe life and the knowledge of God, and then others whom God has vested with authority over us for our good (see CCC 2197).

The Meaning of Honor and Obedience

The "heart" of this commandment is the honor that is due to parents, which builds on natural affection and reflects the honor due to God. Respect for one's parents also is an expression of *gratitude* (see CCC 2215), which "is shown by true docility and *obedience*" (CCC 2216), as the sacred Scripture teaches us (Prv 6:20-22; 13:1).

What are the limits to the command of obedience toward parents? "As long as a child lives at home with his parents, the child should obey his parents in all that they ask of him when it is for his good or that of the family" (CCC 2217). Something asked of a child believes to be morally wrong must not be obeyed. Children's obligations to obey their parents end when they enter adulthood, though they should continue to respect their parents, an attitude that "has its roots in the fear of God, one of the gifts of the Holy Spirit" (CCC 2217). When they grow up, children should help their parents as much as they can in times of need, illness, and old age, and should listen respectfully to their advice and admonitions (see CCC 2217-18).

Respect and honor of parents overflows into relationships between brothers and sisters. "Respect toward parents fills the home with light and warmth" (CCC 2219). Children's honor of their parents is reciprocated in parents' respect for their children as human persons and children of God (see CCC 2222). Nonetheless, Scripture teaches the need for just discipline administrated in love (see Heb 12:3-11; CCC 2223).

> He who loves his son will not spare the rod.... He who disciplines his son will profit by him.
>
> SIRACH 30:1-2

> Fathers, do not provoke your children to anger, but bring them up in the discipline and instruction of the Lord.
>
> EPHESIANS 6:4

The Role of the Family in God's Plan

Parents are called by God to evangelize their children, being the first witnesses of the Gospel to them (see CCC 2225) and the first to educate them in the faith and in human, social, and spiritual virtues (see CCC 2226). They do this, "by *creating a home* where tenderness, forgiveness, respect, fidelity, and disinterested service are the rule" (CCC 2223). The Second Vatican Council calls the home: "the principal school of the social virtues which are necessary to every society";[7] "an outstanding school of the lay apostolate ... which proclaims aloud both the present power of the kingdom of God and the hope of the blessed life";[8] "a domestic sanctuary of the church";[9] and "a first seminary" for priestly vocations.[10]

Needless to say, creating this family environment is a challenge, for both parents and children. Family prayer, humility, readiness to forgive and ask forgiveness, and parents and older children striving to give a good example are all essential elements in forming such a family environment. The *Catechism* speaks of family life as, "an apprenticeship in self-denial, sound judgment, and self-mastery—the preconditions of all true freedom" (CCC 2223). Also, parents should teach their children to subordinate the "material and instinctual dimensions to interior and spiritual ones."[11]

Further, parents show their care for their children and exercise their responsibility by providing for their children's physical and spiritual needs, choosing schools, and giving judicious advice about what profession, vocation, and state of life to pursue (see CCC 2228-31). In turn, "As living members of the family, children contribute in their own way to making their parents holy,"[12] through prayer, example and witness, and enabling them to grow in humility, patience, self-sacrifice, and trust in God!

Truly the family is *"the original cell of social life"* (CCC 2207), *"a domestic church"*[13] (CCC 2204), and *"a privileged community"* (CCC 2206). Yet Jesus taught us that, "family ties are important but not absolute" (CCC 2232). Parents must recognize that for Christians the primary family is the family of God, the church, and that the first vocation of the Christian is to *follow Jesus*. "He who loves father or mother more than me is not worthy of me; and he who loves son or daughter more than me is not worthy of me" (Mt 10:37; see CCC 2232). Hence, parents should rejoice if one or more of their children hear and respond to God's call to follow and serve Jesus through the consecrated religious life or in the priestly ministry (see CCC 2233; Mt 12:49).

The Fifth Commandment

"You shall not kill" (Deut 5:17).

This commandment, found in Exodus 20:13 and Deuteronomy 5:17, is presented by Jesus to include even unjust anger directed against others (see Mt 5:21-22), as well as hatred and vengeance (see CCC 2262, 2302-2303). Jesus even calls us to love our enemies (see Mt 5:22-39, 44).

The fifth commandment is based upon respect for the human life that God has exalted as the "crown," or summit, of his material creation. Catholic teaching, including the following from the Congregation of the Doctrine of the Faith's document on the "Gift of Life" (*Donum Vitae*) speaks of the sacredness of human life:

> *Human life is sacred* because from its beginning it involves the creative action of God and it remains forever in a special relationship with the Creator, who is its sole end. God alone is the Lord of life from its beginning until its end: no one can under any circumstance claim for himself the right directly to destroy an innocent human being.[14]

> The meaning of the fifth commandment is specified in Scripture: "Do not slay the innocent and the righteous" (Ex 23:7). To deliberately kill an innocent person is directly contrary to the dignity of the human being, to the golden rule, and to the holiness of the Creator who is the source and author of life (see CCC 2261).

"Direct and intentional killing [is] gravely sinful" (CCC 2268). This includes murder, especially those acts that break natural bonds, such as infanticide,[15] fratricide, patricide, the murder of a spouse, and procured abortion. In fact,

> Formal cooperation in an abortion constitutes a grave offense. The Church attaches the canonical penalty of excommunication to this crime against human life. "A person who procures a completed abortion incurs excommunication *latae sententiae,*"[16] "by the very commission of the offense."[17] ... The Church does not thereby intend to restrict the scope of mercy. Rather, she makes clear the gravity of the crime committed, the irreparable harm

done to the innocent who is put to death, as well as to the parents and the whole of society. (CCC 2272)

The Catholic Church holds that a human person comes into existence at the moment of conception, and from that moment, "must be defended in its integrity, cared for, and healed, as far as possible, like any other human being" (CCC 2274). The church therefore condemns threatening the life of a child in the womb—whether due to its chromosomic or genetic inheritance or for any other reason—or cultivating human embryos outside the womb for exploitation, implantation, or any other manipulation or "genetic engineering" (see CCC 2274-75). Any manipulations of this kind violate the personal dignity of the human being; the person's integrity; and his unique, unrepeatable identity (see CCC 2275).

God alone is the Lord and author of human life. Human beings are ministers who cooperate with God's plan in bringing forth life and seeking to heal and preserve the life God has brought forth.

One may not arbitrarily *end* a human life. Suicide, the taking of one's own life, is gravely sinful, although "grave psychological disturbances, anguish, or grave fear of hardship, suffering, or torture can diminish the responsibility of the one committing suicide" (CCC 2282). We should not despair of the eternal salvation of those who take their own lives, but pray for them (see CCC 2283).

So-called assisted suicide is contrary to moral law (see CCC 2282). Putting an end to the lives of handicapped, sick, or dying persons ("direct euthanasia") is "morally unacceptable" (CCC 2277). The *Catechism* distinguishes between "the ordinary care owed to a sick person [that] cannot be legitimately interrupted" (CCC 2279) and various categories of "extraordinary" treatments or means to keep a patient alive (see CCC 2278).

Similarly, this commandment enjoins efforts to improve public health and safety and shuns drug use and any excess ("of food, alcohol, tobacco, or medicine ... love of speed," CCC 2290) that endangers, or threatens to endanger, one's own life or the lives of others. However, the church also warns against the opposite extreme: an excessive preoccupation with the health or welfare of the body that "idolizes" physical perfection, fitness, and success at sports (see CCC 2289).

The command not to kill extends beyond the prohibition against ending a human life. Giving scandal is also a type of "killing," as it harms the spiritual health and peace of others (see CCC 2284-87). The fifth commandment also forbids kidnapping, terrorism, torture, and any "amputations, mutilations, and sterilizations" not for strictly therapeutic medicinal reasons (see CCC 2297). The human body, as it represents the person, is sacred, and so even "the bodies of the dead must be treated with respect" (CCC 2300).[18]

The fifth commandment deals with issues of self-defense, war, and peace. Individuals seeking to defend themselves or others from life-threatening attack are not violating this commandment, since this self-defense is their direct intention, not the harm or killing of the aggressor (see CCC 2263-65). In fact, in some cases legitimate defense of the lives of others for whom we are responsible is not just a right, but a grave duty (see CCC 2265).

Many societies, seeking to defend themselves against violence and murder, have employed the death penalty. However, the *Catechism* indicates that since civil authorities today have developed effective ways to protect society from dangerous activities of criminals who have been caught and convicted, "the cases in which the execution of the offender is an absolute necessity 'are very rare, if not practically nonexistent'"[19] (CCC 2267).

Conditions for legitimate defense of a country or a community by a military force (the "just war" doctrine) are enumerated in the *Catechism* (CCC 2309), since "governments cannot be denied the right of lawful self-defense, once all peace efforts have failed."[20]

Even in the midst of warfare, many basic moral norms still remain in force (see CCC 2311-17, 2328-29). Ultimately, though, the seeking of peace and the renunciation of warfare is central to the fulfillment of this commandment, as the "Prince of Peace" (Isa 9:6) taught: "Blessed are the peacemakers" (Mt 5:9). "Peace is the work of justice and the effect of charity."[21]

The Sixth Commandment

"You shall not commit adultery" (Deut 5:18).

This commandment forbids not only adultery (a sexual relationship that violates the marriage bond), but all abuses of human sexuality in violation of God's beautiful design for procreation and expression of love within marriage (see

CCC 2336). Jesus taught: "You have heard that it was said 'You shall not commit adultery.' But I say to you that every one who looks at a woman lustfully has already committed adultery with her in his heart'" (Mt 5:27-28).

Positively, the sixth commandment requires all to live chastely, in imitation of Jesus Christ, according to a person's particular state of life and vocation (see CCC 2348).

Those whom God calls to virginity or consecrated celibacy abstain totally from sexual activity, "for the sake of the kingdom of heaven" (Mt 19:12) and give themselves to God alone (see CCC 2349).

A man and a woman united in marriage live conjugal chastity by expressing their complete giving of self to each other in love, with *every* act of intercourse open to the conception of life as God's greatest gift to the couple.

Those not married practice chastity through "continence," abstaining by God's grace from all that would arouse sexual passions and from all sexual activity (see CCC 2349). Those engaged to be married also must live in continence. "They should reserve for marriage the expressions of affection that belong to married love. They will help each other grow in chastity" (CCC 2350).

In each vocation, chastity is a powerful witness to others, both of the faith of those who practice it, and of God's faithfulness and loving kindness (see CCC 2346). One of the most beautiful expressions of chaste love is friendship between persons of the same or opposite sex (see CCC 2347).

Sins against the sixth commandment include both *lust* (the disordered desire for or inordinate enjoyment of sexual pleasure) and *masturbation* (the deliberate stimulation of the genital organs in order to derive sexual pleasure). Sexual pleasure is morally disordered when sought for itself, isolated from its procreative and unitive purposes (see CCC 2351-52).

The church teaches that any deliberate use of the sexual faculty outside of marriage is sinful because it is essentially contrary to its purpose: the unitive love of the spouses and the procreation of children (see CCC 2352). Examples of this include:

- *fornication* (i.e., carnal union between an unmarried man and an unmarried woman; see CCC 2353);

- *pornography* (i.e., removing real or simulated sexual acts from the intimacy of the partners, in order to display them deliberately to third parties; see CCC 2354);

- *prostitution*, which reduces the person to an instrument of sexual pleasure. The one who pays sins gravely against his own chastity (CCC 2355; see also 1 Cor 6:15-20); and

- *rape* (i.e., the forcible violation of the sexual privacy of another person, which causes grave damage that can mark the victim for life). An even graver evil is

- *incest*, the rape of children committed by parents or other adult relatives (see CCC 2356).

Pornography, prostitution, and rape have direct and dire social consequences, and therefore their prohibition should be vigorously enforced for the common good by civil authorities.

While homosexual attractions or inclination to homosexual activity are not sinful in themselves, sacred Scripture and Christian tradition declare that homosexual *acts* are sins against the sixth commandment (as are all heterosexual acts outside of marriage). The *Catechism* notes that homosexual acts (and relationships that involve homosexual acts) violate natural law, cannot bring forth life, and "do not proceed from a genuine affective and sexual complementarity. Under no circumstances can they be approved" (CCC 2357). However, there is no basis for discrimination or judgment against persons with homosexual tendencies as they strive to live in chastity, to which all people are called (see CCC 2358-59).

The Gift of Sexuality Within Marriage

Our sexuality, which "affects all aspects of the human person" (CCC 2332), is a great gift of God. The meaning of the sexual act is "realized in a truly human way only if it is an integral part of the love by which a man and a woman commit themselves totally to one another until death."[22]

Within marriage, "sexuality is a source of joy and pleasure" (CCC 2362) that encourages the couple to grow in faithful love and to persevere in the challenges and trials of married life. The married couple willingly accepts the responsibility of bringing forth new life. The gift of the child is a precious expression and fruit of God's creative love and the mutual giving of the spouses to each other (see CCC 2366).

Pope Paul VI, in his encyclical letter "On Human Life" (*Humanae Vitae)*, was totally consistent in insisting that both the unitive and procreative meaning of marital union must be expressed and safeguarded whenever the married couple come together in the sexual act: "each and every marriage act must remain open to the transmission of life."[23] This is nothing new. In fact, the church has always maintained the inseparable connection between the unitive significance (expressing love) and the procreative significance (openness to life) of the marital act of intercourse.

The church praises those couples who courageously choose to have large families and see this as a blessing from the Lord (see CCC 2373). The Catholic Church also teaches that responsible parenthood may be exercised by spouses who, for just reasons, wish to space the births of their children through periodic continence (i.e., abstinence from sexual relations during fertile periods; see CCC 2368, 2370). Methods of "natural family planning" are morally acceptable, "respect the bodies of the spouses, encourage tenderness between them, and favor the education of an authentic freedom" (CCC 2370).

All married couples must remember that, "A child is not something *owed* to one, but is a *gift* ... 'the supreme gift of marriage...'" (CCC 2378). No artificial means of insemination or fertilization may be used, since, "they dissociate the sexual act from the procreative act" (CCC 2377). The essential teaching of the Catholic Church on sexuality is simple and clear: sexual activity belongs only in marriage as an expression of total self-giving and union, and always open to the possibility of new life.

The sixth commandment forbids all sins against marriage, beginning with adultery (marital infidelity). "When two partners, of whom at least one is married to another party, have sexual relations—even transient ones—they commit adultery. Christ condemns even adultery of mere desire" (CCC 2380; cf. Mt 5:27-28).

Jesus also teaches that anyone who divorces his or her spouse and marries another commits adultery (see Mt 5:31-32; 19:3-9; Mk 10:9; Lk 16:18; 1 Cor 7:10-11). "*Divorce* is a grave offense against the natural law. It claims to break the contract, to which the spouses freely consented, to live with each other till death" (CCC 2384); "it introduces disorder into the family and into society"

(CCC 2385). Spouses may not be equally responsible for a divorce (see CCC 2386).

The *Catechism* also describes other offenses against the dignity of marriage: polygamy (CCC 2387), incest and sexual abuse of children or adolescents (CCC 2388, 2389); and so-called free unions, or trial marriages. The Catholic Church recognizes that marriage was intended by God to be a permanent, sacramental bond and covenant between a man and a woman. Those engaging in the sexual act outside of the covenant of marriage are objectively in a state of grave sin and may not receive the Eucharist. Those who really understand human love and the nature of commitment recognize the absurdity of the idea of a "trial marriage," for true love, "demands a total and definite gift of persons to one another" (CCC 2391; cf. FC 80).

In summary, the sixth commandment expresses God's law that sexual relationships between a man and woman must take place only within the indissoluble bond of marriage, expressing mutual love and always open to life.

The Seventh Commandment

You shall not steal (Deut 5:19).

This commandment "forbids unjustly taking away or keeping the good of one's neighbor and wronging him in any way with respect to his goods. It commands justice and charity" with regard to earthly possessions (CCC 2401). Of course, this commandment forbids theft (see CCC 2408) and demands honesty in promises and contracts in economic and social life (see CCC 2410). These agreements and exchanges between persons are the realm of "commutative justice" (see CCC 2411), and violation of this justice demands reparation or restitution, as Zaccheus agreed to restore fourfold what he had unjustly taken from others (see Lk 19:8).

The goods of the earth ultimately belong to all people, and so should be justly distributed by the community according to peoples' contributions and needs ("distributive justice," see CCC 2411). St. Paul reminds us that, "If any one will not work, let him not eat" (2 Thess 3:10). There is a "right to private property," acquired or received in a just way; but private ownership is not absolute, since all things belong to God, who gives for the good of all (see CCC

2403). Therefore, to observe this commandment requires practice of certain virtues: *"temperance,* so as to moderate attachment to this world's goods;... *justice,* to preserve our neighbor's rights and render him what is his due; and the practice of *solidarity,* in accordance with the golden rule and in keeping with the generosity of the Lord, who 'though he was rich, yet for your sake ... became poor so that by his poverty, you might become rich'" (2 Cor 8:9) (CCC 2407).

The observance of this commandment forbids the enslavement of human beings ("stealing" rights and freedom, see CCC 2414) and the abuse of any part of God's creation, such as cruelty to animals (see CCC 2416-18). Human beings are stewards of the earth and of all of God's creatures, and thus must respect and care for all that God has made (see Gen 2:19-20; 9:1-4). "Those *responsible for business enterprises* are responsible to society for the economic and ecological effects of their operations" (CCC 2432; cf. CA 37).

This commandment also gives rise to the social doctrine of the church regarding economics (money and possessions) and work. The teaching is based upon the primary value of the human person, the common good of society that flows from this, and the demands of justice. Catholic social teaching stresses that economic life must be ordered to the service of persons and the good of the entire human community. Making profits and multiplying goods are not to be the ultimate end of economic decisions and activities (see CCC 2426). Likewise, human work or labor is a duty and a result of God's command to sub-due the earth,[24] but man is not to become a slave to work, either voluntarily or involuntarily. Nonetheless, having meaningful work fosters human dignity, pro-vides the necessities of life for oneself and one's family, and serves the human community (see CCC 2428). Therefore, everyone has the *right of economic ini-tiative* (see CCC 2429), *access to employment* without unjust discrimination (see CCC 2433), and a *just wage,* which is the legitimate fruit of work. To refuse or withhold fair pay is a grave injustice (see Lev 19:13; Deut 24:14-15; Jas 5:4; CCC 2434).

The seventh commandment also calls for justice and solidarity among nations. The wealthier nations have a moral obligation to aid in the develop-ment of poorer countries (see CCC 2439-40) and to seek to reform interna-tional economic and financial institutions to benefit the growth and develop-ment of all (see CCC 2440).

God has a special love for the poor, and blesses those who aid them (see CCC 2443). St. John Chrysostom said: "Not to enable the poor to share in our goods is to steal from them and deprive them of life. The goods we possess are not ours, but theirs."[25] For this reason, the church has never considered it stealing for a person in dire need to take food, clothing, or other things necessary to sustain life. Preferably, people should not need to take these things; Christians ought to give them to fulfill the demands of justice (see CCC 2446) or as a work of mercy (see CCC 2447; Isa 58:6-7; Heb 13:3).

The Catholic Church teaches that we are to have a *preferential love* for those who are oppressed by poverty, based on God's own special love and care for the poor. Indeed, one of the most beautiful attributes of the church from her beginnings has been her work for the relief, defense, and liberation of the poor through works of charity and justice. This remains always an indispensable work and concern (see CCC 2448). Jesus himself is present in the poor: "Truly I say to you, as you did it to one of the least of these my brethren, you did it to me" (Mt 25:40; see also Am 8:6).

The Eighth Commandment

"You shall not bear false witness against your neighbor" (Deut 5:20).

This commandment forbids all sins against truth, for God is truth (see CCC 2464). Jesus is, "the way, and the truth, and the life" (Jn 14:6), and so, "speaking the truth in love, we are to grow up in every way into him who is the head, into Christ.... Therefore, putting away falsehood, let every one speak the truth with his neighbor, for we are members one of another" (Eph 4:15, 25). God calls us to an absolute moral uprightness that never misrepresents or distorts the truth. Jesus said to "Let what you say be simply 'Yes' or 'No'"(Mt 5:37).

The followers of Christ are called to be always "living in the truth." As disciples of Christ, it is our duty to bring the truth to others as witnesses of the gospel of Jesus (see CCC 2472). We are not to "be ashamed ... of testifying to our Lord" (2 Tim 1:8), even to the point of witnessing to this truth unto death—martyrdom (see CCC 2471, 2473).

What does the eighth commandment prohibit? "False witness" itself is a lie in court, and a lie under oath is perjury (see CCC 2476). Other types of "false witness" can destroy a person's honor and reputation, such as disclosing other peoples' faults (detraction) or simply lying about them (calumny). "Rash judgment" assumes information about others' faults is true (see CCC 2477). To avoid this sin, we should always assume the best, not the worst, about others' thoughts, words, and deeds (see CCC 2478). Opposite to those attacks on others are the forms of flattery, which is speech to deceive others for our benefit (see CCC 2480).

Speech is intended by God to communicate truth and show honor to others. Boasting or bragging only honors oneself, and "irony," or mocking, dishonors others (see CCC 2481). The direct contradiction of God's purpose of communicating truth is lying, "the most direct offense against the truth" (CCC 2483). Although lies may differ in seriousness, lying always affronts God because it subverts the very purpose of speech: "to communicate known truth to others" (CCC 2485). The church calls for those who have sinned against the truth by damaging another's reputation, or in any way, to seek to make reparation for the untruth they have communicated (see CCC 2487). Not all truth needs to be communicated, and some must not be. Respect for others recognizes a right of privacy: No one is bound to reveal the truth to someone who doesn't have the right to know (see Prv 25:9-10; Sir 27:16). The priest cannot violate the "seal" of the sacrament of reconciliation (CCC 2490), and "everyone should observe an appropriate reserve concerning persons' private lives" (CCC 2492). Sadly, the great increase in the use of the social communications media has led many people to believe in an absolute "right" to information, violating or at least threatening the right of privacy (see CCC 2494). Nonetheless, the church also recognizes the great potential of means of social communication ("the media") to promulgate important information, to educate, and to spread truth, including the Good News of salvation in Jesus Christ and through his church.

The *Catechism* proclaims that "truth carries with it the joy and splendor of spiritual beauty. Truth is beautiful in itself.... Even before revealing himself to man in words of truth, God reveals himself to him through the universal language of creation, the work of his Word, of his wisdom..." (CCC 2500). Man, too, expresses the truth by the beauty of his "creation," his art, and worships God in truth by sacred art (see CCC 2501).

The Ninth Commandment

"You shall not covet your neighbor's wife" (Deut 5:21).

"Covetousness" is an interior disposition. This commandment anticipates Jesus' emphasis on the need to be pure and sinless even in our thoughts. "Every one who looks at a woman lustfully has already committed adultery with her in his heart" (Mt 5:28). This commandment requires that by God's grace we overcome lust and "carnal concupiscence," the desires of our body, or "flesh," for sinful relationships with another person's spouse (see CCC 2514-16).

The positive virtue required to fulfill this commandment is purity. "Blessed are the pure in heart, for they shall see God" (Mt 5:8). Purity of heart enables the person to perceive and evaluate things as God does. The pure of heart see others as "neighbors," and the body of each person as a temple where the Holy Spirit may dwell, "a manifestation of divine beauty" (CCC 2519).

To attain and maintain this purity is a struggle, a spiritual battle, requiring real discipline. The gifts of God that foster the purity required to keep this commandment are:

- *chastity,* which enables us to love with upright and undivided heart;

- *purity of intention,* which seeks to live according to the true end of man with simplicity of vision, fulfilling God's will in everything (see Rom 12:2; Col 1:10);

- *purity of vision,* external and internal, by which we discipline our senses and imagination and refuse all complicity in impure sights and thoughts. "Appearance arouses yearning in fools" (Wis 15:5);

- and, of course, *prayer* ... (see CCC 2520).

Also purity requires *modesty,* which, "means refusing to unveil what should remain hidden" (CCC 2521), and involves, "a modesty of the feelings as well as of the body" (CCC 2523). "Modesty protects the mystery of persons and their love ... [also] modesty is decency. It inspires one's choice of clothing. It keeps silence or reserve where there is evident risk of unhealthy curiosity. It is discreet" (CCC 2522).

It is evident that promotion of Christian purity and modesty today, "requires a *purification of the social climate,"* especially the communications media (CCC 2525). There is a battle to be fought, but not without hope of victory, since the gospel of Christ and his grace is at work in the world to renew the life and culture of fallen man and "to purify and elevate the morality of peoples....".[26]

The Tenth Commandment

"You shall not covet your neighbor's goods" (Deut 5:21).

St. John teaches us in his first letter:

> Do not love the world or the things in the world.... For all that is in the world, the lust of the flesh and the lust of the eyes and the pride of life, is not of the Father but is of the world. And the world passes away, and the lust of it; but he who does the will of God abides for ever.
>
> 1 JOHN 2:15-17

While the ninth commandment concerned the "lust of the flesh," the tenth speaks against the "lust of the eyes" and the "pride of life" that covets the goods of others. This covetousness is, "at the root of theft, robbery, and fraud, which the seventh commandment forbids ... [and] leads to the violence and injustice forbidden by the fifth commandment" (CCC 2534; cf. Mic 2:2; 1 Jn 2:16). In speaking of the intentions and desires of the heart, the ninth and tenth commandments summarize all the precepts of God's law. They also prepare for the teaching of Jesus that focuses on conversion of heart and possession of pure and righteous attitudes, rather than mere external conformity to law.

Jesus also warned, "Take heed, and beware of all covetousness; for a man's life does not consist in the abundance of his possessions" (Lk 12:15), and Luke proceeds to relate the Lord's parable of the miserly man who tore down his storage barns to build bigger ones. Clearly Jesus condemns the greed and avarice of those bound by the passion to accumulate and hoard money and earthly goods for one's own benefit. This is the sin of material covetousness. It may lead to the injustice of taking, or seeking to take, the money and goods of others (see CCC 2536). It also may express itself in the capital sin of *envy*, that "cancer of the heart" that is saddened or troubled by the goods or the success of another person, "and the immoderate desire to acquire them for oneself, even unjustly. When it wishes grave harm to a neighbor it is a mortal sin. St. Augustine saw envy as *'the* diabolical sin'"[27] (CCC 2539).

After St. Luke's account of the foolish rich man and his barns, he presents the positive teaching of Jesus about possessions: "Therefore I tell you, do not be anxious about your life ..." (Lk 12:22), and tells of the freedom of the birds of the air and the lilies of the field, who receive from the Father all they need. Jesus tells his followers to "seek his kingdom, and these things shall be yours as well" (Lk 12:31).

Jesus' advice for security is: "Sell your possessions, and give alms; provide yourselves with purses that do not grow old, with a treasure in the heavens that does not fail.... For where your treasure is, there will your heart be also" (Lk 12:33, 34).

Remedies for envy are *humility* (since envy often comes from pride), and *good will*—wishing the best for the person you are tempted to envy. St. John Chrysostom observed:

> Would you like to see God glorified by you? Then rejoice in your brother's progress and you will immediately give glory to God. Because his servant could conquer envy by rejoicing in the merits of others, God will be praised.[28]

The ultimate solution for sins against the ninth and tenth commandments is to replace the "desires of the flesh" with "the desires of the Holy Spirit who satisfies man's heart" (CCC 2541). Christ's faithful have, "crucified the flesh with its passions and desires" (Gal 5:24); they are "led by the Spirit," and, "follow the desires of the Spirit" (Rom 8:14; see CCC 2543).

The opposite of coveting the goods of others is the desire to abandon goods and riches for the sake of God's kingdom, as Jesus "emptied himself, taking the form of a servant" (Phil 2:7). Jesus taught, "Blessed are the poor in spirit" (Mt 5:3), and lived this teaching: "For your sakes he became poor" (2 Cor 8:9; see CCC 2544-46).

God created human beings to find true and lasting happiness in desiring and possessing him alone. God and his kingdom are the only treasure worth giving everything to obtain (see Mt 13:44-45). Paradoxically, those who become materially poor, or "poor in spirit," to obtain this treasure are truly rich. "Abandonment to the providence of the Father in heaven frees us from anxiety about tomorrow" (CCC 2547; see Mt 6:25-34).

The joy of the poor, who already possess God's kingdom (see CCC 2546;

see Lk 6:20), will be completed in heaven, where our desire to see God and all other holy desires will be perfectly fulfilled. As St. Augustine wrote, reflecting on heaven:

> There will true glory be, where no one will be praised by mistake or flattery; true honor will not be refused to the worthy, nor granted to the unworthy; likewise, no one unworthy will pretend to be worthy, where only those who are worthy will be admitted. There true peace will reign, where no one will experience opposition either from self or others. God himself will be virtue's reward; he gives virtue and has promised to give himself as the best and the greatest reward that could exist.... "I shall be their God and they will be my people...." This is also the meaning of the Apostle's words: "So that God may be all in all." God himself will be the goal of our desires; we shall contemplate him without end, love him without surfeit, praise him without weariness. This gift, this state, this act, like eternal life itself, will assuredly be common to all.[29]

This is the goal and the fulfillment of keeping the commandments: fullness of life in the Father, in the Son, Our Lord Jesus Christ, and in the Holy Spirit. It is an abundant life that begins here and now, and reaches perfection in the life of the saints in heaven.

CHAPTER 10

Catholics in the World

The Christian way of life and morality are not carried out in a vacuum but within the world. This chapter will consider some principles of Catholic living and decision making today. A primary source for this study is the longest document of the Second Vatican Council, the "Pastoral Constitution on the Church in the Modern World," *Gaudium et Spes*, and the *Catechism*.

Characteristics of the World Today

Our first task as Catholics considering how to live in the world today must be that of discerning what is actually going on in the world, "scrutinizing the signs of the times and of interpreting them in the light of the Gospel.... Today, the human race is passing through a new stage of its history. Profound and rapid changes are spreading by degrees around the whole world."[1]

Rapid change has been a primary characteristic of the twentieth century. Some of these changes may be attributed to science and technology, others to political or social causes. Our age is a time of progress and uncertainty, in which the human race looks forward to the future with expectancy and hope of the good that may come from change, but also with misgivings, unrest, and even fear of a future that may hold frustration, bondage, suffering, and disaster.

The bishops of the Second Vatican Council pointed out many troubling imbalances in the modern world: "an abundance of wealth, resources, and economic power" held by some, while a "huge proportion" of humanity is "tormented by hunger and poverty." Some experience a keener awareness of freedom, in contrast to "new forms of social and psychological slavery." And while there is a growing sense of the interdependence of mankind and of the need for unity, this is opposed by the reality of growing tension among men and nations because of "political, social, economic, racial, and ideological disputes."[2]

Ironically, while many people continue to search for a better world, their personal lives are often in disarray because they have neglected the betterment of their own spirit. Some have come to realize their need for "a more personal and explicit adherence to faith" in God, and yet, "growing numbers of people are abandoning religion in practice."[3] Indeed, religion (and Christianity in particular) is often viewed as being antithetical to progress, science, and other human endeavors, or is simply seen as outmoded and irrelevant to the present situation of humanity.

In the final analysis, the Second Vatican Council sees the world today in a position of dangerous paradox, with the future of the human race hanging in the balance, depending upon the choices we make:

> ... The modern world shows itself at once powerful and weak, capable of the noblest deeds or the foulest. Before it lies the path to freedom or slavery, to progress or retreat, to brotherhood or hatred. Moreover, man is becoming aware that it is his responsibility to guide aright the forces which he has unleashed and which can enslave him or minister to him.[4]

The Heart of the Problem

Although the external circumstances of the modern world have undoubtedly changed, the Catholic Church holds that the root of its problems today remains the same now as always. The Catholic bishops at the Second Vatican Council taught:

> The imbalances under which the modern world labors are linked with the more basic imbalance rooted in the heart of man. For in man himself many elements wrestle with one another....[5]
>
> Although he was made by God in a state of holiness, from the very dawn of history man has abused his liberty, at the urging of personified Evil [Satan]. Man set himself against God and sought to find fulfillment apart from God....
>
> Often refusing to acknowledge God as his beginning, man has disrupted

also his proper relationship with his own ultimate goal. At the same time he became out of harmony with himself, with others, and with all created things.

Therefore man is split within himself. As a result, all of human life, whether individual or collective, shows itself to be a dramatic struggle between good and evil, between light and darkness. Indeed, man finds that by himself he is incapable of battling the assaults of evil successfully, so that everyone feels as though he is bound by chains.[6]

The basic problem of human life in the world, today and always, is sin: rebellion against God and his plan. That is the heart of the problems we face. The rebellion of human beings against God is becoming increasingly blatant in the world today. In Western society, many people have dropped any pretense of being God-fearing, and have openly turned to pornography, sexual promiscuity and homosexuality, the occult, rebellion against authority, and a host of other evils clearly condemned by sacred Scripture and Christian tradition.

Vatican II speaks of Satan as a source of human rebellion against God. Yet one of the notable "signs" of modern times is the denial of Satan's existence. Belief in the devil or demons is mocked by the "enlightened" modern mind. Fr. Raniero Cantalamessa, O.F.M. Cap., the preacher of the papal household, observes:

A very curious thing is going on: Satan, driven out through the door, has climbed back through the window; driven out of religion and theology, he has come back in superstition. The modern, technological, industrialized world, especially where it is at its most industrialized and advanced, is crawling with gurus, witches, spiritualists, readers of horoscopes, sellers of spells and amulets, not to mention actual satanist sects. Something has happened similar to what the Apostle Paul reproached his pagan contemporaries with: "While claiming to be wise, they became fools and exchanged the glory of the immortal God for the likeness of an image of mortal man or of birds or of four-legged animals or of snakes.... And since they did not see fit to acknowledge God, God handed them over to their undiscerning mind ..." (Rom 1:22, 28).[7]

The "Pastoral Constitution on the Church in the Modern World" devotes three sections (nos. 19-21) to the problem of atheism. Atheism has many forms: the theoretical atheism of existential philosophers and others; the systematic atheism which asserts absolute human independence from God or even the notion of God; and political atheism, which anticipates the liberation of man, especially through his economic and social emancipation. Political atheism argues that, by its very nature, religion "thwarts such liberation by arousing man's hope for a deceptive future life, thereby diverting him from the constructing of the earthly city."[8]

There is also a sort of "practical atheism," subtly promoted by secular humanism, by which a person's attention and concern is so fully directed to life in this world that the question of God is never adequately considered or addressed. Many people today dismiss belief in God simply because he doesn't seem necessary for one to be a good person, which is the highest moral ideal that they can accept or imagine.

The Catholic Church continues to affirm and teach that the root of all the problems of mankind is the rejection of God, whether through knowing denial of God, through ignorance or doubt, or through the rebellion against him that Christians call sin. Without the grace and power of God, the human person is bound to fall into all manner of sin against himself, his neighbor, and the created world. Without the knowledge of God, humanity is blind to the ultimate source of redemption and help when facing the difficult struggles and challenges of life in the world.

God's Solution: Jesus Christ

Man proposes many solutions to the myriad of pressing problems and inequities of the world: social engineering; peace talks and summit meetings; political, social, and economic solutions of various sorts. While these may be necessary to help resolve certain problems, Christians must remember that the world's ills cannot be solved by human efforts alone. Without the help of God and the guidance of his Holy Spirit, all of these efforts remain incomplete and destined to fail.

Sin, in all its forms and with all its consequences, is at the root of nearly all human ills and struggles, and sin has only one remedy: the redemptive love and mercy of God that comes to us through the Savior Jesus Christ. *Gaudium et Spes* constantly turns from its analysis of the situation of the human race today to the ultimate solution of this situation: Jesus Christ.[9] In him alone, the Council says, "can be found the key, the focal point, and the goal of all human history."[10] Pope John Paul II also affirmed the primacy of Jesus Christ in his first encyclical letter, *Redemptor Hominis* ("The Redeemer of Man"):

> In Christ and through Christ God has revealed Himself fully to mankind and has definitely drawn close to it. At the same time, in Christ and through Christ man has acquired full awareness of his dignity, of the heights to which he is raised and of the surpassing worth of his own humanity, and of the meaning of his existence. All of us who are Christ's followers must therefore meet and unite around him.[11]

The fundamental solution to the struggles of this age is for humanity to discover its true identity, which is only fully revealed in the person of Jesus Christ. In Christ, each person has been given the opportunity to be transformed from within and reborn in the image of God, our Creator. As Pope John Paul II said in his address to the world at Christmas, 1985:

> Christ is born so that we may be reborn, new men in the New Man ... the more human world of which Christ the Lord ... is the first-fruit, is a world inhabited by a new people, which goes forward "with sobriety, righteousness, and godliness" towards the full joy of Heaven. [It is] a people that knows how to be sober with regard to the resources of the universe and wise in the use of the energies of its own mind, for it knows how to resist the false mirage of progress that is indifferent to moral values, and looks only to the immediate and material advantage.
>
> A people, too, that is inspired by justice in its thoughts, resolutions and deeds, a people ever aiming at the goal of a more authentic community of persons, in which every individual will feel accepted, respected and esteemed.
>
> A people, finally, that in godliness transcends itself in opening itself to God, from whom it expects the constant support needed for traveling forward, along the road of true progress, towards the goal of meeting with Christ, the Redeemer of man and Lord of history.[12]

The human race cannot become this "new people" through its own efforts, but only by the power of God coming to us through Jesus Christ and the Holy Spirit. As the Second Vatican Council expressed this truth:

> If anyone wants to know how this unhappy situation [of the world today] can be overcome, Christians will tell him that all human activity, constantly imperiled by man's pride and deranged self-love, must be purified and perfected by the power of Christ's cross and resurrection. For redeemed by Christ and made a new creature in the Holy Spirit, man is able to love the things themselves created by God.... He can receive them from God, and respect and reverence them as flowing constantly from the hand of God.[13]

From Christ, we also learn to bear the sufferings and hardships that come from following God and his will:

> Undergoing death itself for all of us sinners, He taught us by example that we too must shoulder that cross which the world and the flesh inflict upon those who search after peace and justice. Appointed Lord by His resurrection and given plenary power in heaven and on earth, Christ is now at work in the hearts of men through the energy of the Holy Spirit. He arouses not only a desire for the age to come, but ... He animates, purifies and strengthens those noble longings by which the human family strives to make its life more human and to render the whole earth submissive to this goal.[14]

The Extraordinary Synod of Bishops in 1985 also affirmed the centrality of the cross of Christ. The Final Report of that Synod stated:

> In the present-day difficulties God wishes to teach us more deeply the value, the importance and the centrality of the cross of Jesus Christ.... When we Christians speak of the cross we do not deserve to be labeled as pessimists, but we rather found ourselves upon the realism of Christian hope.[15]

It is evident from these statements that Jesus Christ imparts the desire to make this world more fully human, abounding in peace and justice. This will entail suffering, but Jesus gives us the perfect example, especially through his death on the cross, of enduring suffering for the sake of God's kingdom. Through his cross and resurrection, Jesus also provides grace and the power of the Holy Spirit to guide and strengthen us as we seek to follow God's will in the midst of doubt, temptation, and trial.

The Dignity of the Human Person

The Second Vatican Council and Pope John Paul II reiterate that a central goal of the Catholic Church's efforts in this world is to promote and safeguard the dignity of each person. The Catholic Church is convinced that the solution to the problems of society depends upon a correct understanding and appreciation of the unsurpassable worth of each human life. *Gaudium et Spes* affirms the belief that,

> By no human law can the personal dignity and liberty of man be so aptly safeguarded as by the Gospel of Christ that has been entrusted to the Church. For this gospel announces and proclaims the freedom of the sons of God, and repudiates all the bondage which ultimately results from sin.[16]

The Catholic Church has always taught and defended the inestimable value of every human life, believing that each human person, "by his interior qualities ... outstrips the whole sum of mere things." Each person, from the moment of conception, possesses "a spiritual and immortal soul," destined for eternal life.[17] Thus one human life is more valuable in God's eyes than all other created things combined. As the noted Christian author C.S. Lewis reflected in his address, "The Weight of Glory,"

> It is a serious thing to live in a society of possible gods and goddesses, to remember that the dullest and most interesting person you talk to may one day be a creature which, if you saw it now, you would be strongly tempted to worship, or else a horror and a corruption such as you now meet, if at all, only in a nightmare. All day long we are, in some degree, helping each other to one or other of these destinations....
> Next to the Blessed Sacrament itself, your neighbor is the holiest object

present to your senses. If he is your Christian neighbor he is holy in almost the same way, for in him also Christ ... Glory Himself, is truly hidden.[18]

In addition to an immortal soul, each person possesses an intellect that is able to perceive truth and wisdom; a moral conscience, which senses an internal law telling the person how to live; and the gift of free will by which each person chooses his or her path of life, including whether or not to submit to God and his call.

The Catholic Church asserts that there are certain rights and obligations that necessarily follow from the fact of the dignity of the human person.

There is a growing awareness of the exalted dignity proper to the human person, since he stands above all things, and his rights and duties are universal and inviolable. Therefore, there must be made available to all men everything necessary for leading a life truly human, such as food, clothing, and shelter, the right to choose a state of life freely and to found a family, the right to education, to employment, to a good reputation, to respect, to appropriate information, to activity in accord with the upright norm of one's own conscience, to protection of privacy and to rightful freedom in matters religious, too.... These rights are possessed equally by all.[19]

As well as expressing these rights, the Second Vatican Council also listed some violations of human dignity that threaten fully human life:

Whatever is opposed to life itself, such as any type of murder, genocide, abortion, euthanasia, or willful self-destruction, whatever violates the integrity of the human person, such as mutilation, torments inflicted on body or mind, attempts to coerce the will itself; whatever insults human dignity, such as subhuman living conditions, arbitrary imprisonment, deportation, slavery, prostitution, the selling of women and children; as well as disgraceful working conditions, where men are treated as mere tools for profit, rather than as free and responsible persons; all these things and others of their like are infamies indeed. They poison human society, but they do more harm to those who practice them than those who suffer from the injury. Moreover, they are a supreme dishonor to the Creator.[20]

The Relationship of Society to the Person

The Catholic Church understands that the basic purpose of human society and government is to serve the individual person: safeguarding and promoting the human rights of each one and protecting against the threats to life itself. *Gaudium et Spes* expresses the principle well:

> The social order and its development must inceasingly work to the benefit of the human person if the disposition of affairs is to be subordinate to the personal realm and not contrariwise, as the Lord indicated when He said that the Sabbath was made for man, and not man for the Sabbath.[21]

Social institutions and bodies, including churches and governments, ultimately exist for the service of individual persons and must therefore respect and safeguard their rights and dignity. *Gaudium et Spes* reiterates, "For the beginning, the subject, and the goal of social institutions is and must be the human person, which for its part and by its very nature stand completely in need of social life."[22] The latter part of this quotation implies that while social institutions exist for the good of the individual person, and not vice versa, persons cannot isolate themselves from others and ignore the needs of society or the church.

Social life, and especially life within the body of Christ, the church, is an essential need of human nature and a major vehicle by which each person discovers his or her own identity and grows as a son or daughter of God. As was noted previously, it is God's plan to call together humanity and to save us as a people, not as isolated individuals. Love of neighbor is just as essential to the Christian life as love of God (see 1 Jn 4:20-21), and to love others we must first enter into social relationships with them.[23]

Building strong Christian social relationships also has practical benefits. It is by working together that Catholics and other Christians are most effective in renewing the social order and proclaiming the gospel of Jesus Christ to others. The Pastoral Constitution warned against an individualistic attitude or approach to restoring the social order to Christian standards:

Profound and rapid changes make it particularly urgent that no one, ignoring the trend of events or drugged by laziness, content himself with a merely individualistic morality. It grows increasingly true that the obligations of justice and love are fulfilled only if each person, contributing to the common good according to his own abilities and the needs of others, also promotes and assists the public and private institutions dedicated to bettering the conditions of human life....

Let everyone consider it his sacred obligation to count social necessities among the primary duties of modern man, and to pay heed to them.[24]

Gaudium et Spes strongly encourages all Christians, especially lay persons who are involved daily "in the world," to become actively involved in the affairs of society according to their vocation and abilities. It is not enough to be "Sunday Catholics." This constitution explicitly denounces the dichotomy between daily life in the world and our faith and calls this false division one of "the more serious errors of our age."[25] Instead, the bishops of Vatican II counseled:

Laymen should ... know that it is generally the function of their well-formed Christian conscience to see that the divine law is inscribed in the life of the earthly city.... laymen are not only bound to penetrate the world with a Christian spirit. They are also called to be witnesses to Christ in all things in the midst of human society.[26]

The Nature and Ordering of Society

The Church "is not to be confused in any way with the political community" (CCC 2245). As the Second Vatican Council reminds us, the purpose God has assigned to the church is a religious one.[27] Yet, "this religious mission can be the source of commitment, direction, and vigor," to guide the human community according to God's law.[28] The church can also assist in discerning the true nature and best direction for society, since, "it has clearly recognized man's origin and destiny in God, the Creator and Redeemer," and, therefore, "invites political authorities to measure their judgments and decisions against this inspired truth about God and man" (CCC 2244).

The *Catechism* describes in detail the church's perspective on the nature and ordering of society. By nature, the human person is a social being. "He rightly owes loyalty to the communities of which he is a part and respect to those in authority who have charge of the common good" (CCC 1880). Since all legitimate authority comes from God (see CCC 1899; see also Rom 13:1-2; 1 Pet 2:13-17), and is necessary for society to function, citizens must obey and show respect for legitimate authority (see CCC 1900).

In God's order, the type of political regime and the appointment of rulers should be chosen freely by the citizens (see CCC 1901). The authority these rulers exercise is legitimate "only when it seeks the common good of the group concerned and if it employs morally licit means to attain it" (CCC 1903). Indeed, authority in society is a service (see CCC 223; Mt 20:26) that is meant "to facilitate the exercise of freedom and responsibility by all" within a just hierarchy of values and with a view to promoting harmony and peace (CCC 2236). *"Political authorities* are obliged to respect the fundamental rights of the human person. They will dispense justice humanely by respecting the rights of everyone, especially of families and the disadvantaged" (CCC 2237).

Citizens, for their part, submit to legitimate authority and have a "co-responsibility for the common good," which makes it "morally obligatory to pay taxes, to exercise the right to vote, and to defend one's country" (CCC 2240; see also Rom 13:7). Nonetheless, "their loyal collaboration includes the right, and at times the duty, to voice their just criticisms of that which seems harmful to the dignity of persons and to the good of the community" (CCC 2238). Indeed, "the citizen is obliged in conscience not to follow the directives of civil authorities when they are contrary to the demands of the moral order, to the fundamental rights of persons or the teachings of the Gospel" (CCC 2242). People are not bound to obey unjust laws or laws that violate the moral order (see CCC 1902-3; Mt 22:21). "We must obey God rather than men" (Acts 5:29; CCC 2242). Armed resistance to oppression by political authority is a last resort, to be used only if a number of conditions are met (see CCC 2743).

Seeking the Common Good

We often hear the phrase "the common good." It refers to the sum total of all the social conditions that enable individuals and groups to reach their fulfillment more fully or easily.[29] The common good flows from the goods of the persons who make up society, and always must respect their rights.[30] The common good seeks the development of the group, making "accessible to each what is needed to lead a truly human life ..." (CCC 1908). It requires "peace ... the stability and security of a just order," and therefore includes the right of individuals and societies to defend that peace and security, if necessary (see CCC 1909).

Because of the growing interdependence of people throughout the world, we recognize a "universal common good" that nations must strive together to preserve (see CCC 1911), never forgetting that "the common good is always oriented towards the progress of persons: 'The order of things must be subordinate to the order of persons, and not the other way around' (GS 26 § 3). This order is founded on truth, built up in justice, and animated by love" (CCC 1912).

Societies should be ordered to provide for the fullest participation of the greatest number of citizens in their directions and public lives.[31] This increases and demands personal responsibility (see CCC 1914). Personal responsibility is enhanced by education and conversion, which instruct people in the true and the good, and (by God's grace) turn them from the selfish and destructive tendencies of sin (see CCC 1916-17). With this education and conversion, people actively participate in society to guide it toward justice for all and in the paths of human solidarity.

Solidarity is a way of speaking about people working together in friendship or social charity to seek human goods for all people (see CCC 1939). These goods are social and economic (e.g., just distribution of goods and fair remuneration for work; see CCC 1942). Finally, the Catholic Church recognizes that a well-ordered society will never be attained without the grace of charity—"God's love has been poured into our hearts through the Holy Spirit" (Rom 5:5).

Charity [that is, the love of God and neighbor] is the greatest social commandment. It respects others and their rights. It requires the practice of justice, and it alone makes us capable of it. Charity inspires a life of self-giving: "Whoever seeks to gain his life will lose it, but whoever loses his life will preserve it" (Lk 17:33). (CCC 1889)

A Catholic Understanding of the World and Christian Hope

Some Catholics are hesitant when they hear exhortations from the church to get involved in the world and its affairs. This hesitancy may be the result of bad past experiences, of unconcern, selfishness, or being too busy with personal affairs; or it may stem from a genuine lack of understanding about whether and how Christians are supposed to relate to the world.

One possible source of misunderstanding is the different possible meanings of "the world" that were discussed in the last chapter. The world can either be viewed as the arena of God's activity (see Mk 16:15) that he loves and has redeemed at a great cost (see Jn 3:16). Or "the world" may be understood as that spirit of evil or vanity that dominates the world by false values (see Jn 15:18; 1 Jn 2:15-16), or even by the bondage of Satan himself (Jn 12:31; 14:30; 16:11).

Gaudium et Spes instructs Catholics concerning the negative usage of this term "the world," as when St. Paul says: "Do not be conformed to this world..." (Rom 12:2): "By world is here meant that spirit of vanity and malice which transforms into an instrument of sin those human energies intended for the service of God and man...."[32] This understanding sheds light on the well-known maxim that Christians are to be "in the world, but not of the world" (Jn 17:14-18). This means that although Christians are physically on earth, they are not to submit themselves to the false values or powers of the world that are opposed to God.

The Catholic approach to the world and human society cannot be characterized simply as either optimistic or pessimistic, but rather as marked by realism and Christian hope. Christian hope affirms that all who consciously commit their lives to Jesus Christ and conform every area of their lives to his teaching will find peace and ultimate victory over all evil (see Rom 8:22-25; CCC 2090). This hope, implanted by the Holy Spirit, is the force that has motivated the great martyrs, missionaries, and saints of the church to endure willingly (even joyfully) their hardships and sufferings on account of the gospel (see CCC 2473).

Catholics today are also challenged by the gospel and church teaching to sacrifice their lives (their time, energy, and money) so that the world and human society can be transformed according to God's will and plan. However, this can occur only if they first have been changed and transformed from within by the Holy Spirit. Only through God's grace can we view and approach the many disturbing realities of the world with true Christian courage and hope (see Col 1:24-29).

Vocation of Prayer and Penance

There are different ways Catholics can take active responsibility for the world—different callings or vocations. Some are called to influence the world through a contemplative life of prayer and penance. This is not a passive approach, or an escape from the world, but a time-honored Catholic vocation based upon the realization that the course of human events is profoundly affected by prayer, as well as influenced by the prophetic lifestyle of the contemplative. As T.S. Eliot wrote in his choruses from "The Rock":

Even the anchorite who meditates alone,
For whom the days and nights repeat the praise of God,
Prays for the Church, the Body of Christ incarnate.[33]

Some Christians mistakenly view the contemplative vocation as useless to society, despite Jesus' teaching about Martha and Mary (see Lk 10:38-42). It is hard to determine whether this view flows from a modern Western orientation toward action, from a lack of faith in the power of prayer, or both. In either case, it is essential for Catholics to grasp the importance of prayer for the direction and transformation of human society.

Even those who are called by God to very active involvement in the world need to pray. As Fr. Cantalamessa has observed: "The overall picture of Jesus that emerges is that of a contemplative who every so often goes over into action, rather than a man of action who every so often allows himself periods of contemplation."[34]

In order to act according to God's will, we first must listen to what God has to say about how to act, seeking the guidance of the Holy Spirit, and also draw strength from the Lord for our activity. We also need to pray, because there is spiritual opposition to the accomplishment of God's will in the world—opposition that can be overcome only by spiritual means, not by human effort alone.

The ministry of Jesus and other writings of the New Testament underscore the reality that, "we are not contending against flesh and blood, but against the principalities, against the powers, against the world rulers of this present darkness, against the spiritual hosts of wickedness in the heavenly places" (Eph 6:12). In response to this realization, Paul exhorts the church to, "Pray at all times in the Spirit, with all prayer and supplication. To that end keep alert with all perseverance, making supplication for all the saints ..." (Eph 6:18).

Jesus himself spent many hours in prayer and fasting in his warfare against Satan, a warfare that ultimately led to his death, "when the devil ... put it into the heart of Judas Iscariot, Simon's son, to betray him" (Jn 13:2). At another time, Jesus told his apostles that, "this kind [of demon] cannot be driven out by anything but prayer and fasting" (Mk 9:29).

One of the most pressing needs of the Catholic Church in our day is recognition of the reality of Satan and his opposition to God's kingdom, and the need for prayer and other spiritual means to combat him. The Catholic Church recognized this principle when it proclaimed St. Thérèse of Lisieux, a cloistered contemplative nun, the patroness of missionaries. Although she never set foot in mission territory, her fervent desire for the conversion of the world to Christ and her zealous prayer for this is recognized by Catholics as having a tremendous missionary impact.

Reflecting on the magnitude of evil in the world should indicate that this evil is not simply the product of human weakness or perversity alone, but is instigated and fostered by a malevolent being, Satan, who is more than human, being a fallen archangel. Yet, salvation means that we have been freed by the Lord's death and resurrection from the power of Satan, sin, and death in our lives. As the Second Vatican Council proclaims:

From bondage to the devil and sin He delivered us, so that each one of us can say with the Apostle: the Son of God "loved me and gave Himself up for me" (Gal 2:20). By suffering for us He not only provided us with an example for our imitation. He blazed a trail, and if we follow it, life and death are made holy and take on a new meaning.[35]

Bringing Christ to the World

The basic message that the Catholic Church brings to the world today must be this same message of liberation and hope for humanity in Jesus Christ that is recorded in the Scripture. When Pope John Paul II asked in his first encyclical letter, *Redemptor Hominis,* what Christians are called to do in this moment of history, he answered:

> Our response must be: Our spirit is set in one direction, the only direction for our intellect, will, and heart is towards, Christ, our Redeemer, towards Christ, the redeemer of man. We wish to look toward Him—because there is salvation in no one else but Him—the Son of God—repeating what Peter said, "Lord, to whom shall we go? You have the words of eternal life."[36]

How do Catholics bring Christ to the world? There are two basic approaches that will be discussed here. The first is *evangelization:* the proclamation of the Good News of Jesus Christ in order to lead others to conversion and faith in him, so that they may be saved and enjoy eternal life with God. This always has been the primary task of the disciples of Jesus, his church.

A second approach to bringing Christ to the world is *to seek the transformation of the social order* (including the political, economic, and cultural spheres of man's activities), so that this social order truly reflects and operates according to God's will, as revealed most fully by Jesus Christ and his teaching.

Both of these approaches are important for Catholics, but the first has priority. Society is made up of individual persons and therefore will not reflect God's will and Christian values fully unless the individuals who make up society personally embrace Christ, for only then will they be able to discern God's will through grace and truth. The grace of Christ may be available to some people who are not explicitly Christian, but certainly the fullness of God's plan for human society will not be achieved unless people come to know, love, and serve the Savior of the human race, Jesus Christ. Hence, evangelization of persons precedes and makes possible the transformation of society according to the fullness of God's will and plan.

Evangelization

The great commission for all Christians to evangelize is based on Jesus' parting words to his followers in Matthew's Gospel (Mt 28:19-20): "Go therefore and make disciples of all nations...."

The charter for evangelization for Catholics today is the apostolic exhortation of Pope Paul VI, December 8, 1975, entitled "On Evangelization in the Modern World" (*Evangelii nuntiandi*). This short document, which applies the "great commission" to the world today, should be studied by every mature Catholic. The document explains, first, the meaning of evangelization:

> To evangelize is first of all to bear witness, in a simple and direct way, to God revealed by Jesus Christ, in the Holy Spirit, to bear witness that in His Son God has loved the world—that in His Incarnate Word He has given being to all things and has called men to eternal life....
>
> Evangelization will also always contain—as the foundation, center and at the same time summit of its dynamism—a clear proclamation that, in Jesus Christ, the Son of God made man, who died and rose from the dead, salvation is offered to all men, as a gift of God's grace and mercy....[37]

But what is meant by "salvation"? The document goes on to explain that our evangelization does not announce an "immanent (this-worldly) salvation" that meets material and spiritual needs of life on earth alone, but, the church announces:

> a salvation that exceeds all those limits in order to reach fulfillment in a communion with the one and only divine Absolute (God): a transcendent and eschatological salvation, which indeed has its beginning in this life, but which is fulfilled in eternity.[38]

In other words, Catholics must witness to the reality of God's love as shown in Jesus Christ and in the gift of eternal life that God has offered to every person.

> Before Pilate, Christ proclaims that he "has come into the world, to bear witness to the truth" (Jn 18:37). The Christian is not to "be ashamed then of testifying to our Lord" (2 Tim 1:8; see CCC 2471). The duty of Christians to take part in the life of the church impels them to act as witnesses of the gospel and of the obligations that flow from it. This witness is a transmission of the faith in words and deeds (CCC 2472).

How does one witness? Witness does not mean reciting doctrine or abstract truths. A witness has firsthand, personal knowledge of that to which he testifies. In order to evangelize, Catholics first must know the reality of God's love and of the power of the death and resurrection of Jesus Christ in their own lives. True evangelization requires genuine faith and conversion on the part of the evangelizer. As the Catholic bishops affirmed at the Extraordinary Synod in 1985, in the document "Message to the People of God, Final Report":

> The evangelization of non-believers in fact presupposes the self-evangelization of the baptized and also, in a certain sense, of deacons, priests and bishops. Evangelization takes place through witnesses. The witness gives his testimony not only with words, but also with his life. We must not forget that in Greek the word for testimony is *martyrium*. In this respect, the more ancient churches can learn much from the new churches, from their dynamism, from their life and testimony even unto the shedding of their blood for the Faith.[39]

The world needs to confront the reality of Christ, the "power of God and the wisdom of God" (1 Cor 1:24), as he is present in the world, changing peoples' lives. As the apostle Paul puts it, "the kingdom of God does not consist in talk but in power" (1 Cor 4:20). That is what is at the heart of evangelization— the testimony or witness of people, through both word and example, to God's transforming power and love in their lives. "In order that the message of salvation can show the power of its truth and radiance before men, it must be authenticated by the witness of the life of Christians" (CCC 2044). St. Francis of Assisi exhorted his followers to preach the gospel constantly, and to use words when necessary. Our lives and example witness our faith more powerfully than our words.

Many Catholics, it appears, need to be evangelized themselves, to encounter God personally before they can become true evangelizers and carry out Jesus' commission to "Go therefore and make disciples of all nations ..." (Mt 28:19).

The 1985 Extraordinary Synod of Bishops proclaimed:

Every baptized man and woman, according to his or her state in life and in the church, receives the mission to proclaim the Good News of salvation for man in Jesus Christ;[40]

and

Evangelization is the first duty not only of the Bishops but also of priests and deacons, indeed, of all Christians....[41] The Church makes herself more credible if she speaks less of herself and ever more preaches Christ crucified (cf. 1 Cor 2:12)....[42]

The primary mission of the church in the world, today as always, is evangelization: to witness in the power of the Holy Spirit to God's love as revealed in Jesus Christ, so that all people will come to know, love, and serve God, and receive the gift of eternal life. "The Holy Spirit is the protagonist, 'the principal agent of the whole of the Church's mission'"[43] (CCC 852).

Finally, it must be stressed that evangelization is only the first stage of an ongoing, lifelong growth in believing in and following Jesus Christ. The Catholic Church has always emphasized that the proclamation of God's word (kerygma), or the act of evangelization, must be followed by an ever fuller instruction in the Christian life (known as "catechesis," or "didache," meaning teaching) that contributes to the person's growth in holiness.

As Pope John Paul II wrote in his apostolic exhortation on catechesis in our time, *Catechesi Tradendae:*

Within the whole process of evangelization, the aim of catechesis is to be the teaching and maturation stage, that is to say the period in which the Christian, having accepted by faith the person of Jesus Christ as the one Lord and having given Him complete adherence by sincere conversion of heart, endeavors to know better this Jesus to whom he has entrusted himself: to know His "mystery," the kingdom of God proclaimed by Him, the requirements and promises contained in His Gospel message, and the paths that He has laid down for anyone who wishes to follow Him.

It is true that being a Christian means saying "yes" to Jesus Christ, but let us remember that this "yes" has two levels: It consists in surrendering to the word of God and relying on it, but it also means, at a later stage, endeavoring to know better and better the profound meaning of this word.[44]

Finally, catechesis is closely linked with the responsible activity of the Church and of Christians in the world. A person who has given adherence to Jesus Christ by faith and is endeavoring to consolidate that faith by catechesis needs to live in communion with those who have taken the same step. Catechesis runs the risk of becoming barren if no community of faith and Christian life takes the catechumen in at a certain stage of his catechesis.[45]

The truths studied in catechesis are the same truths that touched the person's heart when he heard them for the first time. Far from blunting or exhausting them, the fact of knowing them better should make them even more challenging and decisive for one's life.[46]

A strong community of faith is necessary to communicate and support this teaching, fostering growth in Christ. Hence, evangelization must be completed by catechesis.

Transforming the Social Order

The Second Vatican Council also teaches that Catholics have a responsibility to work for the betterment of human society—to serve as a "leaven" (1 Cor 5:6) in order to transform every sphere of human activity, so that they all may attain the full purpose and life that God intends. The church "serves as a leaven and as a kind of soul for human society as it is to be renewed in Christ and transformed into God's family."[47]

But how, practically, do the church and its members seek to transform human society? As *Gaudium et Spes* instructs:

Christ, to be sure, gave His church no proper mission in the political, economic, or social order. The purpose which He set before her is a religious one. But out of this religious mission itself came a function, a light, and an energy which can serve to structure and consolidate the human community according to the divine law. As a matter of fact, when circumstances of time and place create the need, she can and indeed should initiate activities on behalf of all men. This is particularly true of activities designed for the needy, such as the works of mercy and similar undertakings.[48]

The history of the Catholic Church abounds in examples of Catholics of every vocation initiating works of mercy and other services as a response to the call of the gospel. There is no foundation to the view that the church has been or should be separated from the world, if by this is meant a detachment from the needs and concerns of human beings and human society. The very first sentence of *Gaudium et Spes* declares:

> The joys and the hopes, the griefs and the anxieties of the men of this age, especially those who are poor or in any way afflicted, these too are the joys and hopes, the griefs and anxieties of the followers of Christ.[49]

Christ's ministry, carried on by his church, involves healing the sick, feeding the hungry, encouraging the lonely and discouraged, and freeing the oppressed. In Luke's Gospel, Jesus applied the prophesy of Isaiah (Isa 61:1) to himself: "The Spirit of the Lord is upon me, because he has anointed me to preach good news to the poor. He has sent me to proclaim release to the captives and recovering of sight to the blind, to set at liberty those who are oppressed ..." (Lk 4:18). The Catholic Church carries on this mission of Jesus Christ in the world.

Gaudium et Spes firmly rejects the false view of the Christian life as an escape from involvement in this world by focusing solely on life in the world to come. Rather, it is precisely through our involvement in this world (specifically through love of our neighbor, even our enemies) that we attain eternal life in heaven. The Second Vatican Council was direct about this:

> This Council exhorts Christians, as citizens of two cities, to strive to discharge their earthly duties conscientiously and in response to the gospel spirit. They are mistaken who, knowing that we have here no abiding city but

seek one which is to come, think that they may therefore shirk their earthly responsibilities. For they are forgetting that by the faith itself they are more than ever obliged to measure up to those duties, each according to his proper vocation.... The Christian who neglects his temporal duties neglects his duties toward his neighbor and even God, and jeopardizes his eternal salvation....

Christians should rather rejoice that they can follow the example of Christ, who worked as an artisan. In the exercise of all their earthly activities, they can thereby gather their humane, domestic, professional, social and technical enterprises into one vital synthesis with religious values, under whose supreme direction all things are harmonized unto God's glory.[50]

The Catholic Church affirms that all human activities and enterprises are to be carried out for the glory of God.

The principle stated here is clear: Christians, especially the laity, have a responsibility for the life and affairs of the world (see chapter five). The Second Vatican Council acknowledges that in practice there may be legitimate differences of opinion among Christians about specific actions to be taken, or even disagreements in judging what is a truly Christian activity or response. Pope John Paul II and the Second Vatican Council have both taught that the gospel of Jesus Christ cannot be equated with any particular social, political, or economic system. The gospel stands in judgment over all human thought and activity.

The Church's Social Teaching

The pastors of the Catholic Church strive to assist God's people by giving positive guidance and direction to the members of the church about social issues and the concerns of the world.

Since 1891, the popes have issued a series of social encyclicals that have provided authoritative direction to Catholics about the social issues of the day. These encyclicals include *Rerum Novarum* (1891) of Pope Leo XIII, *Quadragesimo Anno* (1931) of Pope Pius XI, *Mater et Magistra* (1961) and *Pacem in Terris* (1963) of Pope John XXIII, *Populorum Progressio* (1967) of Pope Paul VI, and *Laborem Exercens* (1981), *Sollicitudo Rei Socialis* (1987), and

Centesimus Annus (1991) of Pope John Paul II.

The *Catechism* also addresses the issue of social justice. Social justice is attained when society is structured in such a way that every person's dignity and rights are respected, and individuals and groups are able to obtain what is due to them according to their nature and their vocation (see CCC 1928-30). This will be achieved only when members of society act in fraternal charity, "that finds in every man a 'neighbor,' a brother" (CCC 1931). "Everyone should look upon his neighbor (without any exception) as 'another self' above all bearing in mind his life and the means necessary for living it with dignity."[51] "See that none of you repays evil for evil, but always seek to do good to one another and to all" (1 Thess 5:15).

All people have equal dignity and rights, which precludes "discrimination in fundamental personal rights on the grounds of sex, race, color, social conditions, language or religion."[52] However, there are certainly differences among people, "tied to age, physical abilities, intellectual or moral aptitudes, [and] the benefits derived from social commerce and the distribution of wealth."[53]

> These differences belong to God's plan, who wills that each receive what he needs from others, and that those endowed with particular "talents" share the benefits with those who need them. These differences encourage and often oblige persons to practice generosity, kindness, and sharing of goods; they foster the mutual enrichment of cultures. (CCC 1937)

Like the church, society, too, is so ordered that to achieve justice and peace everyone must use the gifts, talents, and social advantages that God has provided for the benefit of others. The *Catechism* speaks of this as "human solidarity," through which people seek the welfare of all and root out sinful inequalities (see CCC 1938-42). As Pope Pius XI stated on June 1, 1941:

> For two thousand years this sentiment has lived and endured in the soul of the Church, impelling souls then and now to the heroic charity of monastic farmers, liberators of slaves, healers of the sick, and messengers of faith, civilization, and science to all generations and all peoples for the sake of creating the social conditions capable of offering to everyone possible a life worthy of man and of a Christian.[54]

Growth in the Church's Teaching and Activity in Social Matters

The Catholic Church, both its pastors and its other members, has failed at times to be faithful to the Spirit of God in carrying out its mission in the world, and seeks "to struggle against [these defects] energetically."[55] *Gaudium et Spes* further states that:

> The Church also realizes that in working out her relationship with the world she always has great need of the ripening which comes from the experience of the centuries.[56]

This statement is important, because it acknowledges that there is an authentic development, or "ripening," that takes place, through the guidance of the Holy Spirit, in the history of the Catholic Church's action in and teaching on the social, economic, political, and cultural life of the world. Essential doctrines of the Catholic faith do not change, but the church's understanding of how it should relate to the world and apply its teaching to the life of human society does deepen and mature through the ongoing guidance of the Holy Spirit.[57]

There are many examples of this growth or deepening of the Catholic Church's teaching regarding issues and affairs of the world. The principles governing issues such as the church's view of political life, culture, socioeconomic activity, and peace in the world are found in the second part of *Gaudium et Spes*. Other issues are addressed in various official church documents, such as the two instructions on liberation theology published by the Sacred Congregation for the Doctrine of the Faith in Rome in 1984 and 1986.[58]

Such instructions are not necessarily the Catholic Church's final word on these matters. Until the Lord comes again, the Catholic Church and individual Catholics are still liable to err in their efforts to live the gospel in the world and to transform it according to God's plan. However, these documents represent the ever-deepening Catholic understanding of the gospel of Christ, as we seek to live and apply the gospel practically in the world through the guidance and empowerment of the Holy Spirit.

Marriage and Family Life

While it is true that there are many areas in which Catholic doctrine has developed over the course of centuries, what is striking about the Catholic Church's teaching on some areas, such as marriage and family life, is its consistency. *Gaudium et Spes* singles out marriage and family life as one area of special concern for the church in the world today. There were few topics that Jesus spoke so clearly and strongly about as the sacredness of marriage:

> But Jesus said to them, "from the beginning of creation, 'God made them male and female.' 'For this reason a man shall leave his father and mother and be joined to his wife, and the two shall become one.' ... What therefore God has joined together, let man not put asunder."
>
> And in the house the disciples asked him again about this matter. And he said to them, "Whoever divorces his wife and marries another, commits adultery against her; and if she divorces her husband and marries another, she commits adultery."
>
> MARK 10:5-12

The most adequate image of the sacredness and indissolubility of the marriage bond is the bond of love between Christ, the bridegroom, and his bride, the church (see Eph 5:21-33).

The bond of marriage must be sacred and indissoluble because it is the basis for the most important and most basic human social group: the family. God wills every person to enter the world and be prepared to participate in society through the family. As the Second Vatican Council put it, "the family is the foundation of society."[59] The *Catechism* teaches, on the dignity and mission of the family:

> The Christian family is a communion of persons, a sign and image of the communion of the Father and the Son in the Holy Spirit. In the procreation and education of children it reflects the Father's work of creation. It is called to partake of the prayer and sacrifice of Christ. Daily prayer and the reading of the Word of God strengthen it in charity. The Christian family has an evangelizing and missionary task. (CCC 2205)

The family is also essential to the life of the church, because from the family new church members are presented for baptism, and within the family people are educated and trained in the knowledge and practice of their faith. *Lumen Gentium* calls the family the "domestic church," because, "In it parents should, by their word and example, be the first preachers of the faith to their children."[60] *Gaudium et Spes* calls the family "a kind of school of deeper humanity," and insists that both the father and the mother are important in raising children in Christ.[61]

> The active presence of the father is highly beneficial to their formation. The children, especially the younger among them, need the care of their mother at home. This domestic role of hers must be safely preserved, though the legitimate social progress of women should not be underrated on that account.[62]

In Western society, it is evident that the traditional structure of the family is being seriously challenged from many quarters. In paragraphs 47-53 of the *Gaudium et Spes* and in Pope John Paul II's apostolic exhortation on the Role of the Christian Family in the Modern World, (*Familiaris Consortio*, Nov. 22, 1981), the Catholic Church presents extended teaching on principles of family life and reaffirms its uncompromising stand against divorce, civil marriage, abortion, sterilization, infanticide, artificial contraception, and "a contraceptive mentality," as well as other threats to family life, such as "a mistaken theoretical and practical concept of the independence of spouses to each other; serious misconceptions regarding the relationship of authority between parents and children; the concrete difficulties that the family experiences in the transmission of values, etc."[63]

Pope John Paul II comments that:

> At the root of these negative phenomena there frequently lies a corruption of the idea and the experience of freedom, conceived not as a capacity for realizing the truth of God's plan for marriage and the family, but as an autonomous power of self-affirmation, often against others, for one's own selfish well-being.[64]

The source of life and success for Christian marriage and the family is Jesus Christ and his example of self-sacrificial love. Marriage and family life only work according to God's plan when all involved are actively seeking to sacrifice and lay down their lives for one another by the grace of God.

> Sacrifice cannot be removed from family life, but must in fact be whole-heartedly accepted if the love between husband and wife is to be deepened and become a source of intimate joy.[65]

Sacrifice is not enough, however. Wisdom, God's wisdom, is necessary for successful married and family life. The biblical teaching on marriage must be reexamined with greater seriousness by Catholics. God has an order and plan for family life. This wisdom from God is to be found in the Scripture and Catholic tradition. Biblical texts concerning the proper order of family life (e.g., Eph 5:21ff; 6:1-4) cannot be lightly dismissed as culturally conditioned or out-moded, as scholarly studies have convincingly demonstrated. Pope John Paul II has reflected on these texts in his apostolic letter "On the Dignity and Vocation of Women" (*Mulieris Dignitatem*) and in other documents.

One of the primary Christian and Catholic values under the most severe attack today is the importance and value of motherhood. While affirming "the equal dignity and responsibility of women with men," Pope John Paul II has taught:

> While it must be recognized that women have the same right as men to per-form various public functions, society must be structured in such a way that wives and mothers are not in practice compelled to work outside the home, and that their families can live and prosper in a dignified way even when they themselves devote their full time to their own family.
>
> Furthermore, the mentality which honors women more for their work outside the home than for their work within the family must be overcome. This requires that men should truly esteem and love women with total respect for their personal dignity, and that society should create and develop conditions favoring work in the home....[66]

Familiaris Consortio adds that the ultimate affront to the dignity of women is anything that would lead to "a renunciation of their femininity or an imita-tion of the male role."[67] In the same documents, Pope John Paul II promotes "the fullness of true feminine humanity," which would include the essential duties of motherhood and family life within the home, as well as valued service and activity outside the family circle. Likewise, men are called to respect and promote the dignity and rights of women, and as fathers and husbands, to reveal the fatherhood of God within the family by "ensuring the harmonious and united development of all the members of the family," and "manifesting towards his wife a charity that is both gentle and strong like that which Christ has for the church."[68]

The Crisis of the Family in Modern Society

The *Catechism* teaches: "The importance of the family for the life and well-being of society (cf. GS 47 § 1) entails a particular responsibility for society to support and strengthen marriage and the family" (CCC 2210).

However, today, living according to biblical and authentic Catholic teaching is not easy for Catholic married couples and families in most places. The genuine values that guide Catholic life are unpopular in many societies, and secular attitudes have heavily infiltrated even the Catholic Church itself.

For example, the family is now viewed by many people primarily as a place for personal fulfillment and as a haven to escape the pressures of the world. The media, especially television, have become, in fact, a primary source of "formation" in the home. How does this measure up to the church's teaching on the family?

> The family is the community in which, from childhood, one can learn moral values, begin to honor God, and make good use of freedom. Family life is an initiation into life in society. The family should live in such a way that its members learn to care and take responsibility for the young, the old, the sick, the handicapped, and the poor.... "Religion that is pure and undefiled before God and the Father is this: to visit orphans and widows in their affliction and to keep oneself unstained from the world" (Jas 1:27) (CCC 2207-8).

Families who desire to live in fidelity to the teaching of Scripture and the Catholic Church and who wish to resist the encroachment of secular values into their homes often find it necessary to seek out support and encouragement from other families with similar values (see CCC 2208). New communities of Christians are forming to provide such support, and Catholic parishes are challenged to provide clear teaching and support for families who wish to stand firm and live according to Catholic values, as a light and witness to the gospel in the midst of an increasingly confused and post-Christian world. With sound Catholic teaching and mutual support, these families can hope to carry out the fourfold mission of the Catholic family expressed by the Synod of Bishops in 1981:

1. forming a community of persons;
2. serving life;
3. participating in the development of society; and
4. sharing in the life and mission of the church.[69]

These aspects of the task of the Catholic family are described in detail in "The Role of the Christian Family in the Modern World" of John Paul II.

The sad reality is that the widespread abandonment of traditional Christian norms of marriage and family life in Western society is resulting in increasingly deeper personal and social problems. Catholics faithful to their tradition and biblical teaching must pray that the Holy Spirit will use this situation to reveal to people the error of infidelity and experimentation, and lead them back to authentic biblical and Catholic values in marriage and family life.

Catholics also should join with other Christians and all people of good will in the battle to preserve or restore the right and freedoms of the family in society. "The family must be helped and defended by appropriate social measures" (CCC 2209). The *Catechism* lists some of the basic rights of the family that must be ensured by the political community:

- the freedom to establish a family, have children, and bring them up in keeping with the family's own moral and religious convictions;
- the protection of the stability of the marriage bond and the institution of the family;
- the freedom to profess one's faith, to hand it on, and to raise one's children in it, with the necessary means and institutions;

- the right to private property, to free enterprise, to obtain work and housing, and the right to emigrate;
- in keeping with the country's institutions, the right to medical care, assistance for the aged, and family benefits;
- the protection of security and health, especially with respect to dangers like drugs, pornography, alcoholism, and the like;
- the freedom to form associations with other families and so to have representation before civil authority.[70]

With God's help, may the family become what it was intended to be in God's marvelous plan, and may all, especially civil authorities, recognize and embrace their "duty to honor the family [and] to assist it" (CCC 2211) in fulfilling its true goals.

CHAPTER 11

Mary

Mary, the all-holy ever-virgin Mother of God, is the masterwork of the mission of the Son and the Spirit in the fullness of time. For the first time in the plan of salvation and because his Spirit had prepared her, the Father found the dwelling place where his Son and his Spirit could dwell among men....

In her, the "wonders of God" that the Spirit was to fulfill in Christ and the Church began to be manifested. (CCC 721)

The "Dogmatic Constitution on the Church" (*Lumen Gentium*) of the Second Vatican Council closes with a chapter on Mary in order to highlight her crucial role in God's plan of salvation.

When Christians understand the unique place of Mary in God's saving plan, she can then assume the role God wants her to play in our lives and we can honor her as God intends. A proper understanding of Mary is also very important for Catholics in discussions and relationships with other Christians, and even with non-Christians. God desires Mary to be a source of Christian unity, not an obstacle to unity.

This chapter will present some of the fundamental Catholic beliefs about Mary, especially drawing upon the *Catechism*. Other sources of Catholic doctrine concerning Mary include the ecumenical councils,[1] papal teachings,[2] teachings of Catholic bishops,[3] and writings on Mary by the great saints and theologians of the Catholic Church.

Mary in the Bible

A basic question to begin with might be: "Why do Catholics honor Mary at all?" The answer is simple. Catholics honor Mary because God has honored her by choosing her to be the mother of God incarnate, Jesus Christ. This role of Mary was prefigured and foretold in the Old Testament, as the Second Vatican Council explains:

> The books of the Old Testament recount the period of salvation history during which the coming of Christ into the world was slowly prepared for. These earliest documents, as they are read in the Church and are understood in the light of a further and full revelation, bring the figure of the woman, Mother of the Redeemer, into a gradually sharper focus.
>
> When looked at in this way, she is already prophetically foreshadowed in that victory over the serpent which was promised to our first parents after their fall into sin (cf. Gen 3:15). Likewise she is the Virgin who is to conceive and bear a son, whose name will be called Emmanuel (cf. Isa 7:14; Mic 5:2-3; Mt 1:22-23). She stands out among the poor and humble of the Lord, who confidently await and receive salvation from Him. With her, the exalted Daughter of Sion, and after a long expectation of the promise, the times were at length fulfilled and the new dispensation established.[4]

In the New Testament, even though Mary is not spoken of at length or in great detail, she is mentioned at many of the central points of the life of Christ and of his church. The infancy narratives, especially in the Gospel of Luke, focus on God's call to Mary to accept her role in his plan (see the Annunciation, Lk 1:26-38), and on the conception and birth of Jesus that resulted from her unqualified "yes" to God: her "fiat" ("let it be done"). "I am the [servant] handmaid of the Lord; let it be [done] to me according to your word" (Lk 1:38, see CCC 494, 2617).

Mary's response to God is seen more fully in her great prayer of praise, the Magnificat (see Lk 1:46-55), in which she acknowledges the honor God had given her—"for ... all generations will call me blessed" (Lk 1:48)—but immediately directs all praise back to God—"for he who is mighty has done great things for me, and holy is his name" (Lk 1:49).

Mary's response to God resulted in hardship and suffering for her. She gave birth to Jesus in a stable, then had to flee to Egypt to escape Herod's wrath (see Mt 2:13-14; Lk 2:6-7). When Mary and Joseph presented Jesus in the temple, Simeon prophesied that her heart would be pierced with a sword (see Lk 2:35).

She witnessed her Son's terrible death. Mary also experienced the normal anxieties of a mother, such as when they mistakenly left behind the twelve-year-old Jesus in Jerusalem (see Lk 2:41-50). Yet the Bible always shows Mary to be a woman of faith in the midst of these trials: "But Mary kept all these things, pondering them in her heart" (Lk 2:19, 51).

In his encyclical letter on Mary, *Redemptoris Mater,* Pope John Paul II accentuates this theme of Mary as a woman of faith. He focuses on Elizabeth's words to Mary at the Visitation: "blessed is she who believed that there would be a fulfillment of what was spoken to her from the Lord" (Lk 1:45).[5]

Mary appears in the New Testament at certain times during Jesus' public ministry. In John's Gospel, Jesus worked his first public miracle, at Cana, at Mary's request (see Jn 2:1-12). Mary followed Jesus during his public ministry, as is indicated when the crowd told Jesus that his mother and brothers were there to see him (see Mt 12:46-50; Mk 3:31-35; Lk 8:19-21). Jesus' response that his mother and brothers were "those who do the will of God" was not a rebuke of Mary, for Mary herself always followed the will of God most perfectly (see Lk 1:38).

Mary followed Jesus right to the foot of the cross, where Jesus gave her to the "beloved disciple," John, to be his mother, and to be the mother of all the "beloved disciples" who came to follow her Son. "At the end of this mission of the Spirit, Mary became the Woman, the new Eve ('mother of the living'), the mother of the 'whole Christ'" (cf. Jn 19:25-27) (CCC 726).

The final glimpse we have of Mary in the New Testament is the scene of her praying with the apostles in the Upper Room, ready to receive with them the outpouring of the Holy Spirit at Pentecost—the birth of the church (see Acts 1:14; 2:1-4): "We see Mary by her prayers imploring the gift of the Spirit, who had already overshadowed her in the Annunciation."[6]

All Christians should thus be able to understand from the sacred Scripture the honor due to Mary. Because of her full response to God and her singularly important role in God's plan, Catholic and Orthodox Christians have a "very special devotion" ("hyperdulia") to Mary. This honor "differs essentially from the adoration ["latria"] which is given to the incarnate Word and equally to the Father and the Holy Spirit, and greatly fosters this adoration."[7] We are led to worship and adore God even more fully when we recognize his mighty works and powerful grace manifested in the humble, faith-filled life of Mary and of all the saints.

The *Catechism* compares Mary to the "burning bush" that Moses saw, for, "filled with the Holy Spirit she makes the Word visible in the humility of his flesh" (CCC 724). She makes Jesus known to the poor and the "poor in Spirit": "shepherds, magi, Simeon and Anna, the bride and groom at Cana, and the first disciples" (CCC 725). May we be numbered among these!

Mary and Christian Tradition

It should not surprise us that the church, as it has reflected more deeply on Mary's role in God's plan, has been led to deeper insight into the truth about her. We even see this process begun in the New Testament, in which the later Gospels, Luke and John, have a fuller treatment of Mary and her importance than the earlier Gospels, Mark and Matthew. Mary is hardly mentioned in Mark, and the infancy narrative of Matthew focuses more on St. Joseph. Luke's Gospel, however, gives us a full account of both the Annunciation and the Visitation, in which Mary is central, and John's Gospel speaks of Mary's role in Jesus' first miracle at Cana, and at the foot of the cross. The Holy Spirit was responsible for this deepening understanding of Mary's role in God's plan of salvation.

Catholics believe that the Holy Spirit continues to unfold and deepen our understanding of the truths of faith found in the Bible. He has done so as Christians have pondered and prayed about these truths over the ages. As a result of this process, the Catholic Church has recognized and defined certain beliefs about Mary that are found implicitly in the Bible (not in their full form), doctrines which the universal church has come to accept and believe with over-whelming consent through the guidance of the Holy Spirit. Here we will examine four of the doctrines about Mary that the Catholic Church teaches as matters of faith.

Mary as Mother of God

All Catholic doctrines concerning Mary are related to and emerge from our understanding of her Son, Jesus Christ (see CCC 964).

In the Gospel of Luke, Elizabeth greets Mary, "at the prompting of the Spirit and even before the birth of her son, as 'the mother of my Lord'" (Lk 1:43; CCC 495). Similarly, the Holy Spirit impelled the early Christians to honor and address Mary as the Mother of God, *theotokos* in Greek (literally "God-bearer"). If Jesus were truly God as well as man, they reasoned, and if Mary were truly his mother, it would be perfectly fitting to speak of Mary as the God-bearer, or Mother of God.

A great disturbance arose in the church of the fifth century A.D. when the bishop of Constantinople, Nestorius, prohibited use of the title *theotokos* for Mary, on the grounds that it implied that Mary gave birth to God—to the divine nature of Jesus. However, soon afterward the Council of Ephesus (A.D. 431) condemned Nestorius' rejection of *theotokos*. This great council of Catholic bishops taught that it is right and good for Christians to address and honor Mary as the Mother of God, understanding this to mean that she gave birth to the one undivided person of Jesus Christ, who is both fully God and fully man.

Jesus possessed his divine nature eternally as God the Son, the Second Person of the blessed Trinity. Jesus' humanity came from the flesh of Mary, when the Holy Spirit "overshadowed" her to conceive Jesus at the Annunciation (Lk 1:35). Since Mary gave birth to the one person of Jesus (as she is the mother of a *person*, not a nature), the Catholic Church has held continually that Mary is rightly honored as the Mother of God.

Mary's Perpetual Virginity

Church leaders of the fourth century and earlier taught that Mary remained a virgin throughout her life. God preserved Mary's virginity even in the conception of Jesus and in the act of giving birth to the Son of God made man (see CCC 499).

Catholics believe that throughout her life, Mary embraced this unique vocation of virgin motherhood to which God first called her through the angel Gabriel. Mary abstained from sexual relations and bore no other children after the birth of Jesus. The biblical data concerning this doctrine is neutral, as even ecumenical studies have concluded.[8]

Matthew 1:25 states that Mary's husband, Joseph, "knew her not until she had borne a son; and he called his name Jesus." Some suggest that this infers that Mary must have had marital relations with Joseph *after* Jesus was born. However, the Greek word translated "before" or "until" (*heōs hou*) refers only to the time prior to Jesus' birth; it does not imply that Mary had sexual relations with Joseph later.[9]

Another objection that is sometimes raised is that the Bible mentions brothers and sisters of Jesus (see Mk 3:31-32; Jn 7:3-10). The church has always understood these passages as not referring to other children of the Virgin Mary. In fact, James and Joseph, "brothers of Jesus," are the sons of another Mary, a disciple of Christ, whom St. Matthew significantly calls "the other Mary" (Mt 28:1). They are close relations of Jesus, according to an Old Testament expression (see CCC 500; Gen 13:8; 14:16; 29:15). Up to the time of the Protestant Reformation, the consensus of the Christian people was that Mary remained a virgin throughout her life.[10] In fact, Christ's birth "did not diminish his mother's virginal integrity but sanctified it."[11] Thus the "liturgy of the Church celebrates Mary as *Aeiparthenos,* the 'Ever-virgin'"(cf. LG 52) (CCC 499).

There is good reason for belief in Mary's perpetual virginity, besides the testimony of Christian tradition. It is a full response to God's unique call to Mary. It is a sign of her total consecration to God and of respect for the fact that God himself had dwelt and grown within her womb. What other human child would be worthy of sharing that dignity? Mary's perpetual virginity also helps us to realize that through her call to be the Mother of Jesus, Mary was also being called by God to be the mother of all Christians, who have been made Christ's body through baptism:

> The Son whom she brought forth is he whom God placed as the first-born among many brethren, that is, the faithful in whose generation and formulation she cooperates with a mother's love.[12]

Mary's Immaculate Conception

If a great dignitary, like a president or the pope, were to come to live in your home for a time, how carefully would you clean and prepare for that guest? If God planned to live for a time as a human being within the womb of a woman and then be taught and formed by this woman after his birth, how carefully would God prepare that woman for this awesome responsibility and privilege?

The Catholic doctrine of the Immaculate Conception states that God prepared Mary for her role of bearing and raising the Son of God by freeing her from original sin from the moment of her conception in the womb of her mother, Anne. God prepared Mary to be a vessel without a trace of sin, not because of her own virtue or merit, but because of her unique role in his plan of salvation. The biblical support for this doctrine is found in the angel Gabriel's greeting to Mary, "Hail, full of grace" (Lk 1:28).

There are some common questions that this teaching raises. First, if Mary was conceived without sin, did she really need a Savior? Put simply, was Mary saved? The Catholic Church teaches that Mary actually was the first to be saved by the grace of her Son, Jesus.

"Through the centuries the Church has become ever more aware that Mary, 'full of grace' through God (Lk 1:28), was redeemed from the moment of her conception" (CCC 491). God first applied to Mary the grace that he knew and foresaw that Jesus would gain by his life and death on the cross. The official definition of Mary's Immaculate Conception, promulgated by Pope Pius IX in 1845, states:

> The Blessed Virgin Mary, in the first instant of her conception, by a singular grace and privilege of almighty God, and in view of the foreseen merits of Jesus, the Savior of the human race, was preserved free from all stain of original sin (cf. CCC 491).[13]

Does this doctrine teach that Mary never sinned? Although Mary was freed from original sin at the moment of her conception, it is conceivable in theory that Mary could have sinned during her life. She had free will and was tempted as we all are. However, Catholic tradition overwhelmingly affirms that in reality Mary always responded to the grace of God to resist sin and thus remained without sin throughout her life.

Mary's freedom from original sin certainly aided her in avoiding sin throughout her life, but it did not guarantee it. Even Eve, who was born without sin, succumbed to the temptation of Satan. Thus, Mary is the New Eve, who reversed the effects of the disobedience of the first Eve and her unbelief and rebellion. Salvation entered the world through Mary, by her faith and perfect obedience to God and his will, as St. Irenaeus first observed in the second century (see CCC 494).[14] "Comparing her with Eve, they [the early fathers of the church] call Mary 'the Mother of the living' and frequently claim: 'Death through Eve, life through Mary.'"[15]

A striking confirmation of the truth of the Immaculate Conception of Mary occurred just four years after its definition as a Catholic dogma of faith by Pope Pius IX in 1854. On the Feast of the Annunciation in 1858, a beautiful lady appeared to a simple peasant girl, Bernadette Soubirous, at Lourdes, France. The lady told her, "I am the Immaculate Conception." At the time, Bernadette did not even know what "Immaculate Conception" meant, but repeated these words to a trusted friend.[16]

Today many Catholics, including the recent popes, believe that Bernadette had an authentic experience of Mary at Lourdes. The hundreds of medically verified healings and other miracles that have occurred at Lourdes since 1858, through Mary's intercession, point to the reality of Mary as the Immaculate Conception.

The Assumption of Mary Into Heaven

This doctrine was formally defined by Pope Pius XII in 1950 after millions of petitions for its definition had been received by the Vatican. Pope Pius XII declared that Mary, "having completed the course of her earthly life, was assumed body and soul to heavenly glory and exalted by the Lord as Queen over all things, so that she might be the more fully conformed to her Son, the Lord of lords and conqueror of sin and death."[17] This definition affirms that at the end of her time on earth, Mary experienced immediately the resurrection of the body that is promised to all faithful followers of Jesus.

The doctrine of the Assumption of Mary into heaven flows from and completes the concept of her Immaculate Conception. Since Mary was preserved from sin by a unique gift and grace of Christ, she was able to experience the immediate union of her whole being with God at the end of her life. Sin did not in any way obstruct her full and immediate union with the Lord in heaven.

The Assumption of Mary is a source of hope for us because it foreshadows what will one day happen to each faithful Christian (see CCC 966). The raising of Mary, body and soul, into heaven anticipates what will happen at the final judgment to all who are to be saved. All who are saved by the grace of Christ will one day live in perfect joy with the Lord with transformed, glorified bodies. Reflecting on Mary's Assumption helps us to turn our thoughts toward our ultimate goal and to pray that we, too, will one day experience the resurrection of the body and the life of eternal glory that Mary has already entered into fully through the grace of her Son, Jesus Christ.

... the Mother of Jesus, in the glory which she possesses in body and soul in heaven, is the image and beginning of the Church as it is to be perfected in the world to come. Likewise she shines forth on earth, until the day of the Lord shall come, a sign of certain hope and comfort to the pilgrim People of God.[18]

Mary and the Church

In addition to these four official teachings about Mary's personal attributes that all Catholics are bound to believe as articles of faith, there are other aspects of Catholic belief about Mary that are helpful in understanding her role in God's plan and her relationship to the church. One way of remembering these truths about Mary and the church is to think of five of her attributes that begin with the letter "M": member, model, mother, mediatrix, and messenger.

The first three of these "M's" are mentioned in one paragraph of the chapter on Mary in the "Dogmatic Constitution on the Church" of the Second Vatican Council:

Therefore, she is also hailed as a pre-eminent and altogether singular *member* of the Church, and as the Church's *model* and excellent exemplar in faith and charity. Taught by the Holy Spirit, the Catholic Church honors her with filial affection and piety as the most beloved *mother....*[19]

Mary as a Member of the Church

The Second Vatican Council included its discussion of Mary in the last chapter of *Lumen Gentium* in order to emphasize that Mary is a member, albeit "a preeminent and ... wholly unique member," of the church (see CCC 967).

This attribute of Mary is a reminder that however much we might rightfully honor and exalt Mary for her response to God and for her role in God's saving plan, she remains fully human. She is not to be adored by Christians as a goddess; she is a fully human servant of God whom he has highly favored through his mercy and grace. This fact can enable Catholics to identify more fully with Mary and to realize that the holiness and full consecration to God that she exhibited is something which is possible for every Christian. It is, in fact, the goal of the Christian life.

Mary as Model

Mary provides an ideal model for each individual Christian of a life of discipleship, consecration, and holiness. God calls each person to make the unconditional "yes" to him and to his will that Mary expressed at the Annunciation and proceeded to live out until the end of her life. Catholics honor Mary because she is the model disciple, the perfect, most faithful follower of her Son, Jesus Christ. Thus, she is a model of true discipleship for each Christian.

Mary is not only a model for individual Christians, but also a model of the church as a whole. For example, the church, like Mary, is both virgin and mother.

> The Church indeed ... by receiving the word of God in faith becomes herself a mother. By preaching and baptism she brings forth sons, who are conceived by the Holy Spirit and born of God, to a new and immortal life. She herself is a virgin, who keeps in its entirety and purity the faith she pledged to her spouse.[20]

The church is called to be God's presence in the world through its faithfulness to the gospel and to following Jesus as he guides the church through the Holy Spirit. Mary manifested God's presence most perfectly by pondering the events and words that constituted her call, and by carrying out faithfully everything God asked of her. Because the church has not attained the perfection of discipleship that Mary attained, we continue to look to her as the best example of what we, as the church, are called by God to be and to do. *Lumen Gentium* states:

> As St. Ambrose taught, the Mother of God is a model of the Church in the matter of faith, charity, and perfect union with Christ ... the followers of Christ still strive to increase in holiness by conquering sin. And so they raise their eyes to Mary who shines forth to the whole community of the elect as a model of the virtues....[21]

This also serves as a key to understanding proper Christian devotion to Mary. As *Lumen Gentium* continues:

> True devotion [to Mary] consists neither in sterile or transitory affection [i.e., warm or sentimental feelings about Mary], nor in a certain vain credulity [i.e., believing every pious statement or claim about her], but proceeds from true faith, by which we are led to recognize the excellence of the Mother of God, and we are moved to a filial love towards our mother and to the imitation of her virtues.[22]

Mary as Mother

Mary is not only a model, she is much more—she is our mother. Mary is the Mother of God, but also by God's grace and call she is the spiritual mother of the church and of each Christian.

> In a wholly singular way she cooperated by her obedience, faith, hope and burning charity in the Savior's work of restoring supernatural life to souls. For this reason she is a mother to us in the order of grace.[23]

The basis of this is found in the Gospel of John, chapter nineteen. As his last act before his death, Jesus told the beloved disciple, who represents all of Jesus' disciples, "Behold, your mother" (Jn 19:27). Christian tradition from the earliest times confirms that Mary is, indeed, the mother in the order of grace of the church and of each Christian. Pope Paul VI confirmed this when, in 1969, he conferred upon Mary the title "Mother of the Church" (see CCC 963).

Mary as Mediatrix

Because Mary is our mother, she is committed to pray and intercede for each of her children and for the church. Catholic tradition has ascribed a number of different titles to Mary to describe her role of intercession. As the Second Vatican Council explains:

> By her maternal charity, Mary cares for the brethren of her Son who still journey on earth surrounded by dangers and difficulties, until they are led to their happy fatherland. Therefore the Blessed Virgin is involved by the Church under the titles of Advocate, Helper, Benefactress, and Mediatrix. These, however, are to be so understood that they neither take away from or add anything to the dignity and efficacy of Christ the one Mediator. For no creature could ever be classed with the Incarnate Word and Redeemer....[24]

Lumen Gentium goes on to explain that just as Jesus' priesthood is shared in various ways by members of the church, he also gives us a share in his unique role as mediator (see 1 Tim 2:5-6)—one who prays or intercedes on behalf of others before the Father. The Catholic Church has long held that because of her sinlessness and close union with her Son, Mary has been given a role of mediation or intercession before God above any other human being. In that role, Catholics speak of Mary as Mediatrix.[25]

Is it not appropriate that God should have given a special role of mediation or intercession to the mother of the church? Who on earth pleads for a person as effectively and fervently as that person's mother? The church, as God's family, has been blessed by God with Mary as a mother to mediate and intercede for all Christians in order to lead them to her divine Son, Jesus Christ, and to receive all the graces He has won for them by his life, death, and resurrection. The Second Vatican Council's concluding statement on Mary as Mediatrix affirms:

The Church does not hesitate to profess this subordinate role of Mary. She experiences it continuously and commends it to the hearts of the faithful, so that encouraged by this maternal help they may more closely adhere to the Mediator and Redeemer [Jesus Christ].[26]

Catholics must always remember that Mary's sole task is to lead people to Jesus, her Son, and that "Mary's role in the Church is inseparable from her union with Christ and flows directly from it" (CCC 964).

Mary as Messenger

Mary's role as messenger has become more prominent in recent times. This refers to the appearances, or apparitions, of Mary that have been reported by Catholics at various times throughout the church's history, and notably more often in the past 150 years.

In these appearances, Mary usually presents a prophetic message. The message is sometimes directed toward an individual or local church, but sometimes Mary's words are intended for the whole church or for a large segment of the church.

How does the Catholic Church view these apparitions of Mary and their accompanying messages? The church does not require its members to believe in the authenticity of any apparitions or particular messages, since these are private revelations. As Pope John Paul II explained in an address at Fatima, on May 13, 1982:

The Church has always taught and continues to proclaim that God's revelation was brought to completion in Jesus Christ, who is the fullness of that revelation, and that "no new public revelation is to be expected before the glorious manifestation of the Lord" *(Lumen Gentium,* no. 4). The Church evaluates and judges private revelations by the criterion of conformity with that single public revelation.[27]

Therefore, private revelations, such as appearances of Mary, must conform fully to the standard of public revelation that comes from Jesus Christ if they are to be accepted and heeded.

It is noteworthy that recent popes have visited and preached at sites of Mary's reported appearances, including Lourdes, France, and Fatima, Portugal, and that the messages of Mary presented at these and other sites have been judged by the Catholic Church to be in full conformity with biblical teaching and authentic Catholic tradition. Numerous miracles have also been confirmed at some of these sites, such as a multitude of medically verified physical healings at Lourdes and elsewhere. Just as God sent angels as messengers of his Word in the Old Testament, it appears that he has chosen in this age to speak particular words of encouragement, instruction, and warning through Mary.

Most of the reported appearances of Mary in recent times have followed the same, biblically based pattern. Mary appears to simple, humble, and usually poor people. The appearances are accompanied by an outpouring of the Holy Spirit, manifesting itself by the good fruit of joy, thanksgiving, worship, and praise of God, and deepened trust in the Lord even in the midst of persecution or oppression. Often healings and other miracles accompany such apparitions.

The effects of such apparitions of Mary and her messages have been profound. Mary's appearance to a poor Mexican peasant, Juan Diego, in 1531, as Our Lady of Guadalupe, led to the conversion to Christianity of an estimated eight million native people within seven years. Thousands of people who have visited Lourdes since her appearances there in 1858 to Bernadette Soubirous have been healed and turned to Jesus Christ.

In 1917, Mary appeared to three children (ages seven to ten) at Fatima, Portugal, and called for prayer, especially the rosary, and for consecration of Russia to her immaculate heart. She warned, "If my requests are heard, Russia will be converted and there will be peace. If not, she will spread her errors throughout the entire world, provoking wars and persecution of the Church...."[28] At that time, Russia was a poor country torn by civil war, and this prediction seemed almost laughable. Yet history has proven it true. Mary's appearance at Fatima reminds Christians that the things we do now, and our prayers and faith, have consequences for our own salvation and for that of the world. As Pope John Paul II stated in his homily at Fatima on May 13, 1982:

If the church has accepted the message of Fatima, it is above all because that message contains a truth and a call whose basic content is the truth and call of the gospel itself.

"Repent, and believe in the Gospel!" (Mk 1:15): these are the first words that the Messiah addressed to humanity. The message of Fatima is, in its basic nucleus, a call to conversion and repentance, as in the Gospel....

At Fatima, Mary promised a sign of the validity and truth of her appearances there. It is estimated that about one hundred thousand people witnessed this sign—the sun dancing in the sky at midday. Many secular observers witnessed this sign, and no one has been able to explain it. It has often been ignored, but never effectively denied.[29]

There are many more reported appearances of Mary. The Catholic Church has always been wary about placing undue emphasis on these private revelations, but many of them have been accepted as legitimate by the local bishops, whose role it is to discern their validity. In the most widely accepted apparitions, Mary has consistently called Christians to prayer, repentance, and conversion to God. Sometimes she has warned of serious consequences for the world if this message remains unheeded. Mary always has presented herself in authentic apparitions as a messenger or servant of God. Although she has affirmed traditional Catholic titles for herself and encouraged the use of Marian prayers, such as the rosary, her focus is always unmistakably centered on Jesus Christ.

Marian Prayers

As God's family, the church, we pray in union with Mary, the Mother of God and our mother, and believe in the power of her intercession. We can find examples of her intercession at Cana and before the day of Pentecost. Mary's prayer, such as in her "Fiat" and Magnificat, are models of trust, thanksgiving, praise, and "the generous offering of her whole being in faith" (CCC 2622).

The Holy Spirit unites us in prayer to Jesus and the Father, and also unites us in a special way in the church with Mary, the mother of Jesus and "spouse of the Holy Spirit." A wealth of prayers and hymns to Our Lady has blossomed in the Christian tradition, honoring her as our mother and mediatrix. The prayer said most frequently by Catholics, of course, is the "Hail Mary" (*Ave Maria*). This biblical prayer beautifully expresses this twofold movement of Marian prayer:

The first "magnifies" the Lord for the "great things" he did for his lowly servant and through her for all human beings (cf. Lk 1:46-55); the second entrusts the supplications and praises of the children of God to the Mother of Jesus.... (CCC 2675; see also CCC 2676-78)

Probably the most widespread and popular Catholic devotion is recitation of the rosary. Though not absolutely essential to a Catholic's spiritual life and growth, millions of Catholics have benefited through the ages by prayerful reflection on the fifteen mysteries of the life of Christ and his mother commemorated in the rosary. For many, the rhythmic recitation of the prayers of the rosary (the Apostles' Creed, the Lord's Prayer, the Hail Mary, and the Glory Be) quiets their spirits and lifts their hearts to God.

Pope Paul VI, in his apostolic letter on devotion to the Blessed Virgin Mary, highly recommended the rosary, comparing it with the liturgy: "like the liturgy, it is of a community nature, draws its inspiration from Sacred Scripture, and is oriented toward the mystery of Christ...."[30]

Another reason that the rosary has gained special prominence among Catholic devotions is because in one of the most widely accepted apparitions of Mary, at Fatima, Portugal, in 1917, Mary told the children that she was the "Lady of the Rosary," and asked them to pray the rosary daily. Since that time, praying the rosary either as individuals or in families or groups has become a characteristic of the prayer life of many Catholics.

There are many other prayers, devotions, and hymns to Mary that pervade and enrich the fabric of Catholic life and prayer. In response to the requests of Mary at Fatima, John Paul II consecrated Russia to her Immaculate Heart, a solemn prayer for the full conversion of that vast and powerful territory. Recent popes also have encouraged Catholics to consecrate themselves and their families to Mary, who is the spiritual Mother of all Christians. The "Angelus" (the angel Gabriel's message to Mary and her response) is prayed daily at noon in many Catholic communities, or the "Regina Caeli" (*Queen of Heaven*) during the Easter season. Another favorite Marian prayer of petition is the "Memorare" ("Remember, O Most gracious Virgin Mary...").

Perhaps the greatest biblical "Marian prayer," though, is the prayer of Mary herself, the "Magnificat," which is prayed throughout the world every day in the Church's official Evening Prayer (Vespers):

My soul proclaims the greatness of the Lord,
my spirit rejoices in God my Savior
for he has looked with favor on his lowly servant.
From this day all generations will call me blessed:
the Almighty has done great things for me,
and holy is his Name.
He has mercy on those who fear him
in every generation.
He has shown the strength of his arm,
he has scattered the proud in their conceit.
He has cast down the mighty from their thrones,
and has lifted up the lowly.
He has filled the hungry with good things,
and the rich he has sent away empty.

He has come to the help of his servant Israel
for he has remembered his promise of mercy,
the promise he made to our fathers,
to Abraham and his children for ever.

LUKE 1:46-55

Conclusion

Catholics are encouraged to foster a proper devotion to Mary, the Mother of God. We honor her, as God honors her, for her special role in his plan of salvation. We imitate her faithfulness as the model disciple of Jesus Christ. We approach her as the spiritual mother that Jesus has given to each Christian and to his church, and we continually ask her, as our mother, to pray and intercede for us before the throne of God. Mary's role in God's plan may be best summed up in the phrase: "To Jesus through Mary." She can never be separated from her Son, as she lives by faith in Him and is now united to Him forever in the glory of heaven. As the *Catechism* summarizes our faith:

What the Catholic faith believes about Mary is based on what it believes about Christ, and what it teaches about Mary illumines in turn its faith in Christ. (CCC 487)

Mary should have a special place in the life of each Christian. As Pope Paul VI taught, "The Church's devotion to the Blessed Virgin is intrinsic to Christian worship."[31] Although the form of our relationship with Mary may differ somewhat from person to person, the Catholic Church recommends certain forms of honor and devotion, especially the rosary, an "epitome of the whole Gospel" (see CCC 971), prayed either individually or in families and groups. The Catholic Church also calls for the observance of the feasts of Mary that occur throughout the church year, such as the feasts of the Annunciation (March 25), the Assumption (August 15), the Immaculate Conception (December 8), and the Mother of God (January 1). Through a proper relationship and devotion to Mary, Catholics (and all Christians) will grow ever deeper in love of God and their following of her Son, Jesus Christ.

CHAPTER 12

The Life of the Age to Come

Christians believe that the brief span of our lives on earth is a prelude and a preparation for life after death, everlasting life in the age to come. As persons created in God's image, we are spiritual beings as well as physical ones. This means that we are all destined to live forever, like God.

For Christians, the real question is not *whether* we will live forever, but *how*. No one would look forward to an eternity of suffering or boredom. Christianity is truly Good News, because it proclaims that God offers to all people a life of unsurpassable joy and peace that will last forever. Christians claim that the truth of this message is confirmed because one man underwent death, a terrible death, but was raised from the dead and returned to announce the reality of eternal life with God. The resurrection of Jesus Christ remains the ultimate reason for our Christian belief in eternal life. As St. Peter exclaimed in the opening of his first letter:

> Blessed be the God and Father of our Lord Jesus Christ! By his great mercy we have been born anew to a living hope through the resurrection of Jesus Christ from the dead, and to an inheritance which is imperishable, undefiled, and unfading, kept in heaven for you, who by God's power are guarded through faith for a salvation ready to be revealed in the last time.
>
> 1 PETER 1:3-5

Accepting God's Offer of Eternal Life

Eternal life with God is an absolutely free gift. There is nothing that any person could do to merit, earn, or deserve an eternity of happiness with God. Catholic theology teaches that without the gift of God that Scripture calls grace, human beings remain in the bondage of original sin and fall into ever deeper rebellion against God and his plan. The result of this sin is death—eternal separation from God. As St. Paul wrote, "the wages of sin is death, but the free gift of God is eternal life in Christ Jesus our Lord" (Rom 6:23; see CCC 1006, 1008).

Eternal life is also a gift that must be accepted through our cooperation with God's grace and our freely-given response to the work of the Holy Spirit in our lives. From this perspective, eternal life is not simply a gift that we receive at the end of our lives when we die. Eternal life begins now, as we choose to accept God's grace and his gift of the Holy Spirit. After all, eternal life actually is a way of talking about sharing in or possessing the life of God himself. Catholics understand that although God's life in us will reach its completion or fullness only when we are totally united with the Lord after death, it begins for us in this life with faith in God (see Jn 17:3) and baptism (see Rom 6:3-4).

The sacrament of baptism inaugurates that work of God in us by which the Father delivers us from the dominion of darkness (Satan's kingdom, into which each person is born because of original sin), and into the kingdom of light, the kingdom of his beloved Son, Jesus Christ (see Col 1:13). "United with Christ by Baptism, believers already truly participate in the heavenly life of the risen Christ, but this life remains 'hidden with Christ in God'" (Col 3:3; cf. Phil 3:20) (CCC 1003).

Thus, baptism is only the beginning of the Christian's road to eternal life. The Gospel of John also stresses the necessity of believing in Jesus (see Jn 3:16) and the Father (see Jn 5:24); of eating Jesus' flesh and blood in the Eucharist (see Jn 6:54; CCC 1003); and of following Jesus, the Good Shepherd (see Jn 10:27-28), throughout our lives. The result of responding to God's call in this way is that the Christian progressively becomes an entirely new creation (see 2 Cor 5:17), freed from the bondage of Satan and sin. Catholics call this process of freedom from sin and growth in Christ "sanctification."

St. Paul taught that even here on earth the faithful follower of Christ experiences a foretaste of the glory of reigning in the heavens with Jesus Christ: "But God, who is rich in mercy, out of the great love with which he loved us, even when we were dead through our trespasses, made us alive together with Christ ... and raised us up with him, and made us sit with him in the heavenly places in Christ Jesus...." (Eph 2:4-6; see CCC 1003).

On the other hand, those who reject God's offer and continue to live in sin experience even here on earth a foretaste of the pain of eternal separation from God. It is unfortunately true that while the road to heaven is like heaven itself, the road to hell resembles hell. We see many people entrapped by the lies of Satan, seeking self-fulfillment, happiness, and pleasure apart from God and his laws. Instead of finding the happiness they seek apart from God, they become locked into deeper disappointment, isolation, and hopelessness. The writings of many modern atheist existentialists, such as Camus and Sartre, reflect the sadness and "quiet desperation" of those who attempt to live without God, struggling to accept the meaninglessness and absurdity of their lives with some semblance of dignity.

Christian Hope and Eternal Life

While life apart from God leads to despair, Christianity proclaims a message of hope. Christian hope is a fundamental virtue that enables us to look forward confidently to receiving the fullness of God's gift of eternal life and happiness. "Hope is the confident expectation of divine blessing and the beatific vision of God" (CCC 2090). Christians experience the same trials and struggles in this world as anyone else, but their hope in God and his salvation transforms their attitude toward life. St. Paul wrote:

> For this slight momentary affliction is preparing for us an eternal weight of glory beyond all comparison.... For we know that if the earthly tent we live in is destroyed, we have a building from God, a house not made with hands, eternal in the heavens.... He who has prepared us for this very thing is God, who has given us the Spirit as a guarantee.
>
> 2 CORINTHIANS 4:17; 5:1, 5

As the Letter of James says so succinctly: "Blessed is the man who endures trial, for when he has stood the test he will receive the crown of life which God has promised to those who love him" (Jas 1:12).

Death

As these passages indicate, the Holy Spirit enables Christians to view and approach death in a way totally different than that of those without the knowledge of God. As St. Paul wrote to the Thessalonians:

> But we would not have you ignorant, brethren, concerning those who are asleep, that you may not grieve as others do who have no hope. For since we believe that Jesus died and rose again, even so, through Jesus, God will bring with him those who have fallen asleep.
>
> 1 THESSALONIANS 4:13-14

There is a finality about death, even for the Christian. It marks the end of our earthly pilgrimage, the one life each person is given to respond to God's grace and plan and to decide his ultimate destiny. "It is appointed for men to die once, and after that comes judgment" (Heb 9:27). "There is no 'reincarnation' after death" (CCC 1013).

Death, for most, is a fearful experience. However, for those perfected in faith, hope, and love, death holds no fear. St. Paul speaks of his own death in a matter-of-fact way: "For to me to live is Christ, and to die is gain" (Phil 1:21). "The saying is sure: If we have died with him, we shall also live with him" (2 Tim 2:11). He even expresses his preference to die so that he can be fully united with the Lord: "My desire is to depart and be with Christ, for that is far better. But to remain in the flesh is more necessary on your account" (Phil 1:23-24). Paul also writes:

> So we are always of good courage; we know that while we are at home in the body we are away from the Lord, for we walk by faith, not by sight. We are of good courage, and we would rather be away from the body and at home with the Lord. So whether we are at home or away, we make it our aim to please him.
>
> 2 CORINTHIANS 5:6-9

While St. Paul speaks of the Christian's approach to death in terms of faith and hope, St. John says that death holds no fear for Christians because we know the love of God:

So we know and believe the love God has for us. God is love, and he who abides in love abides in God, and God abides in him. In this is love perfected with us, that we may have confidence for the day of judgment.... There is no fear in love, but perfect love casts out fear.

1 JOHN 4:16-18

The *Catechism* summarizes:

The Church encourages us to prepare ourselves for the hour of our death. In the ancient litany of the saints, for instance, she has us pray: "From a sudden and unforeseen death, deliver us, O Lord";[1] to ask the Mother of God to intercede for us, "at the hour of our death," in the *Hail Mary;* and to entrust ourselves to St. Joseph, the patron of a happy death. (CCC 1014).

Without this real preparation for death based on faith, people often are given hollow and empty words of encouragement or hope: "Hang in there, Joe, you've pulled through in the past, you'll pull through this one, too!" It seems a law of human behavior that when we don't have a solution to a problem, we deny or attempt to deny its reality. Western society increasingly attempts to hide or deny the reality of death, because it has forgotten that there is a solution, and only one solution to it—the resurrection of Jesus Christ.

The Reality of the Resurrection

Why does faith in the resurrection of Jesus provide Christians with such unshakable hope? "Faith in the resurrection rests on faith in God who 'is not God of the dead, but of the living'" (Mk 12:27) (CCC 993). "But there is more. Jesus links faith in the resurrection to his own person. 'I am the Resurrection and the life' (Jn 11:25). It is Jesus himself who on the last day will raise up those who have believed in him, who have eaten his body and drunk his blood" (CCC 994; see also Jn 5:24-25; 6:40, 54). Christ has been raised, and Christians believe that they, too, will share in his resurrection and eternal life. As St. Paul wrote, answering the skeptics of his age (and ours) who deny the reality of the resurrection:

> But in fact Christ has been raised from the dead, the first fruits of those who have fallen asleep. For as by a man came death, by a man has come also the resurrection of the dead. For as in Adam all die, so also in Christ shall all be made alive.
>
> 1 CORINTHIANS 15:20-22

During his life on earth, Jesus not only foretold his own bodily resurrection (see Mt 12:39; Mk 10:34; Jn 2:19-22), but he even raised the dead—Jairus' daughter (see Mk 5:21-24; 35-43), the son of the widow of Nain (see Lk 7:11-17), Lazarus (see Jn 11:1-45)—to show that he had power over death (see Mk 5:21-42; Lk 7:11-17; Jn 11; CCC 994).

The resurrection of the dead is not a symbol or a myth. The resurrection is a reality that all will experience. The great Christian martyrs and saints could approach death with courage, even joy, because of their faith in the resurrection. During their lives on earth they knew the goodness and mercy of the Lord and so came to believe that the same merciful, loving God would not abandon them to eternal death but would raise them up to eternal life, as he first raised Jesus, the beloved divine Son of God.

Therefore, Christians believe that death is not a final end of life, but a completion of the mission of life on earth. The goal of this life is to come to know God through faith, hope, and love, so that one may see him face to face after death (see 1 Cor 13:12-13). Traditional Catholic theology calls this the beatific vision—the direct vision of God that brings perfect and ultimate happiness (see CCC 1023, 1028). Until Christ comes again, human beings can attain this goal only by passing through the veil of death. Through our faith, we are able to exclaim with St. Paul:

> "Death is swallowed up in victory. O death, where is your victory? O death, where is your sting?" The sting of death is sin, and the power of sin is the law. But thanks be to God, who gives us the victory through our Lord Jesus Christ.
>
> 1 CORINTHIANS 15:54-57

The Bible consistently teaches that what people should fear is not death, but sin. Serious sin brings with it the consequences of eternal punishment—as St.

Paul says, the "sting of death is sin." In Matthew's Gospel Jesus warns, "do not fear those who kill the body but cannot kill the soul; rather fear him who can destroy both soul and body in hell" (Mt 10:28). The result of sin is not merely physical death but the ultimate death of eternal separation from God and the pains of hell.

The warnings of the Bible about the consequences of sin are urgent and must not be overlooked or minimized. However, at the heart of the gospel is the proclamation that sin no longer has power over those who know and follow Jesus Christ. The Good News is that Jesus has conquered sin, and along with it the power of death:

> But if we have died with Christ, we believe that we shall also live with him. For we know that Christ being raised from the dead will never die again; death no longer has dominion over him. The death he died he died to sin, once for all, but the life he lives he lives to God. So you also must consider yourselves dead to sin and alive to God in Christ Jesus.
>
> ROMANS 6:8-11

> There is therefore now no condemnation for those who are in Christ Jesus. For the law of the Spirit of life in Christ Jesus has set me free from the law of sin and death.
>
> ROMANS 8:1-2

What Happens at Death?

> In death, the separation of the soul from the body, the human body decays and the soul goes to meet God, while awaiting its reunion with its glorified body.... (CCC 997)

The Catholic Church teaches that at the moment of death, each person will "appear before the judgment seat of Christ, so that each one may receive good or evil, according to what he has done in the body" (2 Cor 5:10; see also Rom 2:6). This is known, in Catholic theology, as the "particular judgment," to distinguish it from the "general judgment," or "last judgment," when Christ will "come again in glory to judge the living and the dead" (Nicene Creed).

The New Testament teaches consistently that each person will be rewarded immediately after death in accordance with his works and faith. The parable of the poor man Lazarus and the words of Christ on the cross to the good thief attest to this (see CCC 1021).

As Romans 8:1-2 indicates, at the particular judgment there is "no condemnation for those who are in Christ Jesus." For those whose lives have been fully in union with the Lord on earth, unstained by unrepented sin and sin's effects, the moment of death will be a moment of glorious reunion with the Lord and the beginning of a life of unspeakable joy that will last forever. "No eye has seen, nor ear heard, nor the heart of man conceived, what God has prepared for those who love him..." (1 Cor 2:9).

For those who die in the grace of Christ Jesus but with some remaining unrepented sin or the effects of sin in their lives, the Catholic Church teaches that God, in his mercy, purifies the person of these sins so that they, too, may enter into the joy of heaven. This purification or purgation, known as "purgatory," will be discussed more fully later in this chapter.

Those who have rejected God and the grace of Christ receive the consequences of this choice beginning even at the moment of death: eternal separation from God, which Jesus often called "hell" (see Mt 18:7-9; Mk 9:47; Lk 16:19-31; CCC 1022). "At the evening of life, we shall be judged on our love."[2]

At death, the soul is separated from the body, and the human person is judged and continues to exist, even though the person's body has ceased to function. This situation cannot continue forever, though, because God has created human beings as "embodied spirits," creatures who by nature exist and relate by means of bodies. Jesus' resurrection testifies that God's plan includes resurrection and transformation of the body, which occurs for us at the Lord's second coming and final judgment.

Who will rise from the dead? "All the dead will rise, 'those who have done good, to the resurrection of life, and those who have done evil, to the resurrection of judgment'" (Jn 5:29, see CCC 998).

What will the risen body be like? The model is Jesus himself, who is the "first fruits" of the resurrection. Jesus was raised with his own body ("See my hands and my feet that it is I myself" Lk 24:39; CCC 999). And yet, it was a *glorified* body that could go through closed doors (see Jn 20:19 ff) or appear "out of nowhere," as on the road to Emmaus (Lk 24:13 ff). St. Paul explains that Christ, "will change our lowly body to be like his glorious body" (Phil 3:21), which is "a spiritual body" (1 Cor 15:44; see CCC 999).

How does this happen? "This 'how' exceeds our imagination and understanding; it is accessible only to faith" (CCC 1000).

The Sacred Congregation for the Doctrine of the Faith has stated,

Neither Scripture nor theology provides sufficient light for a proper picture of life after death. Christians must firmly hold the two following essential points: on the one hand they must believe in the fundamental continuity, thanks to the power of the Holy Spirit, between our present life in Christ and the future life (charity is the law of the Kingdom of God and our charity on earth will be the measure of our sharing God's glory in heaven); on the other hand they must be clearly aware of the radical break between the present life and the future one, due to the fact that the economy of faith will be replaced by the economy of fullness of life: we shall be with Christ and 'we shall see God' (cf. 1 John 3:2), and it is in these promises and marvelous mysteries that our hope essentially consists. Our imagination may be incapable of reaching these heights, but our heart does so instinctively and completely.[3]

Let us continue to explore the possible destinies for human life after the particular judgment: hell, purgatory, and heaven.

Hell

Many Catholics today have tremendous difficulty understanding or believing the Christian doctrine of hell. If God is the God of infinite love, mercy, goodness, and compassion, how could he create or permit to exist a place or condition of endless torment and unhappiness? Some theologians today admit the possibility of hell's existence but claim that few people, if any, are there. Both reason and Christian revelation prevent us from dismissing the reality of hell. Jesus could not have been more clear about the matter. He told parables about eternal punishment, such as the rich man and Lazarus (see Lk 16:19-31), the marriage feast (see Mt 22:1-14), the wicked servant (see Mt 24:45-51), the servants given talents (see Mt 25:14-30), and others. He warned people directly about hell:

> If your hand causes you to sin, cut it off; it is better for you to enter life maimed than with two hands to go to hell, to the unquenchable fire. And if your foot causes you to sin, cut it off; it's better for you to enter life lame than with two feet to be thrown into hell. And if your eye causes you to sin, pluck it out; it is better for you to enter the kingdom of God with one eye than with two eyes to be thrown into hell, where their worm does not die, and the fire is not quenched.
>
> MARK 9:43-48

Some people cannot reconcile sayings such as this with their image of Jesus—"gentle, meek, and humble of heart." Certainly Jesus is gentle, but not when it comes to sin and warning his followers of the consequences of sin. When Jesus speaks of the consequences of sin and the reality of hell, the tone of his warning matches the danger involved. Although the text quoted above has been variously interpreted by scholars, it is difficult to escape its most evident meaning: nothing on earth is worth keeping (whether your hand, leg, eye, or life) if it means losing eternal life through sin.

Will many people end up in hell?

> The affirmations of Sacred Scripture and the teachings of the Church on the subject of hell are a *call to the responsibility* incumbent upon man to make use of his freedom in view of his eternal destiny. They are at the same time an urgent *call to conversion:*

> "Enter by the narrow gate; for the gate is wide and the way is easy, that leads to destruction, and those who enter by it are many. For the gate is narrow and the way is hard, that leads to life, and those who find it are few" (Mt 7:13-14; see CCC 1036).

The Catholic Church teaches that we cannot judge or determine whether any particular person has been condemned to hell, even Hitler or Judas Iscariot.

The mercy of God is such that a person can repent even at the point of death and be saved, like the good thief crucified next to Jesus (see Lk 23:39-43).

God predestines no one to go to hell;[4] for this, a willful turning away from God (a mortal sin) is necessary, and persistence in it until the end. In the Eucharistic liturgy and in the daily prayers of her faithful, the Church implores the mercy of God, who does not want "any to perish, but all to come to repentance" (2 Pet 3:9) (CCC 1037).

The church also tirelessly proclaims the way of salvation: Jesus Christ. Jesus is the "door" of his sheep (Jn 10:9), and "the way, and the truth, and the life" (Jn 14:6), in whom alone salvation can be found (see Acts 4:12). Jesus is the "life-preserver" that God has thrown into the troubled waters of human existence so that anyone who grabs onto him may be saved from eternal death.

Understanding Hell Today

Hell is the state of those who have decisively chosen to reject God and his wonderful plan for their existence. Hell, and eternal damnation in hell, is not God's idea or will but is the result of the choice of creatures with free will: angels and men who reject and rebel against God and his perfect love. Instead of asking why God could permit the existence of hell, we should rather ask why human beings could reject God and his loving will. Extreme cases of this rejection include attempts to kill whole races of peoples (genocide), slaughtering millions of innocent unborn children (widespread abortion), or allowing the Son of God, Jesus Christ, to be tortured and crucified without just cause.[5]

To see the existence of hell as calling into question the love and mercy of God is to place blame in the wrong direction. All that God has done is to create angels and men in his own image, with the great gift of free will. God maintains such a great respect for the freedom of his creatures that he allows them to freely choose their own destiny, to opt either for things that lead to death or for things that lead to life (see CCC 1033).[6]

Through conscience, natural law, and revelation, God points out the way that leads to life, but he never forces anyone to choose that way. Thus the biblical teaching on judgment emphasizes that God does not actively condemn anyone to hell, but rather all are judged according to the choices they have made.

> To die in mortal sin without repenting and accepting God's merciful love means remaining separated from him forever by our own free choice. This state of definitive self-exclusion from communion with God and the blessed is called "hell." (CCC 1033)

> For God sent the Son into the world, not to condemn the world, but that the world might be saved through him.... And this is the judgment, that the light has come into the world, and men loved darkness rather than light, because their deeds were evil. For every one who does evil hates the light, and does not come to the light, lest his deeds should be exposed. But he who does what is true comes to the light, that it may be clearly seen that his deeds have been wrought in God. (Jn 3:17, 19-21; see also Mt 12:36-37; Jn 12:47-48; Rom 2:4-8; 2 Cor 5:10)

Jesus, of course, is the "light" spoken of by the Gospel of John (Jn 9:5). God's desire is that all people freely come into the light of Jesus Christ so that their sin may be exposed. If they repent of their sin, they are freed from it and thus are saved from the consequence of serious sin—eternal separation from God.

Is Hell a Place?

While hell may begin as an internal reality—such as growing alienation from God or a rejection of his love and plan—it culminates in an actual place or state of existence that lasts eternally (see Mt 18:9; Mk 9:47-48). The Catholic Church has always been somewhat guarded in describing what hell is like, lest it succumb to exaggeration or inaccuracy. Hell exists as a real state or a condition of being. It may be a physical, material place, since Christians believe in the resurrection of the body. Many great Christian writers have observed that the greatest pain of hell is the eternal separation from God, along with the agonizing guilt of realizing that it is due to one's own choice (see CCC 1035). The "wailing and gnashing of teeth" often mentioned by Jesus may be seen as an expression of this eternal despair (Mt 22:13; 24:51; 25:30). "They shall suffer the punishment of eternal destruction and exclusion from the presence of the Lord" (2 Thess 1:9). Jesus also often alludes to hell as a "place of torment" (Lk 16:28) and of "unquenchable fire" (Mt 5:22; 13:30; Mk 9:43, 48; Lk 3:17; Rev 14:11-12), which indicates that hell includes physical suffering. "Depart from me, you cursed, into the eternal fire!"(Mt 25:41; see CCC 1034-1035). Great works of Christian literature, such as Dante's *Inferno*, vividly portray both aspects of the pains of hell.

We must affirm, once again, that the primary reason that God sent his Son, Jesus, into the world was to save people from the pains of hell by showing them the way to eternal life in God. Yet, time and again, Jesus affirms in the Gospels that entry into the kingdom of heaven is not automatic. No one drifts into the kingdom of heaven, but it is possible to drift into hell (see Mt 7:13-14). Mankind deserves only condemnation due to sin. God, out of sheer mercy and love, provides a way to life—Jesus Christ. Jesus shows us this way and constantly calls his followers to watchfulness and vigilance, lest they fall into sin that leads to eternal death. The way that Jesus has taught is the way of faith, discipleship, and constant repentance. We have a God of love and mercy, but we must accept this mercy through repentance:

Or do you presume upon the riches of his kindness and forbearance and patience? Do you not know that God's kindness is meant to lead you to repentance? But by your hard and impenitent heart you are storing up wrath for yourself on the day of wrath when God's righteous judgment will be revealed. For he will render to every man according to his works: to those who by patience in well-doing seek for glory and honor and immortality, he will give eternal life; but for those who are factious and do not obey the truth, but obey wickedness, there will be wrath and fury.

ROMANS 2:4-8

Purgatory

God exhibits both justice and mercy in his plan for the human race, and the doctrine of purgatory reveals this truth ideally. Purgatory is a stumbling block for many Christians in understanding the Catholic faith, and even many Catholics misinterpret it. The word "purgatory," like incarnation or trinity, is not a biblical term, but the concept of God's work of purgation or purification is very biblical, as we shall see. Purgatory is not a second chance for a person to establish a right relationship with God or to repent for past sins after death. When a person dies, the time of free choice is over, and the person's eternal destiny rests entirely in God's hands.

How will God judge a person who has loved God and others, but somewhat selfishly or imperfectly? What happens to this person who has attempted to respond positively to God's grace even up to death, yet dies still in the bondage of some unrepented venial sin or the effects of sin in his or her life? The difficulty here is that no sin can exist in heaven, in the "eternal dwelling place" of the all-holy God. As the Book of Revelation explains, God's presence is so pure and holy that "nothing unclean shall enter it..." (Rev 21:27). All sin must be forgiven, and its effects in the person purified and removed, before one may enjoy the eternal, beatific vision of God in heaven. So what is to be done with those who die in God's grace and friendship, but with some "stain" of less serious sin or the effects of previous sin still present in their lives?

Catholics believe that the mercy of God is so great, his desire to save is so strong, and the infinite merit of Christ's death on the cross for sinners is so powerful, that God has a saving provision for those who die in this state of imperfect love, in a condition of sin that is not mortal or deadly.

All who die in God's grace and friendship, but still imperfectly purified, are indeed assured of their eternal salvation; but after death they undergo purification, so as to achieve the holiness necessary to enter the joy of heaven. The Church gives the name *Purgatory* to this final purification of the elect, which is entirely different from the punishment of the damned.[7] (CCC 1030-31)

Although the term is not found in the Bible, there are two or three texts in the Bible that refer to purgatory, according to the ancient Christian tradition (see 2 Macc 12:46; 1 Cor 3:11-15; 1 Pet 1:7; see also CCC 1031; chapter five of this volume). Pope St. Gregory the Great taught:

> As for certain lesser faults, we must believe that, before the Final Judgement, there is a purifying fire. He who is truth says that whoever utters blasphemy against the Holy Spirit will be pardoned neither in this age nor in the age to come. From this sentence we understand that certain offenses can be forgiven in this age, but certain others in the age to come.[8]

Purgatory is reserved for those whose basic orientation in life is toward God and obedience to his will—not for those who are separated from God by rebellion or serious sin. These latter will not be purified, but suffer the pains of hell as the consequence of their life and choices on earth. God's mercy cannot override his respect for the freedom of choice that he gives to us. God's purification is available for those whose love is imperfect or who still suffer from the bondage or effects of sin, but God does not force anyone into heaven contrary to their free choices on earth.

What is purgatory like? As with all types of existence after death, there is a mystery involved here that requires us to approach it with faith and hope. It is notable that the biblical images of purification from sin often speak of fire as the purifying agent. The Catholic tradition concerning purgatory includes the notion of purgation from sin by the fire of God's love and holiness. Fire implies pain, and thus it should not surprise us if purgatory is painful. We know from our experience on earth that breaking from sin and overcoming all of its ill effects in our lives is often painful, and usually takes time. Penance, prayer, and discipline are necessary to receive God's full freedom and healing from sin while in this life. Purgatory is God's way of completing this process of deliverance and healing from sin and its effects—a process that begins here and now on earth. The goal of God's purifying work is always the same. God desires each person to share fully in his life and holiness, and wills to set us free from anything that impedes or clouds that holiness. Purgatory attests that God completes what he begins. The victory of Jesus Christ over sin and its effects in our lives is perfect and complete when we come into his glorious presence in heaven.[9]

In conclusion, the existence of purgatory should not cause Christians to seek holiness any less fervently, wrongly presuming that God always will purify us after we die. It is far better to accept fully the grace God offers us now to repent and to turn to him for freedom and healing from sin and its effects, lest our hearts become hardened and we fall further away from God. If we are not advancing in holiness in this life, we are retreating from God. However, it is one of the greatest sources of hope and consolation for Catholics to know that even if we fall short of the complete holiness that God wants for us in this life, and even if we die without full healing and repentance from less serious sin and its effects in our lives, God in his mercy desires to purge and purify us so that we may enter into his all-holy presence without shame or fear. The pains of purgatory reflect the justice of God in punishing sin. However, the knowledge that the gift of eternal life is granted even to those who are not perfect in their love when they die reflects God's overwhelming mercy toward sinners.

Indulgences

The Catholic Church has taught since early in its history that this purification from sin, whether for ourselves or others, is significantly aided by prayer and penance. For example, St. John Chrysostom urged:

> Let us help and commemorate them. If Job's sons were purified by their father's sacrifice, why would we doubt that our offerings for the dead bring them some consolation? Let us not hesitate to help those who have died and to offer our prayers for them.[10]

The Catholic doctrine of indulgences is based on the principle that every prayer, good work, or penance offered to God in faith for the remission of the effects of sin is effective.[11] Pope Paul VI reaffirmed and explained the Catholic doctrine of indulgences in his apostolic constitution on this topic (*Indulgentiarum doctrina*), which is summarized in the *Catechism* (CCC 1471-79). What is an indulgence?

> "An indulgence is a remission before God of the temporal punishment due to sins whose guilt has already been forgiven, which the faithful Christian who is duly disposed gains under certain prescribed conditions through the

action of the Church which, as the minister of redemption, dispenses and applies with authority the treasury of the satisfactions of Christ and the saints."[12]

An indulgence is obtained through the Church who, by virtue of the power of binding and loosing granted her by Christ Jesus, intervenes in favor of individual Christians and opens for them the treasury of the merits of Christ and the saints to obtain from the Father of mercies the remission of the temporal punishments due for their sins....[13] Indulgences may be applied to the living or the dead. (CCC 1478, 1471)

"Temporal punishment due to sin" refers to the suffering the soul undergoes in breaking from the "unhealthy attachment to creatures" (CCC 1472) that accompanies every mortal and venial sin, even after the sin has been forgiven, which must occur either on earth or in purgatory in order for the person to enter into the full glory and holiness of God's presence in heaven.

The "treasury of merits of Christ and the saints" refers to

... the infinite value, which can never be exhausted, which Christ's merits have before God. They were offered so that the whole of mankind could be set free from sin and attain communion with the Father. In Christ, the Redeemer himself, the satisfactions and merits of his Redemption exist and find their efficacy.[14]

This treasury includes as well the prayers and good works of the Blessed Virgin Mary. They are truly immense, unfathomable, and even pristine in their value before God. In the treasury, too, are the prayers and good works of all the saints, all those who have followed in the footsteps of Christ the Lord and by his grace have made their lives holy and carried their own salvation and at the same time cooperated in saving their brothers in the unity of the Mystical Body.[15]

In understanding how we can gain removal of temporal punishment due to sin for others, the key concept is the "communion of saints"—the unity of the mystical body of Christ. In this communion, Christians continue to be united in Christ, and can continue to love and serve each other even when they have been separated through death.

So we see that prayer, good works, and penances do foster God's work of the purification of ourselves, of others living on earth, and of those in purgatory. Prayer and sacrifice for each other that we may be freed from sin are among the primary ways that the "saints"—members of the body of Christ, whether on earth, in heaven, or in purgatory—can aid each other. Initially, the Catholic Church specified a length of time for the penance required to gain an indulgence. Later, these ecclesial penances were replaced by prayers or other good works that the church declared to have the value of so many days or years of penance. In recent years the church has ceased to attach these lengths of time to indulgences. (Their meaning was not widely understood.) Today, the church simply declares the indulgence to be either partial (remitting *some* of the temporal punishment due to sin) or plenary (see CCC 1471). Indulgences should encourage Catholics to pray, fast, give alms, and do other good works as an intercession for themselves and others that will aid in the attainment of our common good of eternal life with God.

Heaven

Those who die in God's grace and friendship and are perfectly purified live forever with Christ. They are like God for ever, for they "see him as he is," face to face (CCC 1023; 1 Jn 3:2; see also 1 Cor 13:12; Rev 22:4). The church calls this contemplation of God in his heavenly glory "the beatific vision" (CCC 1028).

Where is this experienced?

This perfect life with the Most Holy Trinity—this communion of life and love with the Trinity, with the Virgin Mary, the angels and all the blessed— is called "heaven." Heaven is the ultimate end and fulfillment of the deepest human longings, the state of supreme, definitive happiness. (CCC 1024)

The goal of human existence, the purpose for which God created human beings, is eternal happiness with God, "For here we have no lasting city, but we seek the city which is to come" (Heb 13:14). Many people consider Christians to be escapists or utopians in looking forward to an eternity of happiness with God. They say it is a distraction from improving this world and serving humanity, a hollow promise that causes people to accept oppression and misery in this life, waiting for "the pie in the sky when you die." They say it is a foolish and false hope produced by our natural human incapacity to accept the certainty and finality of death.

To the contrary, Christians assert that "by his death and Resurrection, Jesus Christ has 'opened' heaven to us. The life of the blessed consists in the full and perfect possession of the fruits of the redemption accomplished by Christ. He makes partners in his heavenly glorification those who have believed in him and remained faithful to his will. Heaven is the blessed community of all who are perfectly incorporated into Christ" (CCC 1026). "To live in heaven is 'to be with Christ'... [and to] retain, or rather find, their true identity, their own name" (CCC 1025; see Rev 2:17). Therefore, Christian belief in heaven is based on the power and promises of Jesus Christ. Jesus reassured his followers:

> Let not your hearts be troubled; believe in God, believe also in me. In my Father's house are many rooms; if it were not so, would I have told you that I go to prepare a place for you? And when I go and prepare a place for you, I will come again and will take you to myself, that where I am you may be also.
>
> JOHN 14:1-3

Jesus also promises that his "sheep," his followers, will hear his voice and receive eternal life from him (Jn 10:27-28), and "inherit the kingdom prepared for you from the foundation of the world ..." (Mt 25:34). He describes heaven as a joyous wedding feast (see Mt 22:1-14; 25:1-13) and a great banquet (see Lk 14:16-24), in which we celebrate the marriage of the Lamb of God, Jesus Christ, to his bride, the church (see Rev 19:7-9).

The *Catechism* summarizes: "Scripture speaks of it in images: life, light, peace, wedding feast, wine of the kingdom, the Father's house, the heavenly Jerusalem, paradise: 'no eye has seen, nor ear heard, nor the heart of man conceived, what God has prepared for those who love him'" (1 Cor 2:9) (CCC 1027).

Catholics believe that heaven is the fulfillment of the deepest yearnings of the human heart. St. Augustine wrote, "You have made us for Yourself, and our hearts are restless until they rest in You."[16] Heaven is the eternal Sabbath day of rest in God after our six days of labor in this life. Yet, for a Christian, there is a sense in which heaven is more than a future reward or state of happiness. As we have seen, heaven begins in this life as we respond in faith to Jesus Christ and his grace. When we put God first in our lives and decide to give up all else in order to follow him, we experience the joy of discipleship that is the foretaste and beginning of the life of heaven. Jesus came that we may have life, "and have it abundantly" (Jn 10:10), beginning now, and in its fullness in heaven.

> Christ will raise us up "on the last day"; but it is also true that, in a certain way, we have already risen with Christ. For, by virtue of the Holy Spirit, Christian life is already now on earth a participation in the death and Resurrection of Christ.... The Father has already "raised us up with him, and made us to sit with him in the heavenly places in Christ Jesus" (Eph 2:6) (CCC 1002, 1003).

Heaven is sharing in divine life and joy to the extent that we are drawn completely into the life of the Trinity. "In that day you will know that I am in my Father, and you in me, and I in you" (Jn 14:20). We aren't absorbed into the life of God in a way that we lose our individual identities, as in pantheism, but we find our true identity as we are immersed in God and his love (see CCC 1025). Catholics believe in the resurrection of the body, implying that heaven is a place and not just a vague state of existence. It is the place where we will not only see God face to face, but will perceive, with our own risen bodies, the risen and glorified bodies of Jesus, Mary, and all the others who have entered the life of heaven. All in heaven will be full of the joy of God, though our joy will be measured according to the capacity of each one of us to receive it. The more loving and generous we are on earth, the greater the joy of heaven for us, like cups of different sizes that are each completely full, but do not have the same capacities.

Children Who Have Died Without Baptism

Catholic theologians of the early church and the Middle Ages reflected on the eternal destiny of infants and very young children who died unbaptized, before the age that they could commit personal sin or make a responsible choice to believe in or follow God. Because they died without the sacrament of baptism, most theologians presumed that because of original sin, they could not enter the presence of God in heaven. On the other hand, it seemed unthinkable that they would be condemned for eternity to the punishment of hell, when they had no opportunity to choose responsibly for or against God in this life. As a result of this dilemma, Catholic theologians in the past proposed the existence of "limbo"—a state of "natural blessedness," or happiness, in which unbaptized infants would experience peace for eternity, but without the full joy of the kingdom of heaven.

The Catholic Church has never formally recognized or denied the existence of limbo in its official teaching. The *Catechism* teaches that "the Church can only entrust them to the mercy of God ... who desires that all men should be saved ... Jesus' tenderness toward children which caused him to say: 'Let the children come to me, do not hinder them' (Mk 10:14; cf. 1 Tim 2:4), allows us to hope that there is a way of salvation for children who have died without Baptism" (CCC 1261).

Although this question appears to many people to be a trivial issue or based on mere speculation, the reality of millions of aborted unborn children and the shocking growth of infanticide every year indicate the importance of this question today. If limbo does exist, as some theologians have proposed, abortion and infanticide not only are heinous crimes that bring spiritual death to those who perpetrate them, but also deprive millions of innocent people, the unborn and infants, of the opportunity of the fullness of eternal life and joy with God. The blood of these innocent victims surely cries out to the God of justice for retribution of this great evil.

The Return of the Lord

Christians profess in the Nicene Creed that Jesus "will come again in glory to judge the living and the dead" (see CCC 668-82). In the Acts of the Apostles, as Jesus' followers were witnessing the ascension of Jesus, two messengers of Jesus asked, "Men of Galilee, why do you stand looking into heaven? This Jesus, who was taken up from you into heaven, will come in the same way as you saw him go into heaven" (Acts 1:11). Jesus, in his risen, glorified body, has been exalted to eternal kingship in the highest place of honor ("at the right hand of God"), and now is revealed to the world as the Lord of everything that has been created through him. Still, not everyone on earth recognizes or acknowledges this rule, or lordship, of Jesus Christ. We live in a period of history in which the reign or rule of God has been inaugurated or established on earth.

> Since the Ascension God's plan has entered into its fulfillment. We are already at "the last hour" [1 Jn 2:18; see also 1 Pet 4:7]. "Already the final age of the world is with us, and the renewal of the world is irrevocably under way; it is even now anticipated in a certain real way, for the Church on earth is endowed already with a sanctity that is real but imperfect."[17] (CCC 670)

Also in this age, Satan and his demons are permitted, for a time, to attempt to draw people away from the reign of God and into their own dominion of darkness (see CCC 671-72).

Christian revelation proclaims that this period of human history will come to a close when the Son of Man returns, not in obscurity and humility as a baby in Bethlehem, but in glory and majesty as the king and judge of all. The Apostles' Creed proclaims, "He [Jesus] will come again in glory to judge the living and the dead."

There are a number of graphic descriptions of this second coming or parousia of Christ in the New Testament, all of which take their images from the apocalyptic, or revelational, literature of the Old Testament. Most of these descriptions use the imagery of the vision of Daniel in that apocalyptic book of the Old Testament:

> I saw in the night visions, and behold, with the clouds of heaven there came one like a son of man, and he came to the Ancient of Days [God the Father] and was presented before him. And to him was given dominion and glory and kingdom, that all peoples, nations, and languages should serve him; his dominion is an everlasting dominion, which shall not pass away, and his kingdom one that shall not be destroyed.
>
> DANIEL 7:13-14

The Bible indicates that a severe time of trial in the world, and particularly for Christians, will immediately precede the second coming of Christ. All three synoptic Gospels describe a time of tribulation on the earth and signs in the heavens. Various texts of the New Testament speak of the appearance of scoffers and false prophets who will lead many people away from the truth in the last days (see Mt 7:15; 24:11, 24; Mk 13:22; 2 Pet 2:1-3; 1 Jn 4:1; Rev 16:13; 19:20; 20:10), and even the emergence of an anti-Christ or anti-Christs (see 1 Jn 2:18, 22; 4:3; 2 Jn 7). The Catholic Church has never attempted to formally identify who these figures will be, but they will be identified by their activity of causing many to fall away from true faith in Christ and Christian love. As Matthew's Gospel attests: "And many false prophets will arise and lead many astray. And because wickedness is multiplied, most men's love will grow cold. But he who endures to the end will be saved." (Mt 24:11-13). The *Catechism* summarizes these events:

Before Christ's second coming the Church must pass through a final trial that will shake the faith of many believers [see Lk 18:8; Mt 24:12]. The persecution that accompanies her pilgrimage on earth [see Lk 21:12; Jn 15:19-20] will unveil the "mystery of iniquity" in the form of a religious deception offering men an apparent solution to their problems at the price of apostasy from the truth. The supreme religious deception is that of the Antichrist, a pseudo-messianism by which man glorifies himself in place of God and of his Messiah come in the flesh (cf. 2 Thess 2:4-12; 1 Thess 5:2-3; 2 Jn 7; 1 Jn 2:18, 22) (CCC 675).

The Church will enter the glory of the kingdom only through this final Passover, when she will follow her Lord in his death and Resurrection [see Rev 19:1-9]. The kingdom will be fulfilled, then, not by a historic triumph of the Church through a progressive ascendancy, but only by God's victory over the final unleashing of evil, which will cause his Bride to come down from heaven [see Rev 13:8; 20:7-10; 21:2-4]. God's triumph over the revolt of evil will take the form of the Last Judgment after the final cosmic upheaval of this passing world (cf. Rev 20:12; 2 Pet 3:12-13) (CCC 677).

However, not all will be bleak immediately before the Lord's coming. This passage in Matthew's Gospel concludes by predicting a great age of evangelism. "And this gospel of the kingdom will be preached throughout the whole world, as a testimony to all nations; and then the end will come" (Mt 24:14). The Scripture also teaches that the Lord's coming awaits the conversion of the Jewish people to Christ:

> The glorious Messiah's coming is suspended at every moment of history until his recognition by "all Israel," for "a hardening has come upon part of Israel" in their "unbelief" toward Jesus (Rom 11:20-26; cf. Mt 23:39).
> ... The 'full inclusion' of the Jews in the Messiah's salvation, in the wake of "the full number of the Gentiles," [Rom 11:12, 25; see also Lk 21:24] will enable the People of God to achieve "the measure of the stature of the fullness of Christ," in which, "God may be all in all" (Eph 4:13; 1 Cor 15:28) (CCC 674).

When Jesus does return, it will be an unmistakable event: "And then they will see the Son of man coming in clouds with great power and glory" (Mk 13:26; see also Mt 24:30; Lk 21:27). No one will miss it, "For as the lightning comes from the east and shines as far as the west, so will be the coming of the Son of man" (Mt 24:27).

What will happen on earth when Jesus, the Son of Man, comes? The Bible speaks of it as a time of great joy for the followers of Christ, an exaltant reunion. "Now when these things begin to take place, look up and raise your heads, because your redemption is drawing near" (Lk 21:28). St. Paul writes that when Christ descends from heaven, "the dead in Christ will rise first; then we who are alive, who are left, shall be caught up together with them in the clouds to meet the Lord in the air; and so we shall always be with the Lord. Therefore, comfort one another with these words" (1 Thess 4:16-18). Protestant Christians call this lifting up of the elect the "rapture." The Catholic Church does not define whether these images are to be taken literally or understood as poetic images or pointers to a reality beyond our imagination. The truth we must believe is that the bodies of both those living and those dead will rise at the second coming of Christ in order to receive their final reward or retribution (see CCC 1038; Acts 24:15), "For we must all appear before the judgment seat of Christ, so that each one may receive good or evil, according to what he has done in the body" (2 Cor 5:10).

The Last Judgment

This last judgment, or general judgment, will mark the time when human history comes to an end. Purgatory, God's provision for purification of sin after death, will also come to an end. The Gospel of Matthew vividly describes the judgment of the nations.

> When the Son of man comes in his glory, and all the angels with him, then he will sit on his glorious throne. Before him will be gathered all the nations, and he will separate them one from another as a shepherd separates the sheep from the goats.... (Mt 25:31-32; see CCC 1038)

God's judgment, as described by St. Matthew, is based on performance of the works of mercy, such as feeding the hungry, clothing the naked, visiting the sick and imprisoned, and welcoming the stranger, emphasizing Jesus' words that "Not every one who says to me, 'Lord, Lord,' shall enter the kingdom of heaven, but he who does the will of my Father who is in heaven" (Mt 7:21 ff). As the *Catechism* explains:

> In the presence of Christ, who is Truth itself, the truth of each man's relationship with God will be laid bare [see Jn 12:49]. The Last Judgment will reveal even to its furthest consequences the good each person has done or failed to do during his earthly life. (CCC 1039)

The second coming of Christ also means that the physical universe and earth as we know it will come to an end. The New Testament envisions a destruction of the universe (see 2 Pet 3:10-12; Rev 21:1)—"Heaven and earth will pass away,..." (Lk 21:33)—but also contains the promise of "a new heaven and a new earth" (2 Pet 3:13; Rev 21:1; see CCC 1043), in which righteousness dwells, in which "happiness will fill and surpass all the desires of peace arising in the hearts of men,"[18] and God will reign forever. The Book of Revelation, especially chapters 21 and 22, presents the most graphic and beautiful picture of this New Jerusalem:

> Behold the dwelling of God is with men. He will dwell with them, and they shall be his people, and God himself will be with them; he will wipe away every tear from their eyes, and death shall be no more, neither shall there be mourning nor crying nor pain anymore, for the former things have passed away. (Rev 21:3-4; see CCC 1044)
>
> For man, this consummation will be the final realization of the unity of the human race.... Those who are united with Christ will form the community of the redeemed, "the holy city" of God "the Bride, the wife of the Lamb" [Rev 21:2, 9]. She will not be wounded any longer by sin, stains, self-love, that destroy or wound the earthly community [see Rev 21:27]. The beatific vision, in which God opens himself in an inexhaustible way to the elect, will be the ever-flowing well-spring of happiness, peace, and mutual communion. (CCC 1045)

Part of the mystery of the "new earth" will be that our bodies will be raised and transformed. Chapter 15 of St. Paul's First Letter to the Corinthians discusses the meaning of the resurrection of the body in detail. Paul points out that the body that each of us is to possess will not be the same as the physical body that dies, but will be a "spiritual body," that will be like the risen and glorified body of Jesus. "Just as we have borne the image of the man of dust [Adam], we shall also bear the image of the man of heaven [the risen Christ]" (1 Cor 15:49). Not only will our bodies be transformed, but so will the whole physical universe, "the creation itself will be set free from its bondage to decay and obtain the glorious liberty of the children of God."[19] As the triumphant Christ proclaims toward the close of the Book of Revelation, "Behold, I make all things new" (Rev 21:5).

This belief in the transformation of the earth affirms the value of our efforts to promote justice and other gospel values in this world. As the Second Vatican Council stated:

> Earthly progress must be carefully distinguished from the growth of Christ's kingdom. Nevertheless, to the extent that the former can contribute to the

better ordering of human society, it is of vital concern to the kingdom of God.

For after we have obeyed the Lord, and in His Spirit nurtured on earth the values of human dignity, brotherhood and freedom, and indeed all the good fruits of our nature and enterprise, we will find them again, but freed of stain, burnished and transfigured. This will be so when Christ hands over to the Father a kingdom eternal and universal: "a kingdom of truth and life, of holiness and grace, of justice, love, and peace." On this earth that kingdom is already present in mystery. When the Lord returns, it will be brought into full flower.[20]

In conclusion:

The message of the Last Judgment calls men to conversion while God is still giving them "the acceptable time, ... the day of salvation" [2 Cor 6:2]. It inspires a holy fear of God and commits them to the justice of the Kingdom of God. It proclaims the "blessed hope" of the Lord's return, when he will come "to be glorified in his saints, and to be marveled at in all who have believed" (Titus 2:13; 2 Thess 1:10) (CCC 1041).

The Time of Christ's Return

The second coming of Christ, the general judgment, the resurrection of the body, and the transformation of the universe in Jesus Christ: when will all this take place? Both the New Testament and the Catholic Church concur in one answer: we don't know (see CCC 673, 1040). The synoptic Gospels do describe proximate and immediate signs of the second coming of Christ that all should be able to recognize, but when this will occur is not revealed. To the contrary, Jesus' parables and direct statements on the subject indicate that his second coming will be sudden and unexpected, "like a thief in the night" (1 Thess 5:2; see Mt 24:43; 2 Pet 3:10). If the householder, bridesmaids, and servants in Jesus' parables had known when the master or the groom would be returning, they would have been prepared. As it is, Jesus says, concerning the day of his return:

But of that day or that hour no one knows, not even the angels in heaven, nor the Son, but only the Father. Take heed, watch and pray;... for you do not know when the master of the house will come, in the evening, or at midnight, or at cockcrow, or in the morning—lest he come suddenly and find you asleep. And what I say to you I say to all: Watch.

MARK 13:32-33; 35-37

Some Christians are convinced that we are living in the last days and that the end of the world is imminent. "Since the Ascension Christ's coming in glory has been imminent (see Rev 22:20), even though 'it is not for you to know times or seasons which the Father has fixed by his own authority' (Acts 1:7; cf. Mk 13:32). This eschatological coming could be accomplished at any moment, even if both it and the final trial that will precede it are 'delayed' (cf. Mt 24:44; 1 Thess 5:2; 1 Thess 2:3-12)" (CCC 673). Catholics agree that the final age of the world has already come upon us[21] but view the entire period of time between the first coming of the Lord Jesus and his second coming as the end-times, the last days, the final age. As the Letter to the Hebrews says, "in these last days he [God] has spoken to us by a Son" (Heb 1:2), we, "upon whom the end of the ages has come" (1 Cor 10:11). We sometimes forget that God's timetable is not the same as ours:

Do not ignore this one fact, beloved, that with the Lord one day is as a thousand years, and a thousand years as one day. The Lord is not slow about his promise [of his return] as some count slowness, but is forbearing toward you, not wishing that any should perish, but that all should reach repentance.

2 PETER 3:8-9

The many warnings of Jesus and the other New Testament authors about the coming of the Son of Man and the day of judgment are meant to convict us, and even disturb us, if we have fallen into complacency, unbelief, or sin. Even if the final coming of the Lord does not come suddenly during our lifetime, none of us know the day or the hour of our own death, our personal day of judgment. The *Catechism* concludes:

The Last Judgment will come when Christ returns in glory. Only the Father knows the day and the hour; only he determines the moment of its coming. Then through the Son Jesus Christ he will pronounce the final word on all history. We shall know the ultimate meaning of the whole work of creation and of the entire economy of salvation and understand the marvellous ways by which his Providence led everything towards its final end. The Last Judgment will reveal that God's justice triumphs over all the injustices committed by his creatures and that God's love is stronger than death (see Song 8:6) (CCC 1040).

The Catholic Response to the Last Things

In times past, some holy Catholic women and men would keep a skull on their desk to remind them of the shortness of life and their final end. Today, when most of us try to hide reminders of death, such a practice appears morbid. However, reflecting on the shortness of life and the possibility of Jesus' imminent return has a positive purpose: to lead us to turn to God, to repent of our sins, to live the new life that God offers to us in Jesus Christ. As Peter wrote in his second letter, God does not desire that anyone die eternally through sin, but that all should reach repentance (see 2 Pet 3:8-9).

To put the human situation today in a nutshell: the problem, at least in Western society, is that people have lost their understanding of sin and the need for repentance. In losing their sense of sin and its horror, they cannot understand the cross of Jesus Christ, because the reason that Christ died on the cross was to take away the sin of mankind. And in losing their understanding of the cross of Christ, they lose the true understanding of Jesus himself. The sacrificial death of Jesus on the cross to take away the sin of the world becomes merely a symbol or an inspiring story, instead of the most important event in the history of humanity. Jesus, without the cross, becomes just a good man or a great teacher, instead of the one who alone gave up his life, his body and blood, in a way that definitively shattered the power of evil and sin in the world and reconciled the whole human race to God.

The basic message of the gospel is to call us to acknowledge our need for forgiveness and cleansing from the bondage of sin, and to accept God's only remedy for sin—Jesus Christ and his death on the cross. To believe in and to follow

Jesus as the one who saves humanity from sin is not just a one-time decision, although it must begin there. It is a decision that each person must make every day, "If any man would come after me, let him deny himself and take up his cross daily and follow me" (Lk 9:23). That is the way that leads to eternal life and gives Christians hope for the day of judgment.

We may look at the lives of Christians who are following this way of daily discipleship, and often it seems their joy and desire for God grow greater as they approach their goal of full union with Christ. St. Paul, for instance, spoke of having run the good race, fought the good fight. All that was left was to receive the crown of eternal life that was awaiting him (see 2 Tim 4:6-8).

Salvation and eternal life are gifts freely given by God. We cannot presume that we possess them before we finish the "race" of earthly life and receive our reward from God. Catholics, realizing this, are encouraged to pray for the grace of "final perseverance," the grace of God enabling them to remain faithful to God and his commandment to the very end of life, so that they may receive the crown of eternal life. The lives of Catholics who are always ready for the Lord's return by following him daily (in daily discipleship) are marked by joy, peace, and a confident hope in their own salvation. These people look forward expectantly to the day when they hear the Father say, "Well done, good and faithful servant; enter into the joy of your master" (Mt 25:21, 23). They remember even during difficult times the promises and words of encouragement that the Bible gives them, such as these words from the Letter to the Hebrews:

> For God is not so unjust as to overlook your work and the love which you showed for his sake in serving the saints, as you still do. And we desire each one of you to show the same earnestness in realizing the full assurance of hope until the end, so that you may not be sluggish, but imitators of those who through faith and patience inherit the promises.
>
> HEBREWS 6:10-12

Those who turn from their sins through ongoing repentance, who believe in Jesus Christ, and who obey his commandments through a life of daily discipleship, have nothing to fear on the day when Jesus Christ comes again to judge the world. The belief of the Catholic Church about the final coming of Christ is best summarized by the "Dogmatic Constitution on the Church," [22]

Since we know not the day nor the hour, on our Lord's advice we must consistently stand guard. Thus when we have finished the one and only course of our earthly life (cf. Heb 9:27) we may merit to enter into the marriage feast with Him and to be numbered among the blessed (cf. Mt 25:31-46). Thus we may not be commanded to go into eternal fire (cf. Mt 25:41) like the wicked and slothful servant (cf. Mt 25:26), into the exterior darkness where "there will be the weeping and the gnashing of teeth" (Mt 22:13; 25:30). For before we reign with the glorious Christ, all of us will be made manifest "before the tribunal of Christ, so that each one may receive what he has won through the body, according to his works, whether good or evil" (2 Cor 5:10). At the end of the world, "they who have done good shall come forth unto resurrection of life; but who have done evil unto resurrection of judgment" (Jn 5:29; cf. Mt 25:46).

We reckon therefore that "the sufferings of the present time are not worthy to be compared with the glory to come that will be revealed in us" (Rom 8:18; cf. 2 Tim 2:11-12). Strong in faith we look for "the blessed hope and glorious coming of our great God and Savior, Jesus Christ" (Titus 2:13), "Who will refashion the body of our lowliness, conforming it to the body of His glory" (Phil 3:21) and who will come "to be glorified in His saints, and to be marveled at in all those who have believed" (2 Thess 1:10).

And, as the *Catechism* states more succinctly:

According to the Lord, the present time is the time of the Spirit and of witness, but also a time still marked by "distress" and the trial of evil which does not spare the Church (cf. Acts 1:8; 1 Cor 7:26; Eph 5:16; 1 Pet 4:17) and ushers in the struggles of the last days. It is a time of waiting and watching, (cf. Mt 25:1,13; Mk 13:33-37; 1 Jn 2:18; 4:3; 1 Tim 4:1) (CCC 672).

Nonetheless, Christians, rather than facing the present crisis or the final judgment with misgivings or fear, should look forward to the future with hope, for, "we wait for new heavens and a new earth in which righteousness dwells" (2 Pet 3:13; Rev 21:1 ff; see also CCC 671). Today Catholics must again learn to echo "above all in the Eucharist" (CCC 671), one of the oldest Christian prayers, which has resounded through the ages in the midst of our troubled and weary world. The prayer is simply Maranatha!—literally, "Lord, come!"

Come, Lord, to establish your kingdom in full glory and power!

Come, Lord, to overthrow Satan's dominion and all the evil in the world!

Come, Lord, to free us each from the bondage of our sin, and to share with us the gift of Your eternal life! Come, Lord, to save us!

Come, Lord, to reveal to all Your rightful place as King, Lord, and Master over the entire universe!

Maranatha! Come, Lord Jesus!

Notes

Chapter One
God's Revelation and Our Response

1. Please note that the author will, at times, use the words "Catholic" and "Christian" interchangeably. This is because Catholics believe that what the Catholic Church officially teaches *is* the Christian faith in its fullness, to the extent that God has revealed it and enabled his church to understand it to this point in time.
2. C.S. Lewis, *Mere Christianity* (New York: Macmillan, 1960), 17–19.
3. STh I, 2, 3.
4. DV 2.
5. *Confessions* I, 1.
6. DV 2.
7. DV 4; see 1 Tim 6:14 and Titus 2:13.
8. Thus, the beliefs of religions that proclaim another savior, such as the Unification Church's beliefs concerning Rev. Moon, and of religions that add to Christianity's basic revelation, such as Mormonism, are rejected by the Catholic Church.
9. DV 10.
10. DV 9.
11. DV 8.
12. DV 8.
13. See GS 27.
14. DV 21 (FL).
15. See DV 24.
16. DV 15 (FL); cited in CCC 122.
17. See DV 16.
18. "Canon" means an "official list," in this case, the official list recognized by the church of the inspired writings that make up the Old or the New Testament.
19. Bishops of the early church developed lists of writings, called "canons," that they considered to be inspired by the Holy Spirit. The canon developed by Bishop Irenaeus of Lyons around A.D. 185 is very similar to the present New Testament, but without mention of 3 John, James, or 2 Peter. Another canon similar to the present one is found written on the Muratorian Fragment, probably from the church of Rome, in about A.D. 200. Yet, even by the fourth century, the question of an official canon remained unsettled. In the early part of that century, Bishop Eusebius of Caesarea refers to the letters of James, Jude, 2 Peter, and 2 and 3 John as "disputed, yet familiar to most." (See his *History of the Church,* Book III, Sec. 25, 1st paragraph in Williamson, G.A., trans. [Minneapolis: Augsburg, 1975], 134.) It took centuries for the bishops to come to an agreement on the complete New Testament canon. The bishops went through a similar process to recognize a canon for the Old Testament, though the dispute about the deuterocanonical, or apocryphal, books was more intense and confusing than the development of the New Testament canon. (See Henry Chadwick, *The Early Church*

[Baltimore, Md.: Penguin, 1967], 40–44, 81–82.)

20. Bishop Irenaeus of Lyons looked to the church of Rome as preserving the apostolic tradition in a preeminent way. See St. Irenaeus of Lyons, "The Refutation and Overthrow of 'Knowledge' Falsely So-Called," Book III, Chapter 3, section 2, in Cyril Richardson, ed., *Early Christian Fathers* (New York: Macmillan, 1970), 372.

21. DV 11 (FL); cited in CCC 105.

22. DV 11.

23. See also DV 11-12.

24. DV 12.

25. Pius XII, *Divino Afflante Spiritu*, no. 28, 29. "In the accomplishment of this task, the Catholic exegete will find invaluable help in an assiduous study of those works, in which the Holy Fathers, the Doctors of the Church and the renowned interpreters of past ages have explained the Sacred Books. For, although sometimes less instructed in profane learning and in the knowledge of languages than the scripture scholars of our time, nevertheless, by reason of the office assigned to them by God in the Church, they are distinguished by a certain subtle insight into heavenly things and by a marvelous keenness of intellect, which enables them to penetrate to the very innermost meaning of the divine word and bring to light all that can help to elucidate the teaching of Christ and promote holiness of life.

    "It is indeed regrettable that such precious treasures of Christian antiquity are almost unknown to many writers of the present day, and that students of the history of exegesis have not yet accomplished all that seems necessary for the due investigation and appreciation of so momentous a subject. Would that many, by seeking out the authors of Catholic interpretation of Scripture and diligently studying their works and drawing thence the almost inexhaustible riches therein stored up, might contribute largely to this end, so that it might be daily more apparent to what extent those authors understood and made known the divine teaching of the Sacred Books, and that the interpreters of today might thence take example and seek suitable arguments."

26. DV 10,"Final Report" in *The Extraordinary Synod - 1985*, section II, B, a, 1. (Boston: Daughters of St. Paul, 1985), 49.

27. Pius XII wrote in *Divino Afflante Spiritu*: "the Angelic Doctor [St. Thomas Aquinas] already observed in these words: 'In Scripture divine things are presented to us in the manner which is in common use among men.' For as the substantial Word of God became like to men in all things 'except sin' (Heb 4:15), so the words of God, expressed in human language, are made like to human speech in every respect, except error" (no. 37).

28. DV 11 (FL); cited in CCC 107.

29. Pontifical Biblical Commission, "The Historicity of the Gospel," April 21, 1964, explains that "the evangelist felt duty-bound to narrate his particular account in the order which God suggested to his memory. At least this would seem to be true for those items in which order of treatment would not affect the authority or truth of the Gospel. After all, the Holy Spirit distributes His gifts to each as he chooses. Since these books were to be so authoritative, he undoubtedly guided and directed the sacred writers as they thought about the things which they were going to write down; but he probably allowed each writer to arrange his narrative as he saw fit. Hence anyone who uses enough diligence, will be able to discover this order with the help of God."

30. (DV 11, italics mine). *Dei Verbum* is the culmination of over a century of papal state-
    ments on the subject of Biblical inerrancy. See Leo XIII, *Providentissmus Deus*,
    November 18, 1893; Benedict XV, *Spiritus Paraclitus*, September 15, 1920; Pius XII,
    Divinio Afflante Spiritu, September 30, 1943; *Humani Generis*, August 12, 1950, and
    many instructions of the Pontifical Biblical Commission, including those of May 14,
    1950, and April 21, 1964. Also, John Paul II has said:

    > In the last century and at the beginning of our own, advances in the historical sci-
    > ences made it possible to acquire *a new understanding of the Bible and of the bibli-
    > cal world.* The rationalist context in which these data were most often presented
    > seemed to make them dangerous to the Christian faith. Certain people, in their
    > concern to defend the faith, thought it necessary to reject firmly-based historical
    > conclusions. That was a hasty and unhappy decision. The work of a pioneer like Fr.
    > Lagrange was able to make the necessary discernment on the basis of dependable
    > criteria. (Address to Pontifical Academy of Sciences, in *L'Osservatore Romano*,
    > English edition, Nov. 4, 1992, p.2, no. 8.)

31. Thomas Aquinas, "On Truth," Q 12, A2, C.
32. Note by R.A.F. MacKenzie, footnote 31 to "Dogmatic Constitution on Divine
    Revelation" in *The Documents of Vatican II*, Walter Abbot, S.J. ed. (New York:
    American Press, 1966), 119.
33. John Paul II, Address to the Pontifical Academy of Sciences, "Faith Can Never Conflict
    With Reason" in *L'Osservatore Romano* (English edition), Nov. 4, 1992, p.2, no. 12.)
34. Ibid., pp. 1–2. This is one of Pope John Paul II's most thorough treatments of the rela-
    tionship of science and Biblical interpretation, based on the conclusions of the Pontifical
    Academy of Sciences' ten-year study of the Galileo case. The pope emphasizes that the
    errors made by theologians in this case were the result of misinterpretations of the bibli-
    cal text. He quotes St. Augustine, St. Robert Bellarmine, and Pope Leo XIII, who point
    out that if the Bible seems to contradict certain reason or scientifically proven facts, the
    problem must lie in our understanding or interpretation of the text.
35. DAS 47.
36. *Humani Generis*, Encyclical Letter of Pius XII, August 12, 1950, N.C.W.C. translation
    (Boston, Mass.: Daughters of St. Paul), no. 22, p. 9.
37. See DV 12.
38. DV 10.
39. UR 11 (FL);
40. DV 9.
41. DV 10.
42. ibid.
43. DV 5 (FL); cf. DS 377; 3010; see also CCC 153.
44. St. Thomas Aquinas, STh II–II, 2, 9; cited in CCC 155.
45. DV 5 (FL).
46. See also DV 4.
47. DV 21 (FL); see also CCC 131.
48. DV 22, 25 (FL).
49. A good, concise history of biblical reading by laity in the Catholic Church may be found
    in Nick Cavnar's article, "Did the Catholic Church Ever Ban the Bible?" *New Covenant*,
    November, 1983, 10-11. "Plenary indulgence" will be explained in chapter 11.

Chapter Two
God, His Creation, and Man's Rebellion

1. DV 11.
2. DV 15.
3. See also Dogmatic Constitution *Dei Filius* (On the Catholic Faith), First Vatican Council, April 24, 1870, and Fr. Stanley Jaki, O.S.B., *Cosmos and Creator* (Edinburgh: Scottish Academic Press, 1980).
4. *Dei Filius* chapter 2 in *Documents of Vatican Council I, 1869-1870,* trans. John F. Broderick (Collegeville, Minn.: Liturgical Press, 1971), 41. See also Dogmatic Constitution on Divine Revelation *(Dei Verbum)* of The Second Vatican Council, no. 6.
5. Council of Trent, 4th Session, decree concerning the Canonical Scriptures (April 8, 1546), quoted in *The Sources of Catholic Dogma,* trans. by Roy J. Deferrari from the 30th ed. of Henry Denzinger's *Enchiridion Symbolorum* (St. Louis, Mo.: B. Herder, 1957), 244.
6. J.B. Phillips, *The Ring of Truth: A Translator's Testimony* (Wheaton, Ill.: Harold Shaw Publishers, 1977).
7. The statement of the *Shema* concerning God's oneness has various implications: (a) Yahweh is one, in contrast to many Baals; (b) Yahweh is the only god *for Israel,* the only god with whom they are to be in relationship; (c) Yahweh is one in the sense of simple being; this has implications for Christians who also believe in the Tri-Unity of the one Godhead.
8. GS 19.
9. ibid.
10. Francis Thompson, *Selected Poems of Francis Thompson* (London: Burns and Oates, 1908), 51.
11. St. Augustine, *Confessions,* trans. F.J. Sheed (New York: Sheed and Ward, 1943), Book I, 3.
12. John Paul II, address to general audience, September 11, 1986, in *L'Osservatore Romano* (English edition), September 16, 1986, 1.
13. Edmund J. Fortman, ed., *The Theology of God: Commentary* (New York: Bruce, 1968), 60.
14. Because God is Spirit, the personal name, *Father,* does not specifically refer to God's gender. God is the author, or "father," of human masculinity and femininity, so they both must flow from God. But God, being spirit, transcends the simple sexual labeling applicable to his creatures. It is notable, however, that when God does reveal himself in human language, it is usually as "father," or in masculine terms. Though the Bible does compare God's care and tenderness toward humanity to motherly concern (see Isa 66:13; Ps 131:2; Lk 13:34), it nowhere explicitly calls God "the Mother" or "Our Mother." This fact should not be interpreted merely as a prejudice of a patriarchal society, since Christians believe that the Holy Spirit of God inspired the biblical text, including the choice of specific language and images employed. God could have inspired the authors of Scripture to name God as "the Mother" as well as "the Father" *(ho pater* in several New Testament passages), but he did not. See also Louis Bouyer, *Woman in the Church* (San Francisco: Ignatius Press, 1979), 29–39.
15. *L'Osservatore Romano* (English edition), December 2, 1985, 5.

16. Ibid.
17. Roman Catechism I, 2, 2; cited in CCC 200.
18. Lateran Council IV (1215); cited in CCC 254.
19. Council of Florence (1442); cited in CCC 255.
20. "The reply which our reason stammers is based on the concept of 'relation.' The three divine persons are distinguished among themselves solely by the *relations* which they have with one another: and precisely by the relation of the Father to the Son, of the Son to the Father; of the Father and Son to the Spirit, of the Spirit to the Father and the Son. In God, therefore, the Father is pure Paternity; the Son pure Sonship; the Holy Spirit Pure 'Nexus of Love' of the two, so that the personal distinctions do not divide the same and unique divine Nature of the Three.
    "The Eleventh Council of Toledo (A.D. 675) made it clear with great exactitude: 'What the Father is, that he is not in reference to himself, but in relation to the Son; and what the Son is, that He's not in reference to himself, but in relation to the Father; in the same way the Holy Spirit, inasmuch as He is predicated Spirit of the Father and of the Son, that He is not in reference to himself, but relatively to the Father and to the Son.' (DS 528)
    "The Council of Florence (A.D. 1442) could therefore state: 'These three Persons are one God ... because the Three have one substance, one essence, one nature, one divinity, one immensity, one eternity; in God in fact everything is one and the same where there is no opposition of relation.'" (DS 1330)
    John Paul II, general audience of December 4, 1985, *in L'Osservatore Romano* (English edition), December 9, 1985, 1.
21. St. Teresa of Avila, trans. K. Kavanaugh. *The Collected Works of St. Teresa of Avila* (Washington, D.C.: Institute of Carmelite Studies, 1985), 3:386.
22. John Paul II, *L'Osservatore Romano* (English edition), December 2, 1985, 5.
23. Liturgy of Ash Wednesday.
24. "Creation is the work of the Triune God. The world 'created' in the Word-Son, is 'restored' together with the Son to the Father, through that *Uncreated Gift,* the Holy Spirit 'consubstantial' with both. In this way the world is *created in that Love,* which is the Spirit of the Father and of the Son. This universe embraced by eternal Love commences to exist in the instant chosen by the Trinity as the beginning of time.
    "In this way *the creation* of the world is *the work of love:* the universe, a created gift, springs from the Uncreated Gift, from the reciprocal Love of the Father and Son, from the Most Holy Trinity." John Paul II, general audience of March 5, 1986, in *L'Osservatore Romano* (English edition), March 10, 1986, 1.
25. CCC 393; St. John Damascene, *De Fide orth.* 2, 4: PG 94, 877.
26. John Paul II, general audience of January 15, 1986, in *L'Osservatore Romano* (English edition), January 20, 1986, 1.
27. GS 24 (FL).
28. GS 12 (FL).
29. "The first human being the Bible calls 'man' *(adam)* but from the moment of creation of the first woman, it begins to call him 'man' *is,* in relation to *issa,* 'woman,' because she was taken from the man, *is.*" Pope John Paul II, general audience, September 19, 1979, in *Original Unity of Man and Woman* (Boston: Daughters of St. Paul, 1981), 24. Hence, the conventional usage of "man" as designating either "mankind" or a male

person of the human race often will be employed in this book. The context should make clear which usage is intended.

30. Council of Vienne (1312); cited in CCC 365.

31. GS 22 (FL); see also CCC 359.

32. John Paul II, general audience, September 19, 1979, in *Original Unity of Man and Woman* (Boston: Daughters of St. Paul, 1981), 24.

33. GS 13; cited in CCC 390.

34. As the *Catechism* explains: "By yielding to the tempter, Adam and Eve committed a *personal sin*, but this sin affected *the human nature* that they would then transmit *in a fallen state* (Cf. Council of Trent: DS 1511-12). It is a sin which will be transmitted by propagation to all mankind, that is, by the transmission of a human nature deprived of original holiness and justice. And that is why original sin is called "sin" only in an analogical sense: it is a sin 'contracted' and not 'committed'—a state and not an act.... Still the transmission of original sin is a mystery that we cannot fully understand...." (CCC 404).

35. *Paradise Lost*, Book 1, l.263. in *The Norton Anthology of English Literature* (rev. ed.), vol. 1 (New York: W.W. Norton and Company, 1968), 1044.

36. *Summa Theologiae III*, 1, 3, 3; see also Rom 5:20.

37. John Paul II, general audience of January 8, 1986, in *L'Osservatore Romano* (English edition), January 13, 1986, 2.

38. St. Augustine, *Enchiridion* 3, 11: PL 40, 236, cf. CCC 311.

39. "Satan and Catholic Tradition," *New Covenant*, April 1974, 8.

40. "In modern times the theory of evolution has raised a special difficulty against the revealed doctrine about the creation of man as a being composed of soul and body. Many natural scientists who, with their own methods, study the problem of the origin of human life on earth, maintain—contrary to other colleagues of theirs—not only the existence of a link between man and the ensemble of nature, but also his derivation from the higher animal species. This problem, which has occupied scientists since the last century, involves vast layers of public opinion.

"The reply of the Magisterium was offered in the encyclical *Humani Generis* of Pius XII in 1950. In it we read: 'The Magisterium of the Church is not opposed to the theory of evolution being the object of investigation and discussion among experts. Here the theory of evolution is understood as an investigation of the origin of the human body from pre-existing living matter, for the Catholic faith obliges it to hold firmly that souls are created immediately by God.... (DS 3896)

"It can therefore be said that, from the viewpoint of the doctrine of faith, there are no difficulties in explaining the origin of man, in regard to the body, by means of the theory of evolution. It must, however, be added that this hypothesis proposes only a probability, not a scientific certainty. The doctrine of faith, however, invariably affirms that man's spiritual soul is created directly by God. According to the hypothesis mentioned, it is possible that the human body, following the order impressed by the Creator on the energies of life, could have been gradually prepared in the forms of antecedent living beings. The human soul, however, on which man's humanity definitively depends cannot emerge from matter, since it is of a spiritual nature."
John Paul II, general audience of April 16, 1986, in *L'Osservatore Romano* (English edition), April 21, 1986, 1, 2.

Chapter Three
God's People of the Old Testament

1. John Paul II, *L'Osservatore Romano* (English edition), April 28, 1986, 5.
2. Biblical scholars debate exactly what body of water was crossed by the Hebrews, whether the Red Sea or the "Sea of Reeds." The crucial point for Jews and Christians is that the plagues, the crossing through a sea, and the entire Passover event were a miracle, a mighty intervention of God in human history that is not reducible to any purely naturalistic explanation.
3. The term *Messiah,* or "anointed one," refers to the special blessing of God on this person. Anointing with oil was a way of setting apart kings for their ministry.
4. John Paul II, *L'Osservatore Romano* (English edition), April 28, 1986, 5.
5. NA 4.
6. cf. NA 4.
7. DV 15.
8. DV 16.

Chapter Four
Jesus Christ and the New Covenant

1. Of course, there is no such thing as purely objective history or reporting. Every account, whether historical, factual, or scientific, is subjective to some extent, since it represents the conclusions or interpretations of the person or persons presenting it. Therefore, to say that the New Testament accounts are not purely objective is not to impugn their truth or accuracy.
2. DV 19.
3. St. Irenaeus, *Adv. haeres,* 3, 19, 1. See CCC 460 and St. Irenaeus, *The Scandal of the Incarnation,* trans. John Saward (San Francisco: Ignatius, 1990), 14.
4. *On the Incarnation of the Word,* section 54, line 3; cited in CCC 460 and in *St. Athanasius on the Incarnation* (Crestwood, N.Y.: St Vladimir's Seminary, 1953), 93.
5. LH, Antiphon of Evening Prayer for January 1; cited in CCC 526.
6. The Council of Chalcedon (A.D. 451), Christological Definition (author's translation).
7. Ralph J. Tapia, *The Theology of Christ: Commentary* (New York: Bruce, 1971), 262.
8. Jesus has two natures, but he is one person, and as a person, he is divine. "Thus everything in Christ's human nature is to be attributed to his divine person as its proper subject, not only his miracles but also his suffering and even his death: 'He who was crucified in the flesh, our Lord Jesus Christ, is true God, Lord of glory, and *one of the Holy Trinity*'" (CCC 468, quoting Ecumenical Council of Constantinople II, A.D. 553: DS 432; cf. DS 424; Council of Ephesus, DS 255). "Christ's human nature belongs, as his own, to the divine person of the Son of God, who assumed it. Everything that Christ is and does in this nature derives from 'one of the Trinity.' The Son of God therefore communicates to his humanity his own personal mode of existence in the Trinity. In his soul, as in his body, Christ thus expresses humanly the divine ways of the Trinity (cf. Jn 14:9-10)" (CCC 470).
9. CCC 475: "Christ's human will 'does not resist or oppose but rather submits to his

divine and almighty will'" (Council of Constantinople III, (681): DS 556).

10. See Pius XII, encyclical *Haurietis aquas*, 1956; cited in CCC 478.

11. LH, Second Reading for Holy Family Sunday.

12. Catholic history is replete with authenticated reports of extraordinary miracles worked through the saints, or in their lives, in every age of the church. In fact, authenticated miracles through a person's intercession are required for that person to be canonized a saint by the Catholic Church. It is ironic that some Catholic scholars will not attribute to Jesus what they must recognize in the lives of his followers: "No servant is greater than his Master..." (Jn 13:16; see Mt 10:24).

13. "The transmission of the Christian faith consists primarily in proclaiming Jesus Christ in order to lead others to faith in him. From the beginning, the first disciples burned with the desire to proclaim Christ: 'We cannot but speak of what we have seen and heard' (Acts 4:20)" (CCC 425).

14. LG 16.

15. Ibid.

16. Michael Schmaus, *Dogma 3: God and His Christ* (Kansas City, Mo.: Sheed and Ward, 1971), 87.

17. For further explanation of the historical reality of the Resurrection, see CCC 643, 644.

18. "Only in a wholly exceptional and unique way would Jesus show himself to Paul 'as one untimely born,' in a last apparition that established him as an apostle (1 Cor 15:8, cf. 9:1; Gal 1:16)" (CCC 659).

Chapter Five
The Holy Spirit and the Church

1. Sermon 267, 4; cited in CCC 797.

2. See also Jn 14:25-26; 16:7-15.

3. Besides the proper name of "Holy Spirit," which is most frequently used in the *Acts of the Apostles* and in the Epistles, we also find in St. Paul the titles: the Spirit of the promise (Gal 3:14), the Spirit of adoption (Rom 8:15; Gal 4:6), the Spirit of Christ (Rom 8:9), the Spirit of Lord (2 Cor 3:17), and the Spirit of God (Rom 8:9, 14; 15:19; 1 Cor 6:11; 7:40), and, in St. Peter, the Spirit of glory (1 Pet 4:14) (CCC 693).

4. *De Spiritu Sancto* ("On the Holy Spirit") 15, 36, see CCC 736.

5. Catechetical Lecture 16, "On the Holy Spirit," in LH (The Liturgy of the Hours), vol. II, 967-68.

6. See also Isa 61:1-2.

7. Alan Schreck, *Hearts Aflame! The Holy Spirit at the Heart of Christian Life Today* (Ann Arbor, Mich.: Servant, 1995), 111.

8. St. Ephiphanius, *Panarion*, 1, 1, 5; cited in CCC 760.

9. LG 1 (FL); see Mk 16:15.

10. LG 3 (FL).

11. LG 3 (FL); cf. Jn 19:34; see also CCC 766.

12. See also SC 5; St. Ambrose.

13. LG 5 (FL). See also LG 4; CCC 767-68.

14. CCC 769. See LG5, 6; 2 Cor 5:6.

15. LG 2 (FL).

16. Pius XII, Encyclical Letter "Mystici Corporis Christi" ("On the Mystical Body of Christ"), June 29, 1943.
17. LG 48 (FL); see also CCC 769.
18. LG 2; cited in CCC 769.
19. LG 3 (FL).
20. "Acts of the Trial of Joan of Arc"; quoted in CCC 795.
21. Sermon 267, 4, quoted in CCC 797.
22. *Adversus haereses,* 3, 24, 1; cited in CCC 797.
23. Pius XII, encyclical *Mystici Corporis Christi.* (1943), no. 69 (New York: American Press, 1943), 26.
24. See LG 7.
25. LG 12 (FL).
26. John Paul II, *CL* 24; see 1 Cor 13.
27. LG 12 (FL); see also LG 30; 1 Thess 5:12, 19-21; CCC 799-801.
28. LG 9; cited in CCC 781.
29. LG 9 (FL).
30. LG 12 (FL); Jude 3.
31. UR 2 § 2; see CCC 813.
32. "The mystery celebrated in the liturgy is one, but the forms of its celebration are diverse. The mystery of Christ is so unfathomably rich that it cannot be exhausted by its expression in any single liturgical tradition.... The liturgical traditions or rites presently in use in the Church are the Latin (principally the Roman rite, but also the rites of certain local churches, such as the Ambrosian rite, or those of certain religious orders) and the Byzantine, Alexandrian or Coptic, Syriac, Armenian, Maronite, and Chaldean rites. In 'faithful obedience to tradition, the sacred Council declares that Holy Mother Church holds all lawfully recognized rites to be of equal right and dignity, and that she wishes to preserve them in the future and to foster them in every way.'" (CCC 1200, 1201, 1203; SC4).
33. LG 8; OE 1.
34. OE 3.
35. See UR 2; LG 14; CCC 815.
36. UR 1.
37. Ibid.
38. UR 4 (FL).
39. Ibid.
40. The *Catechism* lists some additional points in article 821.
41. See UR 3, 5.
42. UR 7.
43. See UR 3.
44. Ibid. As recently as 1949, the Roman Catholic Church vigorously rejected the opinion supposedly expressed by an Irish Catholic priest, Fr. Leonard Feeney, in Boston, that only Catholics could be saved.
45. UR 4; see also chapter 7 on the sacraments.
46. UR 11 (FL).
47. UR 12 (FL).
48. UR 24 (FL).

49. "Letter to the Smyrnaeans," par. 8, line 2 in *Early Christian Fathers*, Cyril Richardson, ed. (New York: Macmillan, 1970), 115.
50. See also LG 13.
51. AG 4.
52. St. Ignatius of Antioch, Letter to the Romans 1, 1; see CCC 832-34.
53. St. Augustine, *Confessions*, trans. Rex Warner (New York: New American Library, 1963), Book IX, Chap. 11, 202.
54. The various Eastern rites of the Catholic Church are "Roman Catholic" in the sense that they are in full communion with the bishop of Rome and accept his universal leadership of the church. However, these churches do not belong to the Latin rite of the Catholic Church.
55. St. Ignatius of Antioch, Letter to the Romans 1, 1; cited in CCC 834.
56. St. Irenaeus, *Against Heresies*, 3, 3, 2.
57. St. Maximus the Confessor, *Opuscula theo.;* cited in CCC 834.
58. LG 8 (FL).
59. Sacred Congregation for the Doctrine of Faith, *Mysterium Ecclesiae*, June 24, 1973, par. 1.
60. LG 8, 14, 15 (FL).
61. LG 14 (FL).
62. LG 15 (FL).
63. UR 3 (FL).
64. Paul VI, Discourse, December 14, 1975; see UR 13-18. Cited in CCC 838.
65. UR 3 (FL).
66. LG 16 (FL); see also CCC 839.
67. *Roman Missal*, Good Friday 13: General Intercessions, VI.
68. NA 4 (FL).
69. NA 2 (FL).
70. Ibid.
71. LG 14; see also Mk 16:16; Jn 3:5.
72. LG 39 (FL); cited in CCC 823.
73. LG 11 (FL); see also CCC 824-825.
74. John Paul II, CL 16, 3; cited in CCC 828.
75. LG 8.
76. AG 5; cited in CCC 857.
77. AG 2.
78. John Paul II, RMiss 21.
79. AG 5; cited in CCC 852.
80. LG 21.
81. LG 27; cited in CCC 896.
82. See LG 23.
83. LG 25; see also CCC 891.
84. LG 29; cited in CCC 1571.
85. LG 23; cited in CCC 882.
86. *Against Heresies*, 3, 2, 2.
87. LG 22; cited in CCC 882.
88. LG 12.

89. LG 25; cited in CCC 891.
90. DV 10 (FL).
91. LG 25; cited in CCC 891.
92. LG 25.
93. Pius XII, address, February 20, 1946; cited in CCC 899.
94. LG 31.
95. LG 33.
96. AA 3.
97. LG 40.
98. See AA 4.
99. AA 4.
100. LG 34; cited in CCC 901.
101. STh III, 71, 4 art. 3; cited in CCC 904.
102. LG 35; cited in CCC 905.
103. CIC, can. 212 § 3.
104. See LG 36; CCC 912.
105. In the church, "lay members of the Christian faithful can cooperate in the exercise of this power [of governance] in accord with the norm of law" (CIC, can. 129 § 2). And so the church provides for their presence at particular councils, diocesan synods, pastoral councils; the exercise of the pastoral care of a parish, collaboration in finance committees, and participation in ecclesiastical tribunals, etc. (Cf. CIC, cann. 443 § 4; 463 §§ 1 and 2; 492 § 1; 511; 517 § 2; 536; 1421 § 2) (CCC 911).
106. CL 29, acknowledging the increasing importance of lay movements and groups in the life of the church.
107. CL 33, 51.
108. CL 34.
109. CL 24.
110. CL 40, 51, 52.
111. LG 43; see also CCC 917.
112. CIC, can. 710.
113. LG 44.
114. As the *Roman Catechism* of the Council of Trent taught, "Everything the true Christian has is to be regarded as a good possessed in common with everyone else. All Christians should be ready and eager to come to the help of the needy ... and of their neighbors in want." A Christian is a steward of the Lord's goods. (See Lk 16:1, 3; CCC 952.)
115. LG 49 (FL); see CCC 959; Mt 25:31; 1 Cor 15:26-27.
116. See LG 29; CCC 956.
117. Expressions of Christian belief in the communion of saints are contained in the earliest creeds of the church, such as the Apostles' Creed. The doctrines of purgatory and the immediate union of the just with God upon death were first formally defined by the Catholic Church at the First and Second Councils of Lyons (1245 and 1274), though they had long been believed by Christians. See Denzinger's *The Sources of Catholic Dogma*, trans. by Roy J. Defarrari (St. Louis, Mo.: B. Herder, 1957), 4–7, 180–81, 184.
118. LG 50; cited in CCC 958.
119. Paul VI, Discourse, November 21, 1964; cited in CCC 963.

120. LG 62 (FL); cited in CCC 969.
121. LG 68 (FL); see also 2 Pet 3:10. Cited in CCC 972.

Chapter Six
Christian Prayer and the Liturgy

1. John Paul II, *Crossing the Threshold of Hope,* 19.
2. AA 11.
3. St. Teresa of Jesus, *The Book of Her Life,* 8, 5 in *The Collected Works of St. Teresa of Avila,* tr. K. Kavanaugh, OCD, and O. Rodriguez, OCD (Washington, D.C.: Institute of Carmelite Studies, 1976), I, 67.
4. See LG 7.
5. LG 13.
6. LG 51.
7. Tertullian, *De orat.* 1:PL 1, 1155.
8. See Didache 8; CCC 2767.
9. SC 10.
10. See CCC 1088; SC 7.
11. SC 7; see also CCC 1089.
12. See CCC 1090; LG 50.
13. SC 14 (FL); see also 1 Pet 2:9; 2:4-5. Cited in CCC 1141.
14. SC 28 (FL); cited in CCC 1144.
15. DV 21 (FL).
16. SC 35.
17. SC 21.
18. Ibid.
19. SC 14.
20. See SC 24, 35; Pet 2.
21. "unchangeable elements," SC 21.
22. SC 34 (FL).
23. UR 8.
24. A modern example of this is the Catholic Church's establishment of the feast of St. Joseph the Worker, May 1, to stress the real purpose and dignity of work in contrast to the communist "May Day," which anticipates the triumph of the working class through Marxist ideology, methods, and military might.
25. See CCC 1172; SC 103.
26. SC 106 (FL).
27. Paschal Homily; cited in CCC 1166.
28. SC 106 (FL).
29. SC 84 (FL); cited in CCC 1174.
30. LG 50.
31. See LG 51, 60, 62.
32. "The Didache," 8:1 in Cyril C. Richardson, ed., *Early Christian Fathers* (New York: Macmillian, 1979), 174. The Jews, it notes, fasted on Mondays and Thursdays.
33. Paul VI, "Apostolic Constitution on Fast and Abstinence," February 17, 1966.

34. The modern Catholic teaching on indulgences is contained in Pope Paul VI's *Apostolic Constitution on the Doctrine of Indulgences* (January 1, 1967), and further specified in the *Enchiridion of Indulgences* (*Enchiridion of Indulgences; Norms and Grants*, trans. William T. Barry [New York: Catholic Book Publishing, 1969]). What must be done to obtain an indulgence? In general, Pope Paul's *Apostolic Constitution* explains that besides carrying out the particular prescribed prayer or work, the faithful must also have the "necessary dispositions, that is to say, that they love God, detest sin, place their trust in the merits of Christ and believe firmly in the great assistance they derive from the Communion of Saints" (no. 10). The "Norms on Indulgences" issued from Rome on June 29, 1968, states that to obtain a plenary indulgence, one must participate in the sacrament of reconciliation, receive Holy Communion, and pray for the intention of the pope, along with the prescribed prayer or work to which the indulgence is attached (no. 27). These three conditions may be fulfilled several days before or after the actual prayer or action of the plenary indulgence, although it is fitting that Holy Communion be received and prayer for the pope's intention be said on the same day (no. 17).

    Plenary indulgences may be received for such things as adoration of the Blessed Sacrament *or* devout reading of the Bible for at least one-half hour, "the pious exercise of the Way of the Cross," (*Enchiridion of Indulgences,* 74 [under "Other Grants of Indulgences," no. 63]) or recitation of the rosary at any time in a church or family group, a religious community, or a pious association of persons.

    Partial indulgences are attached to many prayers and meditations. It is noteworthy that the Catholic Church proclaims three "general grants" of indulgences that are "intended to serve as a reminder to the faithful to infuse with a Christian spirit the actions that go to make their daily lives and to strive in the ordering of their lives toward the perfection of charity" (*Enchiridion on Indulgences,* 1968). The *Enchiridion on Indulgences* lists these indulgences as "(1) a partial indulgence is granted to the faithful who, in the performance of their duties and in bearing the trials of life, raise their mind with humble confidence to God, adding—even if only mentally—some pious invocation; (2) a partial indulgence is granted to the faithful, for a contribution of their goods to serve their brothers in need; (3) a partial indulgence is granted to the faithful, who in a spirit of penance voluntarily deprive themselves of what is licit and pleasing to them."

35. PO 5; see also SC 122-27. Cited in CCC 1181.
36. *De imago* 1, 16; cited in CCC 1159.
37. See SC 112.
38. *En. in Ps.* 72, 1; cited in CCC 1156.
39. Ch. 9; cited in CCC 1157.
40. See CCC 1158; SC 118, 121.
41. "The liturgical traditions or rites presently in use in the church are the Latin (principally the Roman rite, but also the rites of certain local churches, such as the Ambrosian rite, or those of certain religious orders) and the Byzantine, Alexandrian, or Coptic, Syriac, Armenian, Maronite, and Chaldean rites. In 'faithful obedience to tradition, the sacred Council declares that Holy Mother Church holds all lawfully recognized rites to be of equal right and dignity, and that she wishes to preserve them in the future and to foster them in every way'" (SC 4); (CCC 1203).

42. *De fide orth.* 4, 13; cited in CCC 1106.
43. LG 12.
44. Ibid.
45. LG 8, 12.
46. See Kilian McDonnell and George T. Montague, *Christian Initiation and Baptism in the Holy Spirit* (Collegeville, Minn.: Liturgical Press, 1991) and *Fanning the Flame, What Does Baptism in the Holy Spirit Have to Do with Christian Initiation?* (Collegeville, Minn.: Liturgical Press, 1991).
47. STh I, q. 43, a, 6.
    Francis Sullivan draws the following conclusion from St. Thomas' teaching:
    > I conclude from this teaching of St. Thomas that there is no reason why Catholics, who believe that they have received the Holy Spirit in their sacramental initiation, should not look forward to new "sendings" of the Spirit to them, which would move them from the "state of grace" in which they already are into some "new act" or "new state of grace." Now if we recall that in biblical language "sending the Spirit," "pouring out the Spirit," and "baptizing in the Spirit are simply different ways of saying the same thing, the conclusion follows that it is quite in accord with traditional Catholic theology for baptized and confirmed Christians to ask the Lord to "baptize them in the Holy Spirit." What they are asking for, in the language of St. Thomas, is a new sending of the Holy Spirit, which would begin a decisively new work of grace in their lives. As we have seen from the examples which St. Thomas gives (working miracles, prophecy, etc.), he would obviously not be surprised if such a new work of grace involved a charismatic gift.

    Charisms and Charismatic Renewal: A Biblical and Theological Study (Ann Arbor, Mich.: Servant Books, 1984), 71–72.
48. Ibid.
49. SC 24.
50. SC 22.
51. SC 2.

Chapter Seven
The Sacraments

1. Sermon 74, 2; cited in CCC 1115.
2. LG 1.
3. LG 48.
4. Cf. Council of Trent (1547): DS 1608.
5. SC 11.
6. PO 4 (FL); cited in CCC 1122.
7. SC 59 (FL); cited in CCC 1123.
8. CCC 1120; see also LG 10, 2.
9. Cf. Council of Trent (1547): DS 1604.
10. SC 10, 61.
11. *De sacr.* 2, 2, 6; cited in CCC 1225.
12. UR 22, par.2.
13. UR 3 (FL); cited in CCC 1271.

14. AG 14; cited in CCC 1248.
15. SC 7.
16. See CIC, can. 867; CCEO, cann. 681; 686, 1.
17. See LG 11; 41; GS 48; CIC, can. 868.
18. See Rom 8:29; Council of Trent (1547): DS 1609-1619.
19. See CCC 1270; LG 11.
20. LG 14 (FL).
21. CCC 1269; cf. LG 37; CIC, cann. 208-223; CCEO, can. 675:2.
22. Paul VI, *Divinae consortium naturae*, 659; cf. Acts 8:15-17; 19:5-6; Heb 6:2.
23. "The *essential rite* of the sacrament follows. In the Latin rite, 'the sacrament of Confirmation is conferred through the anointing with chrism on the forehead, which is done by the laying on of the hand, and through the words: *"Accipe signaculum doni Spiritus Sancti"* [Be sealed with the Gift of the Holy Spirit.], (Paul VI, apostolic constitution, *Divinae consortium naturae*, 663). In the Eastern Churches after a prayer of epiclesis, the more significant parts of the body are anointed with myron: forehead, eyes, nose, ears, lips, chest, back, hands, and feet. Each anointing is accompanied by the formula: ... 'the seal of the gift of the Holy Spirit'" (*Rituale per le Chiese orientali di rito bizantino in lingua greca*, Pars Prima [Libreria Editrice Vaticana, 1954], 36) (CCC 1300).
24. See CCC 1309; St. Thomas Aquinas, STh III, 72, 8, ad 2; Wis 4:8.
25. Council of Florence (1439): DS 1319; LG 11, 12.
26. LG 11; cited in CCC 1324.
27. SC 47; cited in CCC 1323.
28. c. A.D. 110, *Letter to the Smyrneans*, 7:1.
29. c. A.D. 150, *First Apology*, ch. 66.
30. c. A.D. 185, *Against Heresies*, book 5, ch. 2.
31. c. A.D. 250, *Mystagogical Catechesis*, "Fourth Address: On the Body and Blood of Christ."
32. c. A.D. 400, Sermon 272.
33. "The Eucharistic presence of Christ begins at the moment of the consecration and endures as long as the Eucharistic species subsist. Christ is present whole and entire in each of the species and whole and entire in each of their parts, in such a way that the breaking of the bread does not divide Christ" (Council of Trent; cited in CCC 1377).
34. MF 56; cited in CCC 1378.
35. See SC 47.
36. See SC 6; CCC 1365-68.
37. See SC 47, 48; CCC 1382.
38. Note that in the Latin rite Communion is often legitimately distributed under the species of bread. However, "the sign of communion is more complete when given under both kinds, since, in that form the sign of the Eucharistic meal appears more clearly" (GIRM 240).
39. *Roman Missal;* cited in CCC 1402.
40. LG 3; cited in CCC 1405.
41. LG 8; CCC 1428.
42. Cf. Council of Trent (1551): DS 1712.
43. John Paul II, *Dominum et Vivificantem*, no. 47.

44. Council of Trent (1551): DS 1680 (ND 1626); cf. Ex 20:17; Mt 5:28.
45. "According to the Church's command, 'after having attained the age of discretion, each of the faithful is bound by an obligation faithfully to confess serious sins at least once a year' (cf. CIC, can. 989; Council of Trent (1551): DS 1683; DS 1708). Anyone who is aware of having committed a mortal sin must not receive Holy Communion, even if he experiences deep contrition, without having first received sacramental absolution, unless he has a grave reason for receiving Communion and there is no possibility of going to confession (Cf. Council of Trent (1551): DS 1647; 1661; CIC, can. 916; CCEO, can. 711). Children must go to the sacrament of penance before receiving Holy Communion for the first time" (Cf. CIC, can. 914) (CCC 1457).
46. Tertullian, *De Pœnit.* 4, 2: PL 1, 1343; cf. Council of Trent (1547): DS 1542.
47. Cf. 1 Cor 12:9, 28, 30.
48. Cf. Council of Florence (1439): DS 1325.
49. See LG 26.
50. LG 21; cited in CCC 1558.
51. CD 2; cited in CCC 1558.
52. LG 28; cited in CCC 1564.
53. LG 20.
54. LG 41.
55. PO 12.
56. LG 29.
57. See CCC 1570; LG 29.
58. LG 29.
59. CIC, can. 1024.
60. Cf. John Paul II, MD 26-27; CDF, declaration, *Inter signiores:* AAS 69 (1977) 98-116.
61. PO 16; cited in CCC 1579.
62. St. John Vianney, quoted in B. Nodet, *Jean-Marie Vianney, Curé d'Ars,* 100.
63. See OT 6.
64. Here we discuss the nature of Christian marriage: marriage in Christ. The reader should consult a diocesan marriage official for specific information on interfaith marriage and other specific questions, based on the 1983 Code of Canon Law.
65. GS 48; cited in CCC 1652.
66. According to the Latin tradition, the spouses as ministers of Christ's grace mutually confer upon each other the sacrament of matrimony by expressing their consent before the church. In the traditions of the Eastern churches, the priests (bishops or presbyters) are witnesses to the mutual consent given by the spouses, but for the validity of the sacrament their blessing is also necessary.
67. GS 48.
68. *To Married Couples;* cited in CCC 1642.
69. GS 48.
70. LG 11 (FL); cited in CCC 1656.
71. GS 52.
72. GS 54.
73. See GS 52.

Chapter Eight
Life in Christ and the Holy Spirit

1. LG 40; cited in CCC 2013.
2. *Basic Teachings for Catholic Religious Education,* National Conference of Catholic Bishops, January 11, 1973 (Washington, D.C.: USCC Publications Office, 1973), nos. 17 and 18.
3. "*Mortal sin* destroys charity in the heart of man by a grave violation of God's law; it turns man away from God, who is his ultimate end and his beatitude, by preferring an inferior good to him" (CCC 1855).
4. "For a *sin* to be *mortal,* three conditions must together be met: 'Mortal sin is sin whose object is grave matter and which is also committed with full knowledge and deliberate consent'" (RP 17 § 12) (CCC 1857; see also CCC 1858-60 for an explanation of these conditions).
5. John Paul II, RP 17 § 9.
6. See CCC 1864; 46.
7. See STh I-II, 24, 3.
8. "What are the greatest needs of the Church today? Do not let our answer surprise you as being oversimple or even superstitious and unreal: one of the greatest needs is defense from that evil which is called the Devil.... we know that this dark and disturbing spirit really exists, and that he still acts with treacherous cunning; he is the secret enemy that sows errors and misfortunes in human history.... The question of the Devil and the influence he can exert on individual persons as well as on communities, whole societies, is a very important chapter of Catholic doctrine which is given little attention today, though it should be studied again...." (Paul VI, General Audience on November 15, 1973, *New Covenant,* April 1974, 8).

   In response to the pope's exhortation, the Sacred Congregation for the Doctrine of the Faith published a thorough study on the Catholic understanding of Satan on June 26, 1975, entitled, "Christian Faith and Demonology" (in *Vatican II: More Post-Conciliar Documents, Vol. II,* Austin Flannery, O.P., ed. [Grand Rapids, Mich.: Eerdmans, 1982], 456-85). This study, which was based on sacred Scripture, the teaching of the ecumenical councils, and Catholic tradition from the patristic period to the present, concluded that existence of Satan and demons (evil spirits) is an essential matter of Catholic and Christian faith. While warning against certain extremes, such as denying the existence of Satan (rationalism), placing Satan on the level of God instead of a creature (manichaean dualism), avoiding personal responsibility for evildoing (blaming sins on the devil), or gullibility regarding diabolic intervention, the study concludes: All these considerations notwithstanding, the church is simply being faithful to the example of Christ when it asserts that the warning of St. Peter to be "sober and alert" is always relevant.
9. C.S. Lewis, *The Screwtape Letters,* Letter VII (Old Tappan, N.J.: Fleming H. Revell, 1976), 45–46.
10. GS 15; cited in CCC 1704.
11. Justification is "*the acceptance of God's righteousness* through faith in Jesus Christ. Righteousness (or 'justice') here means the rectitude of divine love.... Justification has been *merited for us by the Passion of Christ* ... [it] is conferred in Baptism, the sacrament of faith. It conforms us to the righteousness of God, who makes us inwardly just by the power of his mercy. Its purpose is the glory of God and of Christ, and the gift of eter-

nal life" (Cf. Council of Trent [1547]: DS 1529) (CCC 1991-1992).

"'Justification is not only the remission of sins, but also the sanctification and renewal of the interior man' (Council of Trent [1547]: DS 1528) ... the Holy Spirit is the master of the interior life. By giving birth to the 'inner man' (cf. Rom 7:22; Eph 3:16), justification entails the *sanctification* of his whole being:

'Just as you once yielded your members to impurity and to greater and greater iniquity, so now yield your members to righteousness for sanctification.... But now that you have been set free from sin and have become slaves of God, the return you get is sanctification and its end, eternal life' (Rom 6:19, 22)" (CCC 1989, 1995).

12. St. Augustine, *In Jo. ev.* 72, 3: PL 35, 1823.

13. Daniel Sinisi, *Christian Moral Living* (Steubenville, Ohio: Franciscan University Press, 1983), 63.

14. DV 5; cited in CCC 1814.

15. Council of Trent, "Decree on Justification," chap. 8 in Heinrich Denzinger, *The Sources of Catholic Doctrine,* trans. Roy J. Deferrari (St. Louis: B. Herder, 1957), 252.

16. The *Catechism* continues, "It is prudence that immediately guides the judgment of conscience. The prudent man determines and directs his conduct in accordance with this judgment. With the help of this virtue we apply moral principles to particular cases without error and overcome doubts about the good to achieve and the evil to avoid" (CCC 1806).

17. *Letter to Serapion,* 1, 24; cited in CCC 1988.

18. See St. Thérèse of Lisieux; cited in CCC 2011.

19. Sermon 298; cited in CCC 2009.

20. GS 16 (FL); see also CCC 1776, 1794.

21. DH 3; see also CCC 1782.

22. See also DH 14.

23. GS 16.

24. DH 3.

25. *To Live in Christ Jesus: A Pastoral Reflection on the Moral Life,* National Conference of Catholic Bishops, November 11, 1976 (Washington, D.C.: USCC Publications Office, 1976), 8–9.

26. *Against Marcion* 2, 4; cited in CCC 1951.

27. *Dec. praec.* 1; cited in CCC 1955.

28. Pius XII, *Humani generis:* DS 3876; cf. *Dei Filius* 2: DS 3005.

29. *The Teaching of Christ,* 315.

30. Sinisi, 14.

31. "Basic Teachings on Catholic Religious Education," art. 17. p. 18.

32. LG 25.

33. See John XXIII, Litt. Encyclical, *Ad Petri Cathedram,* 20 June 1959: AAS 55 (1959), 513, quoted in GS 92.

34. Sinisi, 19.

35. In the United States, these holy days of obligation are: the feasts of Mary, Mother of God (Jan. 1); the Ascension of the Lord (or Ascension Thursday, forty days after Easter Sunday); the Assumption of Mary (Aug. 15); All Saints' Day (Nov. 1); the Immaculate Conception (Dec. 8); and Christmas (the Nativity, the Incarnation of the Lord, Dec. 25).

36. AA 6; cited in CCC 2044.
37. Sinisi, 37.
38. *Basic Teachings for Catholic Religious Education,* 20–21.

Chapter Nine
The Ten Commandments

1. See LG 24.
2. See DH 1.
3. *On the Holy Spirit,* 18.
4. Nicea II; cited in CCC 2132.
5. *First Apology,* 67; cited in CCC 2174.
6. SC 106 (FL).
7. GE 3 (FL).
8. LG 35 (FL).
9. AA 11 (FL).
10. OT 2 (FL).
11. *Centesimus annus* 36 par. 2.
12. See GS 48.
13. FC 21; cf. LG 11.
14. *Donum vitae,* intro. 5; cited in CCC 2258.
15. GS 51.
16. CIC, can. 1398
17. CIC, can. 1314.
18. "The Church permits cremation, provided that it does not demonstrate a denial of faith in the resurrection of the body" (Cf. CIC, can. 1176 § 3) (CCC 2301).
19. John Paul II, *Evangelium vitae* 56.
20. GS 79 § 4 (FL).
21. CCC 2304; see also Isa 32:17; cf. GS 78 § 1-2.
22. FC 11.
23. HV 1.
24. See Gen 1:28; GS 34.
25. *Hom. In Lazaro* 2, 5; cited in CCC 2446.
26. GS 58 § 4 (FL).
27. St. Augustine, *De catechizandis rudibus* 4, 8: PL 40, 315-316.
28. *Hom. in Rom.* 71, 5; cited in CCC 2540.
29. *City of God,* 22, 30; cited in CCC 2550.

Chapter Ten
Catholics in the World

1. GS 4.
2. Ibid.
3. GS 7.
4. GS 9.

5. GS 10.
6. GS 13; see also GS 37.
7. *The Holy Spirit in the Life of Jesus,* trans. Alan Neame (Collegeville, Minn.: Liturgical Press, 1994), 28–29. The *Catechism* lists superstition, idolatry, divinization, magic, spiritism, and other occult practices as transgressions against the first commandment: "I am the Lord your God, you shall have no other Gods before me" (see CCC 2110-2117). Many today embrace these "false gods"; an increasing number of people deny the existence of a God (atheists; see CCC 2123-2126), or claim that we have insufficient evidence to know whether God exists (agnostics; see CCC 2127–2128).
8. GS 20.
9. See GS 3, 10, 22, 31, 32.
10. GS 10.
11. RH 11 (Washington, D.C.: USCC Publication Office, 1979), 31–32.
12. John Paul II, "Urbi et Orbi Message, Christmas, 1985," in *L'Osservatore Romano,* (English edition), January 6, 1986, 1, 2.
13. GS 38.
14. GS 30.
15. Extraordinary Synod of Bishops (1985), final report, section D2.
16. GS 41.
17. GS 14.
18. C.S. Lewis, *The Weight of Glory and Other Addresses* (Grand Rapids, MI: Eerdmans, 1965), 14–15.
19. GS 26, 29.
20. GS 27.
21. GS 26.
22. GS 25; see also CCC 1912.
23. See GS 24, 32; LG 9.
24. GS 30.
25. GS 43.
26. Ibid.
27. See GS 42.
28. Ibid.
29. GS 26 (FL); see CCC 1906.
30. See CCC 1907-1912; GS 26.
31. See GS 31; CCC 1915.
32. GS 37.
33. T.S. Elliot, "Choruses from 'The Rock,'" in T.S. Elliot, *Collected Poems 1909-1962* (New York: Harcourt Brace, and World, 1963), 154.
34. *The Holy Spirit in the Life of Jesus,* 33.
35. GS 22.
36. RH 7.
37. EN 26-27.
38. EN 27.
39. Section II, B, a, 2, p. 50–51.
40. Message to the People of God, III.
41. Final Report, II, B, a, 2, p. 50.

42. Final Report, II, A, 2, p. 45.
43. John Paul II, RMiss 21.
44. John Paul II, "Apostolic Exhortation on Catechesis in Our Time" (*Catechesi Tradendae*) October 16, 1979 (Boston, MA: Daughters of St. Paul, 1981), no. 20.
45. Ibid., no. 24.
46. Ibid., no. 25.
47. GS 40.
48. GS 42.
49. GS 1.
50. GS 43.
51. GS 27 (FL); cited in CCC 1931.
52. GS 29; cited in CCC 1935.
53. CCC 1936; see also GS 29 § 2.
54. Pius XII, Discourse, June 1, 1941.
55. GS 43.
56. Ibid.
57. See DV 8.
58. Sacred Congregation for the Doctrine of Faith, *Instruction on Certain Aspects of the "Theology of Liberation,"* August 6, 1984, and *Instruction on Christian Freedom and Liberation,* March 22, 1986. (Both published in English by the office of Publishing and Promotion Services, USCC, Washington, D.C.)
59. GS 52.
60. LG 11; see also CCC 2209.
61. GS 52.
62. Ibid.
63. *Familiaris Consortio,* no. 6 (Boston, Mass.: Daughters of St. Paul, 1981), 17.
64. FC 6.
65. FC 34.
66. FC 23.
67. Ibid.
68. FC 25.
69. FC 17.
70. CCC 2211; see also FC 46.

Chapter Eleven
Mary

1. See LG 2.
2. See Pope Paul VI's exhortation, *Marialis Cultus,* February 2, 1974, and Pope John Paul II's encyclical letter *Redemptoris Mater,* "Mother of the Redeemer," March 25, 1987.
3. See U.S. Catholic bishops' pastoral letter, *Behold Your Mother: Women of Faith,* November 21, 1973.
4. LG 55.
5. See RM 12-14.

6. LG 59 (FL); cited in CCC 965.
7. LG 66; cited in CCC 971.
8. Raymond Brown, Karl Donfried, Joseph Fitzmeyer, and John Reumann, eds., *Mary in the New Testament* (New York: Paulist, 1978).
9. St. John Chrysostom, in his *Homily V* on the Gospel of Matthew, notes that the word "until" was used similarly in other parts of Scripture. For example, in the story of Noah's ark, the Bible says, "The raven returned not until the earth was dried up" (Gen 8:7). Yet, St. John notes, the raven did not return *after* that time either. This is a particular usage of the Greek word "until," to stress the action prior to a certain time—not afterward. See also Brown, Donfried, Fitzmeyer, and Reumann, 86–87, fn 177; K. Beyer, *Semitische Syntax in Neuen Testament* (Göttingen: Vandenhoeck und Ruprecht, 1962), l. 132, no.1
10. Brown, Donfried, Fitzmeyer, and Reumann, 65–67, 291.
11. LG 57.
12. LG 63 (FL); see also Jn 19:26-27; Rom 8:29; Rev 12:17.
13. Pius IX, *"Ineffabilis Deus,"* December 8, 1854, quoted in *The Sources of Catholic Dogma*, 413.
14. Irenaeus of Lyons, "On the Refutation and Overthrow of Knowledge Falsely So-Called," or "Against Heresies," book III, 22, 4, in *The Faith of the Early Fathers*, vol. 1, W.A. Jurgens, ed., (Collegeville, Minn.: Liturgical Press, 1970), 93.
15. LG 56 (FL); see CCC 494, Epiphanius, St. Jerome.
16. Frances Parkinson Keyes, "Bernadette and the Beautiful Lady," in *A Woman Clothed with the Sun*, John Delaney, ed. (Garden City, N.Y.: Doubleday, 1960), 137.
17 Pius XII, *Munificentissimus Deus,* quoted in Michael O'Carroll, C.S.Sp., *Theotokos: A Theological Encyclopedia of the Blessed Virgin Mary* (Collegeville, Minn.: Liturgical Press, 1982), 55. LG 59; cited in CCC 966.
18. LG 68 (FL); cited in CCC 972. See also 2 Pet 3:10.
19. LG 53 (emphasis mine).
20. LG 64 (FL); cited in CCC 507.
21. LG 63, 65; see also CCC 829.
22. LG 67 (FL).
23. LG 61 (FL); cited in CCC 968.
24. LG 62; see also CCC 969-70.
25. Juniper B. Carol, *Mariology*, vol. 1 (Milwaukee: Bruce, 1954), 32-33, states:
    There is no Catholic theologian who denies to Our Lady the title: Mediatrix of all graces. But since the term "mediation" has many shades of meaning, the sense in which the Mother of God is called Mediatrix must first be explained.
    A mediator is a person who stands in the middle and unites individuals or groups which are opposed. Our blessed Lord, the God-Man, was uniquely fitted to be the Mediator between God and man. St. Paul says, "For there is one God, and one Mediator between God and man, himself man, Christ Jesus, who gave Himself a ransom for all..." (1 Tim 2:5-6).
    He continues, "If there is 'one Mediator,' as St. Paul writes, then any other Mediator can only be such in strict dependence and in a secondary sense." He ends by quoting Pope Leo XIII as he referred to St. Thomas Aquinas in his teaching on the possibility of other mediators: "As the Angelic Doctor teaches, 'there is no reason

why certain others should not be called in a certain way mediators between God and man, that is to say, insofar as they co-operate by predisposing and ministering in the union of man with God.' Such are the angels and saints, the prophets and priests of both Testaments; but especially has the Blessed Virgin a claim to the glory of this title. For no single individual can even be imagined who has ever contributed or ever will contribute so much toward reconciling man with God. She offered a Savior to mankind, hastening to eternal ruin, at that moment when she received the announcement of the mystery of peace brought to this earth by the angel, with that admirable act of consent—and this, 'in the name of the whole human race.' She it is from whom Jesus is born; she is therefore truly His mother, and for this reason a worthy and acceptable, 'Mediatrix to the Mediator.'"

26. LG 62 (FL).
27. John Paul II, homily at Fatima, Portugal, May 13, 1982.
28. William C. McGrath, "Our Lady of the Rosary," in *A Woman Clothed with the Sun*, 175–212.
29. Ibid., 202-3.
30. Paul VI, *Marialis Cultus*, February 2, 1974 (Washington, D.C.: USCC, 1974), 34.
31. Lk 1:48; Paul VI, *Marialis Cultis*, 56.

Chapter Twelve
The Life of the Age to Come

1. *Roman Missal*, Litany of the Saints.
2. St. John of the Cross, Dichos 64, quoted in CCC 1022.
3. Sacred Congregation for the Doctrine of the Faith, "The Reality of Life after Death," (*Recentiores episcoporum synodi*) May 11, 1979, in *Vatican II: More Postconciliar Documents, Vol. 2*, Austin Flannery, O.P., ed. (Grand Rapids, Mich.: Eerdmans, 1982), 502-3.
4. Cf. Council of Orange II (529): DS 397; Council of Trent (1547): 1567.
5. The Catholic Church does not hold any one person or group responsible for the death of Christ. The Church particularly rejects the view that the Jewish people are guilty of "deicide" ("killing God") and insists, "The Church always held and continues to hold that Christ out of infinite love freely underwent suffering and death because of the sins of all people, so that all might attain salvation" (NA 4). Nonetheless, it was human sin and blindness which brought about that death of Christ, which he freely accepted out of love for all people in order to redeem us and reconcile us to God.
6. "We cannot be united with God unless we freely choose to love him. But we cannot love God if we sin gravely against him, against our neighbor or against ourselves: 'He who does not love remains in death. Anyone who hates his brother is a murderer, and you know that no murderer has eternal life abiding in him' (1 Jn 3:14-15). Our Lord warns us that we shall be separated from him if we fail to meet the serious needs of the poor and the little ones who are his brethren" (see Mt 25:41-46) (CCC 1033).
7. Cf. Council of Florence (1439): DS 1304; Council of Trent (1563): DS 1820; (1547): 1580; see also Benedict XII, *Benedictus Deus* (1336): DS 1000.
8. St. Gregory the Great, *Dial.* 4, 39: PL 77, 396; cf. Mt 12:31; cited in CCC 1031.

9. The doctrine of purgatory must be understood in terms of the full meaning of salvation. For Catholics, salvation includes both "justification" (restoration to a right relationship with God through Jesus Christ) and "sanctification" (being cleansed from personal sin and made holy, that is, remade into the image of God, freed from the corruption of sin). Purgatory completes the process of sanctification, by which we are cleansed from sin and restored to the image of God as fully as our nature allows.

10. *Hom. in 1 Cor.* 41, 5; cited in CCC 1032.

11. Catholic doctrine traditionally speaks of this as remission of the "temporal punishment due to sin," meaning the punishment that comes upon each person as a result of the bondage and other ill effects of sin (e.g., bad habits, character weaknesses, inability to overcome a sin) that still linger in a person's life, even after the sin has been forgiven. See chapter six for a further explanation of indulgences.

12. Paul VI, apostolic constitution, *Indulgentiarum doctrina*, Norm 1; see also CCC 1471.

13. Cf. *Indulgentiarum doctrina*, 5.

14. Ibid.

15. Ibid; see CCC 1476-77.

16. Confessions, Book I.

17. LG 48 § 3 (FL); cf. 1 Cor 10:11.

18. GS 39 § 1 (FL); cited in CCC 1048.

19. Rom 8:21; see also GS 34.

20. GS 34; see also CCC 1049-50.

21. See 1 Cor 10:11; LG 48.

22. LG 48.

Index